Social Policy: A comparative analysis

MICHAEL HILL

Department of Social Policy
University of Newcastle Upon Tyne

PRENTICE HALL

HARVESTER WHEATSHEAF

London New York Toronto Sydney Tokyo Singapore
Madrid Mexico City Munich

First published 1996 by
Prentice Hall/Harvester Wheatsheaf
Campus 400, Maylands Avenue
Hemel Hempstead
Hertfordshire HP2 7EZ
A division of
Simon & Schuster International Group

Typeset in 9½pt Melior
by Keyset Composition, Colchester

Printed and bound in Great Britain by
T.J. International Ltd, Padstow, Cornwall

Library of Congress Cataloguing-in-Publication Data

Available from the publisher

British Library Cataloguing in Publication Data

A catalogue record for this book is available from the British Library

ISBN 0-13-353905-9 (pbk)

4 5 00 99 98 97

This book is dedicated to my father, Harold, whose active old age reminds me that if I can remain as busy and alert as he is this book could run through many editions.

Contents

List of figures

List of tables

Preface

This book is an overview of social policy which deals with issues, rather than descriptions of policies. In doing so it introduces key concepts, issues about the performance of policies and the ways in which writers have sought to explain policy characteristics. It thus shows how specific policies and policy systems vary throughout the developed world, using examples from a wide range of societies.

Those societies comprise most of the member states of the OECD, plus some of the newly developed states that have recently joined the 'first world' (notably the 'little tigers' of East Asia). The book does not use examples from countries where social policy is still at an embryonic stage, nor from the countries of the former Soviet bloc where social policy is currently undergoing dramatic changes whose outcomes are difficult to predict. Its use of examples is influenced by the extent to which different issues have been studied comparatively or in a way which facilitates comparative use. It is also affected by the extent to which material is available in English.

While considerable effort has been made to supplement the use of evidence from the author's own society (United Kingdom), this cannot be described as a book offering a grand comparative theory of its own. Rather it is a book about 'social policy issues', which has been designed to have widespread relevance and to avoid the ethnocentrism which marks much British writing on social policy (including much of the author's own earlier work).

Social policy as an academic discipline is largely confined to the United Kingdom (with limited related developments in Eire, Australia, New Zealand and Hong Kong). In other societies social policy teaching will be found within social work departments (notably in the United States and Canada), but the linking of social policy and social work tends to confine the study of the former to a narrow range of concerns, with a strong emphasis on social pathology and on policies directly oriented to the social welfare of the deprived. What has been characteristic of the development of social policy teaching in the United Kingdom in recent years has been a desire to move away from its close identification with social work and to recognise that social policies impact upon all groups in society and that any analysis of those policies needs to deal with interactions between social and economic policies. The 'ghettoisation' of social policy tends to narrow the social policy agenda, seeing it in terms of services for social casualties rather than as universal contributions to the welfare of society as a whole.

As the study of social policy in the United Kingdom has moved outwards in the way described above it has become recognised that its analysis and therefore its teaching need to take into account developments outside Britain, and that it needs to give considerable attention to its links to sociology, political science and economics. These two developments are usefully brought together by the fact that as British scholars cross the North Sea they find that in most other countries developments (and relevant teaching) in their subject are occurring in sociology, politics and economics departments (together with other hybrid and applied departments like departments of public administration, policy studies and management).

The author is describing his own 'awakening' amongst that of others. Indeed he has been in the slightly schizoid position of making a contribution to largely political science-based policy analysis and theory, which has been well received abroad, while continuing to be primarily a contributor to rather parochial work on social policy within his own country. This book aims to address that 'problem'.

These references to other disciplines need supplementing by examining two alternative ways forward for the analysis of social policy. One way is to emphasise the social welfare aspect. This involves recognising that the welfare of individuals is by no means determined only by 'policy' – by direct interventions by the state. The other is to emphasise the policy aspect, to concentrate upon the state's role. Economics handles this dichotomy inasmuch as its approach to welfare is to attempt to delineate those issues which market processes do not handle satisfactorily. This takes it into the domain of philosophy and value conflict. A sociology of welfare alternatively offers an analysis which recognises the complex variety of ways in which families, communities and the state impact upon the individual. Political science puts the role of the last of those three at the centre of its concerns. The stance taken in this book is that it is a book about social *policy*, therefore its central concern is the role of the state. However, the perspectives of the disciplines other than political science are important inasmuch as economics deals in a variety of ways with the market/state boundary or relationship and sociology emphasises the need to keep the relationship between state and society firmly in sight when policy is being considered. Chapter 1 examines these issues further, and each chapter thereafter recognises the importance of the context within which an elaborate state role is found in all the developed economies.

Many people have contributed directly or indirectly to the production of this book. My wife Betty has done both: as someone on whom I could test ideas, as a careful and critical reader of a draft; and as a partner who has to put up with unsocial working hours (very early in the morning mostly) and periods of preoccupation with the task.

Clare Grist of Harvester Wheatsheaf has played a very important role. She interprets her responsibilities as an editor generously, offering support and ideas going well beyond the main practical issues. In developing a comparative project I have had a great deal of help from scholars in other countries. Many are acknowledged below, but two I want to single out here are Peter Hupe and Pieter Degeling. The former has taken an interest in the project since an early stage and generously arranged a programme of activities which deepened my understanding of social policy in the Netherlands. The latter has been my main host in Australia, enabling me to get in touch with a range of interesting and helpful people.

Back home John Veit Wilson has played an important role as a 'sounding board' for ideas, particularly on many enjoyable moorland walks. Others who have generously commented on chapters or answered queries about specific topics include John Bond, Lois Bryson, Tony Dalton, Aksel Hatland, Bjørn Hvinden, Meg Huby, Bob Lingard, Deborah Mitchell, David Reynolds and Mai-Brith Schartau.

PART ONE

Themes in the comparative analysis of social policy

CHAPTER ONE

Welfare and the state

Introduction

There is a basic difficulty about defining social policy in that there are disagreements about whether it should be merely concerned with the correction of malfunctions in the operation of society (and particularly of the economy) or involve some overall and logically prior concern with welfare in society, and about the extent to which welfare should be regarded as a key state responsibility. Rather than engage in an elaborate discussion of these arguments at the very beginning of the book, the preference here is to let the main aspects of these issues emerge in the introductory discussion.

Broadly speaking the study of social policy is the study of the role of the state in relation to the welfare of its citizens. This leads immediately to two questions. First, since the welfare of citizens is affected by their own actions and by the actions of others, including those of collective organisations of various kinds, what is it about the role of the state in relation to welfare that is different? Second, what are the kinds of actions which have an impact on welfare?

Figure 1.1 brings these two definitional issues together. However, reducing the key points to a limited number of words for a chart over-simplifies, so some further explanation is needed.

The individualistic model

The issues about individualism could be taken back to philosophical propositions about 'the state of nature', but it is rather more appropriate for this discussion to recognise that there is an individualistic philosophical position which sees people relating to each other in 'markets' as a key principle for the organisation of social activities (Hayek, 1960; Nozick, 1974;

	Provision of income	Provision of services	Regulation
Individuals	Work, etc.	Purchase	Reciprocity
Families	Sharing	Care	Affection
Communities	Charity	Charity	Norms
State	Benefits	Services	Laws

Figure 1.1 Actions affecting welfare

Gray, 1992). The importance of that perspective in legitimating capitalism and in raising doubts about some aspects of state activities makes it a necessary starting-point for this discussion.

The individualistic 'economic man' perspective sees the distribution of incomes as appropriately determined by market activities. Incomes are 'earned' through 'work' and perhaps through other forms of market participation not covered by the word 'work' used in figure 1.1 – investment, renting of land and property, etc. Once that income is secured the individual makes spending decisions, and thus may purchase 'services' including such things as education and health care. People may even be able to solve future anticipated income maintenance and care needs through savings or through a 'market device', such as private insurance. Even pollution, a problem often created by the market-oriented behaviour of others, can be tackled by individualised economic-type solutions – buying masks or treated water, paying a neighbour to abstain from a noxious activity, and so on.

Regulation of economic activity is seen, in market theory, as arising naturally out of economic reciprocity – the fact that individuals are linked with each other in a series of exchange relationships inhibits the exploitation of short-run economic advantages in ways which will damage long-run prospects. A great deal of the argument about whether or not market principles are adequate for the determination of social order turns upon whether this last phenomenon can work effectively if left alone. Ormerod, amongst others, has pointed out the important message in the work of one of the founding fathers of economics, Adam Smith, that while, as the 'new right' emphasise, 'self interest is seen as the driving force of a successful economy', this needs to be pursued 'in the context of a shared view of what constitutes reasonable behaviour', which the state has a role to promote (Ormerod, 1994, p. 13).

Even in the individualistic model of society it is usually recognised that there are family relationships which may not be governed by market exchange principles. Hence families may be a forum within which incomes are redistributed to deal with dependencies arising from immaturity or infirmity. It follows logically from this that it is within families that much of the interchange of resources between generations occurs, including the inheritance of assets. Much intra-family exchange is in kind rather than in cash, and in this sense the family is the key site for 'social care'. This last kind of exchange includes the possibility of some being cared for while others are carers and some being labour market participants while others are their 'dependants'. This tends to involve divisions of responsibilities between the genders, in which women may be disadvantaged. Hence roles may be imposed rather than determined by free 'exchanges' (Land and Rose, 1985; Pascall, 1986).

The role of the family

In figure 1.1 the regulation of the family is described as determined by 'affection'. That was perhaps a contentious choice for one word to describe the complex, and tension-ridden, web of interlocking obligations and emotions which regulate family relationships. Just as there is much argument about self-regulation in market systems so too is there argument concerning the extent to which the family can be self-regulating and the extent to which its actual characteristics are determined by wider social relationships (Segal, 1983).

Families may be nuclear (including single adult headed families or indeed single persons living alone), or they may extend to quite large kinship networks. Where the latter occur families enlarge the sharing and division of labour possibilities. In terms of social organisation large kinship networks may also merge into small community organisations.

The role of the community

The term 'community' was chosen to describe the next level in the analysis. This is a difficult concept which has been given a multitude of meanings (Hillery, 1955) and has been much used to suggest voluntary obligations that the user asserts 'ought' to exist (Plant, 1974). The term 'society' might also have been chosen, except that in the discussion of modern societies it is very difficult to separate issues about society from issues about the state. What is therefore comprised within the term 'community' here is a very wide range of social institutions from, at a low level, extended kinship networks, tribes and neighbourhoods through to wider forms of social organisations which recognise mutual obligations.

'Charity' is then the term used to encapsulate the variety of ways in which communities may provide both cash and services to specific individuals. But the charitable response may derive from 'other-regarding' emotions (akin to those which may operate within families), from social 'norms' prescribing the right way to behave towards fellow beings and also from the identification of 'reciprocity' (as envisaged in the regulation of market behaviour). There has been extensive argument about the relative importance of these three in determining 'altruistic' behaviour in society (Titmuss, 1973; Reissman, 1977).

The state

The state is both a derivative from the social institutions discussed in the last section (called into being to assist them to work better) and an imposition upon them (arising out of successful efforts at domination). Justifications offered for state action rest upon assertions of the former argument, while attacks upon the 'intrusive' state are likely to draw upon the latter. The state may intervene to influence the original distribution of incomes by interfering with the market or by redistributing after market processes have had their effects. It may provide services and regulate activities through the law to influence what others do to provide incomes or services.

In moving, in the way justified above, from 'communities' to 'states' there is a risk that insufficient attention is being given to self-regulating mechanisms within whole societies. There are clearly important differences between societies in the extent to which state institutions are important for social welfare. These differences may be related to cultural and ideological differences. They may also be related to the extent to which powerful institutions, such as churches, voluntary societies, trade and occupational associations, and even industrial and commercial enterprises, claim to play key roles in social policy.

These differences have led some writers to speak of 'stateless societies' – an expression that has been applied for example to Britain and the United States (see discussion in Pusey, 1991, pp. 14–16). This usage clearly involves exaggeration to make a point – the state is important in any complex society, but there are differences in the extent to which the state is a crucial autonomous actor in policy making (see Chapter 2). In particular it is in the so-called 'stateless societies' that the individualist 'economic man' perspective described above has had more influence, endeavouring to limit the state to a 'night-watchman' role.

In a book that aims to range over its subject comparatively there is a particular need to recognise that 'state services' may be embedded in various kinds of government structure. Within the scope of the general term 'the state' used here is provincial government (in federal systems) and local government below the level of the nation state. There are also sometimes supra-national institutions with roles to play 'above' the nation state.

A societal response to an individual need may come from a variety of institutions ranging in size from the family up to (and perhaps beyond) the nation state. These institutions, however, cannot be analysed as if they were simply alternatives; they interact with each other, they collaborate with each other, they have expectations of each other and they may be able to control or regulate each other. There will be a 'mixed economy of welfare' (Pinker, 1979; Kamerman, 1983), but there will also be much argument about whether that 'mix' is right – hence the need here to emphasise some of the issues about the 'mix'. It is particularly relevant to note here the doctrine of 'subsidiarity' advanced in Catholic social theory which asserts that 'a community of a higher order should not interfere in the internal life of a community of a lower order, depriving the latter of its functions, but rather should support it in case of need and help to coordinate its activity with the activities of the rest of society' (John Paul II, 1991, p. 69). A 'community of a higher order' is most typically the nation state, though the term 'subsidiarity' also features prominently in debates about the role of the European Union.

As there will be particular concern with what brings the state into play it is very important to recognise the extent to which democratic expectations lead the other institutions to have specific requirements of the state and lead them to put pressure on the state to take over roles they are having difficulty in playing themselves. Conversely, however, those who control the state will wish to impose particular obligations upon the other institutions.

To explore these issues further the next three sections will look more closely at some of the issues about the three action categories, set out in figure 1.1, of income transfers, services and regulation with reference to the alternative levels in society.

Options for income transfers

In the model market economy (at least as postulated by classical economics) the primary ways in which incomes are earned are by selling commodities or one's own labour, or by securing returns to investment and entrepreneurial activities. Welfare economics then devotes attention to a series of justifications for departures from the determination of income distribution by the market (Rowley and Peacock, 1975). Such approaches seem to suggest that market determination of income distribution should be the norm. They may also imply that market mechanisms pre-date any other principles for income distribution. By contrast historical and anthropological studies show that concerns about 'just' rewards for economic activities and appropriate levels of resources to enable individuals to meet 'needs' and 'obligations' pre-date markets. They were brought further into consideration as markets developed (Parry and Bloch, 1989).

The point of this brief excursion into historical anthropology is to emphasise that communities (as defined above) have often had concerns about how income transfer processes, *of all kinds*, occur. These have been pursued, as economies have developed, by means of a variety of collective actions from food riots and guild organisations to modern trade unions. They have been taken on board by nation states in a variety of ways embracing concepts like minimum wages and guaranteed prices *as well as* the development of policies described nowadays as income maintenance policies. Hence, although income maintenance policies are one of the main concerns of the discussion to come, it is important not to lose sight of the fact that states intervene to influence incomes in other ways too.

Even today in complex industrial societies, it is not only states which engage in non-market income transfer activities. The most important 'income transfer' institution in human societies is the family. A key feature of marriage as an institution is the role it plays in facilitating income transfers in the forms of the following:

- Initial transfers between generations and between households.
- Mechanisms to enable resources to be available throughout an individual's lifetime.
- Transfers between parents and children.
- The sharing of resources between parents.

This statement should be understood as analytical; it should not be taken as prescriptive, let alone as a challenge to contemporary critiques of the family.

Beyond income transfer obligations determined by kinship lies the second kind of non-market income transfer, that influenced by recognition of a community of interest: collaboration between neighbours, community-based mutual aid in the face of disaster, support for professional and occupational peers, and so on. These forms of recognition of mutual concerns and responsibilities lead to the forming of institutions which facilitate transfers: friendly societies, trade unions, lodges, building societies, etc. In linking people with mutual concerns in this way they form some of the building-blocks of a wider society, contributing to adherence to a wide nation or state, a theme to which the discussion will return. In the shorthand used for figure 1.1 this was subsumed under the general concept of charity. But for the purposes of deeper analysis a distinction can be drawn between concern for those with whom we recognise direct communitarian links and concern for the welfare of 'strangers' (Titmuss, 1973; Watson, 1980).

There is scope for extensive debate about the nature of motivation towards charitable giving beyond the concerns of this discussion; the point here is simply that there are a variety of resource transfers both within and indeed between societies which come under the concept of charity, as used here.

Family and community transfers may owe little to either markets or governments. The key forms of economic transfer were earlier noted as the selling of commodities or one's own labour, and the earning of returns to investment and entrepreneurial activities. It was suggested that the forms they take may be affected by social customs or state interventions. However, there are other economic activities which are extensions of the basic categories just listed, but which also represent the recognition by market actors that there are complex needs outside those covered by everyday market transactions.

The first of these is the inclusion as part of the wage/salary package of specific other benefits which recognise the long-run needs and obligations of employees. The most important of these are pensions, which may be described as deferred wages, but will be nevertheless charges on the economic activities of future workers. Related benefits, involving less of a long-term commitment, are those for sickness and maternity together with retainers paid to employees through periods when no work is available. More complex still are contributions by employers to meet other needs and obligations of their employees: health care, education for children, even sometimes cash support for wives and children. While the analysis of all these can be reduced to assumptions about the market calculations of employers – about what they need to do to secure and retain their workforce – they also owe a great deal to social custom and practice, and long-run assumptions about the availability of resources.

The second kind of complex market-based transfer involves the structuring of investment in a way which is designed to meet individual concerns about long-run security. Included here, therefore, are funded pensions (whether employer administered or not) and various forms of life assurance.

The third relevant transfer system is insurance. This case involves entrepreneurs who make their livings by taking in and investing contributions from individuals who wish to insure themselves against risks lying in the future. Again it is the complexity of people's lives and their obligations, together with limitations to the simpler ways of dealing with the unexpected which fuel this area of business. The collective nature of the activity provides some mutual protection. The entrepreneurs in insurance further protect themselves through the use of actuarial techniques to estimate the likelihood of claims on their funds and to determine the scale of contributions required.

Societies are thus likely to develop a variety of market and non-market devices to achieve transfers between individuals, which will compensate for the inadequacies of simple market transfers. Early in the discussion it was established that the state may not adopt an entirely neutral role in relation to even the most basic kinds of market devices. What then may the state do in relation to devices which represent specific societal attempts to anticipate or deal with income deficiencies? Obviously the state may itself provide benefits. However, the very multiplicity of other alternatives to direct state *provision* offers alternatives for state *intervention*.

First, the state may enforce transfer commitments. It may require families to care for those of their members without incomes of their own, and may also require communities to provide for their poor. The state may force employers to provide sick pay or pensions, and it may even enforce insurance commitments.

Second, the state may regulate transfer arrangements. It may set up a framework of law which determines how family or employers' obligations may be met. Bolderson and Mabbett (1991, pp. 20–2) draw attention to the way in which states have attempted to impose responsibilities upon employers, enforceable through litigation, for injuries and illnesses developed as a consequence of the hazards of work. The state may also require insurance companies and pension schemes to have particular characteristics – rules about where they may invest, who should be their trustees, and so on. It may provide a framework of law for charitable ventures to prevent misappropriation of funds.

Third, the state may underwrite transfer arrangements. This will involve guaranteeing intervention if something goes wrong. There are various ways in which states have been willing to get involved where systems of family, community and charitable care fail. Similarly they have sometimes guaranteed pension or insurance arrangements.

Fourth, the state may become a direct party to a private income transfer arrangement through a subsidy. That subsidy may be a direct contribution to the activity or it may come in the form of relief from taxation, as applied to charities and to forms of assurance and insurance in many societies (see, for example, Stevens in Weir *et al.*, 1988, for the considerable importance of this for social policy in the United States). In a rather more complex sense much contemporary state support for families is seen as premised upon the family doing as much as possible for itself.

These four forms of state intervention have many interconnections. Enforcement and regulation have much in common as strategies; the former is in a sense a variant of the latter. Moreover, once the state becomes involved in enforcement and regulation it may find that it is hard to resist being pulled down the path towards underwriting and through that to subsidising. When non-state transfer institutions which are already heavily state regulated run into difficulties which are a consequence of developments outside their control, the very fact that the state has taken a serious interest in their activities offers a powerful argument for the injection of resources. When, additionally, these difficulties are partly a consequence of state regulation (for example where an insurance scheme has been prevented from rejecting high-risk clients) that argument is even more powerful. The mechanisms which pull the state into deeper involvement are explored more fully in Chapter 2 and in Chapter 4.

Options for services

Before getting on to any discussion of the alternative ways services may be provided it is important to recognise two issues about overlap between services and other modes of intervention. First, as the market model identifies, because services may be purchased needs for them may be met by income enhancement. This may be simply a matter of putting people in a position in which they are able to buy services for themselves (Ryan, 1991; Peacock, 1991). Hence, it may be argued that so long as individuals have sufficient income to be able to buy health care, social care or education they should then be left (by anyone else prone to interfere with their decision-making, and particularly by the state) to decide whether or not to buy them. It will be seen, below, that this issue is confused by the fact that the choices are not simply between the state or market and by social control concerns.

A modified variant of the 'new right' position set out above is to provide income enhancement in a way which in fact locks the recipient into spending it on a specific service. Examples are the education 'voucher', which the recipient parent must 'cash' on some form of schooling for their child, or an earmarked grant conditional upon acceptance of a service (Seldon, 1986). The justification of such linking is seen as being that the service in question is a 'merit good' (Musgrave, 1959; see also the discussion in Ryan, 1991) which the superordinate help provider decides must be imposed upon the recipient. That is, of course, the general case for service provision rather than cash. It may be found operating the other way round with a benefit generally given in cash being provided in kind – the provision of food and commodities directly to the poor, for example.

Second, a superordinate body may use regulatory powers to compel the family or the employer or the community to supply a service (this issue has arisen already in relation to income maintenance). Normally here the superordinate body is the state, but it is important not to disregard the pressure communities and voluntary bodies (in particular religious bodies) may be able to impose upon families and neighbours to assume caring responsibilities.

Once the state tries to impose obligations in this way it tends to move down the road towards funding them, pushed by forces perhaps even more powerful than those applying in the case of income maintenance. This effect can be seen particularly strongly in the history of education (Green, 1990). It is difficult to impose obligations upon poor parents to send children to school if they have to cope not only with the loss of child earnings but also have to pay fees as well. Employers will be reluctant to be educators, if competitors can then 'steal' their newly literate and numerate employees. However much religious bodies may have a commitment to education they are unlikely to be happy to have pupils forced upon them. Education, once pursued at a sophisticated level, has required formal institutions, which have largely taken it out of the family. Community efforts in education have needed heavy subsidies, either from individuals or from the state.

Modern medicine has similarly taken much of the responsibility for health care out of the realm of the family and the community (see Stacey, 1988). It is in the field of social care that one finds the 'mixed economy' most in evidence (Knapp, 1984). This phenomenon is surely not unrelated to the fact that 'care' is seen as an everyday personal and family matter, needing exceptional interventions only when 'normal' processes break down (this issue is explored further in Chapter 6). Significantly ill-health is an important source of such a breakdown. It will be seen in Chapters 5 and 6 on health care and social care that this generates a variety of borderline issues between these two services. The preoccupation with the failure of 'normal' processes in this area of policy also has the effect of bringing issues of regulation to the fore. These are issues about making people take responsibilities, preventing them doing harm to others or to themselves, and (in the last resort) intervening to remove individuals into alternative forms of care.

Options for regulation

Figure 1.1 presented regulation as one of the options at all levels. In the previous discussion it was suggested that it is real or perceived shortcomings of the weaker forms of regulation which bring in the state. The possibilities for self-regulation are, however, very considerable. In the real world this can give a superordinate body like the state the option of threatening intervention if self-regulation is not attempted or is not effective. This remark applies as much to families as to firms!

It is important also to bear in mind the earlier observations on the state, referring to it as both a form of collective action and as an imposition, suggesting that its legitimacy may be open to dispute. In this context ostensibly subordinate institutions – notably families and communities – may internalise regulatory problems precisely to keep the state at bay. Powerful examples of this appear in systems of vigilante law where communities seek to discipline their own deviants.

The topic of regulation will be discussed in this book in three rather different contexts. One area of explicitly regulatory policy is examined – pollution control policy – on the grounds that this is important for social welfare. Second, aspects of service policy, and particularly social care, are seen as regulatory in nature (as discussed above). Third, economic welfare issues are seen in various ways, as already noted, as matters about interference with and regulation of market behaviour as well as matters for 'post-market' intervention.

Conclusions and an introduction to the rest of the book

Conclusions

The study of social policy has been defined as the study of a range of issues where matters of individual welfare are of 'social' concern and therefore potentially of state concern. This book gives a great deal of attention to *how* the state comes to be involved and *why* it gets involved. There are some related issues about whether it *should* become involved, which will not be directly addressed. These have been seen, in relation to the distinctions made above, as choices between 'conservative' perspectives which emphasise family and community obligations, 'socialist' views which emphasise collective provision by the state and 'liberal' emphases upon markets (Evers in Evers *et al.*, 1994; see also George and Wilding, 1994).

These philosophical issues need handling in a rather different way to the approach adopted in this book. That is not to say that the author is indifferent to the philosophical questions. His view is that it is unlikely that philosophy can resolve the key questions, rather it supplies us with justifications for the stances we *choose*. This book will indicate some of the philosophical issues, and the author would be disingenuous if he claimed that he does not have strong views on the key issues. These are probably difficult to hide. For that reason he might as well be open about his general perspective here. Not surprisingly someone who writes a book about social policy and welfare issues and the role of the state, and who has devoted much of his life to the study of these issues, thinks that social welfare issues are important and thinks there is a role for the state with regard to them. In fact the author has quite a strong statist view. He is sceptical about many of the efforts to roll back the state in social policy. He believes many modern critiques of state action have focused too much on the shortcomings of that form of social organisation and not enough on the problems about the other alternatives (particularly those involving markets).

The rest of the book

The next two chapters complete Part I by examining how the state gets involved in social policy (Chapter 2) and looking at comparative work which seeks to explain and explore the implications of different state responses in different societies (Chapter 3). In Part III, the more general themes are also explored in chapters dealing with the issues about social divisions within welfare and with future prospects for social policy (Chapters 11 and 12).

In Part II are chapters on some specific areas of social policy. This section of the book begins with those areas which are generally embraced in definitions of social policy – income maintenance, health and social care. It goes on to other areas which are a little less central – housing, employment and education. While there is little basis for leaving education out of a discussion of social policy, this does often happen. It is suspected this has more to do with the way in which scholars define their areas of study than anything else. Housing and employment policy, by contrast, are rather different because of the extent to which in many societies job and housing opportunities are left to the market. Welfare-oriented interventions are often the exception rather than the rule. However, jobs and houses are vital for individual welfare, and the issues which determine whether or not there will be interventions by the state are important, raising interesting issues about the limitations of market systems.

There is obviously a difficulty about drawing a line between the concerns to be addressed in this book and the concerns of the study of economic policy. This author would neither wish to see social policy as somehow concerned with the problems left over once the economic institutions have been 'set right' nor would he wish to see economic policies determined without reference to their social consequences (see Weale, 1983, for an interesting discussion of this issue). Yet the study of economic policies is a highly specialised subject. The pragmatic compromise adopted here is to see it as necessary to raise issues about the roles of markets in relation to every topic covered in the book, and to include some topics where issues about markets and the working of the economy are particularly salient. There is a related issue here about taxation, another very specialised topic. In this case some references are made to issues about taxation, and forms of tax relief in various places throughout the book, but particularly in the chapters on income maintenance and housing.

To follow the chapters on housing, employment and education policy there is a chapter on environmental policy. This is included because of a dissatisfaction with the narrow approach to the study of social policy. Surely it is a little odd for discussions of social policy to disregard issues about dangers to individual health and safety which get right to the heart of the traditional role of the state in protecting its citizens. However, in including only environmental policy amongst a range of issues where the regulation of economic activities is important the author is laying himself open to the charge that he is trying to redraw the boundary between social policy and other aspects of policy at a particularly unsatisfactory place. What distinguishes environmental policy from other policies concerned with public safety? To stop there involves leaving out some other possibilities – notably issues about the protection of consumers and issues about access to market opportunities where the emergent social policy issues are very interesting (see Cahill, 1994, for a discussion of these). Two particular topics, which only the existing size of the venture deterred the author from including, were energy policy and transport policy. Both of these interact extensively with pollution policy (as Chapter 10 will show), both involve issues about subsidy as well as about regulation and both have a considerable impact upon welfare – including the capacity to benefit from the social policies which will be discussed here (transport to school, hospitals, etc., and heating to enable the home to be a satisfactory site for care, study, etc.).

Beyond these regulatory issues are external defence issues which are never defined as social welfare ones and internal law-and-order issues which are only sometimes included, and then often only inasmuch as they interact with other aspects of social welfare. The pragmatic reason for leaving them out is that they involve specialised areas of study with a large specific literature (criminology and penology) which is often not very well related to the central concerns of the social welfare literature.

The book concludes with two more general chapters in Part III. These enable issues about the relationship between social policy, society and the state to be explored further, and examine some of the current worldwide influences on social policy development. Chapter 11 explores issues about the relationship between social policy and social stratification. Social policy has been presented as involving a set of state institutions which provide 'social rights' (Marshall, 1963), mitigating the divisive impact of capitalist economic institutions. Yet even those writers who subscribe to Marshall's optimistic vision of the development of industrial societies point to flaws in the design of welfare states – the existence of 'social divisions of welfare' (Titmuss, 1958).

The theme of social divisions has also been taken up in two different ways. On the one hand, comparativists suggest that some systems are more egalitarian than others (Furniss and Tilton, 1979). They have stimulated the vein of work, explored in Chapter 3 of this book, concerned with the reasons for these differences. Much of this work has dealt with the extent to which principles of 'solidarity' are embedded in state policies, linking labour market relationships in fully employed economies to rights outside work (Esping-Andersen, 1990 – see Chapter 3).

On the other hand, there has developed a critique of the stress upon labour market relations in both the early 'social divisions' and the later comparative work since it involves the disregard of issues about gender divisions in access to welfare and a lack of concern about racial or ethnic divisions in societies which have an impact upon access to both work and social benefits (Williams, 1989; Bryson, 1992).

Chapter 11's exploration of the divisions in welfare raises issues not merely about the extent to which the 'welfare state' was even in its heyday a flawed system but also about the ways in which those flaws have become more evident. Fundamental to this is the extent to which the original welfare state ideal was premised upon full employment for male bread-winners, heading an inegalitarian conjugal family. The undermining of these premises is forcing the rethinking of social policy. For some amongst the 'new right' social policy must be restructured, and the state's role in family and economic life diminished, because it is to blame for these developments (Murray, 1984). An opposite view is that what is occurring is merely the unwinding of the threads of an untenable system. For those unwilling either to try to turn back the clock or to wait for the revolution there are a variety of worrying developments needing attention. These suggest, certainly, that the idea of a comfortable partnership between the welfare state, the capitalist economy and the patriarchal family (the Keynesian welfare state as it is sometimes called, see, for example, Pierson, 1991) needs revision in the age of a global economy, new technology, far from omnicompetent states, changing demographic structures and challenges to traditional concepts of citizenship and rights. These themes are taken up in Chapter 12, but will inevitably be given some consideration in discussions of individual policy areas in earlier chapters.

Guide to further reading

This chapter has outlined various themes which will be picked up further later in the book; reading suggestions are therefore very limited at this stage. Many writers have attempted to capture the issues about the mix of influences upon welfare. Catherine Jones does so in Part I of her *Patterns of Social Policy* (1985). So do Drover and Kerans in the first chapter of their edited collection, *New Approaches to Welfare Theory* (1993). That book goes on to explore many of the underlying philosophical issues about social policy. The different ideological viewpoints about the role of the state in social policy are very effectively explored in George and Wilding's *Welfare and Ideology*.

A number of books have dealt with the issues about economics and social policy, discussed briefly in this chapter and more thoroughly in the next. Good introductions from economists include Gordon's *Economics and Social Policy* (1982) and Le Grand and Robinson's *The Economics of Social Problems* (1984).

CHAPTER TWO

Explaining the development of social policy

Introduction

Without precisely defining an advanced industrial society, it can be noted that in all such societies collective efforts have been made to develop elaborate social policies. Governments are heavily involved in these efforts – generally as providers, but if not at least as regulators. Examine, for example, a recent addition to the group of societies thus defined, Taiwan. That country has a large state educational system involving compulsory school attendance and a range of opportunities for education up to university level, and it has a system of social insurance with a rapidly extending coverage. At the time of writing a 'universal' health insurance system has just been established. There is also a national social welfare system offering social assistance and various forms of institutional care and the government is struggling towards effective pollution control policies.

In the face of evidence of the universality of social policy development by states in 'advanced' societies some comparative work and related theoretical work has concentrated on a search for explanations of this phenomenon. There are a number of possible approaches. First, there is a need to mention, if only to pass on to more sophisticated theories, that some of the earliest writing on 'welfare states' saw no need to do more than acknowledge social policy development as a natural concomitant of a 'modern' or 'advanced' society. Social policy is in this context a self-evident indicator of social progress. Joan Higgins (1981, pp. 27–32), in her review of approaches to comparison, criticises specific writings on British social policy (for example, a once widely used textbook by Hall, 1957), which 'explain' welfare state development in terms of the advancement of caring values.

Second, there are a number of sociological explanations of social policy development which draw upon functionalist theories, some of which also involve notions of 'progress' or 'development'. These were particularly rooted in a body of American work which has seen social advance as a 'modernisation' process. In some forms of this theory this 'evolutionary' process was believed to be reaching a point in some societies at which conflicts over distribution were being solved through material progress enabling the welfare state to take care of all. It was proclaimed that the 'end of ideology was in sight' (Bell, 1978). The use of 'was' in this paragraph is generally appropriate. This evolutionary optimism, which critics showed to be very flawed even in its heyday (Gouldner, 1971), now looks very dated.

However, the general idea that the development of social policy might be a concomitant of other kinds of development in modern societies is worth further consideration. The discussion in the next two sections will go through the main ingredients in various theoretical approaches which emphasise both modernisation and the growth of the role of the state. Some problems about the wholesale adoption of the theories on offer will be suggested, but it will be indicated that there are elements in each which can usefully be applied in some kind of mixed explanation of events.

Modernisation theory

The 'modernisation' package has the following four features:

1. The evolution of complex urban communities.
2. The development of sophisticated industrial processes.
3. The achievement of a high average standard of living.
4. The elaboration of political and administrative systems (particularly ones involving forms of popular participation – evading here the question begging concept of democratisation).

The evolution of complex urban communities

This element in the modernisation 'package' is the most problematical. There are many very large urban agglomerations in some of the poorer countries in the world (Mexico City, Sao Paulo, Calcutta) where social policies are rudimentary. Nevertheless there is no doubt that such communities are a source of substantial 'collective action' problems which communities and governments have sought to solve through social policies. Historical studies show how significant worries about the spread of disease in cities and fears of the urban mob have been in the early development of pollution control policies, health policies and relief policies. De Swaan (1988) makes interesting use of theory derived from welfare economics (see further discussion on pp. 30–4) about problems that could not be solved by individualistic and later localistic responses. He links this with the evolution of new knowledge and techniques – theories about the spread of disease, methods of disposing of refuse and institutions to reduce the threat from the idle poor. He sees the latter as a kind of social progress, drawing upon Elias's work on the 'civilising process' (1978, 1982).

The development of sophisticated industrial processes

Industrialisation, itself one of the sources of urban development, but also the generator of distributional changes in society and a source of demands for new ways of handling labour as 'a factor in production', has been given rather more attention in accounts of the growth of social policy (Rimlinger, 1971). The original functionalist work identifies a connection between industrialisation and social policy development in terms of social differentiation (Kerr *et al.*, 1973; for a discussion of this work see Mishra, 1977). Mishra describes this as follows:

> *With further socio-economic advance, leading to the industrial society, institutional specialisation develops further. So does mobility – both geographical and occupational. The extended family and the local community weaken as collectivities . . .. More specialised structures arise to cope with the growing volume of welfare functions. (1977, pp. 57–8)*

The initial steps here have been seen as comprising the development of welfare activities by enterprises and the development of voluntary organisations (both of an egalitarian co-operative kind and charities). To then explain why the state comes in without bringing in other theories, more arguments from welfare economics may be applicable (again see de Swaan, 1988). Firms recognise that to try to cope with issues about the education and the health and welfare of their workforce imposes costs which may make them uncompetitive by comparison with others who do less. As far as education and training are concerned they may even suffer from poaching. Voluntary organisations face other kinds of 'free rider' problems – the benefits of their activities extend indirectly to the whole community. They, moreover, find that problems they set out to solve are too big for them. There is then an increased tendency to look to the state as a means of enforcing the 'socialisation' of the costs, sharing them more widely through society.

There is a Marxist version of the above argument that has been most forcefully put by O'Connor (1973), but also by others such as Gough (1979) and Ginsburg (1992). This sees industrial capital as facing two kinds of problems. One of these is that set out above, that the efficient operation of capitalism requires attention to be given to the maintenance of a fit and trained labour supply. It is in the interest of individual capitalists that the cost of doing this should be 'collectivised', that is, taken on by society as a whole. This function is most readily performed by the only overarching body – the state. That view, of course, begins to lose its force once capitalist enterprise becomes multi-national, then perhaps the need is for a supra-national body to deal with social policy issues (a key issue today in a body like the European Union).

The other problem facing capital brings this discussion much closer to classical Marxist theory – this is the problem of unrest in a society in which employment is insecure, rewards are low, and the old and sick are particularly vulnerable. Marxist theory postulates that capitalism needs a 'reserve army of labour' and that workers are regarded by capitalists as 'factors' of production to be employed as cheaply as possible, with no regard to their nuclear or extended family responsibilities. These are inherent characteristics of capitalism for Marx, which will contribute to its ultimate downfall. However, if the state can deal with some of these problems, without at the same time undermining the basic economic relationship between capital and labour, then the otherwise gradually accumulating discontent about the system can be reduced. Theorists like O'Connor go on to argue that this 'legitimising' function of the welfare state is, in the long run, unstable. Its rising costs have ultimately to be borne by production, with damaging consequences for the capitalist system. This takes the discussion into 'crisis theory', affecting the future of advanced welfare states (a theme explored further in Chapter 12). The point here is that this kind of theory offers a Marxist version of the connection between industrialisation and the development of social policy.

Both non-Marxist theory and Marxist theory are largely functionalist in character. It is argued that these developments are the necessary consequences of industrialisation. These approaches have been attacked as deterministic, paying little attention to the choices made by actors or to variations in response from place to place (Ashford, 1986). Nevertheless these theories, if used with others, certainly help to take the discussion away from naive emphases upon 'progress' or the growth of compassion. They also offer an approach to explaining the roles of some unlikely actors in the growth of social policy (like, for example, the Prussian Chancellor Bismarck – see Hennock, 1987; Clasen and Freeman, 1994).

The achievement of a high average standard of living

The third element in the modernisation 'package' concerns the standard of living. Industrialisation makes an important contribution to increases in this.

The more detailed comparative analysis in the next chapter shows that there is no straightforward association between a high national standard of living and high welfare expenditure. That, however, does not mean that there will not have been the following:

1. An association between economic growth and welfare state growth across the broad band of prosperous nations in the past.
2. A certain critical threshold that nations have to pass before significant levels of public services, which impose high costs on the nation, become feasible in developing societies.

There is a further analytical problem relevant throughout this discussion, but particularly pertinent here: expenditure on social policy is not necessarily direct state expenditure. High levels of personal income may make it possible for the state to raise high levels of taxes to pay for social policies but it may equally either reduce the necessity for those policies or create conditions in which it is possible to solve welfare problems by other means. These considerations may be particularly relevant to the contrast between high levels of income and low public expenditure in the United States and Japan. At this point in the analysis little progress can be made without widening the range of considerations taken into account.

Some exponents of the modernisation thesis go on at this point in the argument to consider the demographic effects of industrialisation, urbanisation and high levels of income (for example, Wilensky, 1975). These are lowered birth rates and raised life expectations at the end of life. The second of these, particularly when associated with an earlier fall in the birth rate to limit the size of the prime age population relative to the elderly, is seen as of importance for social policy expenditure (see Chapter 12). The issue of the cost implications of proportionately large elderly populations for pension, health care and social care expenditure will need consideration at various places in this book. But there are difficulties about extrapolating backwards to see this contemporary issue as a crucial driving force in social policy development, except inasmuch as – in the way discussed above – there are a variety of motives for trying to socialise the costs of care for elderly people.

The elaboration of political and administrative systems

The fourth element in the modernisation 'package' shifts attention to the development of the state. The theories discussed so far seem largely to take the state for granted – for example, as the organisation 'capital' turns to when it has problems. It is also a feature of classical Marxism to treat the state as merely the 'executive' of the ruling class. Theories which emphasise the state role in social policy development are more varied than those which emphasise the importance of industrialisation.

First, why should Marxists assume that legitimacy is just a problem for capitalism? The problems of the internal security of the state and the need for support in external struggles suggest that the advancement of welfare policies may be just as much a state concern as a capitalist concern. There is, under certain circumstances, a need to see the pre-democratic state as a modernising force and a need to recognise that the process of creating, and protecting, the modern nation state required social policy developments. Unifying a subject people containing varied linguistic groups called for early educational initiatives (de Swaan, 1988; Green, 1990). Securing an effective army to protect the state or advance its claims needed some attention to the health of the subject population. The period in which most of the major European nation states achieved their modern forms (from the mid-eighteenth century to the early twentieth century) saw extensive conflict between them, both about their European claims and about their colonial ambitions (Porter, 1983). This conflict involved the expression of intense, racialist forms of nationalism, involving claims of national superiority. In such a context evidence of internal weaknesses – an unfit population or a (generally relatively) falling birth rate – contributed to social policy growth (Semmel, 1961; Pedersen, 1993).

Second, in social theory there is a danger of treating the state as an abstraction. The state is, or depends upon the support of, a network of organisations. It has been shown that state apparatuses in many societies emerged out of royal households (Kamenka, 1989). Then as state activity became more complex a range of functions – from soldiering through tax collecting to the administration of justice – became specialised. Bureaucratic elites emerged with an interest in the perpetuation of their own roles. They might also have seen that they could further increase their power by extending their range of activities, and that this might be a source of opportunities for their families and kin. Once, however marginally, social policy responsibilities were taken on by the state, with the appointment of teachers or health inspectors or even workhouse keepers, then within its own bureaucratic ranks there would be people likely to defend their tasks and perhaps to argue for their extension (see further discussion on pp. 34–5).

Third, some approaches to this issue recognise the complex relationship between 'state formation' and policy development. The former process has involved the establishment of a complex set of institutions – constitutions, political practices, administrative arrangements – which affect the way particular social issues and problems will be approached (examples of this are explored further in Chapter 3).

The fourth issue about the state is that there are a variety of effects which stem from the development of democratic participation in state decision-making. What stance one takes depends upon one's view of the importance of these developments. At one extreme lies a body of theory which sees the electoral process as a market process. Elites compete with each other to win the support of the people. In the course of that competition they offer promises of new social policies (Buchanan and Tullock, 1962). This perspective is developed by exponents of the 'economic theory of democracy' – suggesting ways in which costs are spread and hidden. It is argued that there is a kind of 'rake's progress' in which individual benefits can be traded for socialised costs so that people do not recognise the full cost implications for themselves (Brittan, 1977). The theory also makes connections with an 'economic theory of bureaucracy', suggesting that there is a bureaucratic elite only too ready to encourage this process (Niskanen, 1971).

Alternatively there are perspectives, particularly deriving from neo-Marxists, which view the participation offered to citizens with extreme scepticism. For them what the state does is seen as kept to a minimum by capitalism and conditioned by the requirements of legitimation (as discussed above). The fact is, they would argue, that having initiated a participatory process the capitalists may have made the legitimation process a little more complex – they have to be seen to be acknowledging the demands upon them. Furthermore capitalism has enhanced the role of the state, making the state a buffer organisation between the capitalists and the proletariat. While the state's task is to manage capitalism, it may be that it does this with a measure of autonomy. That autonomy may merely be seen as a functional necessity in the face of complex forces on either side (Offe, 1984).

Neo-Marxist theories which acknowledge, and welcome, popular participation get into some difficulties about their theoretical underpinning. Democratic exponents of the class struggle have seen parliamentary institutions as ways to advance the transformation of society. Opportunities for representatives of the proletariat to participate in parliaments and governments may be merely chances to get on to a launching pad ready for a take-off to fundamental social change. For many, however, it is also a chance to start to make changes. The question then arises about whether social policies may not be the initial achievements in a peaceful social revolution. This involves a model of gradualist social change in a democratic society in which, while interests may differ in the extent of their power, the weaker groups have a great deal to play for. Their increased participation shifts public policy in an egalitarian direction. This is a model which renders much of the earlier Marxist theory beside the point. Or is it the case that democratisation is merely a 'tender trap' in which a great deal of effort yields but marginal gains, and, as legitimisation theory argues, the welfare state is the key 'institution of the truce' between capital and labour?

The review of this argument brings this discussion close to one of the central concerns of comparative studies which aim to go beyond the general analysis of similarities between different national systems to look at explanations of differences. It is all very well to emphasise that all advanced industrial societies have complex social policy systems and to spend a great deal of time seeking common explanations, but there are some very important differences. The most fundamental of those differences is that some countries spend substantially more on social policy than others, and that these differences cannot be simply explained by differences in national wealth or income. Not surprisingly, in the light of the influence of Marxism and of interest in working-class movements in general, one of the central concerns of comparative studies has been the extent to which such differences can be explained in terms of differences in the success of political parties of the 'working class' or the 'left'. This theme is further discussed in the next chapter.

Pulling the threads together

Modernisation and the growth of the state have been the general, and related, trends in social policy growth. They come together so powerfully that to some extent there is a problem that the argument may be expressed the wrong way round – the modern industrial state is to some extent defined in terms of its adoption of social policy as a 'welfare state'. One reason the state is a large enterprise, in the absence of war, is that it has to be to sustain its welfare activities. At the same time, though this is more contentious, the complex institutions of capitalism may be sustained by the system of social policy.

At a less grandiose level, it is possible to pull some themes out of the earlier discussion to offer specific suggestions about the growth of state social policy. In doing this the argument will be deployed not in the relatively functionalist way that it was above, but in a way that may be applied to the motivations of specific actors.

The themes are as follows:

1. Concerns about the danger to society of disadvantaged groups.
2. Concerns about national weakness.
3. Demands for egalitarian policies and concerns to achieve the political incorporation of emergent working-class voters. .
4. Concerns about the need to regulate market activities.
5. The roles of professionals and bureaucrats as advocates of state involvement.
6. Altruism.

Concerns about the danger to society of disadvantaged groups

Concerns about the danger to society of disadvantaged groups – sturdy beggars, who might riot or turn to crime – manifested themselves very early in the emergence of nation states (see the discussion of this in Piven and Cloward, 1972). Initial stances looked towards, first, families and, second, communities as sources of support for the poor. The state became involved to define *which* communities should assume this responsibility in the case of those who had moved away from their roots, and initially sought to secure the shift of the mobile poor back to the places from which they originated. As social change undermined the feasibility of this task the state had to face up to the fact that it might be imposing unreasonable burdens upon the communities in which the poor had congregated (de Swaan, 1988). Thus it began to accept the need to subsidise the local effort it had begun to regulate.

The characteristic form of the social policy intervention deriving from this was one which aimed to enforce family obligations wherever possible, reinforce communitarian or charitable responses and enforce individual attachment to the labour force. Herein lies the roots of the widespread response to poverty by way of family means-tests operated locally, within a national framework and with a strong emphasis upon work obligations.

Initially this basic response was very often provided within an institution, designed to deter all but the most desperate from seeking help. This was the 'workhouse' which featured in the early social policy history of many countries. Having responded in that way societies found that many of the people seeking relief had health and social care problems. Simple humanity initially required some caring response, then, later, developing medicine offered some possibilities of treatment. The latter might restore them to health and thus to the workforce. Hence, state involvement in poor relief brought with it the development of state health and social care services for the very poor (Roberts, 1960).

While the workhouses found themselves increasingly involved with the old and sick, the problem of the existence, from time to time and place to place, of the workless able-bodied poor was not solved by a repressive poor law. By the end of the nineteenth century it began to be recognised that there might be a problem of 'unemployment' arising from the malfunctioning of the labour market (Harris, 1972; Burnett, 1994). Since the Marxists were expounding a view that this malfunctioning was endemic and were engaged in trying to mobilise the unemployed, fear of this group stimulated new policy thinking: the search for ways of making the labour market work better, the examination of ways of putting people into work and the consideration of the case for developing unemployment benefit systems. The period after the Russian revolution, which was also a time of great economic dislocation following the ending of the First World War, was also one when, evidence from a study of Britain suggests, fear of the unemployed stimulated the search for new policies (see Gilbert, 1970). Piven and Cloward (1972) have similarly analysed social policy developments in the United States from the nineteenth century through the New Deal of the 1930s to the 1960s largely in these terms.

As far as health policies have been concerned there were other categories of 'dangerous' people as well as 'sturdy beggars'. These were people with illnesses which, if left untreated in the community, would provide a threat to others. There were two kinds of threat that were identified. One of these was the threat of infection. The identification of a need, in the interests of the rest of society, either to treat infectious diseases or to incarcerate sufferers from infectious diseases (or both depending upon the availability of cures) depended upon the development of theories which identified ways in which infections spread (Morris, 1976; Pelling, 1978). Once that occurred the publicly maintained 'isolation' hospital was a natural response. Later as the understanding of causation increased, and particularly as quicker remedies and preventative measures (inoculation, etc.) were identified, the state role could change again (and perhaps reduce). Of course, pollution control measures offered an alternative and, in the long run, a more effective kind of response to these 'dangerous' people. The same was true of housing policies which contributed to the elimination of 'slums'. These responses, however, came slowly with the deepening of the understanding of problem causation and the acceptance of more complex ways of dealing with the issues.

The other threatening group amongst the sick were those whose illness was deemed to produce behaviour that was dangerous to others. Private incarceration of the mentally ill developed amongst the rich, sometimes to prevent inheritance (Jones, 1993). Public incarceration of poorer mentally ill people came later, when the need for public protection was seen as the justification of public expenditure. Similar treatment was often meted out to the group now known as people with 'learning difficulties' (previously called the mentally subnormal). Here, a eugenic concern that they should not breed influenced the public response.

Concerns about national weakness

Concerns about national weakness in the period in which conflicts between nation states were endemic, particularly in Europe, led to concerns about both health care and the role of the family. More recently some of the debates about education policy have been cast in somewhat similar terms.

There was a concern about falling birth rates (in relation to competitor nations and sometimes in relation to differential birth rates within the nation). This generated interest in one of the simplest of income maintenance policies, the provision of direct subsidies for children (family allowances or child benefits). Arguments for this kind of benefit were related in complex ways to arguments about the adequacy of adult male wages for the support of families, including (in very many cases) non-labour market participant wives. The direct involvement of the state in this form of subsidy was seen by employers as preferable to state-determined minimum wages (where family need considerations would exert an upward effect upon all wages). The other alternative, the payment of differential wages to family men, was practised a little in state sectors – in the army and the universities in Britain – and in some parts of the private sector in France. It was an option without direct tax implications, and the added advantage that it might encourage the better off to breed. However, it introduced market distortions, and might have undermined the very objective of the policy by placing a premium on the employment of family men (see Pedersen, 1993, for a detailed examination of the debates about these issues in Britain and France).

A related focus here was upon childbirth and children. By the end of the nineteenth century many countries had quite good data on the incidence of maternal and infant mortality, and there was a growing awareness of ways to tackle these problems. Here concerns about making medical services available, concerns about ways to provide caring services and concerns about the implications of income and housing problems led to a range of responses.

Concerns about the 'fitness' of nations reached their high point around the end of the nineteenth century and remained important until discredited by Fascism at the end of the Second World War (for a historical analysis of this theme in German society, see Weindling, 1989). It is important to bear in mind that a feature of this concern was a set of Social-Darwinist beliefs both about forms of racial superiority and about the need to ensure that nations were strengthened through the propagation of their fittest members. This mind-set posed dilemmas for policy makers who were concerned about the falling birth rate and about the evidence that many of their adult citizens were 'poor' physical specimens. As far as the latter point was concerned the argument was further complicated by the developing challenge to Social Darwinism by those able to show how much these 'deficiencies' were products of deprivation and a poor environment.

The ugliest part of this debate was that which focused not so much upon the need to improve services but on the need to withhold social policy benefits from the unfit on the grounds that their preservation and propagation weakened the nation. Hence a preoccupation on targeting to 'the deserving' or 'the respectable working class' created differentiation in services. Such differentiation was reinforced by the fact that it was this group who were increasingly bidding for political attention at the end of the nineteenth century, the topic of the next section. Since the fall of Hitler overtly biologically based arguments about the fitness of racial groups have largely been discredited, but this theme is still echoed in arguments that particular social policies sustain deviant groups within society. Moore (in Coenen and Leisink, 1993) illustrates the connection between the earlier debates which 'seem extraordinary to us today' (*ibid.*, p. 56) and the 'new populism' of Charles Murray (1984, 1990) in which:

> *The vocabulary of the social sciences is replaced by the language of disease. Murray describes himself as 'a visitor from a plague area come to see whether the disease is spreading' and later asks 'how contagious is this disease?'* (ibid., *p. 57)*

Finally, before moving to the next section, a word on education. The escalating importance in the twentieth century of technology in war and the increasingly global economic competition have raised concerns within governments about the adequacy of their education systems. This has been a particularly significant theme in recent British debate about education. The 'elite tradition' of non-vocational education in private schools and universities and the egalitarian concerns embodied in some of the reforms of the state system in the twenty years starting around 1955 are alternatively, and sometimes together, blamed for the nation's reduced capacity to compete economically.

Demands for egalitarian policies and concerns to achieve the political incorporation of emergent working-class voters

The major debate within the comparative study of welfare states about the political impact of emergent working-class voters will be further explored in the next chapter. It is emphasised in the literature in two rather different ways, hence the rather unwieldy title to this section. There is evidence of what may be described as 'anticipatory reactions' as political elites sought to buy off this emergent electorate with social policy measures. This is seen by many scholars as lying at the heart of the Bismarckian adoption of social insurance. Ashford puts it like this:

> *... social legislation under the Second Reich had the important political purpose of crippling whatever democratic impulse might arise in the form of social democracy or enlightened Catholicism.... The paradox ... was that by 1890 Germany built the most complete system of social insurance in the world, but democratic forces were effectively excluded and unable to use social reform as a way of building a stable democratic tradition. (Ashford, 1986, p. 40; see also Dyson, 1980)*

The German industrial working classes were provided with social insurance, without effective participation in a way which was designed to divide them and inhibit their political mobilisation by tying them, because of their ultimate expectation of social benefits from their contributions, into support of the status quo. As a political strategy this worked only in the short run. In the longer run German social democrats became an effective reformist party seeking social policy advance (see Clasen and Freeman, 1994).

Initially, however, some of the most active representatives of labour, particularly socialist ones, regarded social policies with distrust. In some cases this implied simply a revolutionary distrust of ameliorative measures, a perspective justified by the Bismarckian strategy, but in other cases it involved a recognition that social policies might be poor substitutes for the pursuit of adequate returns to labour, guaranteed incomes at the bottom of the wage distribution and efforts to sustain full employment. That certainly seems to have influenced the response of the Australian labour movement (Castles, 1985; Macintyre, 1985).

The alternative to presenting this theme in terms of anticipated reactions is to recognise that while that went on, in places other than Germany too, much of the history of social policy making between the end of the nineteenth century and the middle of the twentieth century can be seen as involving either working-class parties with social reform platforms – in income maintenance, health, education and housing policies – or acceptance by other parties of a need to secure mass support by recognising the strength of working-class demands for state social policies. It is in sum a recognition of mass pressures within pluralist politics which characterises the 'economic theory of democracy' account of social policy development (see p. 23).

In relation to more detailed events it is important not to forget the significance of 'self-help' amongst workers in the early period of industrialisation. Alongside the development of trade unions were a variety of organisations designed to provide cash benefits at times of personal misfortune, solve housing problems, make forms of care available, enhance education, and so on. These developments had a fragility in the face of increasing turbulence in the labour market associated with the trade cycle, and increasing demands coming from ageing workers with emergent care needs and perhaps looking to health or unemployment benefits in lieu of a pension (Gilbert, 1966). Initially the scope for fraud provided by these institutions also led to calls for state regulation. The state social insurance model built upon the methods being used for self-help. This is what made the Bismarckian approach so appealing to individuals.

Once the state was involved political pressure then slowly pushed it down the path towards more extensive activities (de Swaan, 1988). Demands were made to bring in excluded groups. In particular the exclusion of families from social insurance schemes providing health care for bread-winners provoked new political demands for their inclusion.

The way the vulnerability of private insurance provisions led to demands for state interventions has a particular importance in the field of health care because of the way in which it increased (and is still increasing) in cost. This cost increase is particularly attributable to advances in medicine, which extend the range of costly treatments available, and to the ageing of the population. This theme will be explored further elsewhere in the book. What this development does to private insurance is steadily to increase the premiums required. It also intensifies the difficulties insurers may have in containing costs and avoiding bad risks, leading them both to exclude particular categories of customers and to refuse to support certain forms of treatment (see Deber, 1993). This further stimulates the demands for the state to do the job instead. Clearly in this situation some premium payers (amongst whom may be organisations which have agreed to underwrite the health costs of their employees) may come to believe *either* that the state can do the job more cheaply *or* that a socialised scheme will impose a lesser burden of costs upon themselves. Hence they may join the excluded groups in lobbying for reform. It is this kind of dynamic that lies at the heart of the search for further initiatives from the federal government in the United States (*ibid.*).

Concerns about the need to regulate market activities

The last section emphasised state responses to demands and earlier sections emphasised state responses to threats, but alongside these it must also be recognised that social policies have been seen as correcting the inefficient working of the labour market. This is a contentious subject. The main source for this section is not so much analysis of the historical record (although that has influenced some accounts of this subject, notably de Swaan's, 1988), but theory. That theory is economic theory which has tried to identify the circumstances in which market systems will not work satisfactorily. This has then contributed to a philosophical literature which attempts to define the circumstances in which state (or at least collective) intervention may be justified for those who believe that market systems are the right ones to settle most social distribution questions. Allusions were made to this literature in Chapter 1 and at the beginning of this chapter.

The fact that this literature is principally designed to delineate when state intervention *should* occur, not when it does occur, means that it needs to be used with caution in a discussion of the historical influences upon actual state actions. However, since it draws attention to problems which capitalism cannot, or cannot easily, solve and since economic theory has been very influential in political ideology, what it has to say is surely suggestive of reasons for social policy development.

A variety of concepts are used in the discussion of this topic, but the following three are particularly important:

- Externalities.
- Market inefficiencies.
- Monopoly.

(For more elaborate discussions of the applicability of these issues in relation to social policy, see Culyer, 1980; Gordon, 1982.)

Externalities arise when market activities have consequences, either *positive* or *negative*, for people who are not parties to those activities. The most clear negative example is pollution. In the course of producing something a manufacturer expels waste product up a chimney or into a water course. Neighbours, etc., suffer the consequences of this action. Here, then, is a case for state intervention: to prevent a nuisance that its producer has no incentive to prevent, given that any individual sufferer from it is likely to lack the resources to take action alone.

Positive externalities are not, in themselves, a source of problems. However, the difficulty in this case is that the creator of a positive externality is likely to resent the 'free riders' who will benefit from something they do not pay for. If someone builds a sea wall to protect their property from flooding, their neighbours are likely to share that benefit. There may, of course, also be negative consequences somewhere else down the coast (in which case, to anticipate the argument to come, the combination of positive and negative effects further reinforces the case for collective action).

Faced with a high-cost item and the likelihood of 'free riders' an individual is likely to try to secure agreement to collective action (the sharing of the cost amongst the potential beneficiaries). As far at least as the community surrounding the builder of the hypothetical sea wall are concerned the wall constitutes what is sometimes called a 'public good'. No one can be prevented from benefiting from it. There are other examples where the benefiting community may be much larger. Perhaps the largest example is a national, or even international, defence system. If it is true that a nuclear deterrent preserves peace then everyone benefits. The case for a state monopoly of defence (assuming acceptance of that state's legitimacy by its population) is overwhelming. There are similar issues here with regard to policing within a country.

What is the applicability of this to social policy? A case for regulatory policy to deal with pollution has already been made, but to what extent does everyone benefit if their fellow citizens are kept healthy? Again, the issue about infectious diseases is clear enough, but there are other ways in which everyone benefits from living in a healthy community. Then what about education: Are there not similarly benefits arising out of living in an educated nation? Finally, what about 'externalities' relating to income distribution? If the elimination of extreme inequalities makes people with resources safer – from burglary, assault, revolution even – there are surely externalities which derive from income maintenance policies.

Most economic theorists would probably answer 'no' to that last question, and say that this is stretching the concept too far. If they accepted the case they would probably want to discuss 'trade-offs' with other indirect consequences of state interventions. However, as stressed above, the concern here is not with the philosophical argument but rather with the fact that there has been a recognition within capitalist economies of a range of justifications for state intervention, often stretching far beyond the obvious examples of 'public goods'. Some economists have added another related concept to the list of special cases – merit goods (Musgrave, 1959), where the collectivity (state) regards it as desirable that people should have something whether they want it or not (in economists' terms this means that people are prepared to/can afford to buy it). Education and health services are sometimes put into this category.

Other reasons for state action in respect of these items have been examined in this chapter. One such reason, which lies very close to economic analysis, involves the extent to which state social policy systems make it easier for employers to socialise costs. Help for the old and sick makes it easier for employers to discard inefficient workers. Unemployment benefits similarly may make the laying off of labour at a time of work shortage a less controversial matter, and may help those out of work to deal with their relocation problems in a more economically efficient way.

Private insurance may solve some of these problems for individual employers but the limitations of these derive from 'the tendency of private insurance markets to select low-risk individuals' (OECD, 1994c, p. 12) and the difficulties inherent in insuring against risks whose incidence may change substantially over time (unemployment, for example).

Family benefit systems, portrayed above as originating in some societies from nationalist concerns, have also been shown to be responses to concerns that pressure to pay a living wage for a family leads to demands for wages which are not 'economic' from the employer's point of view. A state benefit can then 'socialise' the costs of children leaving wage determination to a market that can be blind to the family commitments of the labour force (Land in Hall *et al.*, 1975; Macnicol, 1980; Pedersen, 1993).

There are some related issues about the way the state may meet other costs that the market system may be deemed to be unable to meet – arising, for example, out of disability or high housing costs. Bolderson and Mabbett identify a whole category of benefits which they described as 'governed by the principle of cost-attribution . . . on the assumption that some people have additional costs which others do not have' (1991, p. 35). Finally, it was noted early in this chapter that education and training, when undertaken by an employer, will function rather like a peculiarly capricious externality since other employers may 'poach' this more highly qualified worker.

Pure economic theory is based upon assumptions of full awareness by all parties of all their options as buyers and sellers. Real world economics concedes that there are many imperfections in the market arising from incomplete knowledge. That suggests that there may be a role for the state in helping to reduce knowledge imperfections. The case for labour market interventions, introducing buyers of labour to sellers of labour, certainly seems to have been based primarily upon this concern. That example is, however, one designed to deal with an essentially short-run problem. There are also long-run problems inasmuch as citizens may find it very difficult to act in the way the economic model presupposes – this is particularly the case when individuals are unwell or disabled. There was some recognition, even by the tough-minded theorists who designed poor law systems, that there might be individuals who could not be expected to behave like 'economic men'.

The issue of monopoly concerns principally the difficulties which competing suppliers might have in entering a market. Ironically extreme market liberals accept a role for the state in preventing the abuse of monopoly power – the 'night-watchman state' has a duty to restrain those who try to act in restraint of the market. A more serious issue for social policy concerns the variety of situations in which the nature of the activity is such that it is in practice very hard to sustain a competitive situation. The crucial situation here is one in which there is a monopoly or near monopoly supplier and a competing supplier would find the costs of market entry prohibitively high. Social policy examples such as this are found in large institutions like hospitals and schools. There is then an argument for state ownership or regulation to prevent the existing institution from exploiting its position, or perhaps (more controversially) state intervention or subsidy to help create a second supplier.

In this section it has been suggested that the economic theory about externalities, incomplete knowledge and monopoly provides a series of justifications for state intervention, of a kind likely to be taken seriously by states in capitalist societies. It is hoped, however, that some readers will have recognised that there are logical problems about how far to take these arguments. If it is believed externalities are all pervasive, incomplete knowledge is the norm and not the exception and monopoly tendencies are endemic then the logical position reached is a state socialist one. But then, as pragmatic socialists have had to come to recognise, there are arguments to weigh on each side – setting the evidence on 'market failure' against what is sometimes called 'state failure', the incapacity of public institutions to function efficiently or equitably (see Self, 1993, for a good discussion of this issue). This is going beyond the main concerns of this chapter, but the issues are ones which have to be taken into account in social policy planning. Certainly the 'new right' critique of state social policy involves the argument that the influences upon policy growth embodied both in electoral competition and bureaucratic self-interest have led to increased 'state failure' as governments have advanced into activities 'best left alone'.

Finally, almost as a footnote to this section, it is worth noting one activity where the state adopted a regulatory role very early in history, despite the fact that none of the economic justifications for intervention was present. This was in relation to the practice of medicine. In this case the reason the state became involved is surely quite simple. If you kill someone when treating a disease, or if someone dies because you refrain from offering treatment or care that might save them, you may be deemed to be guilty of a crime, even perhaps of murder. Therefore, if individuals are offering services that purport to provide help for the sick they need some assurance that their honest mistakes will not normally bring retribution upon them (Jacob, 1988).

Conversely the sick need help in distinguishing which of the practitioners offering services are likely to have something positive, or at least relatively safe, to offer. This seems to be a rather late justification for regulation as the evidence suggests that much of the initial quest for a legally protected status came from medical practitioners themselves. They wanted a licence to practise, which would protect them from litigation. They also wanted recognition that would distinguish them from 'charlatans' or 'quacks' in the interest of the protection of their own 'business'.

A characteristic of these early steps towards the recognition of a professional monopoly in many societies was a search for a deal with the state in which a specific corporate body of practitioners would be allowed to establish rules about training and entry to the profession, and rules about what then might constitute malpractice and therefore grounds for expulsion from the profession. In other words the deal with the state was that the public would gain protection from malpractice by allowing the profession (the presumed ultimate judge of standards of practice) to govern itself.

It has been suggested that this deal was accepted, as far as the medical groups providing care to the well to do were concerned, because of 'class' understandings between social equals (Parry and Parry, 1976). In any case it occurred when states were still inexperienced in regulatory matters and often happy to delegate responsibilities to self-governing 'guilds'. This early established pattern of medical dominance, which subsequently incorporated some other groups (some of the apothecaries offering services to poorer people, for example) but reduced the status of others (female midwives, see Donnison, 1977), has continued into the era of much greater state involvement in health care (Friedson, 1970).

The role of the professionals and bureaucrats as advocates of state involvement

The impact of professionals and bureaucrats upon state action can be illustrated most powerfully with reference to doctors, but it applies to other professionals in state employment like teachers and, more recently, social workers. It also applies to groups of workers with regulatory responsibilities and, less so, to some groups of bureaucratic officials.

Once established in a dominant position in health care, the doctors were naturally committed to developing their role. People enter a well-remunerated 'caring' profession with a mixture of motives. If they are able to make a positive contribution to society, then further efforts to extend their roles (through the development of new services or the extension of current services to hitherto neglected groups) will extend their wealth (and perhaps power) and serve the 'general good' at one and the same time. Thus, their role was developed by a combination of altruism and self-interest, in which proportions will not be examined.

Hence, doctors came to lobby for state support for health services. Since some of the historical evidence shows powerful medical groups opposing extensions of state involvement in health care (Starr, 1982; Immergut, 1993), there is perhaps a need to justify this assertion. Chapter 5 will look further at some of the issues about medical power in health services, but the point here is that although *some* powerful doctors' groups can be found vehemently opposing *some* extensions of the state's role in health services a careful examination of the historical record will show the following:

1. Other elements in the same profession as strong and active advocates of state involvement (there are, in particular, important differences here between those doctors assured of private business and those whose activities need subsidies for poorer patients if they are to develop effectively).
2. Much of the medical hostility to state involvement has been concerned more with the form it was proposed to take than with the issue of subsidy *per se*.
3. There have been some aspects of health policy development which have been necessarily dependent upon the state extending its role and which have been virtually assured of professional support, for example, medical education and medical research.

In addition it should be noted that doctors in Britain often found self-help organisations before the coming of state health insurance in 1911 tough and unpredictable organisations to work for. Hence, many were quite happy to shift to securer state paymasters (see Moran and Wood, 1993, for a careful comparative examination of these issues about medical power and the state).

Altruism

The final section picks up again the theme of altruism. The chapter began with a negative comment upon simplistic assumptions that the development of social policy could be seen in terms of the advancement of caring values, but should that element amongst the explanatory alternatives be jettisoned altogether, or should it be seen as playing a minor accompanying role alongside the other factors?

Look, for example, a little more at the point made above about doctors. There have been a variety of areas in which medical expertise has inevitably played a part in the extension of a role for the state, without necessarily any expectation of an economic benefit to practitioners. This has clearly been the case with many of the developments in relation to the *prevention* of ill-health. That does not imply, however, that medical people have not been able to build successful careers for themselves as researchers, advisers and advocates in this field. Again professional advancement and social reform have proceeded hand in hand with emergent sub-professional groups like public health specialists playing a key advocacy role (see, for example, Gunningham, 1974).

Similar points may be made about some of the other actors in the history of social policy. Charities and religious organisations have played a role both as providers of services and as pressure groups. They have often managed to move into partnership roles with the state. While the individuals concerned may have had many motives – fear of the poor, hostility to socialism, a quest for new ways to strengthen their organisation – surely again there can be a place for altruism in any explanation of their actions (amongst biographies which explore these issues note Simey and Simey, 1960; Harris, 1977; Darley, 1990). The same logic applies to the many individuals who contribute research, pamphlets, subscriptions to voluntary organisations, work for pressure groups or political parties without any hope of personal gain.

Broadly speaking, altruism seems likely to have achieved little on its own. The puzzle for policy analysis is what weight to give to altruistic action. However, the same applies to many of the factors considered. This leads this discussion to its conclusion.

Conclusions

There is a need to accept the following:

1. The general truth embodied in those theories which have drawn attention to how universal the growth of state social policy has been and therefore that economic, social and political 'development' (trying to use that word neutrally and not to imply progress in any moral sense) played a part.
2. The considerable importance of politics in a general sense with much of it involving pressure from the 'left' and responses from the 'right'.
3. The complex mix of other factors, varying not only from policy to policy but from country to country.

Any analysis of how contemporary social policy emerged needs to draw upon all three sources. Hence this discussion started with the main features of what was described as 'modernisation theory': the evolution of complex urban communities, the development of sophisticated industrial processes, the achievement of a high average standard of living and the elaboration of political and administrative systems. It then unpicked the last of these themes much more thoroughly, in terms of the following influences on state action:

1. Concerns about the danger to society of disadvantaged groups.
2. Concerns about national weakness.
3. Demands for egalitarian policies and concerns to achieve the political incorporation of emergent working-class voters.
4. Concerns about the need to regulate market activities.
5. The role of professionals and bureaucrats as advocates of state involvement.
6. Altruism.

This has, however, not been 'merely' a historical analysis as the factors which explain how policies came about equally explain the continued presence of those policies today. The discussion in the rest of the book will return to these factors in various ways, seeing them as continuing factors in the refusal of states to leave social policy matters to markets, families or communities.

Guide to further reading

Modern works which contribute very effectively to the understanding of the ways in which social policy systems emerged and developed include Ashford's *The Emergence of the Welfare States* (1986), Baldwin's *The Politics of Social Solidarity* (1990), Immergut's *Health Policy, Interests and Institutions in Western Europe* (1993), Pedersen's *Family, Dependence and the Origins of the Welfare State* (1993) and Weir, Orloff and Skocpol's *The Politics of Social Policy in the United States* (1988). Significantly these are all products of the movement in American scholarship which has sought to bring the examination of the role of the state more effectively into policy analysis. However, the piece of historical analysis which the author found most stimulating of all as he prepared this chapter came from the hands of a Dutchman, de Swaan, *In Care of the State, Health Care, Education and Welfare in Europe and the USA in the Modern Era* (1988).

CHAPTER THREE

Comparative theory

Introduction

The last chapter examined a range of ideas and theories that have been put forward to explain the growth of social policies and welfare states. The emphasis was upon universal phenomena, particularly associated with industrialisation and the development of the nation state. Some of the suggestions considered emerged from comparative studies. Amongst the first such studies were a number which emphasised similarities in social policy development between states with similar levels of industrial development (Rimlinger, 1971; Wilensky, 1975). They could point to a general growth of welfare expenditure across their samples of nation states. Such studies were challenged by others who either sought to examine the quantitative evidence more carefully, recognising that there was no simple correlation between, for example, social expenditure and national prosperity (Flora and Heidenheimer, 1981; Pampel and Williamson, 1989; Esping-Andersen, 1990), or who sought to add qualitative considerations (Ashford, 1982; Dixon and Scheurell, 1989; Baldwin, 1990; Ginsburg, 1992; Gould, 1993). These studies, and particularly the latter ones, recognised that even if there were broad general influences to which countries were responding, there was a diversity of ways of doing this. This diversity might arise because of the varying strength of the influences on social policy development from country to country. The influences examined in the last chapter were, prima facie, likely to differ in importance from country to country.

Hence, there is a variety of comparative studies which have used the theories about welfare state growth in ways which attempt to disentangle their relevance in different societies, but an emphasis upon broad social and political influences upon social policy growth can have a rather mechanical, even functionalist, aspect, as was explained in the last chapter. There is a need to recognise initial cultural and institutional differences between countries, which may then be carried forward in the process of state development. There are also questions to be raised about the extent to which nation states can, in a sense, be said to have made choices. These choices may be explicable in terms of the structure of power and interests but they may nevertheless be identifiable as deliberate decisions.

A rather different motive for comparative studies stems from a desire to learn from the experience of other countries. It has involved looking beyond the frontiers of one country to try to explore other ways in which social policies might be framed. Such studies are typically concerned with specific policies rather than with the policy system as a whole (for example, Kamerman and Kahn, 1983; Ham *et al.*, 1990; Kohli et al., 1991; Moran and Wood, 1993; Evers *et al.*, 1994). Some may be motivated by questions like 'Have we got our policies right?' or 'Are there better ways of doing this?' In this case they may lead to celebration or condemnation of 'our' government's efforts. Such approaches rest upon a belief that there are choices to be made. If they are not naive about constraints they will recognise how choices are structured and will want to view policy borrowing in a context of structural influences upon choice.

Another group of comparative studies come to the subject from an 'output' perspective. Such studies have as their primary concern not a comparison of spending or institutional arrangements, but a comparison of outcomes and achievements (Rainwater *et al.*, 1986; Smeeding *et al.*, 1990; Mitchell, 1990; Deleek *et al.*, 1992; Bradshaw *et al.*, 1993). They may want to work back to other issues, inasmuch as they are concerned to explain how achievements arise. They too may be motivated by both pragmatic concerns and by wider theoretical objectives. Differences between nations in terms of poverty, inequality, health or literacy are given attention of this kind, yet such studies also serve a wider purpose of raising questions about the complex relationship between social policy input and actual outcomes. A key theme in such work has been the need to pay attention to the broad context within which any apparent policy 'effort' occurs. For example, any particular measure to reduce inequalities needs to be seen in the light of the size of the initial 'problem' and the effects of other policies. Comparative studies have a key role to play in disentangling interactions of this kind, which cannot necessarily be easily identified in a study of one country.

The literature on comparative social policy is wide ranging and difficult to put into a limited number of intellectual pigeon-holes. Theories do not always relate to each other very well as they often come from rather different disciplinary (sociology, economics, political science) as well as national contexts. They often come from scholars who are not very interested in relating to each other's work, particularly when they have either a specific ideological axe to grind or a preoccupation with a specific policy problem. This chapter will identify some of the key contributions of comparative studies, but it needs to be seen as a preliminary, ground-clearing, exercise for the rest of the book.

Exploring differences between countries: broad quantitative studies

Introduction

The pursuit of comparative data is not easy. Data sources vary from country to country, with the few exercises that there have been to assemble comparable data sets being fraught with difficulty. The main source is the database of the Organisation for Economic Co-operation and Development (OECD). This organisation, which was set up after the Second World War to facilitate collaboration between the industrially 'advanced' economies, collects and publishes comparative information. Its publications are a valuable source of information, but it is important to recognise that the OECD's main concern is the compilation of material on economic performance. It must be borne in mind that the usefulness of the data depends upon the quality of data collection in the countries themselves, and that there are great difficulties in bringing material from a wide cross-section of nations into a common format. As far as social policy is concerned there are additional problems with the data when there are other key actors – local governments and voluntary organisations – alongside central government.

As was suggested in Chapter 1, there are difficulties in determining the boundaries of state social policy. The OECD adopts a more narrow approach to this than that used in the book, comprising social protection (including all forms of public income maintenance and health expenditure). Separate data is also published on education (some of which is reproduced in Chapter 9). Data from the OECD is widely used for simple comparisons between nations, with social expenditure often expressed as a proportion of the Gross Domestic Product (GDP).

Table 3.1 sets out data on social expenditure as a proportion of GDP and on GDP per head for most of the countries surveyed by the OECD, putting the countries in order from the highest proportionate spender to the lowest. One problem with these data is that the proportions are affected by variation in the denominator as well as in the levels of social expenditure. Gross domestic product is a conventionally used index of national output; there are inevitably technical issues about how to compute this which will not be examined here. This table brings out the northern European domination at the 'top' of the public expenditure league, the United Kingdom's low position in relation to other northern European countries and the way the United States, Japan and Australia 'lag' behind.

As indicated in Chapter 2, these data do not refute the thesis which explains welfare state growth in terms of income growth, but they do suggest a lack of connection between income per head and public expenditure levels today. While the poorest countries cluster towards the bottom the richest countries are distributed throughout the table. As suggested, this has led

Table 3.1 Social expenditure in 1990 as a percentage of GDP

Country	Social expenditure	GDP per head ($)
Sweden	33.1	26,652
Netherlands	28.8	18,676
Norway	28.7	24,924
Denmark	27.8	25,150
Finland	27.1	27,527
France	26.5	21,105
Belgium	25.2	19,303
Austria	24.5	20,391
Italy	24.5	18,921
Germany	23.5	23,536
United Kingdom	22.3	16,985
Greece	20.9*	6,505
Ireland	19.7	12,131
Spain	19.3	12,609
New Zealand	19.0	13,020
Canada	18.8	21,418
Portugal	15.3	6,085
United States	14.6	21,449
Australia	13.0	17,215
Japan	11.6	23,801

Note: * = data for 1989.
Sources: OECD (1994c) *New Orientations for Social Policy*, Paris: OECD, tables 1b and 1c, pp. 59–60 and GDP 1990 data from OECD economic statistics series; reproduced by permission of the OECD.

scholars to seek ways of explaining the variation between nations and particularly the observable contrast between some of the most prosperous nations. An obvious place to start looking for an explanation is in the different political traditions of the countries concerned.

The influence of 'left' politics

There are a number of reasons for the examination of the impact of 'left' politics (one of the factors in the development of welfare states examined in the last chapter) as a focus for comparative studies. Social policies have been central features of the political programmes of the parties of the 'left'. Some of those parties have seen the 'welfare state' as their central achievement. Assertions of egalitarian intent have been central to claims for social policy. As suggested in Chapter 2, strongly supported parties of the 'left' may influence the policy agenda even if they are not able to win power. A central interest of political scientists has been to examine the question 'Does politics matter?' (Rose, 1984), to explore the extent to which parties and their programmes have an impact upon policy outcomes in democracies. Social policy has been seen in this context as the area of policy on which the parties are least likely to agree. Finally, the commitments of scholars themselves have led them to examine the links between political action and policy outcome in a context in which many of them have pinned their hopes for the advancement of social policy upon the parties of the 'left'.

The interest in the influence of 'left' politics leads studies to try to relate either levels of 'left' voting or periods of time with a government of the 'left' to the comparative positions of countries as social policy spenders. The Scandinavians, and particularly Sweden, then apparently fall out as 'easy' cases with high scores on both of these indices, but the Netherlands does not fit so easily, and there is in fact a group of European countries (the Netherlands, Belgium, Austria) where politics have been characterised by complex compromises between sectional parties to which simple analyses in terms of a left/right split are difficult to apply. Furthermore, Australia is a strong deviant case at the bottom of the list despite high scores on these indices.

One intuitive way to try to deal with this issue is to categorise countries in terms of their more general ideological climate. A clustering of countries with the Scandinavians plus the Netherlands at the top of the social policy performance league, a middle grouping of most of the early members of the European Union, and some 'new world' countries plus Japan at the bottom seems unsurprising, but may this just be reasoning in a circular way, taking it for granted that the distribution makes sense?

Esping-Andersen's analysis

Scholars have tried to do better than this. One such approach involves using different indices of social policy performance, recognising that it may not be how much money is spent but how it is spent which is important. Esping-Andersen has computed a 'decommodification score' for a sample of countries in an attempt to represent more effectively the impact of parties of the 'left' upon social policy. He explains his concept of decommodification as follows:

> *. . . as markets become universal and hegemonic . . . the welfare of individuals comes to depend entirely on the cash nexus. Stripping society of the institutional layers that guaranteed social reproduction outside the labour contract meant that people*

> *were commodified. In turn, the introduction of modern social rights implies a loosening of the pure commodity status. De-commodification occurs when a service is rendered as a matter of right, and when a person can maintain a livelihood without reliance on the market. (Esping-Andersen, 1990, pp. 21–2)*

Esping-Andersen goes on to argue that as far as welfare state development is concerned there are the following three distinct regime-types:

1. The '"liberal" welfare state, in which means-tested assistance, modest universal transfers, or modest social-insurance plans predominate' (*ibid.*, p. 26). This indicates low levels of 'decommodification'. Esping-Andersen puts Australia, the United States, New Zealand, Canada, Ireland and the United Kingdom in this category.
2. Nations where 'the historical corporatist-statist legacy was upgraded to the new "post-industrial" class structure', in such nations 'the preservation of status differentials' is more important than either 'the liberal obsession with market efficiency' or 'the granting of social rights' (*ibid.*, p. 27). This second category includes Italy, Japan, France, Germany, Finland, Switzerland, Austria, Belgium and the Netherlands. There is some ambiguity in his treatment of the last three (Esping-Andersen splits his chart with them in the third group but discusses them as members of the second). He refers to their recent 'performance' and suggests that social-democratic movements have shifted them towards the third category.
3. Countries 'in which the principles of universalism and de-commodification of social rights were extended also to the middle classes', in these places 'the social democrats pursued a welfare state that would promote an equality of the highest standards' (*ibid.*, p. 27). Denmark, Norway and Sweden are the nations in this category.

Esping-Andersen's decommodification index (*ibid.*, p. 52), which he sees as identifying these three clusters, is derived solely by looking at income maintenance policies and rating pensions, sickness benefits and unemployment benefits in terms of levels of income replacement rates, relative absence of qualification tests and extent of population coverage. The implication is that systems that are made highly conditional through means-tests (as in Australia) score low.

Developments and critiques of Esping-Andersen's model

Work like Esping-Andersen's, still at a preliminary stage at the time this book was written (Korpi and Palme, 1994), tries to take the concerns about the way income maintenance policy is delivered embodied in the concept of 'decommodification' further by distinguishing systems in terms of the extent

Type	Eligibility	Benefit principle
Targeted	Proved need	Minimum
Corporatist	Occupational category and labour force participation	Income related
Basic security	Citizenship	Flat-rate
Encompassing	Citizenship and labour force participation	Flat-rate and income related

Figure 3.1 Institutional types of income maintenance programmes (adapted from Korpi and Palme, 1994, Table 1)

to which they are 'encompassing' (Esping-Andersen's category 3), 'corporatist' (with social insurance orientated towards the economically active population – a category sometimes called 'Bismarckian'), 'basic security' (flat rate or with low ceilings, along lines associated with the Beveridge Report's ideal in Britain) or 'targeted' (with means-testing dominant). Figure 3.1 sets out their approach.

This approach produces a rather different classification to that of Esping-Andersen, in which the adding of a special 'targeted' category makes a difference. Korpi and Palme fit Australia fully into this category (see further discussion of this country below), but they also 'sort' other nations between the other three categories rather differently. Their 'corporatist' group is Austria, Belgium, France, Germany, Italy, Japan and the Netherlands. Their 'basic security' group is Canada, Denmark, Ireland, the Netherlands, New Zealand, Switzerland, the United Kingdom and the United States. New Zealand is regarded as targeted as far as support for the sick and the unemployed is concerned and the United States is classified as having 'targeted' policies for the sick. Interestingly Switzerland is classified as having 'encompassing' policies for the unemployed. Korpi and Palme's clear-cut 'encompassing' group is just Finland, Norway and Sweden. They use their approach to analyse the redistributory effects of income maintenance policies (a theme to be examined further below and in Chapters 4 and 11). It is interposed here to illustrate an alternative to Esping-Andersen's approach to comparative classification.

It has been pointed out that the approaches of both Esping-Andersen and Korpi and Palme are solely based upon the use of data about income maintenance schemes. While these are particularly significant in modern welfare states it is a pity that it has not proved possible to take a wider view of social policies.

A feminist critique of Esping-Andersen has attacked this narrow focus upon income maintenance together with its limited choice of concerns (Orloff, 1993; O'Connor, 1993). A collection of essays edited by Sainsbury (1994) examines ways of fusing Esping-Andersen's work with this feminist critique. It is acknowledged that the concept of 'decommodification' aims to identify system types in terms of 'the degree to which individuals, or families, can uphold a socially acceptable standard of living independently of market participation' (Esping-Andersen, 1990, p. 37), but it is argued that 'it is crucial for the position of women, whether they are entitled to benefits as individuals or whether rights are tied to families, of which men are normally considered the head' (Borschorst in Sainsbury, 1994, p. 28).

This critique points out the paradox that most of the Scandinavian countries in Esping-Andersen's group (1) have comparatively 'woman friendly' welfare systems yet it is in these societies that women are to a great extent labour market participants. In other words women have been 'commodified' in these comparatively decommodified systems and decommodified in the conservative nations in group (2) where their welfare still depends largely on their family position (*ibid.*, p. 43). The Netherlands is given particular attention in this analysis as a high-spending nation which Esping-Andersen recognises as a rather marginal case (see also Therborn in Castles, 1989, on the peculiar features of the Netherlands). Bussemaker and Kersbergen (in Sainsbury, 1994, p. 23) suggest that the Netherlands is a high spender because of a concern that the male bread-winner is a family provider in the context of its conservative view of the roles of women.

These analyses emphasise the need to examine dominant attitudes to the family in the 'conservative' group of nations – particularly Catholic social theory and the doctrine of 'subsidiarity' which sees the state's role as limited to situations in which there is family and community failure. They also suggest that an application of Esping-Andersen's approach to this issue needs to look at differences in expenditure by the state on child care (Gustafsson in *ibid.*, ch. 4) and on 'solo-mothers' (Hobson in *ibid.*, ch. 11).

One of the contributors to Sainsbury's book goes on to suggest a way of developing Esping-Andersen's typology by adding 'family welfare orientation' (based upon the strength of family support policies) and 'female work desirability' (based upon the extent of female access to work opportunities comparable to those for men) (Siaroff in Sainsbury, 1994, ch. 6). Also taken into account in this approach is the extent to which family benefits are paid to women. This leads on to a classification of nations as the following:

1. Protestant social-democratic welfare states (Denmark, Finland, Norway and Sweden).
2. Protestant liberal welfare states (Australia, Canada, New Zealand, the United Kingdom, the United States).
3. Advanced Christian-Democratic (often but not necessarily Catholic) welfare states (Austria, Belgium, France, Germany, the Netherlands).
4. Late female mobilisation welfare states (Greece, Ireland, Italy, Japan, Portugal, Spain, Switzerland).

To arrive at this classification (particularly the last group), Siaroff takes into account, alongside female labour market participation, female political participation and the religious orientation of the society.

Moving away from the income maintenance expenditure emphasis: concern with outcomes

Castles and Mitchell have raised the important point about Esping-Andersen's notion of 'decommodification' that there are other ways than simply income maintenance policies by which states may mitigate the effects of market forces. They challenge 'the expenditure-based orthodoxy that more social spending is the only route to greater income distribution' (Castles and Mitchell, 1992). Is this just two Australians bravely challenging a Swede's model which puts his country top and their country bottom of a 'radicalism' league? No, as will be shown, they have an important point to make. In describing Australia and New Zealand as perhaps belonging to a 'fourth world of welfare capitalism' Castles and Mitchell draw attention to the fact that political activity from the 'left' may have been put in those countries not so much into the pursuit of equalisation through social policy as into the achievement of equality in pre-tax, pre-transfer income. Castles' earlier work had drawn attention to the particular emphasis in Australian and New Zealand Labour politics upon protecting wage levels (Castles, 1985).

Castles and Mitchell make a second point, again about Australia but also with relevance for the United Kingdom, that the Esping-Andersen approach disregards the potential for income-related benefits to make a very 'effective' contribution to redistribution. Australian income maintenance is almost entirely means-tested, using an approach which does not simply concentrate on redistribution to the very poor. Issues about the case for this approach as against the more 'universal' and 'solidaristic' approach highlighted in Esping-Andersen's study will be explored further in Chapter 4 and in the discussion of social policy and social stratification in Chapter 11.

Mitchell (1991) brings to the argument an interest in exploring the relationships between income differences in societies *before* government interventions and *after* them, suggesting that it is the size of the 'gap' between rich and poor and the extent to which policies close that gap that need to be the object of attention rather than simply aggregate expenditure. She expresses this by means of a model (see figure 3.2), and goes on to examine income transfer policies in terms of their contribution to *both* the reduction of inequality and the eradication of poverty (again these are alternative social policy goals which need to be interpreted in their wider political contexts). She also compares income transfer systems in terms of *efficiency* (the relationship between outputs and inputs) and *effectiveness* (the actual redistributive achievement of systems).

Castles and Mitchell do not see themselves as refuting Esping-Andersen but rather supplementing his work. Their approach does not just show that Australia is not as low in the 'welfare state league' as the other data suggest, bit it also raises questions about the 'placing' of other nations, pointing out, for example, that the Netherlands' very high expenditure and high ranking

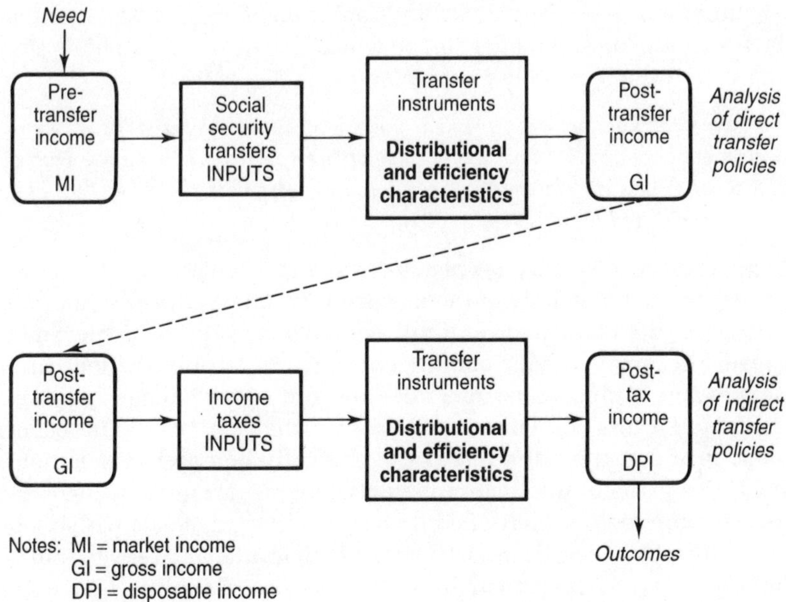

Figure 3.2 Analysing income transfers

on the decommodification index need to be seen in the light of the high levels of pre-transfer inequality in that country.

This work, and that of Mitchell in particular, is important for raising questions about the wide range of influences on incomes, and the variety of policy options available to political actors who want the state to try to change the income distribution. Australia has been characterised as 'the working man's paradise', a country where unions have succeeded in persuading the state to support their wage-bargaining efforts. To take a long-run view of the contribution this makes to the reduction in inequality attention needs to be given to the distribution of resources within the family and between those in and not in the labour force. There are also issues here about the extent of the achievement of full employment, and particularly about the distribution of work opportunities between men and women and between different ethnic groups (see Macintyre, 1985 and Bryson, 1992, for incisive discussions of these issues with particular reference to Australia).

Subsequent discussions of Castles and Mitchell's work by other Australians (Cass and Freeland in Hills *et al.*, 1994; Bryson in Bell and Head, 1994) emphasize the extent to which rising unemployment and the weakening of minimum wage legislation are undermining the egalitarianism of the Australian approach. Bryson (*ibid.*) also points out ways in which the relatively relaxed approach to means-testing is being abandoned, so that the receipt of help is more difficult to obtain and may be more stigmatising (see also Weatherley, 1992). She picks up a point made by Castles (1989) about the lack of built-in safeguards for beneficiaries in the Australian system, making it a 'reversible' welfare state:

> *This reversibility is an ever present possibility because of the oscillation of government between left- and right-leaning political parties in conjunction with the absence of strong middle class support for most elements of the welfare state. (Bryson in Bell and Head, 1994, p. 309)*

It is important to note that Sweden's particular strength as a welfare state model rests upon not merely the achievement of universalist transfer policies but also upon the maintenance of full employment *and* the achievement of high levels of female labour market participation (a point which certainly does not escape Esping-Andersen's attention and which has been particularly celebrated in Furniss and Tilton's comparative analysis, 1979). This occurred, however, in the context of a relatively ethnically homogeneous nation.

Alternatively there are some apparently low-performing 'welfare states' where economic policies have had broadly egalitarian effects which may be argued reduce the need for redistributive policies. Japan, Taiwan and some of the other Asian nations fall into this category. Coupling this with the importance of family support systems in these societies, Jones has written, perhaps rather too glowingly (particularly in view of her gender), of 'Confucian welfare states' (Jones, 1993).

Mitchell's study depends heavily upon data accumulated by the Luxembourg Income Study (Smeeding *et al.*, 1990). This has a database of information upon individual household incomes (including sources), taxes and other primary information from a number of countries. The initial country sample was Australia, Canada, West Germany, Israel, the Netherlands, Norway, Sweden, Switzerland, the United Kingdom and the United States. The sample has since been extended. A database of this kind enables comparative studies to get beyond basic expenditure data and focus upon issues about performance.

The Luxembourg Income Study is the most ambitious comparative study of its kind. However, there is also a smaller European study featuring samples from Belgium, the Netherlands, Luxembourg, France, Ireland, Spain and Greece (Deleek *et al.*, 1992).

Social policy obviously needs to be judged in terms of effective outputs as well as in terms of expenditure. The discussion in the publications from these studies particularly focuses upon the efficiency evident from the relationship between 'pre-transfer income' and 'post-transfer income'. Smeeding, O'Higgins and Rainwater show from a limited analysis of seven of their countries relative 'effectiveness of the income transfer system in reducing poverty . . . in Sweden, Norway and West Germany, and also in the United Kingdom' (1990, p. 72). They comment on the latter 'success' 'given the relatively low percentage of GDP spent on income transfers', this is a similar point to that made by Castles and Mitchell. The lower performers in their sample are Canada, Israel and the United States.

It is very much to the credit of Castles and Mitchell that they do not fall into the trap of only focusing on post-transfer income. It has been recognised earlier in this book that this danger exists in studies of social policy. Not only do economic policies have social effects, but it is also the case that through their impact upon life chances, education, health and employment policies have an impact upon earned income.

The data sets described here have limitations:

> *The data tend to be a few years out of date by the time they become available. There are still some irreconcilable differences in the way the data are collected in different countries . . .. Another problem is that the data for different countries come in at slightly different stages of the business cycle. (Bradshaw* et al., *1993, p. 4)*

All these studies therefore need examining with some care as comparatively slight variations over time or in ways of defining the focus may lead to very different conclusions. However, they have been important in stimulating the consideration of differences between policies in different countries and differences in the approaches adopted within those countries.

Exploring differences between countries: efforts to give the analysis more depth

The next stage in the work on data sets like the Luxembourg Income Study material involves the addition of the value of services of various kinds for different families in different societies. This is methodologically difficult, but important if the full picture is to be revealed. Meanwhile an alternative approach is being pioneered which, though still focusing primarily upon the expenditure and taxation activities in different societies, does look carefully into the 'transfer instruments' (see figure 3.2 above). Bradshaw and his colleagues (1993) have carried out a comparative study of family policies using informants in a sample of countries. Their study collected 'information on benefits and services for families with children and use[d] this information to simulate how the child benefit package impact[ed] on model, comparable families in each country' (*ibid.*, p. 5). Their 'package' included not just cash benefits, tax and tax reliefs, but also education and pre-school care, housing costs, and local taxes and health costs. In their conclusions they compare their findings with those from other studies rather briefly. They comment that:

> *family benefits played no part in the Esping-Andersen de-commodification index. But they might have, for we have seen child benefits have as one of their possible objectives to reduce pressure for increased earnings. They are a source of income*

> *independent of the market which might reduce the need for a second earner in the family and enable lone parents to bring up their children without recourse to the market.* (ibid., *p. 95)*

They go on to offer a 'ranking' which puts France much higher and the Netherlands much lower than in Esping-Andersen's model and puts the United Kingdom and Australia towards the middle of the distribution, well above the United States. They also, however, show how sensitive their ranking is to variations in the policies included (housing subsidy and child-care support differences between countries are very significant) or to the family 'type' considered (countries in particular vary radically in their generosity towards single-parent families).

A rather different study has given attention to cross-national comparisons in respect of the achievement of full employment (Therborn, 1986). In his Introduction Therborn offers another contrast between Sweden and the Netherlands. The former had (at the time of his study) remained successful at keeping unemployment low while the latter was one of the nations which, in the 1970s and 1980s, experienced a dramatic rise in joblessness. The contrasts between high female labour market participation in the former and low participation in the latter make this all the more surprising. He explores the various ways in which differences between countries may be explained and shows that differences in public policies are of fundamental importance. The group of countries which he identifies as generally successful in maintaining full employment are Norway, Sweden and Japan, while those achieving 'selective success' are Austria and Switzerland. At the other end of the distribution he identifies the United Kingdom, Belgium and the Netherlands, plus (with rather special circumstances applying) Denmark and Canada. He goes on to show that this pattern, which readers will recognise as very different to the social policy spending 'league' set out above, is explicable only in terms of government policies specific to the countries themselves. These involve at the top of this particular 'league' deliberate employment-creation policies, except in the case of Switzerland where government effort has been directed to controlling labour supply. At the other 'end' there has been a lack of such efforts and what has been particularly evident has been the abandonment of a political commitment to such policies on the part of the United Kingdom and Denmark.

Therborn not merely adds to the range of issues to be given attention in comparing state social policies, but he also directs attention to issues about choices made by governments. At the core of much of the comparative work on welfare states discussed so far has been a strong emphasis on explanation in terms of political inputs, in particular the issue of great concern to both Esping-Andersen and Castles about the impact of parties of the 'left'. In this debate a preoccupation with 'the Scandinavian model' has been dominant, but there have been questions raised both about the extent to which the

Scandinavian model can be explained simply in terms of popular support for parties of the 'left' and about the usefulness of concentrating upon this issue in looking at a broader range of countries (Baldwin, 1990). That critique has drawn upon a more general debate in political science about the limits of studies of state outputs which concentrate upon societal inputs, as expressed in support for political parties and/or pressure groups (Nordlinger, 1981; Evans *et al.*, 1985; Ashford, 1986). More attention must be given, it is urged, to the state as a partially autonomous actor. This theme was mentioned in general terms in the last chapter; now it must be explored further in terms of the contribution it makes to the elucidation of differences between societies. This takes comparative work on social policy in two related directions. One is towards giving more attention to history. The other is towards more work on policy detail. In both cases the addition of qualitative work to quantitative work has been important.

Historical and institutional analysis

As far as the historical perspective is concerned it is important to recognise that all of the discussion so far has focused upon contemporary comparisons. Of necessity none of these has been contemporary to the writing of this piece; equally this analysis will not be contemporary to many who will read it. In the discussion above no attempt has been made to question whether some of the data may not be already out of date. It could, for example, have been pointed out that the contribution of the public purse to Australian health care has increased since Esping-Andersen's figures were collected. It could also be pointed out that various nations have experienced increasing difficulties in combating unemployment since Therborn carried out his study. Overall some of the gloss has gone off the Scandinavian record (Marklund, 1992).

Equally it can be argued in some cases that events occurring not very long before some of the data was collected were of particular importance for the conclusions, and that very different arguments might have been developed had that analysis been done at an earlier time. In particular the United Kingdom moved in a period between the 1960s and the 1980s from being a welfare state leader to being one of the apparent laggards. This effect had as much to do with the dramatic rise in social policy activity in Scandinavia and the Netherlands as to the questioning of British policy which has occurred since the mid-1970s.

Any analysis which seeks to identify general influences upon policy must, therefore, take into account the fact that those influences change over time. This is, however, not to argue that the impact of these influences will be immediate and dramatic. On the contrary policies change slowly. Present policies may be 'memorials to past problems' (Schon, 1971). In the field of social policy there are considerable difficulties in changing direction. There are political risks in attacking policies which give specific benefits to citizens (as the Reaganites who attempted to change pension policies in the United States and the Thatcherites who wanted to attack the health service in Britain discovered). In the field of income maintenance the use of insurance as a policy device sets up a system designed to last and gives citizens long-run expectations. Public policies, as was pointed out in Chapter 2, also create bureaucratic and professional vested interests.

This issue is effectively explored in Weir, Orloff and Scokpol's (1988) analysis of social policy development in the United States. Three key examples from their work are worth highlighting here. The first is the way in which democratic political institutions (only for white males, of course) pre-dated the elaboration of public administration. There is a particular contrast here with the situation in many European countries where state building, as suggested in Chapter 2, occurred the other way round. This created a situation in which patronage practices were seen as the main form of response to political demands as opposed to distributive policies using a state bureaucracy. For example, pension provisions for civil war veterans were extended way beyond their original intentions as political favours. The second concerns the impact of a federal constitution requiring complex alliances to secure social reform. Here what was particularly significant was the way the reforming possibilities for the 'New Deal' leaders in the 1930s were limited by the fact that the Democratic Party involved a coalition of the northern urban working class with the whites of the rural and racist south. A reforming president still had to carry a legislature in which the latter were a powerful element. The third involves the continuation of that legacy into the post-war period, but with the fact that such social policy legislation as had been achieved in the 1930s tended to add the northern white working class, who had gained through the development of social insurance pensions, to the coalition against more radical reform.

A historical view may also indicate evidence of policy learning between countries. This may take the form of borrowing, for example, in the way the social insurance idea travelled through Europe (see Ashford, 1986; Baldwin, 1990). There may conversely be negative conclusions drawn, where a particular approach has been seen as the wrong way to develop policy. Certainly bodies like the OECD and the International Monetary Fund appear to be playing a role in suggesting economic consequences of social policy choices are likely to affect national competitiveness. Witness, for example, a comment in a recent OECD report on Sweden:

> *Sweden's comparatively slow growth and poor productivity record during the last couple of decades might at least to some extent be due to the country's large and growing public sector. Since social services traditionally have been produced by the public sector in a monopolistic framework, inefficiencies are likely to occur. (OECD, 1994a, p. 88)*

A historical perspective which aims to come right up to date, and perhaps to look ahead, may also see signs of the 'globalisation' of social policies. Multi-national companies may tend to dictate policy choices in areas like social protection and the amelioration of the impact of unemployment. At a less global level continental trading blocs like the European Union will attempt to secure uniformity of response across partner nations in the interests both of 'community' harmony and of competition on a 'level-playing field' (Commission of the European Communities, 1993b).

Explanations of the policies of any specific era need attention to be given to both current and past influences. There have been a number of quantitative studies which attempt to do this (see particularly Flora and Heidenheimer, 1981; Pampel and Williamson, 1989). In practice these studies find it very difficult to do more than complement the work that has been discussed above. They perhaps, on balance, give sustenance to those theories which stress the common features of modern industrialised states. This is, more than anything else because of the complexity of the quantitative analysis tasks they set themselves in trying to add a time series dimension.

The difficulties these studies face point towards the need to attend to the more qualitative historical work. It is difficult to decide what to pull out from this work to highlight here. What has been chosen is work which suggests other ways of looking at the achievements of Esping-Andersen's third category countries (and in particular at Sweden), and work which throws more light on the characteristics of his second category countries.

A number of historical accounts have explored the Swedish record in comparative perspective. What follows particularly rests upon what Heclo (1974), Baldwin (1990) and Gould (1988, 1993) have had to say. While there is no doubt about the importance for Swedish social policy history of the long period of social-democratic rule it is important also to bear in mind the following:

1. That Sweden entered the twentieth century as a very centralised, bureaucratic and autocratic state. Economic interests were weak and there was a substantial dependence on state institutions. The starting-point for welfare development was a society in Esping-Andersen's second category, not a society dominated by economic liberals. Sweden, and for that matter the other Scandinavian nations, was also, as has been pointed out above, ethnically homogeneous.
2. As political democracy emerged there was a rural interest dominated by small farmers who needed state support to help them cope with problems they faced on their generally rather inhospitable land. These formed crucial centre elements in politics, intermittently in coalition with the social democrats throughout the latter's period of political dominance.
3. The political and administrative institutions which emerged in Sweden involved high levels of interest group participation (with labour at all

> levels recognised as a significant element), an emphasis on consensual problem-solving by commissions which might take several years over their deliberations and a set of implementation arrangements which involved central 'steering' of either local government or of agencies in which key interests were represented (like the Labour Market Board).

This sort of analysis puts 'flesh' on the picture emerging from the statistics. It suggests why, for example, Swedish social democrats have built policies which aim to meet the needs of all elements in society, by contrast, for example, with Australian labourites who have sought to protect industrial workers or American New Dealers who developed institutions to protect white middle-income manual workers. Sweden's successful social policy building has reinforced the consensus, making the Swedish system more resistant than others to the new ideologies of the 'right' and the demands that a changing world economy needs harsher responses to welfare.

Historical analysis is even more important in the examination of Esping-Andersen's second category of nations. He is aware of this, writing that 'authoritarian paternalist conservatism has been historically important in the development of welfare-state structures' (Esping-Andersen, 1990, p. 59). What is crucial here is that the identification of this type of welfare state involves the use of an explanatory approach in which the power of labour is not seen as important. There have been some attempts to develop an alternative analysis in terms of the power of organised religion. Catholic parties are important in several of the countries in this group, and Catholic social theory lays some emphasis upon issues of social care and social consensus. Writers have made a connection between Catholicism and corporatism (for example, Wilensky in Flora and Heidenheimer, 1984; McLaughlin in Cochrane and Clarke, 1993; see also the discussion in Esping-Andersen, 1990, particularly p. 40). While Catholic social theory is seen as promoting the corporatist ideal of tripartite collaboration between government, labour and capital as an alternative to socialism, there is perhaps a crucial 'fourth' party – the church itself. The church has been active in trying to protect traditional family patterns. It can also be observed as having a role in social policy delivery in some countries where that religion is dominant (Ireland, Italy and Austria) and in countries where Catholicism and protestantism co-exist in relative harmony (Germany and the Netherlands). (This theme is effectively explored in relation to family policy and the treatment of women in Sainsbury, 1994.)

However, the equation between Catholicism and corporatism should not be overworked. A key feature of social policy development in Germany was the initiatives taken in the late nineteenth century in protestant Prussia by Bismarck. Here there was, as suggested in Chapter 2, social policy development playing a role in the securing of a strong central state, co-opting capital and (particularly) labour in the process. That approach to analysis, however, only takes the discussion back to the general theory used to explain why all the advanced industrial societies developed welfare policies. The interesting things about Prussia are that the development occurred at a comparatively early stage in that country's industrialisation (when it lagged a long way behind Britain), and that it devised social insurance institutions which became a model for others to copy. Later, the German legal and bureaucratic tradition seemed to ensure that these innovations survived an exceptional period of political turbulence from 1914 to 1945 (Clasen and Freeman, 1994, ch. 1). These points bring the analysis back to issues about the specific creativity of an early bureaucratic state.

Developments in some other European states are even more difficult to analyse without careful historical exploration. The Netherlands has been mentioned at various places in this discussion as somewhere that seems to move rather uncertainly between the categories used by the theorists. Dutch politics has been characterised by coalitions resting upon a framework of 'pillarisation' (Lijphart, 1975). This has involved acceptance of separate political and social institutions to enable its two religious groups, and latterly the liberals and socialists who reject confessional politics, to operate side by side respecting each other's beliefs. This initially produced fragmented social policy delivery institutions typical of Esping-Andersen's second category. It is conceivable that the rapid recent growth of Dutch social policy activity is attributable to the decline of 'pillarisation' (Hupe, 1993). It is hard to make sense of the Dutch case without looking at historical and institutional detail.

The development of social policy in France has been comparatively neglected in the English language literature (but see Ashford, 1982, 1986; Baldwin, 1990; Ambler, 1991 and Pedersen, 1993). Pedersen comments:

> *The incoherent and anarchic structure of French welfare institutions presents a discouraging picture for the tidy-minded researcher, and such institutions seem even more puzzling when it is revealed that they do not redistribute income across class lines at all. Historical studies . . . have tended to dismiss France as a 'late developer', while sociologists and political scientists . . . have characterized it as a rather peculiar variant of the 'corporatist' or 'Bismarckian' welfare state . . .. Only during the past decade, when Anglo-American scholars began to notice that France had weathered the welfare crises of the seventies and eighties surprisingly well . . . has a literature emerged that studies the French welfare state for what it did accomplish, rather than for its supposed shortcomings. ((1993), pp. 14–15)*

France can be seen as another of the European states where central bureaucracy has been of long-standing importance. Its social policy development has been patchy: quasi-autonomous institutions in social insurance which are also of key importance for health care (see Immergut, 1993), neglect of marginal groups (until the recent development of the 'Revenue minimum d'insertion'), and educational institutions combining strongly controlled state institutions with high prestige religious schools. As Pedersen's own work shows its developments in family policy have been rather striking, achieving a strong redistributive effect between different types of family units. Surely a case where a careful examination of the behaviour of the state is needed.

Some good work which looks at the development of French policy in a comparative frame of reference along the lines suggested above has been done in the study of education policy (Archer, 1979; Green, 1990). The study of education is interesting for the comparative study of social policy in general (but seems to have been disregarded by the main scholars in the generalist tradition) because some of the 'leaders' both in terms of early development of state education and in terms of investment in education today are not countries who would be predicted to be so from the welfare state development theories. Green looks at education development in Britain, France, Germany and the United States. Despite being well ahead of the other three in terms of the time at which it industrialised, Britain was the laggard in educational development. It also created an education system in which elite education was outside the control of the state. Subsequent unification of the system came late and remains incomplete as there is still a strong private sector. Despite its industrialisation technical education has been persistently neglected. The two leaders in educational development – Germany and the United States – were initially very different. In Prussia the state played an active part in educational development at the very beginning of the eighteenth century. Subsequently it moved towards a strong and unified state system, with an emphasis on technical education. Education thus probably played a role in Germany's economic development. In the United States education was something promoted as part of the democratisation movement in that country, it was certainly not an initiative of the central state but a local movement to which the centre was forced to respond. It, too, can be seen as preceding industrialisation.

Archer sees education policy growth as stemming from the aspirations of emergent social groups. Green, by contrast, emphasises the role of political process – the state itself was the key initiator in the German case but a responding agent in the American case. The British record he sees as explicable in terms of the extent to which, despite the bourgeois dominance in mid-nineteenth-century Britain, key state institutions remained in the control of the aristocratic supporters of private education.

In turning to the case of education for the elucidation of the argument about the historical analysis of the behaviour of the state, the discussion has moved into the second of the issues concerning more detailed comparative analysis – the need to look at specific policy areas and sub-areas. The difficulty about giving an account of this area of work in relation to attempts to compare social policy in different societies is that very little of the work of this kind takes as its starting-point the arguments about the nature of the welfare state, its origins and the influences on its characteristics. This work is almost universally pragmatic in its aspirations: it seeks to advance policy learning, asking questions about the strengths and weaknesses of specific policies in various countries. This may involve trying to see 'what we can learn from them' or trying to help us 'understand the strengths and weaknesses of our policies'. Yet surely there is a need to connect the 'macro' to the 'micro' not only, as suggested above, to throw light on the 'macro' theory, but also because the notion of learning from other countries needs to be informed by a wider perspective on why other systems have the characteristics they do. Without the latter, advocates of 'policy borrowing' are likely to make recommendations that will be ignored or fail because of a lack of appreciation of very different social or political contexts.

The area of social policy where detailed comparative studies of this kind are most widespread is health policy. An interesting feature of this for comparative work is the availability of outcome measures, such as indices of health status like mortality and morbidity rates. This is a field where there are substantial differences in the levels of public funding of health care. There is thus scope for comparison of the relationship between health care expenditure and health status, and evaluation of the public sector contribution towards favourable outcomes. Studies of this kind have been stimulated by concerns about the rising cost of health care which lead to questions about the most efficient ways of raising health standards within a nation. These will be explored further in Chapter 5.

Conclusions

This chapter has shown how comparative analysis of social policy has advanced from simplistic generalisations about relative expenditure levels. Esping-Andersen has played a particularly important role in this advance, addressing the questions about the impact of politics. His work has then produced critiques and attempts at refinement in which the issues concerning the relationships between 'inputs' and 'outputs', and other ways states may influence welfare, have begun to be addressed; and in which issues concerning gender divisions and family ideologies have been added.

Closer attention to detailed policy outputs has been shown to raise more subtle political, cultural and institutional issues. It is often difficult to provide a detailed analysis across social policy as a whole. A range of interesting studies focus upon specific policy areas. An approach to comparative work which is in its early stages (Ginsburg, 1992; Gould, 1993) dips into specifics about policies by making contrasts between developments in societies at different points in the quantitative 'leagues'. Issues are raised about the treatment of specific groups – women, ethnic minorities – within systems

(Ginsburg, 1992). There are also issues to be addressed about policy delivery; about authoritarianism, for example, the examination of which (Gould suggests) puts the Swedish record in a rather different light. There are also issues to be considered about participation and the respective roles of central and local government (see Ashford, 1982). All these things may add to the models, and exceptionally lead to their revision. There is an increasing need to engage in micro-policy analysis looking at the way different systems tackle the same issue: for example, the treatment of single parents, the encouragement of labour market participation, the control of professional power, and the 'free rider' problem in insurance systems.

Guide to further reading

Key sources for this chapter are Esping-Andersen's seminal work on comparative theory *Three Worlds of Welfare Capitalism* (1990), Sainsbury's very exciting edited collection which incorporates issue about gender divisions into Esping-Andersen's theory *Gendering Welfare States* (1994), and Ginsberg's *Divisions of Welfare* (1992) which looks at social policy in Sweden, Germany, the United States and Britain.

Good sources for more historical or institutional approaches are Baldwin's *The Politics of Social Solidarity* (1990) and Immergut's *Health Policy, Interests and Institutions in Western Europe* (1993), while a good source for an overview of comparative social policy with regard to specific policy areas is Heidenheimer, Heclo and Adams' *Comparative Public Policy* (1990); this has gone through several editions, and will doubtless be further revised before long.

PART TWO

Specific areas of social policy

CHAPTER FOUR

Income maintenance

Introduction

This chapter has been called income maintenance rather than social security, which it might have been if it had been written solely for a British audience. In American usage the term 'social security' is generally applied only to social insurance with the term 'welfare' being applied to social assistance. This chapter will deal with both.

The concept of income maintenance refers to the provision of transfer incomes by the central or local state to a wide range of people, who are unlikely to be able to obtain adequate incomes in other ways. This is today seen as so central to the welfare state that attention is seldom given to its precise definition. This needs examining carefully *both* in relation to other ways in which income transfers occur *and* in relation to other state activities which affect income distribution. This was done in general terms in Chapter 1. Readers need to bear in mind when they read this chapter that state income maintenance activities should be seen in a context in which there are non-state alternatives, some of which operate alongside them.

It is possible to develop a two-dimensional taxonomy of the various ways in which the state gets involved with income maintenance, with types of *beneficiaries* on one dimension and types of *benefit systems* on the other. It is important to recognise in any attempt to generalise about income maintenance that the various characteristics of recipients have influenced the benefits provided and the willingness of governments to provide support. Hence, some very different considerations apply, for example, to benefits for the elderly than to benefits for single parents. It will be seen below when the second dimension is introduced that some types of benefit system are found more for some groups than others.

Types of income maintenance beneficiary

Generally states do not regard low income as a sufficient criterion for entitlement to income maintenance. Rather policies have developed with the needs of particular people in mind, whose income deficiencies are seen to have some specific cause or group of causes. Thus benefit recipients may be classified into the following groups:

- Retired people.
- Children.
- People unable to work because of sickness or disability.
- Unemployed people.
- People unable to work because of family responsibilities.
- Workers with inadequate incomes.
- People who need special forms of help to enable them to be labour market participants or who have to meet exceptional costs.

Using this categorisation there will be double counting in some cases and some groups who are at the margins between two categories. There are some particular complexities which arise in relation to support for 'dependent' members of families because of varying views about dependency and about labour market participation, particularly with regard to women. These will be explored within this discussion.

Retired people

The emergence of a category of people defined as 'retired' was itself largely a product of the growth of pensions both public and private. Before the development of pension schemes an elderly person who was regarded, as a consequence of increased frailty, as unable to work might get support from one of the rudimentary sick benefit schemes or might be supported by a relief scheme with any requirement to perform duties in a 'workhouse' reduced. The emergence of pension schemes with either fixed retirement ages or rules providing for a full pension after a fixed period in work added an element of rigidity to arrangements which had hitherto depended upon work capacity and the availability of an income source which could enable withdrawal of elderly people from the labour force. Of course, then, once such arrangements were in place the increased longevity of elderly people made the pensioner group more evident.

Despite the emergence of expectations that people will 'retire' on 'pensions' actual behaviour still depends upon both job opportunities and health considerations. Where there is a strong demand for labour many people over pension age remain in the labour force. Conversely, with weak demand for labour many leave the labour force for the last time before reaching pension age (some illustrative statistics are provided in Chapter 11). As far as the health issue is concerned Hatland has drawn attention to the widespread incidence of what he describes as 'disability retirement' in the Scandinavian countries where state pension schemes have rules which facilitate early retirement on health grounds without serious additional income loss (Hatland, 1984, p. 194). His data indicate that in the Nordic countries in 1981 around a quarter of people in the age group 60–4 were in this category (see also Kohli *et al.*, 1991, for evidence of the development of a similarly 'relaxed' approach to the definition of disability in Germany and the Netherlands). Other countries have similarly been willing to allow long-term dependence upon benefits for the unemployed without expecting strenuous efforts to search for work (for Britain and France, see *ibid.*).

In fact rather contradictory trends can be found in policy – some countries have accepted *de facto* early retirement (in France and the Netherlands, for example) while others have responded to anxieties about the growth in the number of the elderly by raising the official pension age (in Britain and the United States, for example) or by trying to encourage later retirement (this is the case in Norway). Of course, if the pension provision is more generous than that for unemployment or disablement there may be cost advantages for governments in responses of the latter kind regardless of the ages at which actual retirement is occurring.

Data on the incidence of retirement are confused by the complex character of pension arrangements. Many countries have mixed systems of state and private pensions. The provisions for payments under these two schemes may not be the same; in particular, while the state may provide pensions after a fixed age is reached, amounts paid under private schemes will generally depend upon numbers of years of contributions. In such a context employers' views about when retirement should occur will be influenced by the specific pension provisions available to their own employees.

Implicit in the concept of retirement is the notion of a clear-cut contract of employment which will be brought to an end. The behaviour of people in many forms of self-employment may be rather different – particularly where the process of transition from work involves passing a business on to family or changing residence (for example, leaving a farm). Again, however, much will depend upon the availability of a pension of some kind. The position is very different, for example, for a peasant farmer who will remain a charge on a family venture which yields a low return than it will be for someone who can easily sell valuable assets to another company. In the former case the availability of a state pension will do much to aid the transition, in the latter it may make little difference.

A similar issue about 'employment' in the formal sense arises inasmuch as there are workers whose work has been confined to the home and family. The key group here are women who have spent all, or much of the later part, of their lives outside the formal labour force but have been working in the home. For many of them the arrival of a pension entitlement, if any, makes no difference to their patterns of work. Formal pension arrangements for this group often depend upon being regarded as 'dependants' of a male participant in the labour force.

There is a related issue about a category of social security beneficiaries, often found in formal systems, which has been left out of the list used here: widows. The rapid increase in female labour market participation in modern societies, accompanied by the comparative rarity of male death in early adulthood, has created a situation in which widows in need of income maintenance tend to fall into one of two other categories – they are either left as carers of children or they are elderly. In the former case it is their care responsibilities which are regarded as the reason for benefit dependency, putting them in theory, though not necessarily in practice, in a similar category to mothers whose relationship with a male has been broken in other ways. In the latter case the extent to which inheriting a pension from their spouse is essential for their economic welfare depends upon their own previous labour market participation.

There is a small group of widows who fall into neither of these categories. Inasmuch as labour market participation is a feasible option for this group benefit systems designed to cope with temporary absence from this – through sickness and unemployment – are likely to be deemed adequate for their support. Given, however, the relative newness in many societies of high rates of female labour market participation the elimination of widowhood, *per se*, as providing a case for income maintenance dependency will be a source of difficulties for a few, specially if they have to try to enter the labour force relatively late in life with low qualifications and little experience.

Overall there has been a broad shift, in respect of pension schemes, from the treatment of married women as 'dependants' of men to a recognition of the significance of the female labour market participant as someone earning pension rights of her own. Anomalies do arise from the mixing of the two alternative approaches. Difficulties are also associated with the impact that expectations that women should play caring roles (both of children and of others) have upon the achievement of the kinds of career patterns which bring strong and clear-cut pension (and other) entitlements with them. These issues will be considered further in Chapter 11.

Children

Another group categorised as 'dependants' in income maintenance schemes are children. The most straightforward kinds of benefits here are those premised upon the view that children impose costs upon all families and that the state has a role to play in alleviating those costs. In this case the very presence of a child in a family or household is treated as evidence of need for a benefit or for tax relief. Benefits of this kind are widespread. A survey of fifteen countries (Bradshaw *et al.*, 1993) showed all but Italy, Spain and the United States as having universal (or near universal in the case of Australia) benefit schemes while all but Denmark, the Netherlands and the United Kingdom have tax relief schemes.

Much more complex is the wide range of situations in which some attention is given to responsibilities for the care of children in the determination of benefit rates for adults – either in the form of dependants' additions to contributory benefits or in adjustments to the formula used for the application of a means test. In these cases the direct cost of a child and the indirect cost of caring for a child may not be distinguished.

The costs children impose upon families also extend to the costs of their day care, education and health care. In the examination of income maintenance policies for children it is necessary to bear in mind the whole 'child benefit package' (Bradshaw *et al.*, 1993). It is particularly important when the policies of different countries are compared as compensation for the costs of children may come in both cash and kind and will be affected by variations in what parents have to pay for (see *ibid.*, for a full discussion of these issues). A child's need for care has an impact upon the carer's capacity to participate in the labour market or to earn enough to free her or him from income maintenance dependency. Discussion will therefore return to some of these issues.

The special feature of benefits for children is that they are paid to their carers not to the children themselves. This sometimes generates a rather silly argument about whether parents spend child benefits on children. If the function of a child benefit is to raise the incomes of those with children over those without, then the exact budgeting practices of families are beside the point. In any case it would be peculiarly difficult to prove that many children derive no benefit from these schemes. One can imagine a methodologically difficult research project designed to see whether, other things being equal, when in receipt of these benefits parents spend more on drinking, smoking, gambling, etc. Conclusive results would be difficult to achieve. Certainly anecdotal evidence that parents save up child benefit for special occasions offers no proof that children do not benefit in other ways from this practice, since detailed scrutiny of the budgeting practices of such families as a whole is not available.

The equivalent issue for child benefits to the issue above about the age at which pension dependency begins is the age at which childhood is deemed to end for benefit purposes. This is an administrative issue generally tackled arbitrarily by the specification of a particular birthday (generally at the age of 16), but the termination of full-time education may be taken into account – this can extend the benefit as far as the twenty-seventh birthday as in Germany or Luxembourg (Bradshaw *et al.*, 1993, p. 35). This is exceptional;

most countries end extensions of benefit much earlier than this (for example, at the age of 18 in Belgium and the United Kingdom, at the age of 20 in France).

This termination of child benefit entitlement leaves in its wake a variety of issues about who should assume financial responsibility for young people, given both the prolongation of 'dependent' status by education and many young people's difficulties in establishing themselves in the labour market. For those who remain in education there may be special forms of help – this is a topic to be explored further in the chapter on education (Chapter 9). Otherwise it is administratively, and often politically, convenient for the state to define people as adults and therefore hypothetically entitled to the range of benefits available to non-working adults while in fact contributory rules and means-testing practices make it difficult for them to access those benefits.

People unable to work because of sickness or disability

Both state and non-state benefit schemes for people unable to work because of sickness and disability were early arrivals in the development of income maintenance policies in industrial societies. Long-term sickness, particularly in the later years of life, is an important source of problems for schemes solely dependent upon the contributions of the fit. This has made controls to ensure that claimants are 'genuine' of great importance.

There is a tendency amongst the healthy (perhaps reinforced by those sociologists who have written of the 'sick role' – Parsons, 1951) to see illness as a state of total dependence, as people take to their beds, need care and are certainly not able to work. But a great deal of illness is not like that. It may be partially disabling, the extent of which depends upon what people want or have to do. A classic example about which a lot of simplistic views are expressed concerns back problems. They vary widely in their impact and in their intensity over time for specific individuals. They make some tasks impossible, while other tasks may be painful but not impossible. Similar considerations apply to problems affecting the limbs, but also to minor heart conditions and minor chest conditions. Opinions will also vary about how soon it is wise to return to work after major illnesses and operations.

It will be obvious from these remarks that fitness for work will depend upon the work to be performed, but issues about motivation make the problem of discriminating between fitness and unfitness for work even more difficult. Most people will have had occasions in their lives when they decided that they would not let illness stop them doing something they really wanted to do. Conversely they will probably also have used minor illness as a convenient excuse to get out of something. Translate this to the world of work: bear in mind that some people's work experiences are much more satisfactory, and better financially rewarded, than others; recognise that sickness benefits are generally designed to provide sufficient support to make staying away from work feasible when you are ill; and finally take into account that the difference between income in work and income out of work will vary, often in ways which tend to mean that the most unpleasant work provides the lowest actual gain. There is here then a series of reasons why the determination of the boundary between fitness and unfitness for work will prove to be a controversial one. Those given the job of 'policing' sickness claims – doctors, officials, medical boards – are likely to have an unenviable task. They are likely to come under political pressure to take tough decisions which may be controversial.

This particular boundary problem is affected by the labour market. If work is scarce, if the demands upon those in work can be increased under threat of redundancy (faster work, longer working hours, etc.), if pay levels can be pushed down by a plentiful supply of labour, then the job prospects for workers with health problems will be diminished. Incentives to remain defined as unfit for work will be enhanced. If, in addition, the benefits available to sick people are superior to those available to unemployed people, then there will be another incentive for this group of 'marginal workers' to remain defined as unfit for work. This is commonly the case: note, for example, this comment on the Netherlands:

> *. . . persons with an employment disability remain better-treated than the long-term unemployed. In contrast to the former group the latter are caught after a period of time in . . . social assistance with its means-test. (Klosse,* et al., *in Hills* et al., *1994, p. 186)*

Hatland has shown how in Norway the incidence of disability benefits may be influenced by the forms of work available:

> *. . . the chances of becoming a disability pensioner are least in major municipalities with a varied labour market. Chances are greatest in fishing municipalities. (Hatland, 1984, p. 85)*

In Britain, at the time of writing, the government has decided that there is a problem about the large number of claims for benefits available for long-term sick people under exactly the conditions described in this and the previous paragraph. There were similar concerns about levels of sickness claims in similar economic conditions in Britain in the inter-war period (Whiteside, 1988). The British government's approach to this 'problem' involves a combination of encouraging stricter scrutiny of claims for benefit and deliberately turning a blind eye to the issues about the connection between the disability and the nature of the work which the individual could expect to find, together with a reduction in the value of the benefit available to the long-term sick.

An alternative approach to this involves the development of benefits to subsidise disabled people in the workforce. A later section will return to this issue. In a context of high unemployment this means using policies to try to combat the strong incentives for employers to discriminate against those less than fully fit. Such discrimination will be particularly likely when the disabilities involve physical or mental conditions which will lead the individuals to be inconsistent participants in the workforce.

The final point to be made about unfitness for work due to sickness or disability as a category for consideration by income maintenance schemes is that many schemes are set up to deal with these phenomena as either temporary, or if not temporary at least late in life, interruptions of normal working patterns. There is, however, a group of people whose disabilities render it difficult for them to enter the labour force in the first place. This is the group with severe permanent disabilities, either from birth or from childhood, including the group of people with severe learning difficulties. Many efforts are made to get this group into the workforce, but this is an uphill struggle if there is less than full employment. The problem for this group, to anticipate the discussion of types of income maintenance systems, is that they are likely to be disadvantaged by contributory rules for benefits and pensions. At best assumptions can be made about what they would have paid had they been able to be contributors (see Hatland, 1984, for the way this is done in Norway). At worst they may be expected to turn to means-tested systems which offer low levels of benefits and pay little attention to the needs of their carers (or even worse, define their carers as financially responsible for them). Not surprisingly, in the light of what was said in Chapter 2 about the role of eugenic concerns about the fitness of nations in the early history of state income maintenance schemes, fair treatment of this group has only arrived late and rather haltingly on the scene.

The issues about the treatment by income maintenance systems of the extra living expenses of disabled people (many of whom are of course also elderly) which are associated with their care costs will be discussed in the chapter on social care (Chapter 6). There are complex issues about the relationship between cash provision and care provision in this area which need to be examined more carefully.

Unemployed people

There is a similar set of problems to those applying to the definition of sickness and disability which affects the administration of unemployment benefit. There are also (as was already made clear) some issues about the borderline between sickness and unemployment.

Any definition of unemployment for the purpose of a claim for income maintenance has to include not merely the absence of any (or sufficient) paid work but also the capacity to perform such work and the desire to secure it. The first of these conditions may not be problematical for the income maintenance system in any society which provides support for its sick and retired at a level at least as good as the rates of support for the unemployed. It may nevertheless still be an issue for the definition of unemployment, as the use of the 'unemployment rate' as a measure of the efficiency of the economy and the effectiveness of the government may lead to a concern not to have sick and retired people defined as unemployed.

The second condition is more important. Since there will always be some citizens who do not wish to participate in the labour force, it is likely to be regarded as undesirable that they should secure income maintenance simply by registering as unemployed. In the history of support for unemployed people a particular concern has been the need for rules to prevent people who withdraw from the labour force to perform domestic tasks from securing benefits designed for the unemployed (Deacon, 1976). This is another issue about the treatment of women by the benefit system. It is one exacerbated by the assumptions about female dependency, which, as noted above, are often extended into the benefit system. 'Housewives', however, are not the only group who are seen as potentially inappropriate claimants of unemployment benefits. Two other such groups are evident at the beginning and end of the working life: young people who are still studying and old people who have retired from work before reaching the formal state pension age.

Devices built into income maintenance systems may be used to curb unemployment support claims from these groups. One is comparatively strict insurance principles which will have the effect of ensuring that any claimant has been a substantial and recent contributor to the scheme as a paid member of the labour force. Such insurance rules may also extend to provisions for benefit entitlement to 'exhaust' after a fixed number of weeks. Insurance rules are seen as limiting 'free riding' on the scheme and also as giving contributors an incentive to inform against abusers of 'their' scheme.

The other device which will curb claims to unemployment benefit is a means test. This is taking the discussion into a key theme to be considered later, but it is appropriate to note that in the contentious area of unemployment support the use of this device to prevent wives of earners or recipients of substantial private pensions from claiming money has been widely used.

While the examples used so far all concern explicit examples of reasons for non-participation in the labour force the political debate about 'abuse' of unemployment benefit schemes extends to a concern about a less specific group of alleged 'malingerers'. It is widely regarded as necessary to have ways of 'policing' unemployment support schemes to ensure that claimants have not deliberately abandoned work and are genuinely seeking work. Such policing implies that efforts to *help* the unemployed to find jobs or secure training often also have a coercive aspect. Failure to use such help may be regarded as grounds for total or partial disqualification from financial support. In some cases acceptance of training or participation in some specially created labour scheme may be a condition for financial support. Alternatively claimants for income maintenance may be required to prove that they are actively seeking work.

It is hard to quarrel with the general point that public financial support should not be given to people who simply do not want to work, but situations are rarely as simple as that. There may not be work for all. Does it matter if everyone in a large 'pool' of workless people is not competing desperately to secure opportunities from a smaller pool of jobs? In Chapter 8 the phenomenon of unemployment will be explored further. There readers will encounter the arguments about the 'classical' economic view that unemployment is simply a consequence of a failure of the price of labour (wages) to fall to its market level. Such a position denies the existence of involuntary unemployment except as a temporary phenomenon. It is a view seldom set out these days in its extreme form. Inasmuch as it deserves some attention it must be recognised that it presupposes some people working for wages below subsistence levels at appalling jobs.

Hence, rather more real world questions concern the extent to which unemployed people may be justified in refusing work where the wages are very low or the conditions are very poor. A related issue concerns the sacrifices that people may be expected to make to get work – moving away from homes and families, for example. Some more difficult issues concern the extent to which unemployed people with skills and qualifications may be justified in holding out for work at their 'level' and the extent to which they may expect to wait for work offering a comparable amount of remuneration to that achieved before.

Notwithstanding all the administrative efforts to draw a line between involuntary and voluntary unemployment the reality is that people vary in their efforts to get work and that these variations are likely to be affected by the variations in the prospects of success and variations in the quality of the jobs likely to be achieved. They may also, as implied in the discussion of the unemployment/sickness boundary, depend on health status.

This discussion of unemployment has important links with each of the last three categories of income maintenance recipients. Each involves quite complex questions about the feasibility of labour market participation. Furthermore in each case there is controversy about whether income maintenance responses are appropriate.

People unable to work because of family responsibilities

A discussion of issues about benefits for people unable to work because of family responsibilities must raise questions about the way income maintenance systems treat women. This occurs not by definition as men have family responsibilities too, but because of conventions that see care as a predominantly female role. There are two rather different issues to be mentioned here: one is parenthood, while the other is care for other adult family members. The former is discussed here and the latter is left to Chapter 6 for the reasons already set out on p. 68.

Children could be regarded as the general responsibility of society, and thus of the state, rather than the specific responsibility of those who have produced them. Generally speaking this is not accepted in any comprehensive sense by the state. The prime responsibility for the care of children is deemed to belong to their parents. Nevertheless states do vary substantially in the extent to which they are prepared to subsidise arrangements for the care of children. Where provisions for the care of children by others and labour market participation by women are widely accepted (for example, in Sweden), there is some acceptance of the 'knock-on' implications of this for the income maintenance system in the form of benefits to support parental leave to care for sick children.

As suggested earlier, however, Bradshaw and his colleagues have reminded us that in looking at an issue like this there is a need to bear in mind the potential trade-off between the provision of subsidised care services on the one hand and the provision of benefits on the other. As far as very young children are concerned 'if a family has to pay for child care' at high rates (as is likely in Germany, Ireland, the Netherlands, Spain and the United Kingdom) 'all the income related and non-income related family allowances they receive are effectively cancelled out' (Bradshaw *et al.*, 1993, p. 51).

Another slight variation from the general principle that the everyday care of children is not the state's responsibility lies in income maintenance provisions for maternity. This topic might have been considered under the general heading of 'sickness'. Placing the topic here tacitly accepts the argument that 'normal' pregnancy, confinement and its aftermath are not in themselves an illness. Rather, therefore, the justification for income maintenance provisions to support mothers (and exceptionally fathers) across the period of confinement is that the prospect of the production of healthy children, without adverse consequences for women's health, is enhanced if the state assumes some measure of responsibility for income maintenance at this time to enable women to abstain from paid employment. Logically that principle could be extended further into the life of infants. In practice it is limited. Typical examples of the extent of normal coverage are: Denmark, four weeks before confinement to twenty-four weeks after; Germany, six weeks before to eight weeks after; France, six weeks before to ten weeks after; the Netherlands, sixteen weeks in total; and the United Kingdom, eighteen weeks in total (MISSOC, 1993).

However, the most significant extension of state support for the care of children involves provisions for single parents (most of whom are female).

Reference has already been made to widowhood, a status originally given attention in the context of a view that labour market participants were generally to be expected to be males, with wives and children featuring in support schemes as their dependants. In this context the removal of the male supporter through death provided a clear context for the continuation of state support for the 'dependant'.

What if this breach in the family support system occurs because of marriage breakdown? There is an interesting section in the Beveridge Report (Beveridge, 1942) discussing this issue. Beveridge concludes that in principle social insurance provisions could be extended to cover marriage breakdown, but there are difficulties for an insurance system in any context in which beneficiary status can be deliberately created. He goes on to suggest that marriage breakdown in which the woman is 'at fault' should disqualify for insurance support. In practice governments (including the British one) have preferred not to use an insurance-based approach to the support of this group of people.

Those notions of a 'beneficiary status which can be deliberately created' and 'fault' pervade discussions of support for single parents (Murray, 1984), together with a third notion 'responsibility'. The concern about responsibility is that men should continue to be responsible after a relationship breakdown for the care of their children, a principle generally extended to at least some of the costs of supporting the carer. Where single parents are supported by benefits, there are also arrangements to try to enforce contributions from the 'absent' parent. The main practical problems about enforcing this are that many men lack the resources to shoulder these responsibilities, particularly when they have entered new family relationships, and some deliberately evade them. Furthermore, the whole issue is complicated by a range of relationships in which there is not a pattern of stable cohabitation in one place or in which children move between two households.

The other complication about the provision of income maintenance for the heads of single-parent families simply because they are carers lies in assumptions that these individuals should be labour market participants. In comparing schemes to provide for this group of people a range of responses can be found: from schemes which assume that single parents should seek work once children pass the age of 3 (the United States and France), to schemes which assume a commencement of labour market participation as children grow up (the Netherlands and Norway), to schemes which allow single parents to remain out of the labour force until their children reach school leaving age (the United Kingdom – albeit increasingly reluctantly).

Two phenomena complicate the arguments about the issue of state support for single parents. One is increasing labour market participation by women (the gender-neutral language in places in the paragraphs above should not lead readers to lose sight of the fact that most single parents are women). The other is the increased incidence of single parenthood, both as a consequence of marriage breakdown and of unmarried relationships which produce children but do not become stable partnerships.

These two developments are at least indirectly linked to the changed status of women in modern societies. It is hoped readers will not interpret this as a sly way of 'blaming' single parenthood on female liberation. Rather it is designed to bring the discussion back to a recurrent theme, to be examined more comprehensively in Chapter 11, about the extent to which there is an increasingly bad fit between real family life in modern society and models of income maintenance provision in which families are identified as the central units, comprising a benefit claimant and *his* dependants. More individualistic models in more individualistic societies would identify separately men, women and children as each having needs which they were more or less able to meet through employment. With such models the single-parent family would not feature as a political obsession in the way it does in several societies today.

Workers with inadequate incomes

The last two categories of income maintenance recipients both involve the subsidy of wages. Emphases in modern industrial societies on both the importance of formal labour market participation and the determination of wages by market forces leave governments with dilemmas about whether or not to subsidise low wage earners. Any tendency for the levels of income deemed to be the minimum necessary to support people out of work to reach levels comparable with the lowest wages paid will tend to put this issue on the political agenda. Governments will worry about the 'unemployment trap' created if worklessness may be seen to produce better incomes than work.

This issue generally only arises for workers who have either high family commitments or high expenditure levels which will be taken into account in the determination of levels of means-tested benefits. The simple remedy to the first problem lies in something discussed above – a child benefit paid without reference to income. The second problem principally arises where individuals have high housing costs. Again there are straightforward ways of making subsidised housing available. Britain offers a classic example where a commitment to market wages (involving rejection of minimum wage laws), a commitment to market rents and a reluctance to pay high levels of child benefit have come together to lead the government down the road of wage subsidy through means tests. The key benefits here are 'family credit' and 'housing benefit', both offering subsidies to wage earners modelled on the means test applying to people out of work.

At the time of writing the increased incidence of part-time work is leading to the examination of new ways to subsidise work (OECD, 1994b; Commission on Social Justice, 1994). There is a concern that inflexible income-maintenance policies based upon assumptions that paid employment is either full time or non-existent may be preventing labour market participation. While this issue is closely linked with that of child-care responsibilities – particularly for single parents – there is a wider concern that the changing labour market is increasingly offering part-time opportunities. Hence, the only route out of unemployment for some may be by way of jobs of this kind. Issues then emerge about benefit subsidy of such work, with again matters to address about how to avoid 'trapping' people in particular options.

People who need special forms of help to enable them to be labour market participants or who have to meet exceptional costs

The last income maintenance category, related to the one just discussed, concerns people who need special forms of help to enable them to be labour market participants. One such group already identified are disabled people who either face exceptional costs in getting to work (associated with mobility problems) or whose earning capacity is deemed to be low because of their disability. They have already been identified as a group about which income maintenance systems have dilemmas. Some countries offer 'disablement pensions' calculated to take into account the extent of the disability (as, for example, in Norway), others relate benefits to earning loss (as, for example, in Belgium), while others offer special additions to income designed to provide contributions towards the costs of labour market participation (for example, Disability Living Allowance in the United Kingdom).

Single parents have been similarly identified as a group with labour market participation problems. These are likely to be associated with the cost of alternative child care. Given that this group is predominantly female (likely, therefore, to be low paid) returns from employment will often be insufficient to offset child-care costs. Help may be provided towards these costs or the care may be provided at a subsidised cost (see Chapter 6).

There is a wider issue here about whether the case for additional help arises because the state wants these people to be labour market participants or because they have to bear additional costs. This issue is complicated by a related one, the issue of the extent to which it is appropriate to 'compensate' people to make up for a loss or damage. This issue particularly arises in relation to disability as a result of participation in war or economic activity (Bolderson and Mabbett, 1991; this theme is picked up again on p. 76). However, inasmuch as child support arises from pro-natalist concerns, there is a related possibility of 'compensating' people for 'sacrifices' in adding to the population (see Pedersen's analysis of the emergence of child support policies in France, 1993).

This category could be widened by adding other 'additional cost' problems which income maintenance systems may deal with. There is obviously a classification problem about where to put benefits designed to reduce housing costs. The case for these may be related to the causes of low incomes – unemployment, retirement, sickness, low earnings, etc. – but they may also be seen as 'exceptional costs' to be alleviated. There is an overlap here with the issues about housing to be discussed in Chapter 7. This topic will therefore be left alone at this stage.

This concludes the examination of the range of sources of need that income maintenance systems have to deal with. Various comments have suggested that there are alternative kinds of responses to those needs and that in many societies public systems may disregard some of them. The discussion moves now to a taxonomy of approaches to state income maintenance policies. As this is examined it will become evident that there are various kinds of 'fit' between the reasons for needs and the kinds of response.

Towards a taxonomy of income maintenance systems

Income maintenance options can be classified in terms of the following taxonomy:

1. Approaches involving entitlement if specific demographic, social or health status criteria are fulfilled, without reference to contribution conditions or means tests.
2. Approaches involving previous contribution conditions, such as social insurance.
3. Approaches involving means tests, such as social assistance.
4. Approaches providing relief from taxation – notably because of commitments to dependants or contributions to private income maintenance schemes.

It will be shown below that these types are found mixed together in various ways. Ways in which they merge, in practice, into each other will also be pointed out from time to time.

Approaches involving entitlement if specific demographic, social or health status criteria are fulfilled

The simplest approaches to the provision of income maintenance involve guaranteeing payments if specific demographic, social or health status criteria are fulfilled, without reference to contribution conditions or means tests. The clearest example of this is the provision of cash support for all children regardless of the income of their parents (child benefit in the United Kingdom, France, Germany and Norway, but not in Italy, the United States or Australia – see Bradshaw *et al.*, 1993).

A similar example may occur at the other end of life, when the only criterion for payment of a pension may be age, and claimants merely have to prove that they are above a qualifying age. Systems of this kind have emerged out of the extension of contributory schemes to the point where past benefit records are disregarded in the interests of the inclusion of everyone (pension schemes in Norway (see Hatland, 1984) and Sweden (see Gould, 1993, p. 185) provide guaranteed minima in this sense). This is a manifestation of the 'solidarity' (Esping-Andersen, 1990) or 'encompassing approach' (Korpi and Palme, 1994) which has come to characterise social security policy in those countries.

In these cases very heavy demands upon the public exchequer are likely to be involved. The price of the abandonment of methods to limit the number of claims may be low levels of benefit. In the child support case the benefit is always likely to be merely a partial state contribution to the cost of a child. Bradshaw and his colleagues showed levels of universal child benefits for one child varying from a minimum of £12 a month (in Portugal), through amounts like £22 (Australia), £29 (the Netherlands) and £42 (the United Kingdom), to a maximum of £86 a month (in Norway) (Bradshaw *et al.*, 1993 – translation to sterling based upon their own purchasing power parities data in 1992). In the case of pensions these universal provisions may be set at a low level in the expectation that contributory state or private systems will supplement them (this is, for example, the case in Sweden and Norway).

Another less straightforward example is the provision of specific benefits simply on proof of disability. In this case there is inevitably a task to be performed, probably by doctors, to discriminate between claimants using a set of rules which define a level of disability necessary to qualify. The British benefits provided to supplement other incomes for the severely disabled (Disability Living Allowance and Disability Working Allowance) come in this category, as does the Dutch General Disablement Benefit (AAW) but with the extra requirement that some recent labour market attachment must be proved.

In the area of benefits in respect of disability it is relevant to note Bolderson and Mabbett's taxonomy which identifies alongside insurance and means-testing 'compensation' and 'cost attribution' (Bolderson and Mabbett, 1991). There are principles which may be used to identify entitlement in the terms suggested here by reference either to the 'cause' of the disability (war, employment, etc.) or to the demonstrable consequences of it.

In all these cases complete 'universalism' may be partly undermined by rules which confine the benefits to citizens of the country concerned. In that case migrant workers may contribute through taxes but be denied support – this is but one of a number of ways in which discriminations based upon nationality or ethnicity may get built into income maintenance systems.

There are no systems in the world where the approach described above is adopted comprehensively, as opposed to being used in combination with the others to be discussed below. A universal approach along these lines has been advocated: this is 'basic income' or 'citizens income' (Parker, 1989). This involves universalising the child benefit idea to the whole population, providing everyone with a minimum income out of taxation. Earnings, etc., would then be additions on top of that, clawed back by necessarily high rates of taxation. The theory is that those without earnings would have enough for their basic needs without having to make any kind of income maintenance claim. The obvious problem for the advocates of this approach is that they have to persuade politicians to countenance a combination of an indiscriminate cash distribution scheme with high taxation.

On the road to that goal the pragmatists amongst the basic income advocates accept that they might first win the case for a comparatively low universal sum, which would leave many needing either insurance benefits (public or private) or means-tested benefits to bring them up to an acceptable standard of living (Parker, 1989, 1993). If reform got stuck there the basic income might be little more than symbolic, and its advocates might wonder whether the battle had been worth fighting. An alternative is the guarantee of a 'participation income' to those in work, available for work or in various approved alternatives like voluntary work, education or training (see Atkinson, 1993).

Social insurance: introduction

Social insurance, with entitlement to benefit depending upon previous contributions, occupies a central role in many of the more sophisticated income maintenance systems. Many countries have schemes for pensions, protection for widows, sickness benefits and unemployment benefits developed along social insurance lines. Some countries add to these maternity benefits and benefits to provide for parental absence from work.

However, the umbrella term 'social insurance' covers a multitude of possibilities. Some remain close to the commercial insurance ideas upon which social insurance was originally based, some even involve private, but non-profit organisations in the system (for example, sickness insurance in Switzerland (see Segalman, 1986) and Germany (see Clasen and Freeman, 1994)).

Commercial insurance requires, if it is to remain solvent, methods to ensure that the insured will contribute adequate contributions matched in various ways to the likelihood that claims will be made. A consequence of this may be the rejection of some potential customers on the grounds that they will be 'bad risks'. Social insurance departs from this hard-headed commercialism by pooling risks much more radically, recognising that this may mean that 'good risks' may subsidise 'bad risks' to a degree that would simply deter the former from purchasing commercial insurance. Compulsory inclusion deals with that problem. At the same time state 'underwriting' of social insurance is expected to eliminate the other commercial problem that too many 'bad risks' may bankrupt a business. In fact in many social insurance schemes the risk-pooling is taken further not merely by the acceptance of redistribution between contributors but also by the requirements for contributions from employers and by the deliberate building into schemes of the acceptance of contributions from the state.

On top of all this most social insurance schemes are not actually 'funded' in the way commercial schemes must be. Funding involves the making of long-term calculations which accept that in order to cope with periods when demands upon an insurance scheme will exceed income there must be, if bankruptcy is to be avoided, other periods in which income exceeds outgoings and the surplus invested to protect against future demands. This is of fundamental importance for a private insurance-based pension scheme. At the start of such a scheme individuals are invited to make contributions which will entitle them to pensions many years ahead. Much of that money will have to be invested to protect it from inflation. Only many years later will that scheme expect to achieve some sort of balance between contributions coming in and pensions being paid out.

Only very occasionally do governments behave like that (the main example is the funded social insurance scheme in Singapore). What is confusing to the public is that many social insurance schemes were initially described to the public as if funding were to occur. In many cases, particularly where pension provisions are involved, funds obviously start off with an excess of contributions over payments. In such situations there are two alternative temptations to which politicians (people who often have short-term time horizons) respond. One is to regard the 'fund' as something which may be 'raided' to meet other needs; the other is to make promises to provide benefits (particularly pensions) rather sooner than the maintenance of strict funding principles could justify.

However, public accounting practice often maintains an illusion of funding by producing social insurance fund accounts showing income and outgoings. This may be seen as having 'symbolic' importance – encouraging the view that contributions are being paid for a specific purpose. Moreover, governments may use evidence of deficiencies in the 'fund' to justify adjustments to either benefits or contributions as opposed to additional subventions from general taxation. Some countries even maintain accounts with balances which earn interest (see Hatland, 1984, p. 189 on Norway's scheme; similarly there is a trust fund for pensions in the United States).

The fact that social insurance schemes are in reality 'pay-as-you-go' schemes, in which current income funds current outgoings, has inevitably led to many decisions based upon short-run expediency when responses are needed to exceptional demands. Insurance schemes to protect against unemployment provide the clearest examples of this phenomenon, since severe depressions have undermined 'pay-as-you-go' schemes and demanded either additional government subventions or a breach of the original promises made to scheme contributors (see Gilbert, 1970, for a discussion of this issue in Britain in the 1920s).

Issues about social insurance pensions

The ageing of populations provides another, more predictable, complication for social insurance. It is sometimes alleged that in the absence of funding, the growth of the number of pensioners will lead to them becoming an unreasonable burden upon the workforce. This has been seen as a reason to replace state provision by private 'funded' provision. However, it is fallacious to believe that this will solve the 'alleged' problem since the paying out of private pensions will, as suggested above in the outline of what funding involves, require the disbursement of invested funds. Such disinvestment will, in macro-economic terms, impose a burden on the working population, who will have to face severe economic problems unless they replace that money from funds otherwise available for current expenditure to cope with problems of capital withdrawal. In other words, to maintain the economic *status quo* they will need to invest more and enjoy less of their income. The effect of the imbalance will mean that this investment will tend to have to be at a higher rate than earlier generations have accepted as necessary for their income security in old age (issues about the implications of ageing are discussed further in Chapter 12).

The other way of looking at this issue is from the point of view of young people offered a choice, as they are in Britain, between paying into a state 'supplementary' pension scheme (the State Earnings Related Pension Scheme) or a private scheme. Which involves the bigger risk? Private schemes may deteriorate or even collapse (at the time of writing newspapers are full of stories about problems with schemes which the Conservative government encouraged with subsidies in the late 1980s). Can, however, the long-run promises of governments be trusted? The British government's attack on sickness insurance, retrospective changes to earnings-related pension rules and niggardly approach to the uprating of pension rates encourage distrust. Which is the greater hazard in the long run – market failure or state failure?

There is another aspect to this argument – there may be grounds for the encouragement of funded pensions (either private or public) based upon a need for more investment *now*. The arguments about this take the discussion into complex aspects of macro-economic policy beyond the brief of this book. What is important here is that readers should not be misled into believing that funding offers a simple solution to pension demands lying in the future. The OECD sums up this point in the following way:

> *. . . reducing the costs of ageing populations cannot be met by merely changing the balance of responsibility. The real costs are appropriately measured by the current-period consumption they support, and only reducing the consumption of the elderly from all sources – public and private – reduces their costs to society. The means of financing, advance-funding versus pay-as-you-go methods does not change those costs. (1994c, pp. 14–15)*

Overall, however, it is suggested that, while social insurance is modelled upon private insurance, political concerns – to maximise social protection while distributing the burden of the cost of doing that in ways that are politically acceptable – have led to an evolution away from that model. In some cases that evolution is so considerable – where maximum inclusion is linked with considerable attention to variation in the capacity to pay contributions – that it may perhaps be more appropriate to see a scheme (or parts of a scheme) as falling into the non-contributory category discussed above with the contribution functioning as no more than a social security tax. In these circumstances it is perhaps more appropriate to see pensions as a contract between the generations (Hills, 1993) in which the current workforce expect to pay for the retired in the expectation that they in turn will be similarly supported in due course.

Social insurance and the principles of 'solidarity'

This last point can be elaborated further in terms of the principles of 'solidarity' in social insurance (Esping-Andersen, 1990; see discussion in Chapter 3). This involves the following considerations:

1. It has been mentioned that there may be three contributors to social insurance – the insured person, his or her employer and the state. Clearly the proportions may be fixed along a scale in which the input from the first named varies from a very small to a very large proportion.
2. Contributions may be flat rate or they may be related to income (or some combination of the two).
3. 'Risks' do vary. Some demands upon social insurance schemes are likely to come more from the worse off than the better off. Likelihood of unemployment is strongly skewed towards the worse off; likelihood of sickness is similarly but less strongly skewed. Conversely the better off are likely to live longer, and thus to make greater demands upon pension schemes.

4. This socio-economic skewing of claims may be affected by entitlements. Some benefit schemes provide flat-rate payments, others contain adjustments to take into account previous incomes. If the latter phenomenon, earning relation, applies to schemes then clearly the better-off claimants will, proportionately to their numbers of claims, take more out.

In a survey of benefits amongst the twelve European Union countries in 1993 all except Ireland related short-term sickness benefits to lost earnings and all except the United Kingdom related insurance benefits to the unemployed to previous earnings (MISSOC, 1993). Here we see that comparison between Bismarckian and Beveridgean principles discussed by Korpi and Palme (see pp. 43–4):

> *The basic feature of the German system of social security is high benefits for high contributions. A German worker would typically contribute 25 per cent of his or her salary in unemployment and sickness insurance .... The benefits are proportional to contributions. The first tier of unemployment benefit pays 63 per cent of former earnings, rising to 68 per cent for those with dependent children ....*
>
> *Germany's 'status maintenance' system of social security can be contrasted with the British system of flat-rate benefits in Income Support and Unemployment Benefit .... (Wilson in Cochrane and Clarke, 1993, pp. 146–7)*

The author of that quote might have gone on to make a similar comparison in relation to pensions and sickness benefits (though the facts are a little more complicated in these cases).

To make an overall judgement about the extent to which any social insurance scheme is redistributive there is a need to look at all the issues outlined above together. Other things being equal, a scheme with graduated contributions but flat-rate benefits will be highly redistributive. A scheme with both graduated contributions and graduated benefits will achieve a comparable rate of income replacement across the income groups. A scheme with flat-rate contributions and graduated benefits – an improbable combination – would be regressive. Again real cases can be very complex mixes, but it is possible with reference both to these issues and to the strictness with which insurance contribution conditions are enforced to compare schemes in terms of the extent to which they embrace principles of solidarity covering all risks and redistributing resources from those at high risk of dependence to those at low risk. Solidarity is most clearly embodied in schemes which cover the whole population and redistribute effectively. It is least embodied in situations in which different economic or social status groups are differently protected (as, for example, in Germany).

However, while solidarity may well equate with egalitarianism it does not necessarily do so. An inverse social redistribution effect has already been noted, associated with longevity in the better off. There are issues here about the form of distribution being attempted – between individuals, between generations or within individual lifetimes (see Hills, 1993, pp. 15–21). Other things which will affect the equation are the levels at which the minimum benefit is set and the extent to which the egalitarianism of a social insurance scheme is offset by very strong incentives to the better off to make separate provisions. In the British case the egalitarianism of a flat-rate pension scheme funded by graduated contributions is undermined by the fact that a low basic pension is supplemented by an earnings-related scheme in which strong incentives (including relief from contributions) are provided to better-off individuals to 'opt out' into private schemes. By contrast in Sweden and Norway effective but graduated schemes make this a comparative rarity. Korpi and Palme use their comparative data (see the discussion of their study in Chapter 3) to show a 'paradox of redistribution' in which 'encompassing social insurance institutions providing relatively high levels of income security to the middle class and high income earners tend to be more efficient than basic security and targeted programmes in reducing inequality and poverty' (1994, p. 17). There is a complex issue here about the way schemes commanding universal support, because all are potential beneficiaries, may offer a better deal for the poor than more specific measures, an issue to which discussion will return from time to time throughout this book (and particularly in Chapter 11).

These issues are rendered all the more important if work is not available to all who want it, or is available in part-time or temporary forms, or if caring responsibilities reduce labour market participation. This is where the issues about 'solidarity', discussed in Chapter 3 with reference to the work of Esping-Andersen and to feminist critiques of his work, are important. The traditional social insurance model is based upon an expectation of continuous labour market participation. It needs to be radically modified if that is, for any reason, an unrealistic expectation.

Employers' contributions to social insurance

In the course of the above discussion attention has been given in various ways to the issues about the individual contribution on the one hand and the state contribution on the other. But it should not be forgotten that there is generally a third contributor – an employer. In many countries – Sweden, Finland and Italy, for example – employers provide the majority of income for a social insurance scheme. Exceptionally employers may be the sole contributors (unemployment insurance in the United States, and family allowances in France and Belgium).

Hatland suggests that historically workers' organisations have seen employers' contributions as a way of making 'capital' pay for social security but that 'today there is widespread agreement among economists that employers have plenty of opportunity to pass the costs on to others through price and wage determination' (Hatland, 1984 p. 178).

This leads to other considerations. It is important to recognise that social insurance contributions are a form of tax upon the size of the workforce for an employer. This may thus be a factor, at the margin, in choices about the extent to which tasks should be performed in capital-intensive as opposed to labour-intensive ways. In some countries (Belgium, for example), this connection has led to deliberate manipulation of levels of employers' contributions as an economy management tool to try to influence levels of unemployment or inflation. The OECD has seen this as one of a number of issues about the *real* cost of labour, which may hamper efforts to reduce unemployment (1994b).

It is also the case that quite specific rules may affect employment practices. Examples of this kind include the following:

1. Rules that part-time employees doing less than a specific number of hours a week need not be insurance contributors.
2. Sub-contracting of work may be encouraged by the fact that the contractor does not have any responsibility for the contributions for the consequent 'self-employed' workers.
3. Contribution rules may be amongst the factors which make it cheaper to offer existing staff overtime rather than to take on new staff.
4. Exceptionally onerous rules about contributions (plus the administrative complications coming with them) may be a factor in the evasion of requirements to register staff for tax and social insurance purposes (informal economy practices in short).

As a number of these examples suggest, the issues need to be seen in a wider context. This wider context will include the fact that employers may have adopted practices, or may be required by the government to adopt practices, which extend some forms of income maintenance to their employees at a cost to their enterprise – sick pay and pension provisions, for example.

As indicated in Chapter 2 social insurance is in many respects a development from private provisions, in which employers succeeded in getting governments to take on the burden of responsibility for practices which otherwise employees might expect of model employers. In this respect it is also important to recognise that there is one large category of employers in the modern world who have played a key role in the advancement of income maintenance practices for their own employees: that is governments themselves. In many societies a characteristic feature of public employment, both civil and military, has been the provision of high job security with the expectation of pensions and often generous coverage for sickness absence. Often this has assumed forms comparable to social insurance – underwritten contributory pensions, for example – on terms far superior to the coverage the state offers to those it does not employ. In this sense governments may partly undermine the solidarity emphases in their own mainstream social insurance schemes. A striking example of this is provided by Germany where tenured public service employees (a large group) are provided with a quite separate system of social protection (Clasen and Freeman, 1994). There are similarities to this in the Netherlands.

Social assistance (means tests)

The provision of income maintenance through schemes involving tests of means has a long history in many societies. At a simple glance this approach seems to satisfy the requirements of both a desire for equality and a commitment to efficiency. Equality because means-testing is generally designed to concentrate help upon those in greatest need. Efficiency because such 'targeting' is designed to keep expenditure to a minimum. However, a deeper examination of means-testing reveals many problems which may undermine these two goals.

While it may seem appropriate to concentrate help on those with least at any point in time it may be regarded as unfair that this means that those who have squandered resources will get help while those who have saved or made some other kind of private provision for adversity will not. There is likely to be a 'savings trap' which will mean that all or part of one's savings have to be spent before help can be received (see Hills, 1993). The recognition in a society that such an effect will apply to income maintenance may actually operate as a disincentive to self-protection.

The position is then made more complicated by the fact that means-testing systems are likely to look at more than individual resources. This brings the discussion back to some of the dependency complications within income maintenance provisions. Logically if children and a spouse are deemed to be the 'dependants' of a benefit claimant, then in the context of means-testing their resources will also be taken into account. In addition, however, many means tests take into account the resources of other household members, particularly if they are related. There are some problems about assumptions of this kind since households may be difficult to define – this is not a simple matter of residence since a variety of practices with regard to resource sharing may be found under the same roof. The alternative of regarding marriage as a key principle for determining how to treat a household is complicated by the range of relationships not involving formal marriages. Officials may have to impose simplifying rules or may be required to use their judgement, or there may be an element of negotiation between claimants and officials (see Hupe, 1993a, on this issue in the Netherlands). Some means tests have regard to family obligations extending beyond the framework of the household as defined by residence in the same dwelling (for example, the scheme operated in Taiwan may look to provisions from the parents and siblings of adult

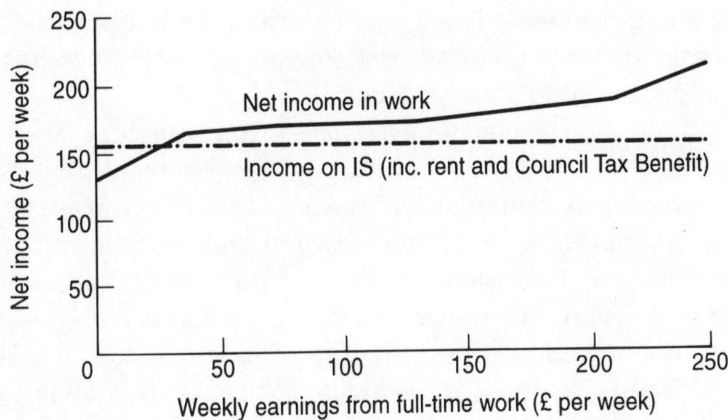

Figure 4.1 The poverty trap
From Hills, (1994), figure 15, reproduced with the permission of the Joseph Rowntree Foundation.

claimants even when they live elsewhere in the country). Any rules extending obligations will extend the disincentive effects described above.

Means tests are likely to be seen as very unfair to those who have self-provided incomes slightly above the level they guarantee. Achievement of a job paying wages a very modest amount above that guaranteed level may come to be seen to imply going to work for a minute real reward when a comparison is made with the benefit available to the workless. Such an unfavourable comparison is likely to be encouraged by the unpleasant and onerous nature of many of the lowest-paid jobs. This comparison problem may be avoided by provisions that enable means-tested support to taper off gradually above the guaranteed income level. However, much will then depend upon the rate at which this tapering-off effect occurs. If it is rapid then it will resemble a draconian tax on earnings. This is the phenomenon of the 'poverty trap', particularly noted in Britain, which has the effect of holding substantial numbers of families at income levels only a little above the level guaranteed to those out of work (see figure 4.1).

Disincentive effects will undermine the efficiency of means-testing. They also create incentives to fraud, as people may be able to conceal resources to secure help. Certainly also if a small increase in income will undermine benefit entitlement then there will be a strong incentive to conceal it. These issues about fraud than feed into administrative concerns. If an application for help requires proof that an individual has an income deficiency, a lack of savings and no help from other family members; and if any payment made needs to be accurately tailored to available resources and to the family (and perhaps housing cost) commitments of the applicant, then a claim for help is likely to be complex. In these circumstances, if the scope for fraud is extensive, assessment of the claim will require a costly investigation. Once the benefit is in payment, high administrative costs are likely to continue.

Changes of circumstances will necessitate reassessment and the continued risk of fraud may be deemed to necessitate surveillance procedures over the lives of beneficiaries (Weatherley, 1992).

The final problem with means tests arises from the general implications of the points that have been made so far – about disincentive effects, family obligations and administrative surveillance – that the process of obtaining and retaining help of this kind will be regarded as degrading and stigmatising to applicants. This may be regarded by those not in need of help as a desirable feature of means-tested income maintenance: deterring claims to benefit, keeping costs down and counteracting the characteristics which seem to discourage self-help. However, a political reaction to this attempt to define means-test recipients as the 'undeserving poor' has been strong demands for benefits that are not provided in a stigmatising way. This has fuelled the demand both for fair ways of means-testing which do not involve very strict rules and tests of means, and for other ways of determining entitlement to income maintenance (such as the contributory principle).

Means-testing alongside contributory benefit systems

Hostility to means-testing from politically active low- to middle-income people (what used to be widely called 'the respectable working class') has led to the creation of two-tier income maintenance systems in many countries. These involve contributory benefits to meet many contingencies – particularly those deemed to arise through no fault of the claimant (particularly worklessness as a result of sickness or old age). These are then accompanied by means-tested 'safety net schemes' for those not protected by contributory benefits. While these may be seen as necessary to meet temporary deficiencies in the contributory schemes or to assist those whose rather exceptional circumstances prevent them benefiting fully from contributory schemes, there is a tendency for them to be seen as the appropriate form of support for less 'respectable' categories amongst those unable to secure support through the labour market, particularly the single parent and the long-term unemployed person (see further discussion of these 'class' connotations of dual schemes in Chapter 11).

This dualism of contributory benefits underpinned by means-tested benefits is widespread. There is a danger of the development of inconsistencies in an income maintenance system as a whole as a result of the operation of very different principles for the determination of benefits which are side by side. This particularly arises if the income guaranteed by a means test is similar to that provided by contributory benefits. It creates situations in which there will be many people who, despite the fact that they have entitlements to contributory benefits, find that means tests determine their final income. This is an effect which erodes support for the contributory principle. It engenders the possibility that individuals will see the making of contributions as unnecessary – evading them by working in the 'informal economy' – on the grounds that if they lose their work the state will protect them just the same. The United Kingdom is a country where these issues have particularly arisen – from the relative frugality of the insurance benefit rates, the desire to provide comprehensive protection through means tests, the fact that the latter take into account housing costs but the former do not, the poor protection to women, the provision that insurance support for the unemployed 'exhausts' after six months out of work and the encouragement given by governments (since 1980) to self-employment (see Hill, 1990). Many other countries have avoided getting into such difficulties by ensuring a wider gap between contributory and means-tested benefits either through the generosity of the former (the Scandinavian countries) or the meanness of the latter (the United States).

Variations in approaches to means-testing

Just as insurance comes in many forms, it must also be recognised that there are many different approaches to means-testing. These have been given little attention in comparative studies. At the time this book is going to press the results from an ambitious study of this subject from the University of York are awaited (see Bradshaw, 1995, for a small foretaste).

The previous discussion has linked together income testing and asset testing. Exceptionally the latter does not apply (as in the Netherlands) or the capital cut-off used is sufficiently high to exclude only those with unusually high levels of savings. A distinction has already been noted between systems which take a broad view and those which take a narrow view of family networks. It is also important to acknowledge that systems vary in the extent to which they require intrusive investigation of circumstances. Linked with this variation is variation in the powers given to officials to exercise discretion, variation in the extent to which entitlements are clearly spelt out to applicants in advance, and variation in the scope given to people to challenge decisions. Finally, and fundamentally, the rate at which benefits 'taper off' influences the intensity of the poverty trap.

It has been suggested that Australia (as indicated in the discussion in Chapter 3) has developed a system where some of the problems discussed above are minimised by means tests that are particularly inclusive. There is no social insurance, and means tests have accordingly been developed to exclude only the well off (Bolderson and Mabbett, 1991). At the time of writing, measures are being developed to move to a largely individualised form of means-testing to enable one partner to receive benefit even when the other works (Briggs, 1994).

Hence, there is in Australia a kind of 'capped universalism'. This is a topic of some controversy (see Weatherley, 1992, for example, for a less sanguine picture of Australian means-testing). As suggested in Chapter 3, the system has been seen as sustained by a relatively egalitarian wage structure and low unemployment. These are advantages which are probably now disappearing (see Cass and Freeland in Hills *et al.*, 1994; Bryson in Bell and Head, 1994).

The United Kingdom's system may be moving in the same direction. By contrast in many of the countries where social insurance is strong (Scandinavia and Germany, for example), social assistance is characterised by local variation (often with local government administration), harsh means-testing procedures or work tests, and an absence of 'rights' for applicants (Bradshaw, 1995).

Tax relief

The final category of income maintenance system merits only brief mention. It functions as a complement to other schemes and is particularly used to benefit better-off workers. This is the provision of relief from taxation. Some tax schemes allow children, wives and other dependent relatives to be taken into account in the tax assessments of earners. While there is debate about whether a relief from taxation should be classified as an income maintenance benefit, such measures obviously contribute to redistribution between types of family in much the same way as benefits like child benefit.

Tax relief devices are also used to support private forms of income maintenance. Contributions to private pension schemes and to insurance attract tax relief in some countries. More indirect still are devices which may give employers relief from taxation in respect of their inputs into pension and sick-pay schemes. Finally, tax relief may be given towards housing costs. This is a topic for a later chapter, but it needs to be noted here that this may have *de facto* income maintenance effects.

General tax relief is implicitly regressive; the higher someone's income the higher their marginal rate of tax and therefore the higher their benefit from any relief. It is, however, possible for governments to reduce this effect by confining tax relief to lower incomes or lower parts of the tax band, or by tapering it off in some way. In the United States an Earned Income Tax Credit for working parents with children under the age of 18 is designed in this way (Bradshaw *et al.*, 1993, p. 136).

However, tax relief obviously presupposes adequate amounts of earned income. Some advocates of the use of the tax system to provide income maintenance have recognised this problem and have advocated the provision of 'tax credits' (payments to support those below the tax threshold). This 'negative income tax' offers an approach to means-testing which integrates tax systems and benefit systems (Friedman and Friedman, 1981; Minford, 1984). It offers the attractive prospect of administrative integration, simplifying means-testing and reducing its stigmatising effects. However, it is subject to the general difficulty outlined above in relation to the 'poverty trap'. The transition of individuals from benefit recipient status to tax-paying status as their income rises has to be a gradual one if the poverty trap is to be avoided. There are consequent alternative problems for the designers of these schemes in that a gradual 'taper' may imply either a very low guaranteed income or a very low tax 'take' until rather high up the income distribution (see Hill, 1990, pp. 157–62).

This discussion of tax relief could be extended further into a discussion of tax relief for economic enterprises, and then from that into issues about subsidies to business activities. These may function as income maintenance systems in some circumstances. Where this is particularly evident is in tax, subsidy and price maintenance support for agriculture. In various countries, including those in the European Union and the United States, these may be seen as 'income maintenance policies' which enable farmers and their families to continue with their occupations and remain in their homes. It is not proposed to extend this discussion into this complex area, but readers should not forget that market interventions of this kind have income maintenance effects.

Finally, the issues about tax relief have been shown to bear some relationship to the application of the 'tax threshold', the point at which people begin to be taxed. Clearly the explicit deduction of income by means of taxation is the opposite of 'income maintenance'. It may be that the tax burden itself makes people poor and its lifting can relieve poverty (there are some problems here about what is meant by poverty, to be followed up on p. 91–2). It should also be emphasised that part of the British problem about the 'poverty trap' arises because of the comparatively low point on the income distribution at which liability to taxation and to the payment of social insurance contributions commences. The author is grateful to Deborah Mitchell for pointing out the need to mention these issues. Clearly, the discussion of taxation decisions as *de facto* social policy decisions could be further developed.

The types of system: concluding comments

This completes the taxonomy of systems of income maintenance. As always with a taxonomy there are borderline cases and cases which combine two approaches. Some of these have been discussed. Insurance, means tests and tax reliefs all work with entitlement categories. Where either insurance principles (Scandinavia) or means-testing (in respect of pensions in

Australia) are weakly applied systems may by different routes come very close to the first category in the taxonomy used here.

National systems, as a whole, always involve some sort of mix of types. It is possible to identify some sort of fit between the types of policy problem and the types of policy response. Benefits for children, support of elderly people and some benefits for long-term disabled people are sometimes provided without contributory conditions or means tests. Contributory rules have generally been applied to pension schemes and to schemes for the support of the sick and unemployed. Means tests often occur as a residual or 'safety net' category but are also seen as the most appropriate form of support for single parents and for those who have not been particularly well integrated into the labour force. They are widely regarded as inferior alternatives to the other two types.

It is possible to classify countries in terms of the popularity of the various options and in terms of the relative importance of insurance or assistance. In Chapter 3 approaches to classification used by Esping-Andersen and by Korpi and Palme were discussed. The comments below follow the general lines of those two approaches. In the Scandinavian countries a strong emphasis on insurance is found with strongly developed principles of solidarity so that few people are left out. Schemes come so close to being universal that one wonders whether the term 'insurance' is really appropriate. In these countries means tests are in a genuine residual role. In Germany, France and the United States, by contrast, the insurance principle is more clearly upheld. In these countries means tests are evident but harsh, the insurance/means-test gap is wide, and long-run labour market attachment is crucial for the former. Linking of benefit amounts to labour market participation and to income level further enhances social differentiation. Women are likely to be seen as 'dependants' rather than as participants in their own right. There is a tendency towards a divided structure (see further discussion in Chapter 11) which is particularly marked in the United States. That country has good insurance schemes for the strongly labour market attached elderly and disabled, but harsh means-testing for many poor families (Weir *et al.*, 1988; Marmor *et al.*, 1990). In Britain, as already noted, there is a muddle because of the decay of insurance and the growth of means-testing on a 'mass' basis involving comparatively simple rules, wide coverage and attempts to cope with disincentive problems. The Netherlands maintains strong insurance and means-tested schemes side by side, but in this case the generosity of the former largely protects the 'gap' between it and the latter. Australia has placed a relatively generous and rule-based means-testing system at the centre of its income maintenance system, and has not developed social insurance. Yet, as suggested in Chapter 3, in making cross-national comparisons a great deal may depend upon both the specific issue and the criteria used to compare and contrast.

Benefit levels, redistribution and poverty

In the discussion above some references have been made to generosity or meanness in schemes. Obviously the evaluation of income maintenance schemes and their comparisons requires some attention to be given to issues about the amounts involved and the effectiveness of schemes in achieving redistributive effects and in eradicating poverty. The developing work of this kind was discussed in Chapter 3 where it was shown that it is important to bear in mind that the case for income maintenance transfers has to be made in terms of the maldistribution of pre-transfer income. This implies some sort of critique of the distribution of pre-transfer incomes. This can take a number of forms. Focus may be upon the extreme bottom end of the distribution, involving an argument about the unacceptability of the 'poverty' at that end, or a rather wider critique may draw attention to the pattern of the distribution as a whole, arguing that there is an unacceptable range.

These two concepts of poverty and inequality are closely linked. There have been many attempts to identify a way of defining poverty, in order to highlight the problems at the bottom end of the distribution. There are difficulties in arriving at a definition of poverty in terms of an absolute minimum necessary for survival in the context of societies with a high average standard of living. In such societies people rarely starve to death, yet there are differences in life expectancies and in the physical quality of life which do suggest that the term 'poverty' should not *merely* be seen as a way of stressing 'inequality' (Townsend, 1970, 1979, 1993). The difficulties with such an emphasis come about because of problems about establishing where the cut-off point should occur, below which people are defined as 'in poverty'. For example, as will be seen in Chapter 5, mortality and morbidity differentials occur through the whole income distribution.

These difficulties lead some authorities to prefer to define poverty in comparatively arbitrary relative terms as a fixed percentage of a national average (Department of Social Security, 1993; Smeeding *et al.*, 1990; Deleek *et al.*, 1990). As far as income maintenance is concerned it will often be the relation between low-income groups and the average which will be of concern politically. This approach is also easily used in comparative research, which would otherwise face some severe problems of developing a common yardstick for use in several rather different cultures. However, these arbitrary measures cannot be justified as 'poverty lines' (see Veit Wilson, 1994).

As was suggested in Chapter 2, much of the political pressure for the adoption and improvement of income maintenance schemes has come more from the relatively deprived lower income groups as a whole rather than from the very poor. In this context, also, it has been issues about expectations of income in and out of work, and particularly in the latter case in old age, that have been important. Inasmuch as this is the concern it is the effect of income maintenance in smoothing out variations in individual lifetime incomes rather than in redistributing between rich and poor that has been the focus. Here again contrasts may be drawn between *within group* and *between group* redistributions. Pension schemes may be judged in terms of replacement incomes achieved, of equality or inequality within the ranks of the old regardless of their previous incomes and of their generosity relative to that of income maintenance schemes for the non-elderly (this was considered earlier in relation to the concept of solidarity in social insurance).

Hence, the achievements of income maintenance schemes may be seen in terms of the alleviation of poverty, of the reduction of overall inequalities in the income distribution in societies and of the evening out of income variations in the lives of individuals. Modern data on incomes, benefits and taxes enable these issues to be studied. However, any effect detected must, if a sensible overall assessment of income maintenance policy is to be made, be related back to the original distribution. As suggested in Chapter 3, if pro-equality value judgements are to be made in comparing countries, a nation whose pre-redistribution income spread is small, without very low incomes at the bottom, needs less effective income maintenance policies than others. As stressed before, income maintenance must be seen in the context of other policies. Government interventions to protect wage levels, particularly at the bottom, and to maintain full employment may make redistribution from the outcomes derived from the working of the labour market less necessary.

Taking this point further, differences in national policies may be detected between those areas of life where it is taken for granted that income maintenance policies will adjust market-generated inequalities and those where it is regarded as appropriate for little to be done to alleviate the effects of market forces. Thus a contrast may be made in many countries between the effectiveness of policies to relieve poverty in old age and the ineffectiveness of policies to counter the consequences for family poverty of differential work opportunities. This is an effect particularly detectable in recent trends in the data on poverty in the United States (Harrington, 1985; George and Howards, 1991). Table 4.1, adapted from George and Howards' book, illustrates this point.

Conclusions

The central importance of income maintenance in modern industrial states, reflected in the high levels of public expenditure upon it, has meant that this has had to be a rather large chapter. At its core has been an analysis of income maintenance in terms of two alternative principles for a taxonomy – one based upon the cause of the need for income transfers (which may be described

Table 4.1 The risk of poverty for various population groups in the United States

	1969	1988
Elderly	25.3	12.0
Children	14.0	19.7
Female-headed family	38.2	37.4
White race	9.5	10.1
Black race	32.2	31.6

Source: George, V. and Howards, I. (1991) *Poverty Amidst Affluence*, Aldershot: Edward Elgar, p. 73.

as the client-group approach), the other based upon the nature of the system used for determining entitlement. In the latter case two alternatives of social insurance and social assistance are dominant, and are used in tandem in some way in most countries. The evolution of the former towards automatic entitlement on proof of membership of a specific group (children, the elderly, the disabled) is leading to some fusion between insurance schemes and simple contingent benefit schemes (the first category considered). Some brief attention was given to tax relief as a form of income maintenance.

Around the key issues raised by the two taxonomic approaches are a number of others. Some of the following were highlighted:

1. The issues about the relationship between state schemes and market schemes.
2. The fact that income transfers occur in a context in which other factors (both market and non-market) determine income distribution.
3. The fact that there is a need to know about the sums of money transferred and the relationships between those sums, and the resources available to citizens before tax deductions or benefit additions if their effectiveness is to be judged satisfactorily.

Income maintenance systems are likely to be structured in ways which reflect other socially structured inequalities in society. In this sense it may be possible to talk of an income maintenance 'class' structure – at the top are people whose replacement incomes when out of work may be determined principally by private pension and sick-pay schemes (perhaps underwritten by the state through tax concessions and other subsidies), in the middle are people whose income maintenance mainly depends upon their membership of social insurance schemes, and at the bottom are people dependent upon means-tested benefits. This issue will be explored further in looking at social divisions of welfare in Chapter 11, because it is not only income maintenance which tends to be structured in this way.

Two other themes dealing with social security were discussed and will receive further attention in Chapter 11. One of these is the effect of assumptions about the nature of the family and the household, and the related ideas about 'dependency' for the treatment of women in social policy. Women may be disadvantaged both by 'dependency' assumptions and by rules which disregard their disadvantages as labour market participants. This theme occurs as an issue in other areas of social policy (particularly in social care – see Chapter 6).

The other theme related to 'dependency' is 'citizenship'. Historically receipt of aid from the public purse was often deemed to lead to denial of citizenship rights. Such individuals were denied the right to vote, in particular. Nowadays such direct disenfranchisement is not practised, nevertheless both the procedures used to determine entitlement and the levels of benefits granted may have a degrading effect which sends a psychological message to the recipients which suggests that they are less than full citizens.

Furthermore there are some issues to be considered about the way income maintenance schemes treat racial, ethnic and national minority groups in a society. At worst schemes may take the taxes and contributions from 'guest workers' that are necessary to fund benefits but deny entitlements and force a return to the country of origin. Slightly less draconian are rules which mean that new arrivals in a country, or people who move intermittently in and out of a country, have difficulties in securing entitlements. This is generally true of contributory insurance schemes where there are no reciprocal arrangements with the countries from which the migrant workers come. Countries may also only let certain categories of migrants into the country if their families guarantee that they will not be a charge on the public purse (Britain treats family members of people already established in the country in this way). All these rules tend to cast a shadow over other members of ethnic groups treated in these ways (even when they have formally established residency or citizenship rights), since officials are likely to view their income maintenance claims with suspicion. All of these problems are compounded by general problems of racial discrimination and oppression, placing particular groups in situations of vulnerability where income maintenance claims are likely, yet official responses are often unsympathetic. Again, these phenomena are not peculiar to income maintenance alone.

Finally, there are two more ways in which income maintenance issues will be discussed further later in the book. First, there are a number of areas of policy where cash provision and service provision issues interact (notably in state-provided housing, in the provision of social care and in the provision of education). Second, the very high cost of social security, together with the factors which are driving those costs up (for example, the ageing of the population and the rise of unemployment), brings issues about how it is provided into the centre of the stage in debates about the extent to which there is a 'crisis' for welfare and about the extent to which welfare provision on current levels can be afforded in the future (see Chapter 12).

Guide to further reading

Since the analysis of income maintenance policy is at the very centre of the study of social policy, most of the books recommended at the end of Chapters 2 and 3 have much to say on the subject. This is particularly true of Esping-Andersen's book. One comparative book specifically about income maintenance is Bolderson and Mabbett's *Social Policy and Social Security in Australia, Britain and the USA* (1991). Two books marking the fiftieth anniversary of the publication of the Beveridge Report which contain much comparative and analytical material alongside essays which specifically relate to the British experience are Hills, Ditch and Glennerster (eds.) *Beveridge and Social Security* (1994) and Baldwin and Falkingham (eds.) *Social Security and Social Change* (1994).

Scholars at the University of York are engaged on some important new contributions to the comparative analysis of income maintenance. Their book on child support (Bradshaw *et al.*, *Support for Children*) came out in 1993, and currently completed material from their comparative study of social assistance is eagerly awaited.

CHAPTER FIVE

Health policy

Introduction

The pursuit of good health, the quest for cures for diseases and the concern about the care of the sick have been universal preoccupations of human societies. Health policy, implying the involvement of the state in these concerns, is a comparatively modern phenomenon. Its emergence, like all the policy concerns discussed in this book, parallels the development of the active state in general. It has also been linked with the development of scientific medicine; this has involved the identification of a complex range of activities which have required regulation. These activities have become costly not merely because the application of modern therapies is expensive, but also because the development of those therapies rests upon costly education, research and equipment. These have provided a variety of motives for the development of ways of socialising the costs of medicine, spreading them so that they do not necessarily fall upon the very sick at the time of their greatest need. Yet, even if it is the implications of the development of scientific medicine which have been central preoccupations of political responses to health care problems, it is important to recognise that this is embedded in a wider range of issues. There are two that need to be identified before the discussion proceeds any further.

The first is that good health does not depend solely upon direct medical provision. The achievement and maintenance of good health depends upon the following:

- Adequate incomes.
- Satisfactory housing.
- A safe water supply and system for the disposal of waste.
- The avoidance of accidents.
- An unpolluted environment.
- A supply of good, appropriate and unpolluted food.

- A safe lifestyle.
- Satisfactory relationships with others.
- Avoidance of excessive stress.

There are connections between many of the items in this list. It is not exhaustive. It includes vague words ('adequate' and 'satisfactory'), about which a great deal more could be written. There is room for debate about how 'avoidable' some risks are, and whether efforts to avoid stress or accidents may not bring health problems in their wake.

There are important issues to be addressed about the extent to which the maintenance of good health depends upon a combination of the decisions people take for themselves and the protection from risks provided by public policies other than medicine (some of which – income maintenance, housing, social care, environmental protection – are discussed in other chapters of this book). An extreme version of this position sees medicine as an almost unnecessary intrusion into health maintenance, indeed even as a source of illness ('iatrogenic disease' – see Illich, 1977). A more moderate version to which public health physicians may themselves subscribe stresses the way in which health improvements in societies have depended more upon environmental improvements and raised living standards than upon medical advances (McKeown, 1980).

There are, however, connections between the other actions or policies needed to address the issues identified in the list above and the roles played by medical activities and policies. Medicine has played an important role in identifying connections between environment or behaviour on the one hand, and health problems on the other. The fact that people can now take action, without medical help, to avoid problems or even to treat themselves rests upon the work medical experts have done to diagnose diseases and identify causes and cures. While in theory non-medical scientific and social-scientific activity could have sorted out many of these issues, and has indeed participated in sorting them out, much of the impetus for this progress has come from the particular concerns of the medical profession. In this sense it is important not to let the high profile assumed by direct interventions through medical treatment and surgery to try to deal with or alleviate illness lead to the undervaluing of the role the medical profession plays in identifying it and assisting with its prevention.

The other important issue alongside medical treatment of sick people is that of caring for sick people. This has been the concern of families and communities throughout the ages, regardless of whether any medical intervention is feasible or not. The reason for identifying this issue now is that there is a danger of confusing 'care' in this sense with 'treatment', the direct application of medical skills and technologies. Medical expertise may be needed to recommend the best kind of care but that expertise is not necessarily required to provide it. Looking at the issue the other way round the successful application of medical expertise may require that people are cared for in a satisfactory way.

This distinction is being laboured because of a variety of important policy questions which flow from the alternative ways 'care' and 'treatment' (as defined above) may be combined. The hospital has evolved from a long-term caring institution where social and nursing care were generally more important than medical care to a site for the practice of high-technology medicine. The modern hospital generally endeavours to confine its provision of in-patient care to very brief episodes in which patients need to be present to be given intensive medical or surgical attention. Accordingly there are issues about the extent to which the nursing and social care of the sick then occurs largely in patients' homes, with implications for themselves, their families and perhaps social care services as much as for health services. Such a focus on the caring side highlights, as the above emphasis upon prevention did, the fact that doctors themselves need to work in partnership with other carers (both formal and informal) to ensure that poor 'care' does not undermine 'treatment' and that within health services themselves there are other workers, professional and non-professional, whose roles particularly concern the caring side.

These two key issues about health care and health policy are connected. Hence, while the focus will be upon the way in which health policy has developed as a way of regulating and providing modern scientific medicine (and dentistry), it will be recognised that there are a variety of issues to be considered about the following:

1. The extent to which health status improvements in societies are attributable to medicine.
2. Tendencies for 'health services' so called to be primarily 'illness services'.
3. The importance of care in a wide sense for the well-being of those who are treated by health services (an issue that has implications for other services as well as for those parts of the health care activity which are often regarded as the responsibilities of individuals and their families).

These three points together mean that the putting of health policy into practice in a society involves a variety of activities, including the prevention of disease, health promotion and efforts to support caring systems. It is important not to let the particular visibility of the hospital and of the profession of medicine blind one to the range of activity which goes on outside institutions or does not involve doctors, or indeed both.

The issues outlined above about the need to see health policy in a wider context, and to recognise the complex relationship between 'treatment' and 'care', lead to one other issue. Any system of publicly supported health care has to draw boundaries around the services it will provide. These will identify treatments that will not be provided (cosmetic surgery or perhaps sterilisation). They may exclude some treatments because of doubts about their efficacy (for example, some forms of 'folk medicine'). There may also be often controversial attempts to exclude 'heroic' surgical interventions where chances of success are low and costs are high (some transplant surgery, for example). As systems run into difficulties with scarce resources these boundaries may be redrawn (the exclusion of the provision of spectacles or dental care, for example). Thus the issues about what health care can do for people and the issues about what governments will let it do (at least with public money) can become very mixed.

Alternative roles for the state in relation to health care

There are a number of roles the state may play in relation to health care. These are as follows:

- Regulator.
- Funder/purchaser.
- Provider/planner.

Any one system is likely to involve a combination of all or most of these roles. While logically there is no reason why the state cannot be involved in planning and providing without funding, in practice the three are likely to be mixed together with the state being only a part funder.

This section will look at what these roles may involve, some of the alternative ways these roles may be fulfilled and some of the ways they may be combined. In the course of this discussion some of the different ways these roles are fulfilled and combined in different countries to produce very different configurations for health policy will be highlighted.

The regulator role

It has already been shown in Chapter 2 how states accepted the case for regulation of the activities of doctors by delegating regulatory responsibilities to professional organisations. Similar regulatory issues subsequently arose with regard to other health professionals and semi-professionals (dentists, opticians, pharmacists, nurses, midwives, etc.), as did regulatory policies in respect of hospitals, clinics and nursing-homes.

With the extension of private insurance into health care some states became concerned about the need to regulate business practices in this area of activity. Customers were vulnerable to exploitation because of their need for help. In some societies the private insurance option was seen as the way forward for the care of all. This meant that the state moved to require individuals to take on insurance, to require companies to offer policies to all and to lay down certain standards for these arrangements. As suggested in Chapter 2, such an approach put the state in a position in which it might be hard to resist demands for it to 'underwrite' the protection offered, subsidising bad risks and companies which got into difficulties. In many societies efforts to universalise private insurance can be seen to have been a stage down the road towards state-supported 'social' insurance (Immergut, 1993).

The funder or purchaser role

For the purposes of this discussion the role of the state as a funder of health care has deliberately been separated from consideration of other roles. Like the regulator role the funder role can be seen as independent of the other roles, notwithstanding the fact that a strong funder role tends to lead to the state wanting to be involved in provision and planning of services and, at the very least, leads to the strengthening of the regulator roles. However, when health care is examined comparatively it is clear that countries combine these roles in very different ways.

The alternative approaches to state funding involve *either* funding from taxation (including local taxation) *or* funding by way of a state-administered or regulated insurance system. However, these two may occur in combination (for example, an insurance system may receive tax subsidies). It will also be shown that in certain circumstances the distinction between the two approaches becomes so blurred that an insurance scheme may in practice be described as a 'health tax' scheme.

The analysis is then further complicated by the public/private mix in health care funding. State systems will be found which aim to be as far as possible comprehensive, together with systems where there are substantial areas of activity left to private (but probably insurance-supported) provision, and systems where it is the public sector rather than the private sector which is the residual one.

Amongst the examples from specific countries which will be discussed below, the following four variations on these funding themes will be found in practice:

1. Comprehensive tax-funded schemes – the United Kingdom, Sweden.
2. Tax-funded schemes involving elements of earmarked taxation, often called health insurance – Canada, Australia.
3. Comprehensive insurance schemes – France.
4. Partial schemes involving public and private insurance plus elements of tax funding – Germany, the Netherlands.

5. Residual systems with some injections of tax funds and state-controlled insurance into broadly privately funded systems – the United States.

Tax-funded schemes offer perhaps the simplest place to start the discussion of funding. Tax funding is probably the most straightforward way for a state to assume the funder role. Yet even that model is susceptible to many variations. First, states take many forms. They may be federal, they may have highly developed systems of local government and they may have partially autonomous administrative systems. Thus while the health service systems of Australia, Canada, Sweden and the United Kingdom all fall, in general terms, into the tax-funded category, that of Canada involves delegation to provinces, that of Australia federal funding but state level providers, that of Sweden delegation to local government and that of the United Kingdom a rather complex (and changing) system of partial administrative devolution. These are important issues for the performance of the service in each country, producing inevitable variations in the forms it takes.

Tax funding may involve alternatives – there may simply be funding out of general taxation, there may be specifically earmarked taxation for health (as identified by the use of a separate category for Canada and Australia above), and there may be elements of cost sharing with local taxation. The hybrid forms of sharing between tax and insurance (as in Canada and Australia) lead to questions – as suggested in Chapter 4 – about whether it might not be more appropriate to call a universal insurance contribution in which the link between payment and entitlement is exceptionally weak a 'tax'.

An aspect of this distinction – and perhaps another reason for describing the Australian system as an insurance-based one rather than a tax-funded one (see, for example, the usage in Palmer and Short, 1994) – is the role the patient is allowed to play in making an initial 'purchase' of care. In the Australian case there are options for physicians as to whether to charge the patient and leave him or her to reclaim from the state or to direct-bill the state. The picture is then further confused by the range of situations in which the provider can offer a private alternative option or charge for supplementary services.

An important and growing form of cost sharing, even in tax-funded health care systems, is the expectation that patients will pay some part of the cost of their treatment. Such payments may include such things as charges for prescriptions, fixed charges for consultations, contributions towards dental treatment and charges for the 'hotel' costs of in-patient stays. There may also be situations in which the government imposes reimbursement limits for services but allows practitioners to charge more (this has been a controversial aspect of the French system, see Wilsford in Ambler, 1991). In some systems which initially aspired to offer a free service, these charges have grown as a response to government concerns about the growing cost of health care, being seen as both ways to raise money and ways of trying to curb unreasonable demands upon systems. As they have grown two effects have occurred. One is that universalistic systems have turned back towards some of the forms of means-testing that were often characteristic of earlier systems in that society. The other is that incentives have increased for a minority of citizens to opt for private health care.

No democratic state which has developed a comprehensive publicly funded health care system has entirely outlawed private medicine. This leaves a situation in which wealthy citizens may opt for private care. This may be done to get swifter attention, to get care superior to that offered in publicly funded institutions (more luxurious 'hotel' conditions, more privacy, etc.), or to get treatment the state is unprepared to offer (see discussion above, p. 98–9). This demand by the well off, at the margins of the state system, has led to opportunities for insurance companies and has spread private care beyond the ranks of the very rich (Higgins, 1988).

In Australia, where the public funding of health care has been so significant an area of controversy between the political parties, that comprehensive schemes have in the recent past been set up, then abolished and then imposed again (Palmer and Short, 1994, chs 1 and 4), private insurance is particularly strong. About 40 per cent of the population hold some health insurance at the time of writing, but the percentage is declining (Grant and Lapsley, 1993, p. 140).

One feature of a mix of public and private medicine in which the former is dominant is that the public sector is likely to subsidise the private one. If doctors are trained in public hospitals but can then practise in private ones the latter will secure the benefit of their expensive training. Similarly the private sector is likely to benefit from developments in knowledge from research in the public sector. These 'positive externalities' (see discussion on p. 31) are difficult to avoid. Much the same occurs when doctors move between countries and when research findings are disseminated internationally.

There are other forms of cross-subsidy, theoretically more easily preventable. If patients have a general entitlement to state health services then they can choose to confine their private care to situations where the private sector offers special advantages – when waiting lists are long, for example. Private hospitals can choose to carry out only those procedures where returns to their investment will be high – for example, straightforward surgery making relatively low demands on expensive equipment. They can enjoy the protection that if complications arise the public system cannot morally refuse to take over the case.

A justification for this cross-subsidy in tax-funded systems is provided inasmuch as the purchasers of private health care are also taxpayers contributing to the cost of the public sector. The benefits of cross-subsidy have the effect of muting the complaint that private patients should not have to pay for a state sector they do not use. In any society, the more the private sector is able to do to secure itself wide support amongst the well off and become a sector offering comprehensive health care, the more vociferous will become the call for a break from a universal tax-funded model for the state. This has been a direction in which the British system has been 'feared' or 'hoped' to be travelling with the decline in the public sector and the rise of the private sector during the 1980s and 1990 (see Glennerster in Glennerster and Midgley, 1991, for an assessment of these developments). In such a context any weakening of the capacity of the public sector to meet need, particularly lengthening waiting lists for the operations the private sector is willing to take on, stimulates private-sector growth.

Another way in which a mixed pattern of care may grow, also evident in the history of the British health service, occurs if the private sector is allowed to offer extra benefits in partnership with the public sector or to cushion (through private insurance) the impact of the cost sharing that sector requires of patients. In Britain in the 1970s a government of the left tried to eliminate a practice under which people could secure private care in National Health Service hospitals, a pattern likely to involve heavy subsidies of the private sector by the public. They were replaced by a government of the right before they could progress with the implementation of that change. In the 1990s the direction of change is the other way – private insurance companies have been able to get the support of National Health Service Trust hospitals with the selling of private insurance which will enable public sector patients to get extra services and benefits. This is also a salient feature of the Australian scene (Palmer and Short, 1994).

The insurance approach to the state funding role in health services – with the state underwriting, subsidising, perhaps managing and certainly regulating contributory insurance – copes with this public/private tension better than a universal tax-based state health service, but to put the issue like that is probably to confuse result with cause. It has been the very power of the protectors of the private model, manifested largely in modern times by private insurance, which first confined the state intervention to the filling of gaps in private insurance. Coming at the problems about universalising health care in this way many states, not unnaturally, went on gradually to shift their systems from private insurance domination to state insurance domination (Immergut, 1993).

Where states have sought to develop comprehensive health insurance systems the details can be very complex. That complexity often derives from a gradual evolution away from private insurance. France's compulsory national health insurance covers 99 per cent of the population, but is organised into a complex network of quasi-autonomous funds (Caisses Nationales) together with friendly societies and private insurers.

At the time of writing the legislature in Taiwan has just passed a measure which will enable a single unitary insurance system to take the place of limited separate schemes for private employees, public employees, farmers, etc. The relative simplicity of this scheme is probably a consequence of the absence of a strong insurance industry when the original partial social insurance schemes were set up. In the light of the aspiration towards universalism, with low-income people inevitably the beneficiaries of a combination of cross-subsidy and mainstream tax-based support, this system may evolve so that it may become more appropriate to label it a 'health tax' rather than a 'health insurance' system.

Germany and the Netherlands provide interesting examples of what were described above as 'partial schemes'. In Germany there are 1,100 autonomous sickness funds in the Western Lander (federal 'provinces'), about 75 per cent of the population are insured compulsorily and 13 per cent are insured voluntarily (OECD, 1992, p. 57). Membership of funds is compulsory for lower-income people, and there are complex cross-subsidy arrangements to compensate schemes for low contributor members. In total:

> *... about 60% of health expenditure is derived from compulsory and voluntary contributors to statutory health insurance, about 21% is derived from general taxation, about 7% is derived from private insurance and about 11% is represented by unreimbursed, out-of-pocket expenditure. (*ibid., *again this data derives from the Western Lander, a similar system was set up in the former GDR in 1991)*

The Netherlands' system has rather similar characteristics. Health care is:

> *... financed by a mixture of social and private insurance contributions combined with significant direct payments and government subsidies. The whole population is compulsorily insured for chronic health care risks . . . 70% is compulsorily insured for acute health care risks .... Tight and detailed central regulation of prices, volume and capacity has been imposed on an essentially private system of provision and a mixed system of finance. (*ibid., *p. 87)*

What is interesting about the Dutch model is that, while it too allows higher-income groups to contribute to private schemes, it has a compulsory arrangement for 'chronic health care risks'.

Differentiation between types of contributor, as in the German and Dutch schemes, may involve explicit provisions for choice by contributors about levels of premiums to pay with corresponding alternative benefits. In such a situation the state's role may be to regulate to secure a minimum standard (and to expect that for those it has to subsidise), but to allow a wide range of possibilities above that minimum.

One issue which arises where there are, as in Germany, alternative insurance schemes which individuals may join is inequities in the costs and/or services available to different socio-economic groups. In Germany health insurance contributions lie in a range between 8 and 16 per cent, with many schemes at the expensive end of the range containing 'disproportionate numbers of the poor and unhealthy' (Moran in Clasen and Freeman, 1994, p. 97).

The most obvious example of what was above described as a 'residual system' of public funding of health care is that of the United States. There the key state ingredients are the following:

1. 'Medicare' – a federal insurance programme for persons over 65 years of age which is tax supported but to which individuals are required to pay low premiums and for which there are 'cost sharing' charges often covered by individuals through supplementary private insurance.
2. 'Medicaid' – a system of health care cost subsidy for low-income people linked to the public welfare (social assistance) system and supported by federal and state taxation (Ham *et al.*, 1990).

At the time of writing, it seems certain that the Clinton administration has failed to realise its commitment to moving the American system on from that position to one in which the state makes contributions to ensure more universal insurance cover.

It should be evident from Chapter 2 that, while variants of either tax funding or insurance funding of health services dominate in modern societies, there are two other ways in which the state subsidises health services. One of these is in situations in which it provides specific services and/or controls over sick individuals in the name of the 'public interest'. If the state insists that people with fevers should be treated in isolated institutions or mentally ill people should be incarcerated it is likely to have to pay all or most of the cost of this. While actions in these two categories are rare today, their importance in the nineteenth century was a major influence on the development of large state-owned institutions. Their modern equivalents are likely to be less draconian measures designed to promote public health, limit the spread of disease and provide responses to natural disasters.

The state may also inject funds into health care because of concern about the health of its own employees, particularly its military. Finally, state investments in medical education and research may provide an element of public funding into otherwise very private health care systems.

This discussion of funding has provided little in the way of figures on levels of funding or on the nature of the public/private mix in various countries. This will be done in a later section, but first there is a need to look at the issues about the way services are provided, as opposed to how they are funded.

The provider and/or planner role for the state

The relationship between the role of the state as funder and the role of the state as provider can logically take any of four forms – for it to be funder and

Table 5.1 State roles in health care

	State as provider	
Funding	**Yes**	**No**
Tax	1	2
Insurance	3	4

provider, for it to be neither funded nor provider, for it to be a funder but not a provider, or for it to be a provider but not a funder. However, since in the modern state the state is normally involved in funding to some degree, the crucial alternatives involve the relationship between the nature of provision and the funding method. The alternatives are set out in Table 5.1. A third dimension could be added to this table by making a distinction between institutions and services, and in view of what has already been said about insurance, it should not be surprising to find that some very complicated mixed forms occur.

The history of health provision in Britain has involved what may generally be seen as an evolution from category 4 in Table 5.1 towards category 1 and then some shift away towards category 2. In the period 1911–48 the main state contribution was social insurance (plus the poor law), the main providers of primary care were general practices (operating as private businesses), while hospital care was available in voluntary and local authority-owned hospitals. Since 1948 there has been a tax-funded universal health service. Between 1948 and 1990 the state owned all the hospitals providing health service care. General practitioners, while allowed to continue as self-employed workers under contract to the health service, lost the right to buy and sell practices. Since 1990, hospitals may become self-governing 'trusts', still in the state system but with some autonomy and a right to do private work. Health authorities may buy services from private hospitals and primary care practices may assume forms very much more like private businesses.

Saltman and von Otter (1992) have demonstrated similar complexities in the Swedish system, where local authorities are the key units in the system and recent developments have also involved the evolution of mixed provider systems. Federal systems like those of Australia and Canada have, as already noted, similar characteristics. But there is a contrast to be made between them inasmuch as in the former the providers are still public bodies (albeit state rather than federal government run), while in the latter many private organisations are providers (Deber, 1993). France comes more clearly into category 3 as far as hospitals are concerned, while the Netherlands is in category 4 (OECD, 1992).

The case against the simple model (category 1) is that which has been made by critiques of bureaucracy and professionalism which see state institutions as very open to 'provider capture' inasmuch as the staff of the service determine the needs of the system and can impose demands upon public funds which are very hard to control. A massive literature has developed in recent years around this issue (contributions specific to health services include Enthoven, 1985; Altenstetter and Haywood, 1991; Saltman and von Otter, 1992; Harrison and Pollitt, 1994).

The forces against state monopoly – amongst which it is interesting to note that professional self-interest has been significant (Immergut, 1993; Moran and Wood, 1993) despite what is now being said about the problems of controlling professionals in such a context – have the effect of making state provision with tax funding the rarity, at least in a complete form. Even in very unified systems like that of Britain before 1990 general practitioners were able to preserve a measure of autonomy.

The other models for the relationship between funding and provision require quite complex arrangements to deal with issues like the following:

1. The making, variation and termination of contracts.
2. The determination of the amounts and forms of reimbursement for services provided.
3. The ways in which publicly and privately funded activities may be mixed.
4. The rights of patients in respect of choice of services and the avenues for the redress of grievances.
5. The determination of where the benefits or costs of 'externalities' may fall – health prevention, medical education, research, etc.
6. The monitoring of standards and the determination of needs for new services.

The various mixtures of provision tend to lead governments to assume a planning role in the absence of overall direct control. Current interest in the viability of mixed market or quasi-market models for the provision of health care seems to suggest that the 'hidden hand' of the market beloved of the classical economist can replace planning (for discussion of this see Le Grand, 1990; Glennerster, 1992, ch. 10; Hudson, 1994). The examples of the United Kingdom, Sweden and Finland studied by Saltman and von Otter suggest three reasons why this is not the case.

First, many ventures in health care, particularly in hospital care, are very big business. Market entry costs are therefore enormous. It would be a rash entrepreneur indeed who engaged in investment in a new hospital without some clear guarantee of 'business'; only some kind of planning process can offer that.

Second, there are a variety of situations in health care where 'externalities' (largely positive ones, inasmuch as the consequences of inaction are very negative) are very considerable. This issue has already been discussed in Chapter 2 and mentioned in this chapter. Medical education and research have already been identified as creating situations where others are bound to benefit from investment in these activities. These together with the organisation of efforts to deal with rare diseases and to supply special forms of treatment call for some degree of regulation and planning.

Third, health care is a topic about which everyone has strong feelings. Health care organisation decisions are therefore very much concerns of politics. Cries to 'keep politics out of health care' are a waste of breath. Hence issues about 'gaps' in services, the closure of services, etc., are kept on the public agenda. If the outcome is not necessarily 'planning' in some ideal sense it certainly is interference with market forces and efforts to match resources to political rather than economic demands.

While there are good grounds for scepticism about the scope for achieving a split between purchasing and providing which truly 'mimics the market' the divided model may be seen as a method for making the decision processes in relation to health care expenditure more explicit. This may facilitate control by central purchasers, and perhaps by the general public, as the costs of medical procedures and the differences in efficiency between providers are made more explicit (Saltman and von Otter, 1992). Forms of provider capture can at least be more easily identified.

Evaluating health services: inputs

Tables 5.2 and 5.3 set out, for various countries, two aspects of health expenditure inputs – total expenditure (regardless of the spender) and the proportion of that expenditure undertaken by the state. While the focus of this book is upon public policy, from the viewpoint of society as a whole it is the issues about overall health status and total expenditure which are important. A view can be taken that it is only state expenditure that should be a matter for public policy, since what individuals spend their money on is their own concern. Alternatively it can be regarded as worrying that individuals are spending high proportions of their incomes on their health care, on the grounds that this is an inefficient use of resources. In this discussion the determinants of *both* indices will be considered, while recognising that there may be issues about the relationships between the two. Thus an exceptionally high level of private expenditure in the context of a low state level (as in the United States) may suggest that the state could do a more efficient job than private enterprise. Conversely a relatively low level of state expenditure which is at the same time a high proportion of total expenditure may offer evidence of a deficient effort by the state, evidence that the state is very good at cost control or evidence for a need to stimulate

Table 5.2 Health expenditure 1991 (public and private)

	As % of GDP	Index of health expenditure per head (USA = 100)
Australia	8.6	48
Austria	8.4	54
Belgium	7.9	48
Canada	10.0	67
Denmark	6.5	41
Finland	8.9	49
France	9.1	60
Germany	8.5	58
Greece	5.2	16
Ireland	7.3	31
Italy	8.3	48
Japan	6.9	46
Netherlands	8.2	49
New Zealand	7.6	38
Norway	7.7	46
Portugal	6.8	22
Spain	6.7	30
Sweden	8.6	58
Switzerland	7.9	63
UK	6.6	38
USA	13.4	100

Source: OECD (1994c) *New Orientations for Social Policy*, Paris: OECD, table 2, pp. 70–3 and chart 3, p. 80 reproduced by permission of the OECD.

the private sector. These are alternative interpretations of the situation in the United Kingdom. It all depends upon what may be taken as an appropriate yardstick for a satisfactory level of expenditure, and that all depends upon the determinants of levels of expenditure.

Thus there are a number of things to be taken into account in evaluating expenditure figures and in comparing data from different countries. First, there is an association between overall economic achievement and expenditure on health. It is instructive to take the figures on the proportion of GDP spent on health and relate them to figures on GDP per head (the most generally used index of the overall prosperity of a nation). Table 5.4 does that.

This suggests that not only are richer countries able to spend more but also spend proportionately *even* more. This may have something to do with the extent other needs are satisfied or perhaps to exceptional health care

Table 5.3 Public expenditure on health as a percentage of total expenditure on health care 1991

Australia	68
Austria	67
Belgium	89
Canada	72
Denmark	81
Finland	81
France	75
Germany	72
Greece	79
Ireland	76
Italy	78
Japan	70
Netherlands	73
New Zealand	79
Norway	97
Portugal	61
Spain	82
Sweden	78
Switzerland	68
UK	83
USA	44

Source: OECD (1994c) *New Orientations for Social Policy*, Paris: OECD, table 2, pp. 70–3; reproduced by permission of the OECD.

aspirations which come with prosperity (from heroic surgical interventions to cosmetic surgery). However, there are some interesting deviant cases. The United States's level of expenditure is very high relative to its level of prosperity. This seems to offer a case for public intervention to control costs, particularly when it is compared with a country like Denmark with a high GDP per head, a high level of public relative to private expenditure and a low level of health expenditure per head. There is another contrasting case, Switzerland, with a system with a relatively large private sector, where high prosperity and high health care expenditure co-exist without at the same time consuming an exceptional proportion of that country's very high GDP. Such contrasts obviously indicate the need to examine issues about the cultures of the countries concerned and issues about the insurance industry. Perhaps US insurers could learn from Swiss ones, or perhaps the fact that the latter system involves a public/private partnership helps to curb costs.

It is important to return to the issue posed above about the United Kingdom.

Table 5.4 Health expenditure as a percentage of GDP, 1991

	Health exp. as % of GDP 1991	GDP per capita 1990 (US$)
Australia	8.6	17,215
Austria	8.4	20,319
Belgium	7.9	19,303
Canada	10.0	21,418
Denmark	6.5	25,150
Finland	8.9	27,527
France	9.1	21,105
Germany	8.5	23,536
Greece	5.2	6,505
Ireland	7.3	12,131
Italy	8.3	18,921
Japan	6.9	23,801
Netherlands	8.2	18,676
New Zealand	7.6	13,020
Norway	7.7	24,924
Portugal	6.8	6,085
Spain	6.7	12,609
Sweden	8.6	26,652
Switzerland	7.9	33,085
UK	6.6	16,985
USA	13.4	21,449

Sources: OECD (1994) *New Orientations for Social Policy*, Paris: OECD, table 2, pp. 70–3 and GDP 1990 figures from OECD economic statistics series; reproduced by permission of the OECD.

A tightly state-controlled system may, as suggested above, simply be ignoring needs. Systems vary in the extent to which they encourage or suppress demand. The question whether that is desirable raises a minefield of value questions about justifiable and unjustifiable demands, about the extent to which the demands of patients are unreasonable and about the way systems raise expectations. When looking at expenditure inputs there are obviously comparisons to be made between levels of efficiency. There are also issues to be considered about the levels of staffing and levels of remuneration of the professions. Data on numbers of doctors per 1,000 population are interesting in again providing another part of the explanation of levels of health costs per head. Table 5.5 sets side by side data on health expenditure per person in various countries and data on numbers of doctors.

Germany is notable for its very high ratio of doctors to population. The finding for the United States seems surprising – high costs but an average doctor–population ratio. The key to explaining this can be found if doctors'

Table 5.5 Health expenditure per person and doctors per 1,000 people

	Health exp. per person (US$ 1991)	Doctors per 1,000 people 1990
Canada	1,915	2.2
France	1,650	2.7
Germany	1,659	3.1
Japan	1,307	1.6
UK	1,043	1.4
USA	2,868	2.3
OECD av.	1,305	2.4

Source: Schieber, G., Poullier, J.-P. and Greenwald, L. (1993) 'Health spending, delivery and outcomes in OECD countries,' in Clasen, J. and Freeman, R. (eds.) *Social Policy in Germany*, Hemel Hempstead: Harvester Wheatsheaf, table 4.1, p. 85.

pay rates are examined; they are particularly high in the United States (Heidenheimer *et al.*, 1990, p. 89, quoting data from OECD, 1987). It is evident from figures like this that there are trade-offs between levels of medical remuneration and numbers of doctors per head. To carry the analysis even further there is a need to go into the roles in which these doctors are employed. This is done in Heidenheimer, Heclo and Adams's discussion of this topic (1990, ch. 3) revealing the extent to which doctors in the United States are employed in the high-status and high-paid hospital jobs, where they are particularly ill positioned to control demand upon services.

There are, however, three fundamental problems about comparing data of this kind. First, there are difficulties about identifying the borderline between health care expenditure and other related expenditure (for example, on social care). Different countries may draw their borderlines differently. Second, economic difficulties or the unavailability of services drive people into forms of self-treatment and family care. Third, the health of nations (see further discussion below) depends upon many things, a lot of them unconnected with health care. In theory it should be possible to identify nations where demands are lower because people are fitter *before* health care inputs, but in practice this is difficult to do.

Evaluating health services: performance indices

All of the problems about input measures seem to make output measures preferable. It is possible to collect explicit *output* measures from health

Table 5.6 Life expectations and infant death rates (1990 data)

	Life expectancy at birth	Infant deaths per 1,000
Australia	73	7.8
Canada	74	6.8
Denmark	73	7.2
France	73	7.3
Germany	72	7.1
Italy	74	8.6
Japan	76	4.4
Netherlands	74	7.1
New Zealand	72	10.0
Norway	73	7.0
Sweden	75	5.7
Switzerland	74	5.9
UK	73	7.3
USA	72	9.8

Source: World Health Organisation (1992) *World Health Statistics Annual*, Geneva: World Health Organisation.

services – data on numbers of people dealt with, and so on. In the case of health care few measures are available that provide direct evidence on system 'achievements', inasmuch as the objectives of health services are to improve health status in general. What is available is evidence on, in a sense, the failures of the system – numbers dying and numbers unwell. Turn this on its head and it may be possible to regard low numbers as evidence of system achievement. Comparisons of data of this kind offer evidence on health status differences between different nations and groups and on trends over time. Mortality and morbidity statistics are in this rather back-to-front sense ultimate *outcome* measures for health services.

Interpretation of mortality and morbidity data is by no means problem free. Mortality data are important. General mortality rates need to be read carefully, adjusted to take into account the age structure of the population. Demographers calculate age-specific mortality rates. Untimely death may offer particularly telling evidence on the health problems of a society. One death rate, therefore, that has been given particular attention has been the infant mortality rate, deaths of children under one year of age standardised to take into account the overall numbers at risk. Table 5.6 sets out some statistics on both life expectancy and on mortality rates for a sample of developed countries.

Differences in life expectancy between countries in this sample are not very significant. The data on infant deaths make rather more striking reading. The

Table 5.7 Persons in Australia who took various health-related actions during two survey weeks in 1989–90 (thousands)

Hospital in-patient episode	157
Visit to casualty/outpatients	426
Doctor consultation	3,400
Dental consultation	876
Consultation with other health professional	1,603
Took vitamins/minerals	3,960
Used other medications	10,900
Days away from work/school	1,169
Other days of reduced activity	1,645
Total persons taking some 'action'	12,827
Total persons taking 'no action'	4,162

Source: ABS National Health Survey quoted in Grant, C. and Lapsley, H. M. (1993) *The Australian Health Care System*, Kensington: School of Health Services Management, University of New South Wales.

two countries with high rates are the lowest overall spender per head (New Zealand) and the highest spender (the United States) (see table 5.2). Conversely the country with far and away the best record (Japan) is one of the comparatively low spenders. These data raise very different questions about what is going on in those countries. The answers to these will not be addressed as the intention here is only to draw attention to the questions.

Looking at the population more generally rates of deaths from specific conditions may offer evidence on preventable deaths, where knowledge about the feasibility of treatment may enable further reflection on the effectiveness of health services. A difficulty with condition-specific death rates is that evidence may be crucially dependent upon the classification practices of the doctors who sign the death certificates. These naturally vary over time and from society to society according to the state of knowledge and perhaps medical fashion.

Morbidity statistics are needed to supplement mortality statistics. Populations suffer from many health problems which do not kill them. Yet morbidity statistics are even more difficult to interpret than mortality statistics. There are two alternative sources – medical judgements about the health problems brought to practitioners or self-reported morbidity data (based upon surveys of the population). The latter produces much larger numbers than the former method, with obvious variations according to the condition. Table 5.7 illustrates this, and includes some interesting evidence on the various forms of self-treatment adopted. It indicates that during that survey period 76 per cent of the population of Australia took some 'health-related action' but only 20 per cent of the population consulted a doctor.

All kinds of morbidity statistics have subjective elements. People very often treat themselves or manage to live with conditions without seeking treatment. Statistics derived from patients depend upon their assessments of the seriousness of their own problem; those derived from doctors depend (notwithstanding their expertise) also on interpretations of the seriousness of other people's conditions. Stacey has shown how complex the sociological distinction is between 'illness' and 'disease':

> *Illness is the subjective state which is experienced by an individual, a feeling of ill-being. Disease is a pathological condition recognized by indications agreed among biomedical practitioners. (Stacey, p. 171)*

The definitions of 'biomedical practitioners' are no more valid than people's subjective judgements. They are subject to variation over time and between 'experts', and are conditional upon the dominant paradigms in medical knowledge.

It is perhaps most useful to take the two data sources together, considering the extent to which the 'gap' between them is influenced by the availability, accessibility and approachability of doctors. Evidence of larger gaps in some places or for some categories of patients (identifiable, for example, by class, race or gender, or the nature of the condition) can lead to questions about the way services are provided.

The discussion in the last paragraph raises issues about more specific approaches to comparisons between illness incidence rates. These are important for mortality as well as morbidity rates. These differences may raise considerations about the performance of health services. There are some important issues about 'inequalities of health' within nations as well as between nations. Any single national 'rate' may conceal variations, particularly if it is derived from a very large population. Thus an infant mortality rate for a large country like the United States may give a very different picture to a set of rates from different regions, racial groups and socio-economic groups within that nation. For example, in 1983 the infant mortality rate for 'whites' was 9.7 per hundred thousand live births, that for 'non-whites' 16.8, and that for 'blacks' 19.2 (US Bureau of Census, 1987, quoted in Ginsburg, 1992, p. 135). In Australia the infant mortality rate for Aborigines was 22.5 per thousand live births (Grant and Lapsley, 1993, p. 33) as opposed to the 7.8 shown in table 5.6 for the whole population.

Studies in various countries have similarly demonstrated the extent of mortality and morbidity variations between social classes (or socio-economic groups) (see Townsend *et al.*, 1988). In Britain the death rate in 1990 for children between one month and one year, per thousand live births, was 2.0 for children whose parents were in the top two social classes in the Registrar General's five-point scale and 4.0 for those whose parents were in the bottom two classes (*ibid.*, p. 268). Similar findings are reported for France, showing infant mortality rates for the children of labourers double those for children in the professional classes (*ibid.*, p. 90).

Clearly some powerful comparisons between survival chances can be made if between nation contrasts and within nation contrasts are brought together. Leon, Vägerö and Olausson (1992) have done this with infant mortality data from Britain and Sweden. Whitehead reports:

> *The authors calculate that if all Swedish infants had the same level of mortality as the non-manual classes in Sweden, then 10 per cent of neonatal and 29 per cent of post-neonatal deaths would be avoided. If English and Welsh babies had the same level of mortality as the Swedish non-manual classes, then 40 per cent of neonatal deaths and 63 per cent of post-neonatal deaths would be avoided. (Whitehead in Townsend* et al., *1988, p. 310)*

As suggested in the introduction, health status data do not only depend upon health services. Many improvements in the health of nations are attributable to economic and environmental advances (McKeown, 1980), and many inequalities of health within and between nations are attributable to differences in incomes and environments (both within and outside the home). There is clearly a need to look at such data in relation to evidence on the differential use of health services. Results are, however, difficult to interpret: there is a package of interlocking factors here, particularly where income and environment deficiencies themselves have a direct impact upon access to health services.

These interactions may raise policy questions for those responsible for the design of health services. To what extent can good health services compensate for other disadvantages? The answer is 'probably not very much' – this involves concentrating on cure when prevention would have been much more effective. But if this is the case then, to what extent can a health service see the elimination of disadvantages as part of a preventive health programme? This is an issue which has clearly been grasped for a long while in relation to adverse environmental factors, with health experts becoming involved in the attack upon pollution and other health hazards. It has been less readily grasped in relation to problems of income deficiency, where health specialists have often been reluctant to get involved with the political issues (often with a big 'P') about the management of the economy, the incidence of taxation and the availability of income maintenance benefits. Rather they have often turned to issues about the behaviour of the poor – their eating patterns, their use of alcohol and their smoking – legitimate targets, but surely not unconnected with issues about income (see the discussion in Whitehead in Townsend *et al.*, 1988).

Control of health services

This section will look at some related issues about control over health services. It will start with that major preoccupation of modern industrial states – control over health service costs, looking at the approaches used to control them. It will then go on to a wider and related issue about the way the character of health services is shaped by their professional staff. This will lead on to issues about control by the public over their health services – a topic which will be organised around two alternative approaches, control through 'democratic' representative institutions and control through markets.

Cost control

Chapter 12 will look at the general issues about the sources of growth of the costs of the welfare state as a whole, amongst which growth of the health sector looms large. The discussion here will briefly outline the issues specifically affecting health care. Demographic pressures are particularly evident as a source of growth in health care costs. The beginning and end of life, particularly the latter, impose heavy costs on health services. In Australia in 1989–90 the average total health expenditure was $1,690. But it rose steadily through the age groups to reach $3,070 for people aged 65–9, $4,089 for people aged 70–4 and $7,567 for people aged over 75 (Grant and Lapsley, 1993, p. 117).

Countries are experiencing growth not merely in the numbers of the elderly but particularly in the numbers of the very elderly (see the data on p. 303). Incidence of chronic health conditions amongst the very elderly is high and the more medicine can do to prolong life the more it has to cope with high demands on its services in that extra period it has added to people's lives.

Politicians may be reluctant to attack services to this group directly. Cutting of services may occur relatively covertly by way of the lengthening of waiting times for operations to deal with conditions, prevalent amongst the elderly, which are not life threatening (vein treatment, hip replacement, etc.). Judgements about priorities may also be biased against the elderly.

Another source of upward pressure on health service costs which is equally difficult to handle politically comes about because of advances in medical science and technology (including advances in drug uses). In areas where very high costs force the rationing of treatment (transplant surgery or kidney machines, for example), it is very difficult for politicians to say 'no' to efforts to bring such services to all who need them. The remorseless upward cost pressure exerted by scientific advance can easily have consequences for other services which are less dramatic in their impact and less likely to secure media attention. There is an ever present danger that the indirect 'casualties' of scientific advance will be the sufferers from minor chronic conditions or from mental illness.

High technology medicine requires politicians and other decision-makers to face up to the issues about equity in the provision of health services in society. These will not merely concern the way the state orders its priorities, but also the extent to which market mechanisms are allowed to 'solve' the rationing issues in favour of those with the resources to buy.

Health costs are pushed up by changes to the prices charged by those who supply the medicines and the technology. There are also other critical 'suppliers' of health services whose costs increase. These are the staff, whose wages, salaries and fees have to be paid. Governments will try to resist rises in these, but they may also tackle this particular cost control problem another way, by seeking an efficiency gain in return for a pay rise. These issues, common to all services, are discussed further in Chapter 12.

Some of the founders of modern health services naively believed that the introduction of a good service readily available to all would, in raising the health status of the nation, have a self-limiting impact upon the demands on itself (see Klein, 1989). The reality seems to be almost the opposite of that – as health services have improved so the demands upon them have increased. The following are possible reasons for this:

1. The existence of extensive unmet health care need.
2. Advances in scientific medicine that make it possible to do more things for more people and to keep people alive longer.
3. The extent to which the supply itself stimulates demand.

This last point leads on to some of the issues about alleged 'unreasonable' demands. It is suggested that people take to doctors many problems they could deal with themselves. These may include problems they need to learn to live with, problems they can easily treat themselves and problems that people other than doctors could equally help with (perhaps at a lower 'cost' – family, clergy, social workers, etc.).

It is further argued that these 'unreasonable' demands are likely to occur where people do not directly pay the costs of health care themselves or where the costs are met by the state, by employers or by insurance companies. This leads to a search for methods of curbing expenditure. The most direct approach obviously is to make the individual pay all or part of the cost. Examples of the wide ways in which this may be done were set out on pp. 101–3.

Less direct are methods which make people wait, rules which prevent certain conditions being examined or certain treatments being used, or the use of 'gatekeepers' to filter demands. The use of inverted commas around the word 'unreasonable' was designed to draw attention to the fact that there are likely to be problems with all of the ways of curbing demand inasmuch as subjective judgements are required about whether demands are reasonable or not. Arguments about this regularly figure in investigations of health service complaints. Any device to deter access to health care will deter some individuals from getting attention to serious problems. Furthermore, the problem about deterrence extends beyond the issues about life-threatening conditions: there is a large 'grey area' around most minor complaints about where the line should be drawn between a condition that is best left alone or self-treated and a condition that requires expert attention.

The best approach to the 'grey area' problem is often seen as having a doctor to play the 'gatekeeper' role. Employers certainly often look to doctors to play this role, in relation to their employees' claims to have health problems. However, there is a potential difficulty about placing doctors in gatekeeper roles for health services. They may have an interest in maximising the numbers of health problems. They may have no incentive to turn patients away and, in some circumstances, even a positive incentive to encourage patients to come to them. This brings the discussion back to the tension, discussed in Chapter 2, between the altruistic interest of doctors in advancing health care and their self-interest in advancing a demand for their skills.

The implication of this argument is not necessarily that doctors should not play gatekeeper roles, though it is perhaps a suggestion that there is a need to control those roles rather carefully, but there is a particular case to be made for the value of systems which have an easily accessible primary care physician (as in Britain) who may both increase the accessibility of the service for the public and control costs by exercising a judgement about who should or should not go on to more expensive secondary services. What is, however, important for cost control is that the remuneration of those in gatekeeper roles should not depend simply upon the number whom they let through the 'gates'.

A contrasting example with very different consequences for cost control is found in Germany where, for constitutional reasons, the state cannot control the supply of doctors and where both generalists and specialists, offering 'ambulatory care', are directly accessible to the public. In addition the doctors have established a powerful position in the fragmented system of quasi-autonomous insurance funds (Moran in Clasen and Freeman, 1994, ch. 4).

There are a number of points about the remuneration of doctors wherever they are not simply salaried employees. The avoidance of salaried service has been an important consideration for the professional organisations, keen to maximise the freedom of their members (including, of course, their freedom to make money) (Moran and Wood, 1993). A 'fee for service' approach which seems to both meet this demand and maximise the operation of 'market principles' in health services involves precisely a risk of over-provision of services unless it is very carefully structured. A capitation fee approach is often seen as the best alternative – embodied in the British general practitioners' contract and advanced in many American innovations through 'health maintenance organisations' (see further discussion below, p. 122) – involving a payment for each patient on the doctor's list regardless of the service provided. Yet both options can face problems – the 'perverse incentive' to over-treat with fee for service is replaced by a perverse incentive to reject certain kinds of patient with capitation fee systems. There are thus various ways in which more complex combinations of the two have been created: weighted capitation systems to take into account patient characteristics, systems combining capitation plus fee for special services, incentive payments which reward specific approaches to treatment or health prevention, and so on. Many health services and insurance companies have struggled in recent years to find remuneration systems for doctors, particularly doctors who are directly accessible to patients, which do not provide excessive encouragement to the provision of drugs, treatments or diagnostic tests (Ham *et al.*, 1990).

The whole issue is made more complex by the divisions within the medical profession. These have at least three different but interrelated manifestations, which occur in different ways in different countries. One is a distinction between general physicians and those physicians and surgeons with specialist roles and tasks. A second is between those who are primarily hospital based and those who work outside such institutions (bearing in mind various combinations between these two). The third is a distinction between primary and secondary care roles. Primary care practitioners will tend to be non-specialist and to work outside hospitals but this is not always the case (the rather different situation in Germany has already been noted). Equally such practitioners are likely to be the 'gatekeepers' for more specialised services, but many systems allow patients direct access to specialists and/or hospitals.

The arrangements which affect patient access, the incentives and disincentives operating in relation to referrals between doctors, and the mechanisms which enable the cost implications of choices of kinds of treatment to be evident before referral affect the way issues about control over access to expensive services can be influenced in various countries.

There is a sense in which the concerns about a cost crisis in social policy (to be discussed in Chapter 12) have particularly focused upon medicine. The growth of costs has led nations which seem to have the problem of costs under control, relative to other nations, to join in the general panic about this subject. There has been a great deal of policy 'borrowing' in this area. Nations like Britain which have a relatively strong structure of bureaucratic controls have sought advice on their cost controls from American gurus (in particular Enthoven, 1985), while at the same time the Americans' private insurance sector was turning to devices of a kind which had been long present in the British system, to advance primary and preventive care and reduce incentives to over provide.

Wider issues about control over professionals

The issue of control over professionals has been picked up in two different ways in relation to issues of cost control – in relation to overall remuneration and in relation to specific payment methods. But the issue has an importance beyond the specifics of cost control. Perhaps the best way to highlight this is to examine the challenge sometimes offered to the assumption embedded in the discussion above that it is in general a *good* idea to have doctors in gatekeeper roles, so long as they cannot exploit them to enhance their rewards.

That challenge points out that health services have largely been set up on terms dictated by doctors. The latter have been closely involved in the politics of the creation of health care systems, encouraging aspects that suited them as a profession and trying (often successfully) to veto aspects they did not like. They have acquired high financial rewards and they have secured positions of power from which to influence the day-to-day running of services. In doing all this, they have defined good health, health care needs and the responsibilities of health services in ways which put them in a central and indispensable role (Friedson, 1970; Alford, 1972; Harrison *et al.*, 1990; Ham, 1992; Harrison and Pollitt, 1994).

As a dominant profession in society, if not *the* dominant profession, their ranks are biased in favour of the dominant elements in society. They are disproportionately male, a bias that appears even more strongly in the highest prestige positions and specialties. There are similar racial, linguistic and nationality biases amongst their ranks (depending, of course, upon the country). In exercising the gatekeeper roles described above, doctors mix their expertise with judgements which may be influenced by their gender, their race and their social class. Hence, a case can be made for enabling people to get past these gatekeepers easily or at least for ensuring that they 'open the gate' without 'prejudice'. This leads to the final set of issues about control by consumers and/or citizens.

Control through consumer choice

Obviously a straightforward system of marketed medical care allows a patient to make a choice as a consumer, so long as there is nothing which constrains competition. In practice there may be a variety of constraints, particularly ones imposed by geography. Only a limited selection of primary care practitioners are likely to be located close to the consumer's home, and the more specialised the services which are required the more geography and lack of information are likely to impose constraints. The importance of economies of scale in health service investments has inevitable consequences for choices in any area.

Simple purchasing of health care without any pre-planning in the form of insurance is only really feasible for the very rich. The crucial issues are about the extent to which private insurance or public insurance (or some mixed type) can be operated in ways which enable consumers to make unconstrained market choices. Where private insurance is allowed to select its clients it will be likely to avoid bad risks (see Deber, 1993 on the situation in the United States).

In any case at the very least insurers will be concerned about the cost implications of choices (just as motor insurers are when people seek car accident repairs), but in fact in the field of health care insurers' concerns are likely to go beyond a simple concern for the cheapest appropriate tender. This brings the discussion back to an issue examined earlier about the difficulties for cost control which may arise if decisions about need are made freely by patients and decisions about whether and how to treat the need are made by a doctor whose income is influenced by those decisions. The result is that insurance agencies have developed devices to try to strengthen their control over these situations by having their own restricted lists of practitioners with whom they have developed contracts and whose activities they can supervise. A further development from this has been 'health maintenance organisations' (Stoline and Weiner, 1988; Ham *et al.*, 1990, p. 66), with pre-determined package deals for the overall care of a group of patients, who may be offered health checks and health care advice as well as services when they are sick. The insurance companies will pay capitation fees for patients taken on in this way. These developments have been widespread in the United States as both insurance companies and the employers, who often pay their employees' premiums, have sought to bring costs under control. It will be evident that as these processes develop consumer choice disappears.

Some attempts have been made to mimic the contracting models used in insurance in tax-funded state health care schemes. In Britain an organisational model has been developed for services other than primary care under which health authorities make contracts with health care providers (hospitals, etc.). Also primary health care practitioners are being allowed to develop contractual relationships with secondary care suppliers, but both of these developments at best provide for elements of competition between providers and choice by 'experts' in placing contracts. They do not widen consumer choice. They may in fact narrow it since where once primary care providers might have drawn from a network of contacts to offer secondary care choices for patients, now they are likely to be locked into specific previous contracts. In fact the main form of consumer choice available to patients is the choice of a primary care practitioner, one that has always been available under the National Health Service. The catch here is that the practitioner can choose, too, and strike a patient off the list. 'Difficult' patients may end up without choice.

Despite the rhetoric of consumerism, the drift of insurance systems away from choice and the difficulties faced by tax systems in creating genuine choice, together with cost concerns and the very specialised nature of health services, make the exercise of choice through the market very difficult to achieve in health care (see Hunt, 1990; Hudson, 1994). It is ironic that the main political advocates of market forces are restrained from following this principle through in the area of health care by the cost implications of doing so, inasmuch as these people are also – as far as publicly funded services are concerned – particularly concerned about expenditure restraint.

Control through representative systems

A more positive point that may be made about purchaser/provider schemes is that they make hitherto bureaucratic links between organisations more explicit and in this sense may facilitate the alternative approach to accountability, through representative institutions. Control by representative institutions is also constrained by some of the limitations on market choices. The distribution of specialties and the sharing of activities between hospitals create problems of scale which call for political decision-making at a high level. It is difficult for every community to have its own hospital, let alone one offering a comprehensive range of modern services. This is one thing which tends to influence decisions to centralise control over health services. Another is the political salience of health policy issues. Central governments are reluctant to delegate responsibility for policies on which the public as a whole has strong views, and arguments about appropriate responses are sharply contested between political parties.

Another argument which sometimes appears for limiting the scope for direct popular control over health policies is that expert professional decisions, particularly those with very specific implications for individuals, should not be open to local interference. In the debate about the structure of the British health service in the 1940s medical objections to control by local government were taken very seriously. However, that is now a rather dated view. The 'trust the expert' argument for medical dominance has come under widespread challenge (Friedson, 1970; Illich, 1977; Wilding, 1982). It has also become recognised that it is possible to establish controls over the outputs of an administrative system providing personal services to individuals without at the same time engaging in interference in detailed decision-making with regard to specific cases.

In respect of the issues about the appropriate level for democratic control it is necessary to recognise that distinctions can be made between setting broad political and planning parameters, including decisions about overall funding, making arrangements for delivery at local levels and giving individuals access to influence or subsequently complain about their own treatment. Such distinctions lead to various ways of providing structures for the control over health services which spread responsibilities between levels, with an expectation that they will collaborate with each other. In the Swedish case, for example, this involves a division of labour between central government and county governments (Saltman and von Otter, 1992). In the

British case distrust of local government (an irrelevant story here) has meant that instead there have been a succession of experiments with tiers of control, but with little political or popular input below the national level. In federal systems (Canada, Germany, etc.), ways have been found to try to accommodate expectations at the two levels.

The issues about confidentiality and the sensitivities of powerful professionals have meant that the personal complaints of patients of state health systems tend to be handled by procedures of a private nature in which care is taken to ensure that professionals can put their point of view. There are various tensions here: the desire of the professions to control their own disciplinary procedures, the fact that a grievance may involve decisions with fundamental implications for someone's life or well-being, and if something has gone wrong what may be involved can be a combination of individual malpractice and weakness in the system. The range of complaint and appeal systems provided in different countries probably has more to do with different legal and administrative traditions than with the characteristics of health services; they will therefore not be considered further here.

Conclusions

This chapter has given particular attention to the ways in which the state becomes involved with the provision of health care. Much of the discussion has focused upon the implications of the two alternative, yet subtly merging, approaches to state funding – through central funding from taxation and through insurance (often involving an accommodation with private insurance systems). The interactions between funding and organisational arrangements, the concerns about cost control, the issues about professional influence, the ways services may be judged and the expectations of patients have been explored. Chapter 11 will return to some of the equity issues raised and Chapter 12 to some of the cost control problems.

In this discussion the boundary issues about family care and about private markets have surfaced from time to time, but another kind of boundary issue – about the relations between health care and other social services, and particularly about the relations between health care and social care – has been given comparatively little attention. This is given more attention elsewhere, particularly in the chapter on social care which follows.

Guide to further reading

There is a distinctive, and growing, comparative literature on health policy. Key books in this area are Ham, Robinson and Benzeval's *Health Check:*

Health Care Reforms in an International Context (1990), the OECD's *The Reform of Health Care* (1992a) and Saltman and von Otter's *Planned Markets and Public Competition* (1992).

One largely country-specific book on health policy which is recommended because it also contains a more general overview of the subject, is Palmer and Short's *Health Care and Public Policy: An Australian Analysis* (1994). That comment can also be applied to Ham's *Health Policy in Britain* (1992). Deber's article 'Canadian medicare: can it work in the United States? Will it survive in Canada?' (1993) has also a rather specific concern, but sets out some of the key issues very well.

Three books, largely dealing with British issues but which nevertheless deal with important themes in the analysis of health policy, are Stacey's *The Sociology of Health and Healing* (1988), Townsend, Davidson and Whitehead's *Inequalities in Health* (1988) and Harrison and Pollitt's *Controlling Health Professionals* (1994).

CHAPTER SIX

Social care

Introduction

By comparison with the other chapters of this book the issues about defining the social care sector in social policy are rather more difficult. Accordingly there is a relative absence of comparative material. Systems for dealing with 'care' issues vary widely between societies and are attached in various ways to other services. There is a lack of a common pool of ideas, data and concepts which facilitate comparison as found in income maintenance or health policy.

There are two reasons for this. One is that there are particularly strong problems about identifying the circumstances in which social care problems emerge from that category of issues which are regarded as personal or family concerns to become those of the wider society, and especially of the state. The other is that the boundaries between social care and the other social policy categories are difficult to identify and are arranged differently in different societies. Discussion of these two issues, and their implications, will accordingly provide the main focus of this chapter.

Care issues: from private to public

In his book *Understanding Social Policy* the author used the example of his need for someone to do the housework so that he could write books to explore problems about the meaning of 'need'.

Social care responses are seen as designed to meet needs (Hill, 1993a, p. 126). This argument will be examined further and then complicated by adding other considerations, of a kind more likely to induce a concerned response from others!

In Chapter 1 it was recognised that the main options for responses to social problems are for the problems to be regarded as the following:

1. Needing to be solved by the individual (taking into account his or her 'market' position).
2. Family concerns (in either a narrow or a broad sense of family).
3. Social but not state concerns (again the options range from narrow neighbourhood and community responses to wider voluntary organisations).
4. State (including local state) responsibilities.

The best the author in need of help with housework can expect is some concern from the family (though even here there may be issues about the extent of reciprocity expected – approaching the notion of an economic exchange). Formal organisations, if approached for help, will probably expect a payment which will render any transaction a pure market one or will apply some rules to define need which disqualify this kind of application. But then the so-called 'need' may not simply arise because of a personal priority but may be:

1. Derived from physical inability to perform domestic tasks.
2. Leading to self-neglect.
3. Leading to child-neglect.
4. Involving some combination of (1), (2) and (3).

The following sections will explore the implications of these considerations.

Need deriving from physical incapacity

Where 'need' derives from physical inability to perform domestic tasks a more sympathetic response is likely all round. However, responses from outside the family may be muted by a view that the family has the main responsibility. These assumptions may be further reinforced by assumptions about caring roles, particularly ones that might be taken on by female members of the family. The response of the state may be to look first to others, particularly family members but also perhaps neighbours and friends. It should be noted that this is a statement about what is likely to happen not about what should happen – the author is engaged here in a sociological analysis not a philosophical one. In addition, potential carers, and particularly formal carers, may well raise issues about the capacity of the person in need of help to pay for that help.

Hence, there may be a three-part test of need, one part based upon the nature of the condition, one based on the availability of informal carers and one based upon the availability of resources to buy care (a means test). This triple test may be applied in other areas of social policy – with regard to medical or educational need, for example – the point here is that it is particularly likely to occur in a case like this. What makes social care situations different is the much greater strength of 'normal' assumptions about how basic domestic caring problems should be solved. That is another sociological generalisation. As such it is offered in the knowledge that there are exceptions. Societies, or sub-societies, exist where all caring is seen as a communal responsibility, for example, many Israeli kibbutzim.

If the need is accepted as something requiring a formal response there is then a number of options. First, there is a choice to be made between providing a domestic service in the person's own home, or taking them into another home or institution. The latter option has tended to dominate care provision. The OECD comments:

> *The provision of long term care in institutional settings has too often dominated the policy agenda. . . . an absence of sufficient and affordable alternatives has made the institutional solution the only one on offer for many families. Further, in some cases the more generous funding available for institutional care appears to have created a 'perverse incentive' directing demand towards . . . [it]. (OECD, 1994c, p. 38)*

Second, responses to need may be in the form of direct intervention by the agencies assuming responsibility or involve the commissioning of someone else to take on the task. On the face of it the latter is another version of the purchaser/provider split observed in some health services. However, in the case of something as simple as domestic care the commissioned provider may be a friend or neighbour. The purchaser may then be engaged in monetising a caring relationship, which might develop without this outside intervention. The logical point to follow on from this is to ask, if it is acceptable to formalise and monetise that sort of relationship, what about the same for family care?

Finally, amongst the response options the points made in Chapter 4 should not be forgotten, that cash benefits are sometimes provided to subsidise informal carers. Again issues arise about state payment for roles often provided by kin. The discussion in that chapter went on to identify another alternative: to provide benefits to the disabled person to enable the service to be bought.

Evers, Pijl and Ungerson (1994, p. 4) explore this issue with the use of a diagram which sets out the options and indicates how they may be combined (see figure 6.1). Their subsequent analysis makes extensive use of the alternative ideological perspectives on the roles of state, family, community and market. While these undeniably play a part in determining responses in different societies, this ideological 'battle' occurs in a context of resource constraints. Even the most collectivist state is unwilling to see itself as an indiscriminate provider of care. Where it cannot simply dismiss the issue

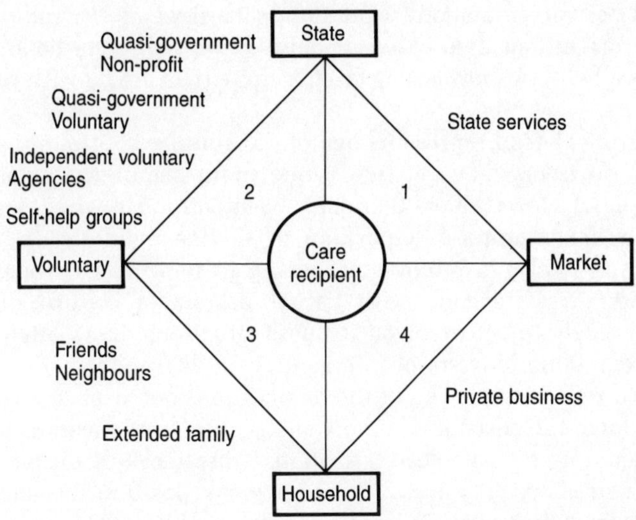

Figure 6.1 The welfare diamond. From Evers, Pijl and Ungerson (1994) *Payments for care: A comparative overview*, p.4. Reproduced with the permission of the European Centre for Social Welfare Policy and Research.

as an individual problem, it is likely to look to the family and, to a lesser extent, the community as a resource. It is then faced with difficulties inasmuch as social and economic factors reduce the capacity of these systems to take on burdens. These difficulties can be explored more by moving on to the two further possible complications.

The implications of self-neglect

What will be the implications for the response to 'need' of a situation in which there is someone who neglects their own domestic care so seriously as to put themselves in danger of disease, accident or starvation? Such situations arise in a variety of ways – as a consequence of very low levels of intellectual ability, because of mental illness (including particularly degenerative diseases amongst the elderly such as Alzheimer's disease) and because of addictions. It should not be forgotten that these phenomena may be found in various combinations with each other.

It may be expected that there will be variations in the extent to which there are sympathetic responses to these problems from the various potential carers. Cause – or views, beliefs and superstitions about the cause – may influence the response. In the case of the potential informal carers emotional involvement – implying anger, frustration, guilt, etc. – may influence the response or even the capacity to respond. But what will be particularly likely to alter the configuration of responses is that in these situations significant others will be worrying about what *should* be done as the individuals are unlikely to make their own cases for help. There will often be a concern to try to *impose* help. In short, a concern to care will be linked with compulsion and control.

The example chosen represents one of the simpler control situations that social care providers may get into (some more complicated ones will be explored below). Nevertheless there may be situations in which it is deemed necessary *either* to impose some kind of service upon the individual *or* (perhaps more likely) to remove the person to some place where care can be provided. As an agency with formal powers of control the state is particularly likely to get involved in these situations. Laws often give state agencies exceptional powers of intervention to deal with them.

It is worth reflecting on one of the devices the state uses to keep it out of or to keep down the costs of its involvement in the care business: a charging policy linked with a means test. If it imposes itself as a caring agency in the way described above it places itself in a weak position to charge for the services it offers. However, in practice some of the people assisted in this way will possess substantial financial resources. Further legal powers are often available to unlock these to pay for care, involving 'guardianship' procedures which shift responsibility for assets to kin, legal representatives or the state.

The implications of child neglect

The final set of care issues to be considered are those arising in respect of children. Suppose the hypothetical individuals discussed above are parents who are neglecting children. In short, the author – in the initial example – could expect punitive responses from others, the physically disabled person could expect help and the 'confused' individual (to adopt a shorthand way of referring to the rather more complex third example) could expect to be relieved of the responsibility. Real examples are not so simple. In all three cases the modern state is likely to arm itself with a range of powers and services. The removal of the child from parental care will be an option to be considered in all three cases, and the state will therefore have either the capacity to provide alternative care itself or to pay for it (which may bring it back to some of the dilemmas about formalising informal substitute care which were discussed above). Furthermore the removal of a child from the care of its parents is a draconian and costly process which the state will initiate with reluctance. To try to prevent that necessity it may provide a range of services, some of which are much more complex than the substitute domestic provisions discussed in relation to the earlier examples. These will include advice, counselling and therapy – in short, 'social work'.

This stage in the development of the examples thus acknowledges that a specific professional activity may be linked up with social care concerns. But it would be wrong to suggest that social work has no part to play in relation to the other caring tasks outlined above. It may have a diagnostic role in relation to all the rationing problems faced by formal organisations. It is likely to have a role to play in relation to the issues of individual neglect discussed in the third example: to identify the nature of the problem, to decide whether it is so serious that intervention is essential and to manage that intervention. It is then also likely to play a part in the after-care of the individual, including the supervision of the arrangements made.

There is a difficulty in generalising across societies about the social work role. Not only are there problems about equivalent terms in other languages than English, but there are also different usages in English itself. The notion of social work as a profession with specific characteristics and expertise is disputed, much more fiercely than the professionalism of doctors. The expression 'semi-profession' (Etzioni, 1969) is sometimes used and social workers are sometimes bracketed with groups like the police as 'street-level bureaucrats' identifiable in terms of their wide discretionary powers rather than their expertise (Lipsky, 1980). The key problem is that the concept is used both to refer to workers with the very specialised tasks identified above in relation to child care and mental illness, most of whom will have had a significant formal training with a strong emphasis on skills to deal with human relationships, and for a wide range of routine workers involved in the administration of social care tasks. In making any comparative analysis it must be recognised that countries vary in the extent to which educational developments and other 'professionalising' activities have occurred which enable the former to distinguish their roles from the latter.

Additionally, in those societies where social care tasks and last resort income maintenance tasks are formally linked (see discussion below) the responsible street level workers are often called social workers even when most have little training and carry out relatively mechanical tasks (in the United States, for example). Finally, the term 'social worker' is sometimes used colloquially to describe voluntary unpaid carers.

It would not be helpful to try to define social work more precisely here, since to do so would require adopting a specific stance with regard to a dispute about that role which is explicitly embedded in an Anglo-American cultural context. The point is that in that context the fourth example introduces both a *strong* social control concern and an area of work where social work expertise is particularly used. The long digression on the latter was necessary to identify an area of potential confusion about the relationship between the general topic of social care and a more specific activity – drawing upon a pool of ideas from psychology and psychotherapy – seen by some writers as to be at the very core of 'social work' (Butrym, 1976).

Care: the family and the individual

This section recaps some of the key themes which the four examples above have highlighted. First, there are a variety of ways in which there are likely to be special expectations of the individual or the family. In many respects, even in societies in which highly sophisticated state services have been developed, formal social care services are only expected to come into play when family care fails. For example, in respect of care for frail elderly people the OECD suggests:

> *Attempts to estimate the value of family care, using even modest rates for bought in care, suggest that it exceeds by a ratio of at least 3 or 4 to 1 the value of formal services, even in countries with highly developed social services. (OECD, 1994c, p. 41; see also Sundström in OECD, 1994d)*

Attention was given in the discussion above to consequences of formalising or monetising informal, and particularly family, care relationships. This is bound to be regarded as a 'danger' both for those who believe that it is right that the family should be the primary caring institution and for those who think the state cannot bear the cost of going seriously down the alternative road (it implies a great deal of the hidden costs of family care being translated through taxation into formal care).

Even if the state does regard the family as the appropriate locus of care it will not necessarily then abdicate all responsibility. It may accept a role of surveillance over the quality of that care. It may also adopt a supportive role, recognising that carers may need advice and counselling, help with specific practical tasks and occasional relief (respite care). It must be noted that 'family' is being used very loosely here. As pointed out in Chapter 1 there are variations between societies in the extent to which family responsibilities are identified as extending beyond the nuclear family.

On the issue of family some mention was made of gender assumptions. Men are more likely to receive care and are less likely to be regarded as appropriate unpaid informal carers (even when they are kin). An important body of feminist writing has identified the extent to which 'community care' means in practice the deployment of women as family (including extended family) carers, as neighbourhood carers, as volunteer carers and as the low-paid caring staff of voluntary and statutory caring organisations (Finch and Groves, 1983; Land and Rose, 1985). Bryson sums up this literature (1992, pp. 211–15) suggesting that the extension of female roles along these lines is occurring not only in countries like Britain and Australia where social services were always poorly developed, but equally in countries like Norway (Waerness, 1984). She goes on to criticise the way an account of the strength of family care in Japan treats women as invisible. Without mentioning the respective roles of men and women, Maruo says:

> *The absence of public provision of welfare services for the elderly in Japan does not mean they receive no care. Traditional Japanese values lead most adult children to care for their elderly parents within the same household. (1986, p. 71)*

This point should be linked with some of the assumptions about men as 'earners' and women as 'carers' discussed in relation to income maintenance in Chapter 4. As promised there, this theme will be explored further in Chapter 11.

Cash or care

Reference to earners brings up the next general theme. Several times it has been pointed out that even when the case for care in the physical need sense is clear formal systems may balk at providing it on the grounds that the individual is able to buy it. This issue creates a number of interactions between social care systems and income maintenance systems (see p. 138–42). It also creates a situation in which care systems are likely to be primarily for low-income people. The Scandinavian societies offer a partial exception to that rule. However, this universalism is far from complete. For example, many in those societies still have to find private care when they want it and some public care, moreover, involves means-tested charges. These recoup around 15 per cent of the cost of publicly provided care for children in Sweden (Ginsburg, 1992, pp. 55–6). Perhaps the systems where this area of activity is best protected are those where social insurance gives rights to forms of care (surprisingly, for example, Switzerland; Germany is introducing a care insurance scheme at the time of writing). There has been some development of private insurance in this area, particularly in the United States (Weiner in OECD, 1994d) but the OECD suggests that 'it seems questionable whether the insurance industry can treat long-term care as an insurable risk at affordable terms' (OECD, 1994c, p. 47).

The mention of social insurance, however, highlights the fact that in various respects (both through that mechanism and through more simple ways of assessing entitlement – see Chapter 4) income maintenance systems may provide cash to subsidise care. Instead of providing the care itself, the state may ensure that the disabled person has sufficient income to be able to pay for a carer (in actual cases often not the whole cost) or it may provide income maintenance for the carer.

States are tempted to adopt the last approach as one which builds partially on older assumptions about extended family responsibilities and enables them to minimise their costs (see Glendinning and McLaughlin, 1993, for a survey of some of these developments particularly in Britain, Eire, France and Italy). It is a cheaper alternative inasmuch as it looks at carers' needs in benefit terms rather than wage terms and expenditure can be limited by means tests which consider the family and economic circumstances of one, or indeed both, of the two parties. Australia has a carer's pension which is means-tested and available at a level comparable to the ordinary state pension. A regular doctor's certificate is necessary to prove that the care is needed. Britain has a non-means-tested benefit, but it is set at a very low level relative to other benefits (a good review of these issues is contained in Ungerson, 1995).

As a cheap option, support of this kind for carers has long-run implications. Carers may have to survive on low incomes for many years and because they are prevented from being normal labour market participants they may fail to build up future benefit entitlements (particularly to adequate pensions). This is, again, unsurprisingly, particularly a female problem.

Care issues and income maintenance issues may merge in various quasi-market forms. In such circumstances the policy issues that emerge concern the extent to which the state will merely see itself as the provider of incomes or will find it necessary to regulate the forms of care which are thereby purchased. The whole matter is complicated by the issues about family carers. Are these to be subsidised in some way, and if so, to what extent? Can it be justified to pay a non-kin carer but not a family member (there has been an extensive Norwegian debate on this)? If professional care needs supervision, does the same apply to kin care? (see Evers *et al.*, 1994, for a discussion of these issues).

Care and control

It should be noted that even where the state is unwilling to subsidise care it may assume regulatory responsibilities. Private homes for the elderly, private arrangements for the day care of children, and so on, are often subject to licensing and inspection powers by public authorities (examples of this form of regulation can be found in Sweden and Britain). This brings the discussion to the next theme, the relationship between care and control. The discussion about the care of children particularly brought out the way formal organisations may intervene in social care situations normally regarded as the responsibility of the family, but that example was preceded by one of adult care. There are other areas where social care and control are linked together in relation to adults. One is where mentally ill people are behaving in ways which are threatening to others. Another is where the courts or prisons decide to make the freedom of an offender conditional upon accepting some kind of social care; this generally means a form of social work supervision. These examples offer a foretaste of some of the service borderline issues to be discussed in a later section.

The mixed economy of care

The final general theme is that it was, rather briefly, recognised that formal care and control tasks may be organised in a variety of ways. First, in many places in the discussion expressions like 'formal care' were used instead of 'state care'. There were several reasons for this. Care institutions that are entirely voluntary, funded by charities and churches, may offer formal care. They may also be subsidised by the state to do this. Even control tasks may be delegated to voluntary organisations.

Second, even where one formal organisation has responsibility it may commission services from others. At one stage in the discussion it was recognised that formal carers may use informal carers. For example, in the case of children fostering arrangements may be made in private homes. These carers may even be relatives. A final complication (certainly present in British child-care law) is that children may be returned to their original family while the state retains exceptional formal responsibilities for them.

Third, where there are state organisations for social care the diversity of possibilities defies generalisation. There may be one general social care organisation with a relatively comprehensive remit (the British Social Services Department), care tasks may be distributed across a number of agencies with client group remits – for children, elderly people, etc., mentally ill people, etc., or different organisations may take on different aspects of care – home services, social work supervision, the provision of residential care. There are then complications about social care attached to other agencies – for health care, income maintenance, etc.

In many societies an important element in the 'mixed economy' is voluntary non-profit organisations. These may be seen as efforts to preserve the idea of social care as something which emerges naturally from the concerns of the family and the community. Volunteers often play a role in the care system. In some societies there are strong religious traditions associated with this care, with voluntary bodies linked to denominational organisations (Germany, France, the Netherlands, Eire, etc., see Munday, 1993; Cochrane and Clarke, 1993; Clasen and Freeman, 1994). In the case of the Netherlands the traditional 'pillarised' (Lijphart, 1975, see the earlier discussion on p. 55) structure of social support sustains this. In Japan a strong voluntarist structure seems to have emerged with powerful state encouragement (Gould, 1993, drawing on the work of Collick, 1988). Increasingly, in all countries these voluntary patterns of care are sustained by state funds (albeit often at lower costs than 'pure' state ventures).

Some writers have sought to portray this diversity through the concept of the 'mixed economy of care'. This mixed economy can be seen as involving 'three dimensions of provision, funding and regulation' (Knapp, 1989). Diversity of provision includes, as already suggested: public, voluntary, private (marketed and profit-seeking), informal and household care. The state may regulate care in a variety of ways and to varied extents, through a wide range of agencies. Funding methods, as with health care, may be diverse. Wistow *et al.* (1994) identify the following funding alternatives, only two of which directly involve the state:

1. Coerced collective demand – public purchase on behalf of citizens.
2. Voluntary collective demand – voluntary organisations purchasing services.
3. Corporate demand – funding from private sector firms.
4. Uncompensated individual consumption.
5. Compensated individual consumption – purchase subsidised by public transfer payments (income maintenance).

The purpose of itemising these options is to stress that 'Many social care services are funded from more than one source, and certainly most of the multi-service "packages" of care used by people with greater needs for support will be funded directly from a variety of sources' (*ibid.*, p. 35).

The literature on the mixed economy of care draws attention to the complexity of the issues at stake. As the discussion earlier in this chapter has suggested, there are moral and political questions at stake about the circumstances in which state intervention *should* occur. But this literature draws attention to the confusing ways in which care options may be combined. Baldock and Ungerson (1994) in a study of the actual ways in which 'care packages' for stroke victims were put together, point to this confusion in practice and to the influence of individual expectations upon ways people try to resolve it. Figure 6.2 sets out the way they identify attitudes to participation and to collectivism as influencing this.

Baldock and Ungerson describe their 'consumerists' as expecting to make active market choices for themselves and their 'collectivists' as actively seeking state help. Their 'clientalists' depended upon welfare professionals making allocation decisions for them. Their 'privatists' did least well amongst those in their study: they were not active in pursuit of either state or private services but rather passive consumers, facing difficulties because they required 'products that are not available "off the shelf"' (*ibid.*, p. 19). Their observations on this group are pertinent to the confusion presented by the state's relatively passive role in the provision of social care. Gatekeepers reluctant to extend services which individuals might buy or families might provide are unlikely to be satisfactory sources of advice to ill and dependent consumers.

To sum up this section, there is in the social care field a diverse range of care problems and a variety of ways of responding to them. The issues about the family and about private purchase are likely to loom large in any discussion of how the often scarce resources for this activity should be

High participation

CONSUMERISM | WELFARISM

Individualist | Collectivist

PRIVATISM | CLIENTALISM

Low participation

Figure 6.2 Participation and collectivism in community care

distributed. Responses to the questions these concerns raise vary from society to society. Even within any one country cultural change and diversity are likely to fuel controversy about who should do what, yet when the value questions seem to be solvable decision-makers may shrink back at the implications of precedents they may be creating. This is an area where, while official practices will generally reflect dominant social values, innovations in practice can accelerate social change – formalising and monetising relationships which had hitherto been informal. It is also an area where social care policies may be forced to respond to policies adopted by other agencies. This theme is picked up in the rest of this chapter.

Social care policy and other social policies

Social work theorists have expressed the philosophy of their profession in terms of a concern for the whole person (Goldstein, 1973). Yet there is a need to put together both the fact that formal social care policies generally come into operation only when 'normal' institutions cannot cope and the fact that many other policies – education and health in particular – accept a universal remit for *only some* aspects of people's lives. This leads to a conclusion that notwithstanding the philosophy of the 'whole person' the reality is rather different. This suggests a rather 'residual' definition of social care as a public policy area. With every one of the policy areas discussed in this book, with the exception of pollution control policy, there are situations in which mainstream services need extra help in dealing with a lack of fit between the needs, lifestyles or behaviours of some of the users of their services and what they offer to the population in general.

That extra help may be provided by a specialist service attached to the mainstream services (decreasingly the case in Britain, but still widespread elsewhere – for example, in Germany, see Clasen and Freeman, 1994, ch. 7). Alternatively it may be delegated to another agency. Where societies have established generic social care and social work services these organisations may pick up many of these extra tasks. Furthermore, as far as one particular policy system is concerned – income maintenance – social care services are very much a derivative from the separation of money provision concerns from related concerns about care and control for recipients of cash. This section will therefore explore these issues, starting with those deriving from the income maintenance function.

Income maintenance and social care

This section will not repeat the discussion above about the alternative approaches to support for those in need of care, but rather raise some other issues about the way these two topics are linked. The crucial historical link between income maintenance and care was mentioned in Chapter 2. Many poor-law systems provided relief within institutions. The theory was that the 'penal' character of such places would deter applications for relief. The reality was that many of the sick and elderly poor were forced to turn to them. Once this was recognised as a problem attempts were made to develop systems of cash support outside institutions. But a minority could not be so easily turned out because they could not look after themselves and had no one else to turn to. Hence a system set up for control purposes gradually evolved into a care system. As that happened some societies separated cash benefit administration from this care activity, though a means test was still used to determine whether any contribution could be made to care costs. In Britain in 1948 legislation gave the former responsibility to a central government agency and the latter to local government.

However, this was not the only link between means-testing and what is today regarded as at least in part a care task – along with some salient control elements. The deterrent concerns of relief systems bring them with difficulties wherever there are considered to be grounds for recognising that claimants are not just behaving in terms of the simple pleasure/pain calculus of the Benthamite theory which inspired poor-law thinking, at least in the English-speaking countries. A recognition of this, together with a shift towards a rather less harsh view of how the poor should be treated, generated other developments within relief systems.

Such systems had to develop procedures to deal with exceptional situations – where it was claimed that special problems made it impossible for people to live on the money provided, where unanticipated needs arose and where resources were dissipated on drink, drugs or gambling. A simple punitive approach might involve arguing that the 'exceptional' – particularly, of course, if an outcome of behaviour – was solely a problem to be solved by the individual, but alternatively it might be recognised that the consequences of a lack of attention to such issues might be severe suffering, not only for the claimant but also for his or her dependants. If this was the view taken then one possible way to help while at the same time protecting relief funds was to give assistance under some kind of supervision and guidance.

An alternative preoccupation for a relief agency in a situation of the kind described may be to try to discriminate between applicants. This may involve using criteria that are designed to prevent fraudulent claims or concentrate aid upon those most likely to use it satisfactorily. It may involve the application of some moral principles which are seen as distinguishing the 'deserving' from the 'undeserving'. Discriminating in this way is likely to involve some sort of 'case investigation' designed to provide information to put an application for help in a wider social context. Such work may call for social work expertise of some kind. The notion that applications for help should be investigated in this way was particularly advanced in the past by charities, which had (compared with the state) modest resources and were particularly open to exploitation by persons who moved from organisation to organisation trying to trade on the absence of this background 'intelligence' (Woodroffe, 1962).

These concerns – and in particular the notion that it should be possible to discriminate between those who could increase their independence if given carefully managed help and those who would simply squander the money and keep on coming back for more – led to wider attempts to link financial relief and social support. Thus emerged the principle of 'help to self-help' still given attention in relief systems today (see, for example, Hvinden, 1994, on the Norwegian system). This may involve a range of options: help with budgeting and money management, help to get work or training, help with family problems or help with health and psychological problems. The issue that still ties these forms of help to financial relief is efforts to make cash help explicitly or implicitly dependent upon acceptance of these other forms of help.

However, a more critical view of this linking – with rather less emphasis upon the word 'help' – points out that what is likely to be involved is a process of making financial aid dependent upon behaviour (including some effort to effect behaviour change). This is seen as coercive – for example, a linking of cash help with control (Handler, 1973; Jordan, 1974). Objection to this may then involve a specific concern that it is not appropriate to be exercising social work skills in such a coercive context. The problem with the latter argument is that the linking of social work with income maintenance in this way is by no means the only 'control' issue within social work; a much more clear-cut control function is involved in those situations in which social work help is given as an alternative to the removal of children into care or the committal of offenders to prison. In these situations the possibility of the more draconian response in the event of non-compliance with the helping efforts lies heavy over the relationship.

In the view of this author what is more important about the cash/help link is the extent to which the poor are forced to accept intrusion into their lives in order to secure financial help, inasmuch as this may involve behavioural requirements (about how they organise their family or work lives) that are not imposed by society on anyone else, and may (particularly when they belong to a minority culture) require unacceptable lifestyle changes. Such a view is based upon a belief that the problems of the poor stem principally from a lack of resources and that linking that problem with behavioural concerns involves evading that central social issue (Jordan, 1974). It is a view obviously linked with a belief (which would need a large digression here) that the maldistribution of money in society is an important cause (not necessarily the sole cause) of many other social problems – delinquency, child neglect, etc.

The reason for referring to this view here is that social workers and others with social care concerns have developed a range of alternative responses to income maintenance problems, related to but diverging from the conventional response with its mixture of care and control. The alternative responses may be described as *advice*, *advocacy* and *mobilisation*.

The complexity of income maintenance systems, particularly means-tested systems, may give scope for the development of advice services which can play an important role in ensuring that poor people maximise their incomes. Other workers with low-income people – particularly social workers – may supply this expertise themselves or may be important sources of referral to these services.

This advice-giving activity is often described as 'welfare rights' work (Fimister, 1986); as such it may extend into advocacy. This may involve negotiating on behalf of poor people with benefit-providing agencies and assisting them in making their cases before appeal bodies. It may involve the development of legal expertise and indeed lawyers may become involved in these activities (a point particularly pertinent to the issue about who pays for this sort of work – see discussion below).

An extension of this individual advocacy work may be efforts to establish legal and administrative precedents, with implications for more than the individual applicant (Prosser, 1983). This may involve a political activity which endeavours to assert that entitlements to state benefits (including the more grudgingly given means-tested benefits) should be regarded as 'rights', a form of 'property' which may compensate the poor for the absence of other property (Reich, 1964). It leads advocacy into political as well as legal battles – linking struggles for individuals with pressure group activity (McCarthy, 1986).

All this has been set out in terms which imply that it is non-poor individuals who are fighting for the poor. It does not have to be like this, and many of the exponents of advocacy try to develop the activity in partnership with those they seek to help. Many regard self-determination and involvement in the struggle as an important principle. Thus advocacy *for* the poor merges into mobilisation *of* the poor (see Piven and Cloward, 1977, for a discussion of this in the United States). A significant branch of social work (again using that term rather loosely) has developed forms of 'community work'. Like social work this is hard to define. It ranges across a continuum from assisting deprived communities to solve their own problems (a version of 'help for self-help'), to stimulating them to make political demands for themselves.

With specific reference to income maintenance the participatory equivalent of 'welfare rights' is the 'claimants' union', seeing its objective to make demands upon the system in much the same way as a trade union. This is a difficult task as the poor and particularly the workless poor have few weapons to use in such a struggle. They depend upon using demands for 'rights' inasmuch as they are embodied in legislation, and appeals to altruism and guilt. Political mobilisation is difficult, with a group of people whose participation in democratic institutions is often low. Threats of violence may be an ultimate weapon, lying in the background and needing careful use.

Clearly advice and advocacy can be provided by altruistic people on a voluntary basis and community mobilisation is, as just pointed out, a political activity. What has all this got to do with any publicly funded care system? Arguably nothing much. Yet, workers with care concerns have sought a variety of ways to replace or supplement their duties, as defined in some of the more conventional ways outlined above, with activities of this kind. They have reinterpreted a duty to care, even a duty to stimulate self-help, as comprising also a duty to carry out these tasks. In this context making a case for giving advice is relatively easy.

Extending this to advocacy and mobilisation is more difficult. Winning public funds for such activities involves invoking political principles and slogans, perhaps advanced for very different reasons – citizenship, consumerism, pluralism, rights – in the cause of the poor. It also involves taking advantage of political and administrative complexity. Thus a social care agency may see it as feasible to 'attack' an income maintenance agency in the name of its obligations to its clients, or a local government may encourage pressure on a central government organisation on the grounds that it maximises the flow of resources to citizens in its area. Not surprisingly it is all a fraught and controversial business in which powerful elements in control of the state are always likely to want to prevent the subsidising of opposition to their policies.

Much of what has been said here about aid, advocacy and mobilisation might have been inserted elsewhere in this book. These activities do not simply apply to income maintenance policy (they also apply, for example, to aspects of health, housing, employment and education policy). It may be noted that they apply to social care policy itself too – one of the biggest problems for social care workers committed to advocacy comes when they need to try to turn their skills against their own organisation. It is also the case that social care workers and social workers are by no means the only social policy system employees who engage with these issues – community health workers, housing workers and education workers may also carry out these activities. In choosing to put this discussion here the author has been influenced by the particular salience of the debate about welfare rights work in social services in Britain. Scandinavian colleagues have assured him that similar issues arise there.

Health care and social care

The chapter on health care has alluded to the health care/social care overlap. To summarise, the key issue is that if people are ill they may need some combination of care in a simple physical sense – someone to provide food, do household tasks, perhaps to wash and feed them – and care in the strictly medical treatment sense. These two overlap in quite complex ways. In addition a health condition may be such that people also need advice, counselling, social and emotional support and even, exceptionally, control to prevent them from damaging themselves and others. These interactions are particularly evident in situations in which mental illness is involved or physical illness has behavioural or emotional consequences.

Clearly it is logically possible to conceive of a health service system which deals with all the implications of these issues itself. It will, however, be a health service that draws on a variety of skills and has to cope with *within system* boundary problems – the transition from hospital to home care and the construction of the relative responsibilities of doctors, nurses, social workers, domestic care workers, etc. It is much more likely in practice that many of these will be *between system* boundary matters, with issues about who is responsible for what and who pays for what a source of tensions between health and social care systems. These difficulties are then further complicated by the fact, which is coming up again and again in this book, that aside from any argument whether particular matters are health care or social care concerns there are also issues about whether they are properly the concerns of the individual as a person with the capacity to purchase the service or of the family and/or community rather than the state.

This section will explore the boundary between health care and social care with regard to two particularly salient issues: community care and the role of social work in relation to health problems. What makes community care a particularly ambiguous concept is the fact that it has so many different meanings, and accordingly implications, for different people. An important distinction here concerns a usage linked with *where the care is provided*, a usage linked with *who is providing it* and a usage linked with *who is paying for it*. Many of the public/private ramifications of this have already been discussed. As far as the health care/social care boundary is concerned there is a need to note the following:

1. A health service concern to minimise hospital stays – implying discharge to a variety of places from other institutions run by social care agencies

through to private homes (sometimes it appears as if health service references to community care mean 'anywhere so long as it is not a hospital').

2. Despite point (1) some health care systems may maintain, subsidise, recognise or regulate forms of institutional care outside hospitals – nursing homes, hospices, hostels, even supported lodging-houses.
3. Social care systems, as has been seen, often provide institutional care – across a range of types similar to those listed in point (2); there are then issues about under what circumstances interchanges should occur between health and social care institutions (How long should health care institutions go on caring for those getting better and how long should social care institutions care for the sick?).
4. Given that both health care and social care organisations try to support people in need of care in their own homes a series of other boundary issues need attention (Where does the home nurse's job stop and the home care worker's role start? What are the respective roles in relation to mental illness of community psychiatric nurses and social workers specialising in the provision of help to the mentally ill?).

On the whole these boundary issues have to be solved pragmatically. In some cases the 'best' solution from the point of view of the recipient of the services is one in which disruption is minimised and continuity of care maximised. The old person with deteriorating health in a social care home experiences less disruption if nursed there as long as possible. The mentally ill person in the community may be considered or may consider themself to get the 'best' help from whoever he or she can develop a satisfactory long-term relationship with, and so on. What disrupts this pragmatism is organisational and financial pressures which either provide incentives for the shifting of responsibilities across boundaries or, perhaps less often, encourage competition to 'invade' across boundaries (see Dunleavy, 1991, for an interesting discussion of motivations for this strategy). Considerable attention has been given through organisational, planning and financial devices to minimise problems with regard to this boundary (this issue has been widely discussed in Britain; see, for example, Means and Smith, 1994). However, what Tunissen and Knapen (in Kraan *et al.*, 1991, p. 18) call 'substitution' – 'active government intervention' . . . (to achieve) shifts from expensive to cheap provisions' – influences this process.

There is a danger of over-emphasising the health care/social care boundary as problematical and a source of conflict. It is important to bear in mind just how fundamental recognition of the interlinking of the two systems is for an adequate health care system. Better a problematic boundary than a system in which the health care system readily limits its involvement without regard to the social consequences.

The issues about the role of social work in relation to health care bring home these considerations more clearly. One of the roots of social work involvement with health care lies in an issue akin to some of the things discussed above in relation to income maintenance. Systems of health care that confine their free services to the poor need someone to determine whether patients can pay or not. In pre-National Health Service Britain such a task was given to a kind of social worker – the 'almoner'. This semi-professional group gradually widened their concerns from that basic consideration to a much wider range of issues about difficulties faced by patients coming into hospital (unresolved child-care problems, for example), and difficulties faced on leaving hospital. Thus they continued to have a role after the arrival of free hospital care for all.

There are other issues on which social workers have a contribution to make. Often these involve wider concerns in which the concrete problems outlined above are mixed up with emotional and psychological problems. Examples include when patients need to cope with amputations or terminal illness and when people are bereaved. In addition there is one area where a central social work concern and a medical concern come together; this is in relation to the abuse of children, where medical experts may diagnose and may have to treat, but there are then issues about whether the children should be taken 'into care' to be resolved (see Munday, 1993, for examples of procedures to deal with this issue in various countries of the European Union).

There is a similar merging of medical and social work concerns in the field of care for mentally ill people. One of the threads in the development of the social work profession – particularly in the United States – was the assumption of a role in relation to therapy for mentally ill people (Woodroffe, 1962). Here social work played a role in the introduction of approaches to mental illness which derived from Freudian and post-Freudian theory and sought alternatives to the more physically interventionist strategies favoured by many of the medical practitioners in this field (drug therapy or even brain surgery). This has led to a situation in which social workers may both work alongside doctors in a variety of therapeutic roles or may still offer alternative approaches.

The social work role in relation to mental illness is particularly salient outside hospital settings. Here social workers may have a role in coping with emergencies which arise out of mental health problems, in dealing with interactions between mental illness and other family problems, and in providing community and after-care services.

It must be noted, again, that there is no self-evident institutional location for much of this social work effort in health care. There is an argument for seeing social workers as part of a health care team, presumably therefore in the employment of health care agencies, but there is an alternative view that recognises the way in which much of the social work effort looks outward from the health care institutions to concerns about the lives of patients in the community, and links up with other social care services that are clearly community based.

Housing and social care

The remaining issues about the links and boundaries between social care and other areas of social policy are of much less fundamental importance than those between social care and either income maintenance or health care. They will be discussed briefly.

In the field of housing there is a negative set of control issues as well as a positive set of care issues to be mentioned. Non-marketed social housing is seen principally as a commodity provision activity with most characteristics, other than the determination of rent levels and the selection of tenants, like those of the marketed sector (these issues will be discussed in the housing chapter). But what does this sector do about the non-conforming tenant – the person who fails to pay rent, who mistreats the property or who is a nuisance to the neighbours? It may, of course, have to resort to exactly the same remedies as the private rented sector – legal sanctions including the possibility of eviction. However, in many circumstances recourse to these remedies will be inhibited by notions of obligation to tenants – particularly if those tenants have been selected in the first place because they have social problems. That inhibition may be particularly reinforced by the fact that the social landlord may be the last resort for tenants. An evicted tenant may have nowhere else to go, and the social landlord may have a specific statutory responsibility to help the homeless (Emms, 1990). Once again this point is leading us to care and control issues: the possibility that the social landlord will want to have, or to have access to, some sort of social service which will give attention to the deviant tenant.

The more positive care issues arise for the basic reason that anyone in receipt of social (or for that matter health) care needs to live somewhere. Caring institutions embrace housing within their other concerns. This is one of the factors which makes them expensive. Since means tests are often used to assess charges there is a problem about whether these should include 'asset testing' in which the value of the original home is taken into account. Where return to that is possible this is clearly unsatisfactory. Where it is not there is an issue about the extent to which it is reasonable to make inroads into assets which would otherwise be passed on to the next generation. It has been observed that in nations where owner-occupation is widespread there is a significant and growing group of elderly people who are 'asset rich' but often 'income poor'. National policies vary in the way they address this issue (OECD, 1994c, p. 46).

Alternatively, when options for social care are considered which are as far as possible 'within the community' a social housing system may have a role to play with regard to the following:

1. Seeing that the homes provided have appropriate physical characteristics (that is, are designed or adapted to enable people with disabilities to live in them).
2. Ensuring that tenants are linked up in user-friendly ways with social support services (which implies a variety of linked support systems – a warden on site, an alarm system, special communal facilities, etc. – a constellation often described as 'sheltered housing').

(See Tinker in OECD, 1994d, for a discussion of the wide variety of approaches to these issues.)

Once again when the 'support' system needed relates not so much to physical frailty as to mental health issues, learning difficulties, addiction or behavioural problems the social 'support' needed may include an element of social control.

The issues then about whether these things are part of the housing service or whether there needs to be provision for reference to and/or supply by and/or payment from some separate agencies have characteristics in common with the issue discussed above in relation to social work within health services. There is a case for such work to be integrated with other aspects of housing management. Alternatively the housing system can be seen as simply concerned with the 'bricks and mortar' part (Griffiths Report, 1988, p. 15), and the services (including even perhaps some of the special costs of adaptions) as the responsibility of other caring (and controlling) agencies.

Employment policy and social care

Many of the issues about the relationship between employment policy and social care have been mentioned in the section about income maintenance and social care. To a large extent employment services only worry about the social and behavioural factors which may be influencing people's chances of finding work when the individuals are also dependent upon benefits. An exception is sometimes special services for disabled people, helping them to overcome the barriers to work and offering training regardless of benefit status.

One aspect of concern in using care services to help people get into work is the provision of child-care services, particularly for single parents. There is a significant distinction to be made between the extension of such services universally as an option for all parents and the much narrower focus in some societies on the function of such services to reduce dependency.

Mention of the extension of child-care services to enable people to take work suggests a point that needs to be made concerning social care services. Care services are labour intensive, the widespread availability of care services (in Sweden, for example) may make a major contribution to the provision of employment (see Rein in Klein and O'Higgins, 1985), but, as has been discussed at length earlier, care services are often carrying out tasks which are performed in many communities and households without any employment contract or formal remuneration, principally by kin. Hence, shifts of policy which alter the respective roles of formal and informal care in a society may have very significant effects upon labour market participation. To put it more concretely: a drive to make the family do more caring shifts people (mainly women) from the paid labour force into the unpaid one; conversely extensions of formal care enable people to be paid to perform tasks for others that they might otherwise be performing within their family. There are social choices to be made here, which are often masked by the separation of debates about the labour market from debates about the caring roles of the family. These choices have particular implications for women, an issue to which Chapter 11 will return.

Finally, a brief comment about the impact of unemployment upon social care needs. Again the main issues are those discussed in relation to income – about unemployment as a cause of poverty which then causes other social problems, but there are also more direct relationships, both positive and negative. Inasmuch as unemployment in itself has an impact upon individual self-esteem it may be seen as a direct cause of social problems. There is, however, a beneficial side too: unemployment may release people to participate more effectively in family life. Much depends upon individual adaptation, and in practice for many the impact of unemployment upon their income and self-esteem is so fundamental that it undermines any positive aspect.

Education and social care

A compulsory education system which is committed to doing its best for all children encounters a variety of situations in which the behaviour of children or their families (or often some combination of the two) makes its task difficult. Action is needed to deal with children who fail to attend school and children who disrupt classes when they are there. Teachers may also be concerned about deprived children whose undernourished condition or whose emotional problems (and so on) makes it difficult for them to participate satisfactorily in school life.

All these situations may make necessary some 'outreach' work from the school. While some of this work may be seen in control terms – compelling children and their parents to meet the obligations of compulsory education – a variety of 'care' concerns are likely to be linked with it. These may range from trying to solve money problems through referral to other helping agencies to providing children (and perhaps their parents) with specific therapeutic or guidance services. Much of this work requires skills like social work and psychiatry. These services may be provided as part of the overall education service or by other agencies.

There is also a group of children who are very hard to educate because of either severe physical handicaps (in particular deafness and blindness) or severe mental handicaps (often now described as 'learning difficulties' – an expression that would have caused confusion if used without explanation in this context). In some societies education is regarded as so close to impossible with some of these children that they are not taken into the system at all. It is left to a health or social care agency to give them what little training it can. The alternative view is to try as far as possible to integrate these children into the school system with teachers supported by care workers and able to draw upon other special services when necessary.

Universalistic philosophies in education – with views of education as something for life and not just for its early years, and commitments to link schools into their communities – mean that education services become involved, in some places, in a range of social and community activities. The issues about advice, advocacy and mobilisation discussed above in relation to the social care/income maintenance interface are sometimes concerns of education services. Community development may be regarded as an educational task. There is here, as with both health and social care, the possibility of a broad view of the mission of an education service where a holistic vision may complicate boundary issues with other services.

Criminal justice and social care

As pointed out in Chapter 1, this book is not going to get into the complex issues around criminal justice policy, but as the connections between social care and social control have been explored previously in this chapter, completeness requires a note on the variety of ways in which criminal justice and social care issues intersect. In various respects social care and social work are offered in efforts to treat convicted criminals as redeemable and to avoid more draconian punishments. Institutional provisions which fall short of the total imprisonment may also be included under this heading.

This means that representatives of these caring services are needed to advise the courts on sentencing options, to provide support for convicted people who are not imprisoned and for prisoners when released and paroled. This may also imply various forms of residential provision where care and supervision may be offered. Elements of compulsion are inevitably present in these situations; refusal to accept this not necessarily welcome help may result in a worse alternative, generally incarceration.

Conclusions

Social care concerns arise in a variety of ways and link fundamentally with many other social policy issues. It has been suggested that in ideal terms it may be possible to see social care as fundamental to all social policy, treating people, families and communities as 'wholes'. Hence comprehensive approaches to income maintenance policy, health policy, education policy, and so on, may recognise the spill-overs from specific concerns to general ones. Yet, societies expect adult individuals to be responsible for their own lives and to use their incomes to meet their needs, and they expect families to be the main caring institutions for children and often for adults unable to be responsible for their own care. These considerations render social care services into a residual position, to be there when the other institutions fail. This is an observation on what occurs in practice, not a value judgement.

There are arguments, as was indicated in Chapter 1, about the inadequacies of both individualism, as expressed in market participation terms, and about families as the 'normal' foundations for social care. Where these arguments are taken seriously they widen the concerns of the social care sector. Notions of rights to care for frail elderly people or for children, regardless of the capacity of other family members to provide or pay for this care, emerge on the agenda. Only in the most developed of the welfare states, in Scandinavia, are these ideas on the agenda, and even there they are fragile growths.

Yet without the advancement of universalist propositions of this kind social care services are inevitably emergency services, deployed to help those both unable to help themselves and unable to secure the help of close kin. This has two consequences that have been explored in this chapter. One is that they are typically services for the poor and isolated. Means tests and family obligation assumptions keep other customers at bay. The other is that they frequently contain a 'control' element, inasmuch as they are imposed upon people, regarded, rightly or wrongly, as unable to help themselves or to use other services in the 'normal' way.

Guide to further reading

It is difficult to find appropriate suggestions for further reading for this chapter. A comparative literature on social care is only just beginning to emerge. Munday's *European Social Services* (1993) offers a largely descriptive account of policies in various European countries. Evers, Pijl and Ungerson's *Payments for Care: A Comparative Overview* (1994) deals with one of the key issues in this field.

Otherwise there is a need to turn to studies of specific countries. Clasen and Freeman's *Social Policy in Germany* (1994) includes a chapter on personal social services in that country. Gould's *Conflict and Control in Welfare Policy* (1988) deals with some of the issues about social care in Sweden. In Britain the recent government interventions to promote privatisation and the 'mixed economy of care' are producing an increasing volume of literature. Good introductions to this are contained in Wistow, Knapp, Hardy and Allen's *Social Care in a Mixed Economy* (1994) and Hudson's *Making Sense of Markets in Health and Social Care* (1994).

CHAPTER SEVEN

Housing policy

Introduction

Housing is a commodity that is bought and rented in the market, yet states become involved or intervene in that market in a variety of ways. Housing's importance for individual welfare provides a justification for that intervention, but the same is true of food and fuel with whose provision states are much less likely to intervene. What is it about housing which influences this intervention? Probably the relatively high cost of its provision and the fact that accommodation is one very large element in a household's needs which, once provided, lasts for a very long while. However, it will be seen that when states become involved in the provision of housing they tend to do so in ways in which public roles and market roles are mixed, often complicatedly. Comparatively few people pay nothing for their housing, and where states help to meet housing need they often do so in a way in which public and private effort are combined. It is conversely the case that there is very often a state role in what seems to be a purely private market; states intervene in a variety of ways which affect the prices at which private deals to rent or buy accommodation are made.

The fact that houses and flats last for a very long while means that interventions into their supply have consequences which continue for many years. Initial subsidies will have long-run effects. Once states start to intervene in the property market they generate effects which cannot easily be eradicated.

A subsidy for some kinds of people or for some sectors of the market has repercussions for others. It passes on benefits which may in practice pass to the supplier. It conveys advantages with corresponding disadvantages to others. It may distort supply and/or demand in the market as a whole. Moreover, interventions which may appear to be merely efforts to regulate – to influence private letting or purchasing transactions – have the same impact as more direct subsidies. Inasmuch as they prevent some individuals

Table 7.1 Distributions of the three main kinds of housing tenure in various societies

	Social rented	Private rented	Owner-occupied	Date
Australia	5	25	70	1988
Denmark	21	21	58	1990
France	17	30	53	1990
Germany	25	38	37	1990
Ireland	14	9	78	1990
United Kingdom	27	7	66	1990
Belgium	6	30	62	1986
Italy	5	24	64	1990
Netherlands	43	13	44	1988
Spain	1	11	88	1989
United States	2	32	66	1980

Sources: for European countries, Power, A. (1993) *Hovels to High Rise*, London: Routledge; for Belgium and Spain, Clasen, J. and Freeman, R. (eds.) (1994) *Social Policy in Germany*, Hemel Hempstead: Harvester Wheatsheaf; for the United States, Ball, M., Harloe, M. and Martens, M. (1988) *Housing and Social Change in Europe and the USA*, London: Routledge; for Australia, National Housing Strategy (1991) *The Affordability of Australian Housing*, Canberra: Government Publishing House.

from fully taking advantage of market forces they may be said to force them to 'subsidise' other individuals.

The point of these general observations will become more apparent as specific issues are examined. Issues about housing policy are looked at by considering separately issues about state intervention in the private rented market, the provision of state-subsidised rented housing (social housing), and state influences upon the provision of owner-occupied houses. Table 7.1 shows the shares of these three kinds of housing tenure in various societies. The discussion of these tenure types, and comparisons between them, will highlight some of the more general issues about the dynamics of the housing system, influenced by or influencing state interventions. In looking at social housing attention will be given to interactions between housing subsidy and income maintenance policy.

In terms of the framework provided in Chapter 1, relating state interventions to issues about individuals as market actors, people in families and relationships within communities, much of the thrust of this chapter will concern the relationship between state and market. However, issues about families and housing will be discussed at the end of the chapter.

It should be noted that when the expression 'housing' is used without qualification it refers to accommodation of all kinds including flats, lodgings and (to some extent) institutional arrangements. In some places specific comments will be made about types of dwelling.

The state and the private market

In the past in many simpler societies people with limited resources solved problems of house construction, whenever they were beyond the resources of a single family, through collective action. In pre-industrial Europe individual ownership, with houses passing from generation to generation, was widespread. Housing for the poor was often provided by their employers. Market societies developed an alternative approach in which entrepreneurs carried the cost of investment in the production of homes and recouped their expenditure through rents. Hence, as industrial societies developed (one might indeed say here urban societies since it was in the towns that this development was so important), the letting of houses by private landlords emerged as a dominant mode of housing provision for low-income people.

Since the incomes of industrial workers, before the twentieth century, were generally so low that only modest housing expenditures could be contemplated, the quality of early urban rented housing was low and occupancy levels were high. As towns grew demand for this basic rented housing naturally rose. A 'natural' market response to increased demand is rising prices which brings in new suppliers. A peculiarity of housing is that it is a commodity which occupies space for a long period of time. Hence, towns in which job opportunities were concentrated became congested. Meeting new needs would be likely to involve either the relatively uneconomic business of pulling down old houses still providing a return to their owners to replace them with bigger ones or the establishment of new houses outside the developed area. The latter process produced, in some cases, a pattern of urban growth in which entrepreneurs were able to take advantage of rising incomes to build better houses on the periphery of earlier developments to let to the better off. The earlier poorer property then passed down to poorer people moving into the town in search of work. It was observation of that sort of approach which led early urban sociologists in Chicago to talk of what they saw as a kind of natural development of concentric circles of residences reflecting in a spatial form the social stratification of a city (Park *et al.*, 1923).

Chicago, however, was a new development in a relatively empty country where land was cheap. The outward development process was not so easy in places where there were geographical constraints upon growth (water, mountains, etc.) or existing patterns of land ownership and use which limited an urban expansion process. Moreover, even where expansion was possible transportation problems might limit the attractiveness of suburban life – elites might prefer to seize the opportunities for inner-urban living. Hence, the alternative to a community which grew harmoniously in response to 'natural' market forces might be one in which competition for scarce houses grew rapidly in the inner area – with resultant opportunities for exploitation by landlords and severe overcrowding – while transportation problems brought difficulties for those, not necessarily much better off, people who sought to get away from the city.

Various things might then tempt dominant groups to seek to intervene in the situation. One was the spread of disease from the overcrowded underprivileged areas. Another was the threat of fire, spreading rapidly and indiscriminately from its source to destroy property. There was also the potential for an aggrieved urban population, living in an area crucial for the economic and/or political life of a nation, to disrupt and threaten the lives of the better off (to riot, to rob, etc.). It was also the case that the fit, or lack of it, between the location of work and the location of homes was of concern to the entrepreneurs who provided the former. Some of these issues, particularly the first two, had implications beyond the housing policy area, and were considered in general terms in Chapter 2.

'Model' communities and charitable housing

One response from elites to these problems was to try to provide better, or more appropriately sited, housing themselves. A number of entrepreneurs built 'model' communities where they let better-quality houses to their own workers (for example, Saltaire and Bournville in Britain and developments at Guise and Mulhouse in France – see Power, 1993). In Germany the provision of housing by employers was widespread, particularly in areas like the Ruhr valley (Harloe, 1985). These developments were particularly likely where work ventures were being developed in places where housing was scarce – mines or mills established in remote valleys, for example. In these circumstances, as indeed had long been the case in agriculture, it is important not to be over-impressed by the apparent charity. It served employers very well to have workers who had more than just their jobs to lose! Moreover, some of these developments did not offer particularly good-quality housing – the special cases stand out today because where the houses were good they have survived.

An alternative approach involved charitable ventures – the provision of non-profit or low-profit houses by organisations of private individuals. In the late nineteenth century there were a number of ventures of this kind (see Power, 1993, on European examples). A variety of 'limited dividend' ventures were set up, encouraging investors to take less than full profits in the interests of philanthropy (described in Britain as 'five per cent philanthropy', Tarn, 1973). In some countries modern social housing ventures originated in this way, with the state moving in as a partner or a source of subsidy at a later date (this was particularly the case in Germany, see Power, 1993).

Clearly this is leading up to another alternative – a role for the state in dealing with these issues. Before discussing state interventions that can in some sense be described as 'housing policy' it should be mentioned that since much of the problem being discussed here arose out of urban congestion there is one alternative kind of policy intervention which is not being examined in this book – transport policy. State investment in transport and state subsidy of transport may offer an important contribution to the relief of housing stress arising from urban concentration. Such interventions have 'knock-on' effects on housing markets. Another alternative, state employment policy, inasmuch as it concerns itself with the location of job opportunities can also have an impact. This can be both positive and negative – states may encourage job dispersal but they may also contribute to job concentration (for example, wartime stimulation of heavy industry concentrated in key urban centres). Some of these aspects of employment policy are discussed in the section on policies affecting the demand for labour in Chapter 8.

Regulation of the private sector

The first state interventions to deal with urban housing problems were regulatory. Planning policies, typically forward looking, as it is difficult to impose planning limitations retrospectively, were developed to try to determine the character of new housing – its size, quality and the amenities it offered. Copenhagen, for example, passed a 'building act' as early as 1683 (Harloe, 1985, p. 18), but public health considerations were deemed, in some circumstances, to justify a more draconian public response – to force adaptions to existing houses, to limit levels of occupation and exceptionally to require the demolition of unfit houses. In Britain:

> *The first Nuisances Removal Act was passed in 1846 in an attempt to enable authorities to deal with urgent threats to public health, such as neglected middens. The Nuisances Removal Act of 1855 was noteworthy for introducing the words 'unfit for human habitation' which remains central to slum clearance legislation. (Malpass and Murie, 1990, p. 32)*

Both planning and public health measures are *interventions* in the housing market. It can be said that they force landlords to *subsidise* tenants. In other words they prevent landlords from extracting the full return that an unfettered market would have allowed them to secure. The emphasised words are used to define, not to either condemn or justify what is involved. People may have strong feelings about landlords, regarding them as parasites or benefactors. It is important to analyse their behaviour as market actors, making investments in expectation of certain returns, and therefore likely to alter their behaviour if those returns do not materialise (Robinson, 1979; Le Grand and Robinson, 1984, pp. 96–9). Unless this consideration is borne in mind it is difficult to make sense of the history of housing in the period since these initial state interventions. Measures to control the activities of housing investors, which reduced the returns on their investments, inevitably produced responses. Landlords have several options in the circumstances described above. They may just accept them – they lower their profits and, if their money could be better invested elsewhere, they may be said to be making a 'charitable' contribution to housing policy. This was noted above as one not uncommon response. The peculiarly long-term nature of housing does mean that a safe but low return investment in a venture offering better-quality housing over a long period may still be regarded as preferable to more risky speculations.

Alternatively landlords may try to evade legislation which reduces the profitability of their investments, intensifying the control problems for those charged with the enforcement of the law. Certainly much of the history of regulation in housing can be seen as a succession of battles between law enforcers and landlords as various approaches to evasion were developed (Doling and Davies, 1984). Where tenants are desperate for low cost-housing they are likely to be forced to collude with much of this evasion.

Another alternative for landlords is to follow the logic of economic rationality and pull out of the business of providing housing for poor people. One of two consequences is likely to follow from this: either the passing of the property into the owner-occupied sector in which case it will cease to make a contribution to the housing needs of the poor, or its shift into ownership by someone less scrupulous about conformity with the law. It is this last phenomenon which has created 'pariah' landlordism – individuals who have bought into the business with heavy loans and are desperate to make a return on their capital (Rex and Moore, 1967).

Rent regulation

There is another alternative open to the landlord forced to raise housing standards, which is important in its significance for further policy developments. It is to try to recoup the cost of improvements by increasing rents. Inasmuch as the trigger for change is scarcity and the tenants are low-income people this alternative puts pressure upon the state to adopt a more radical form of market intervention – rent regulation. It was in recognition of the significance of this form of regulation that the discussion above emphasised the need to see landlords as market actors. Rent restriction, particularly when linked with both security of tenure and controls over occupancy levels and standards, goes right to the heart of the capacity of a landlord to secure a 'normal market' return on a capital investment.

Rent regulation seems to offer a way for governments to adopt an approach to housing problems with slight implications for public expenditure. Urban unrest, electoral pressures and concerns about inflationary wage demands (to meet rising rents) may lead to the use of this option. Wartime – when consensus is important, urban industries need to grow fast and house supply is falling (from some combination of bomb damage and the diversion of resources to other priorities) – has been a time when rent control has seemed a particularly attractive option (France introduced rent control in 1914, Britain in 1915, Denmark in 1916, the Netherlands and Germany in 1917 – Harloe, 1985, p. 29). These controls experienced a complex history after their initial imposition, with relaxation in peacetime and reinforcement in and after the Second World War. Once initiated rent control is difficult to discontinue, at the very least it has to be done gradually to avoid the economic and political repercussions of a dramatic rise in the cost of living.

As already stressed, however, rent regulation has cost implications for landlords. The adjustments to their behaviour outlined above are then likely, and economic theory suggests that there may be a movement out of the business of providing houses for other people. The latter may involve various effects. Those who already own houses may be able to sell, the feasibility of this depends upon either the availability of others less scrupulous and willing to try to evade the impact of rent regulation or tenants willing and able to become owner-occupiers.

In practice rent regulation may trap many owners, with assets falling in value because of the declining financial attractiveness of the role of landlord, into remaining in the business. Where a house is old, the original investment may have been recouped, indeed the asset may even have been inherited. A low return on a relatively notional capital asset may be tolerated. Accordingly the actual fall in the availability of rented houses after rent regulation (in the absence of willing buyers) may be quite slow. Problems begin to occur as these properties deteriorate or if the demand for rented housing is growing (as a result of population increase or migration, for example). Then, a second effect begins to become more serious – the fact that rent restriction limits returns on capital is likely to have a very strong impact upon the readiness with which individuals will make investments in the provision of rented housing. In other words, wholesale rent restriction may be expected to create a situation, other things being equal, in which the supply of new rented housing dries up. Governments may try to avoid this by confining rent restriction to older properties. However, there are problems about doing this. An imbalance will develop between the two sectors which will encourage attempts to evade control. The poor are likely to be concentrated in the old sector, facing steadily deteriorating housing conditions. Since housing is a very long-term investment, once intervention has occurred for some sectors potential investors are likely to be deterred by the possibility it will extend to others.

This analysis suggests that the effects of rent control may be complex. Where it occurs other effects may be operative too, in particular controls on occupancy levels and housing quality (as suggested above) which also affect profits to landlords. Critics of the simple market theory-based analysis of the effects of rent control suggest that there is a need to consider issues about the capital market and to recognise that different considerations influence the propensity to provide new rented housing to those that influence willingness of landlords to stay in the market letting old property. Above all they stress the fact that the working of this market is affected by the low incomes of those most dependent upon it. Harloe sums up his complex analysis of developments in various countries with the blunt statement 'in a situation in which private rented housing is increasingly confined to housing those on the lowest incomes, the claim that landlords would necessarily gain higher rents if control were abolished is not sustainable' (1985, p. 176).

Notwithstanding difficulties about rent control it is a policy that has been widely used. Reference has already been made to its use in the two world wars. After the Second World War many countries retained it in some form (see Harloe, 1985 and Power, 1993, on its use in France, Britain, Germany, the Netherlands and Denmark; Harloe also discusses its use in New York but reports its absence in much of the United States; it also emerged in Australia in the Second World War and persisted in some states until the 1960s – see Jones, 1990).

Harloe suggests that aspirations to phase out rent control came up against concerns about inflation, with rising housing costs a factor in high pay claims; hence, he traces a switch from gradual withdrawal from the end of the 1940s to partial reimposition in the 1970s (1985, ch. 5). Efforts were made to limit its impact, exempting new lettings or high-value properties, but these tended to offer loopholes for evasion. At the very least they required the maintenance of one aspect of regulation, protection of tenants from unreasonable eviction.

Many countries tried to develop formulae to apply rent control flexibly, using special courts or tribunals to resolve difficult cases. Sophisticated approaches had to deal with difficulties in determining, in societies in which government interventions over many years had fundamentally restructured housing markets, what should be regarded as reasonable returns on investments or situations in which landlords could be deemed to be unreasonably exploiting housing shortages. This issue also arises in the discussion of appropriate subsidy levels (see next section). Together they have contributed to a shift away from interventions to affect rent levels to ones designed to enhance rent payers' incomes (another issue examined further later).

Rent control has been seen as emerging early in the development of state housing policy as a facet of a 'liberal interventionist' approach, aiming to remedy specific problems in a market context:

> *Rent control, apart from some minor administrative and policing expenses, costs the state nothing. It benefited housing consumers at the expense of one relatively small group in society, landlords. Later commentators were to highlight important feedback effects ignored by rent controllers. (Ball* et al., *1988, p. 12)*

These feedback effects, highlighted in the discussion above, added up to situations in which governments' initial 'cost free' interventions were likely to come under pressure for a very different kind of intervention in housing policy – direct provision and/or subsidy in order to supply rented housing as a supplement or alternative to the private rented sector. While Harloe is right to attack any simple linking of rent control with the decline of the private rented market, it is clearly the case that as governments developed concerns about the housing of the poor they could not easily control the behaviour of private providers without at the same time providing subsidies to bridge the gap between the costs of provision and the rents to be paid by tenants. This was particularly evident where the need was for new investment. Above all where action involved a combination of the clearance of old unfit housing and its replacement, entrepreneurs (particularly the small entrepreneurs who dominated private provision in many countries; see Harloe, 1985, ch. 1) could not be expected to be willing to undertake it. Hence the development of a subsidised social housing sector in most countries. This is the subject of the next section.

Social housing

The term 'social housing' is used here to cover rented housing which is supported by public subsidy of some kind, where 'social' considerations are seen as the justification. There is a multiplicity of forms this may take, so that at the margins it merges into the other kinds of tenure.

While in many societies there is a core social housing sector characterised by ownership by non-profit-making organisations and with tenants paying rents clearly below market levels, the ambiguity which will be shown to be present in both of those defining elements creates classification problems for many kinds of housing (particularly inasmuch as many states have been seeking to reduce investment in social housing in the recent past). Thus examples will be found of tenants paying rents comparable to those paid in the open market to non-profit-making landlords, perhaps in the process subsidising other tenants (this is a phenomenon which has emerged in Britain from government efforts to reduce subsidies to local authority tenants, see Malpass, 1990). At the other extreme profit-making organisations will be found collecting state subsidies, directly or indirectly, for some of their tenants (in a number of countries social benefits to support rents have this effect, this issue is discussed further below).

There is also some merging of renting and owner-occupation where publicly subsidised tenants are allowed to become part-owners or to commute their tenures into owner-occupation in a way which enables them to retain some benefit from their earlier subsidised status (this has been a particular characteristic of the British 'right-to-buy' policy since 1980, see Forrest and Murie, 1991).

In all these cases it is possible to get into a debate about whether certain groups are really subsidised or not, given that high levels of state intervention make it difficult to work out what market rents would really be in a hypothetically unsubsidised society. They also begin to indicate the wide variety of ways in which public interventions may occur. There is clearly, as with the purchaser/provider distinction in health care, a need to recognise both that there are a variety of ways ownership may be organised in social housing and a variety of ways in which state subsidy may be organised.

Forms of social ownership

The ownership options are easier to analyse than the subsidy options. Government, central or local, may be the owner of social housing, but in the European Union countries Power (1993) studied, only the United Kingdom and Ireland have social housing sectors dominated by public (in fact local government) landlords. Social housing ownership may alternatively be in the hands of a variety of non-profit-making organisations. This is the case in the other countries studied by Power – France, Germany and Denmark. It is also the case in the Netherlands (see Emms, 1990). These forms of ownership may be constituted in a variety of ways, allowing in some cases for tenant representation or even tenant ownership (the latter is particularly evident in Denmark – where the classification used in table 7.1 puts these perhaps misleadingly into the private sector – and in the Eastern Lander of Germany). Government organisations may be partners in these ventures.

As pointed out above, ownership may also be vested in profit-making organisations, where the subsidy is designed to bridge the gap between the actual return from rents and the forgone market return. Power (1993) shows how the German 'social housing' sector has involved profit-making ventures as well as non-profit organisations, and Emms (1990) cites policies in the Netherlands which enable private entrepreneurs to secure public subsidies so long as they accept rent controls.

Types of subsidy

The main distinctions to be made between types of subsidy are between the following:

1. Those provided in a capital form when an investment in housing provision is first made.
2. Those provided in ongoing form.
3. Those deliberately targeted towards the tenant.

Another distinction is between direct subsidies and exemptions from taxation (the latter have been particularly important in the United States; see Harloe, 1985, ch. 6).

It is important to recognise that even with public ownership there may be a variety of ways in which provision is actually subsidised. Governments may apply rules to themselves, and obviously to local governments, which have very similar consequences for the benefits that accrue to tenants as those applied to the subsidy of other providers.

It would be nice if at this stage in the discussion a neat table could be interposed comparing countries in terms of their approaches to types of subsidy, but in practice many countries have used mixed approaches and have varied these over time. In general there has been a shift from capital subsidies to more complex kinds of subsidies and from 'bricks and mortar' subsidies to the direct subsidising of low-income people.

Capital subsidies may be in the form of a lump sum given at the outset, they can also take the form of land or even a building which is given to the provider at a subsidised cost. There are obviously dangers from the point of view of governments that subsidies of this kind will in fact bestow benefits to developers or owners rather than to tenants (see Ball *et al.*, 1988, ch. 1, for an analysis of issues about the way subsidies may be more beneficial to producers than consumers, and Heidenheimer *et al.*, 1990, pp. 108–10, for further evidence on the use of producer subsidies). It is to be expected that where governments are not themselves the owners they are likely to maintain some continuing control over rent levels. However, these controls may disappear eventually.

Ongoing subsidies may involve a guarantee of a specific amount of money continuously or for a fixed period of time, but they may also involve a regularly revised amount in support of tenancies, taking into account movements of rents and incomes. An important consideration here is the extent to which such subsidies are specific to properties or are general grants to providers. In the latter case, as with British local government, it may be possible for the provider to concentrate the help in such a way that it is the case that some tenants are subsidising others (Malpass, 1990). This moreover may not be a transfer from the better off to the worse off, but a transfer from long-term tenants whose property was erected relatively cheaply to more recent arrivals whose houses cost a lot more to build. This 'pooling' effect seems to be a peculiarly British problem, elsewhere more diverse providers and legal controls generally prevent it (Emms, 1990, p. 135).

Examples of subsidies which are hybrids between capital grants and running-cost grants will be ones where governments enable organisations to borrow at below prevailing market rates or provide tax reliefs on returns to investments. As with the borrowing opportunities of owner-occupiers, there are a variety of complexities about what happens as interest rates change while the loan is still outstanding. These changes may deepen the subsidy or alternatively enable government to back away from its initial commitment. Ultimately the owner has an asset whose purchase has been completed and may or may not be freed from any obligation to charge less than market rent.

Readers may feel rather lost at this stage. In a society where there is a large subsidised rented sector and social housing owners are not in a position to simply evict their tenants and sell or select new tenants on an open-market basis, the concept of 'market rent' may in fact be rather meaningless. Implicit or explicit cross-subsidies may occur as a social landlord's stock builds up over time, secured at different costs and supported by different subsidies. A fair approach to rent determination may involve sticking rigidly to relating rent to the original cost of provision, updated to take into account maintenance and making allowance for an ultimate need for replacement. It may alternatively involve an attempt to determine what is reasonable: relative to income, what others are paying within the stock and what is going on in the private market (Hills, 1988).

It is important to bear in mind that one of the motives for the development of social housing was a concern about the difficulties faced by low-income people in the private rented market. Governments have therefore been concerned to try to develop ways of ensuring that the benefit from subsidy is principally secured by that group. In societies where there is a strong owner-occupied sector and obvious advantages to the better off to acquire an asset rather than rent, use of housing tends to be stratified (but see below some issues about the way the owner-occupied sector is in fact subsidised too). Moreover, in many countries the establishment of social housing systems pre-dated the development of a strong owner-occupier sector. Accordingly a variety of devices may be discovered which have been used to try to ensure either that the social housing sector favours low-income people or that within that sector subsidy is concentrated amongst such people. The problem about the former approach is that, unless people are to be evicted when their income rises (as is often the case in the United States), it offers only very approximate targeting in the long run. The history of long-established social housing schemes obviously involves complex changes over time, affected by rising incomes, changing opportunities, migration and rising access to owner-occupation.

Many of the earliest social housing systems, set up with modest amounts of subsidy from government, were found to offer little to the poor – their standards demanded comparatively high rents even when subsidised. It is arguable that, as with income maintenance benefits, social housing in much of Europe and also to some extent in Australia (Jones, 1972), but not in the United States, developed as a benefit targeted towards the newly politically oriented skilled working class rather than the very poor. Subsequently, as issues like slum clearance and homelessness intensified pressure on governments to do more for the housing of the poor, subsidies needed to be either increased or better targeted. Inasmuch as incomes were rising amongst the skilled working class targeting tended to be the favoured option, involving the use of means-tests to determine rent levels.

Many states shifted, from the 1960s onwards (Heidenheimer *et al.*, 1990, p. 111), their approaches to the subsidisation of social housing systems towards the operation of means tests, at least in respect of expensive new schemes. This shift, accompanied as it was by growing owner-occupation, brought with it changes to the character of social housing.

Social housing and social segregation

Any system for determining what tenants shall pay in a new housing development which imposes some sort of market rent (bearing in mind the discussion above about the problems with this concept) will be likely to offer a relatively unattractive deal to those well enough off to fail to get any means-tested support. This will be particularly the case if opportunities are available to get into owner-occupation. Hence, a housing development to which strict means-testing principles are applied will be a relatively unattractive proposition to this group of people. It will therefore start off, relative to schemes where such strict pricing did not occur, as dominated by low-income people.

Any subsequent changes in occupancy will tend to involve better-off people moving away to be replaced by poorer people. Social sorting will then be reinforced by notions of stigma. These may arise either simply because the project is perceived as 'for the poor' or because a significant resident group have other characteristics perceived as stigmatising – they are unemployed, they are single parents, they belong to a minority racial group, etc. These attitudes will influence the efforts of people to move away and the responses of those offered vacancies. The whole problem can be made worse if there are preferred alternatives in other sectors of the social housing system. These arise partly as a result of the different social histories of different developments. In addition design defects – faults in industrialised building, problems about safety in the common parts, etc. – will contribute to the unpopularity of some areas (see Emms, 1990, for a discussion of some of these issues with reference to 'problem' estates in Britain, France and the Netherlands).

Actions by officials, with regard to the initial allocation of places and their responsibilities to deal with vacancies, can exacerbate the whole issue discussed above. Suppose, for example, people are only allowed moves if they are not in rent arrears and conversely people in arrears in popular accommodation are evicted to unpopular accommodation. These practices, commonly noted in British housing management, will tend to exacerbate social segregation along the lines described here (*ibid.*).

The paragraphs above illustrate the way a mixture of issues come together to create 'problem estates' and to stigmatise much social housing. It would be wrong to attribute the whole problem to means-testing, but it has played its own part in exacerbating the problem. In the United States the small size of the social housing sector and the consistent attempts to ensure it is 'welfare housing' for the poor have tended to stigmatise the whole sector. In the British case there has been a general process of 'residualisation' of the sector, exacerbated by means-testing and the sale of much of the best of the stock to tenants in the more prosperous areas. In the Netherlands, problem estates have been a more recent development in some areas under a particular combination of circumstances, in a society where social housing in general has been more widely accepted.

Implications of direct subsidy of tenants

The shift of subsidy for social housing towards specific targeting through means tests is starting to create a situation in which it is arguable that it might be better to regard housing as a generally marketed commodity and simply subsidise those unable to pay full market prices through means tests. Logically that principle could extend to the owner-occupied sector as much as to the private rented sector, though it needs to be recognised that owner-occupiers are in the process of acquiring a marketable asset.

A shift to subsidy through means-testing implies that some of the general issues about that phenomenon have to be addressed. The issue of the contribution that housing allowances, tapering off as income rises, may make to the 'poverty trap' was discussed in Chapter 4. Ball, Harloe and Martens (1988) also identify the following potential problems:

1. The fact that benefits may not be taken up by all in need. They see this as depending very much upon the extent to which there is stigma attached to the claiming of means-tested benefits – favourably contrasting the Netherlands and Denmark with West Germany.
2. The difficulties which may ensue when tenants are required to make minimum payments regardless of their income. They observe that one of the cuts applied during the Reagan administration in the United States involved increasing this minimum without reference to tenants' capacity to pay (Hartman, 1986). At the time of writing the issue of introducing a minimum payment is on the British political agenda.

3. Schemes apply controls to prevent 'over-consumption of housing, requiring for example, that the space is closely matched to family size' (Ball *et al.*, 1988, p. 71). There is a related issue, particularly if rents are not controlled in any way, about whether there should be an upper rent limit for support. If there is not one the possibility of collusion of landlord and tenant to maximise the benefit arises, in effect undermining the operation of the market. If there is one, it will be the case either that tenants have to meet a top slice themselves or that this reinforces the social segregation of the poor.
4. Housing allowances may not adequately substitute for 'production subsidies', in other words they may inhibit the production of new building.

Kemp (1990) has examined some of the variations in approaches to income-related assistance with housing costs in Britain, France, Germany and the Netherlands. Kemp's analysis shows why the poverty trap stands out as a problem for the British system – because of a combination of complete support for housing costs with a high taper rate. Contrastingly the other systems he studied are likely to leave rent payers with high residual amounts to find from low incomes, particularly where (as in the Netherlands) there is no integration with other aspects of income maintenance.

The general issue about the subsidisation of consumption is that the savings from this apparently efficient 'targeting' of housing support may exacerbate divisions in society. Some writers have suggested that a system of 'housing classes' may be detected in some societies, affected not only by socio-economic divisions but also by opportunities for access to public housing (Rex and Moore, 1967). Bureaucratic choices – preferences for some groups over others (discrimination on grounds of race and gender, for example) – may influence the structure of housing opportunities. However, even if social housing is only targeted on income grounds its distribution is likely to mainly reflect socio-economic divisions in a society.

Some of the social housing pioneers had an aspiration that it should become a 'universal' housing sector, serving all classes of society living together in mixed estates. However, a variety of comments during the discussion have suggested that the development of the owner-occupied sector in many societies provides one of the main reasons why this has not occurred. This must be examined before it is possible to review the stratification issue as a whole.

Owner-occupation

It is important not to take it for granted because people buy and sell houses on the open market that the owner-occupation system in housing is simply a market system unaffected by public policy. There have been three important kinds of public policy intervention in relation to this sector: interventions in financial markets to make loans for house purchase easier to obtain, house production subsidies and tax relief for house buyers which have reduced the costs of borrowing money. Each of these will be looked at in this section. In addition government interventions in planning and land supply have also played a part. The activity has also been supported by the creation of a legal structure for institutions involved in the business of promoting or providing finance for owner-occupation.

Loans to owner-occupiers

The issues about support for house purchase are of fundamental importance for the growth of the owner-occupied sector. In looking into this subject what is found is the development of institutions willing to provide loans for individuals. Without such loans only a very small number of people with very large incomes or who are able to transfer assets between generations would be able to afford owner-occupied housing. Most owner-occupiers live in houses worth several times their annual incomes. Furthermore, those incomes are generally such that they could only support housing costs which are a modest percentage of the total. In such circumstances saving up to raise the full cost of a house purchase would be a daunting, lifetime challenge for many.

Hence, to become owner-occupiers most people need loans. Institutions are needed to provide the finance for house purchase, allowing borrowers to pay back over a long period. People living in a society where the provision of these loans – or mortgages – is widespread may take this mode of house financing for granted. It is a system of housing finance built up gradually over a long period. This build-up varied considerably from society to society. Table 7.2 charts the growth of owner-occupation in various countries.

Early ventures in the provision of housing finance were often fraught, systems were needed in which considerable sums of money could be channelled into long-term investments. Some of these house-financing developments were co-operative in nature, some depended upon banks being prepared to lend, others depended upon the development of specialist institutions dealing in the channelling of savings into housing (see Boddy, 1980). Government interest in this development, manifested in the regulation of credit-giving institutions and perhaps in their underwriting, was very important for its establishment and growth.

Ball, Harloe and Martens (1988) describe developments in capital markets in various countries since the 1960s which have transformed finance for owner-occupied housing from one in which 'protected specialised financial circuits' (*ibid.*, p. 131) were dominant. Clearly any explanation of this

Table 7.2 Owner-occupied housing as a percentage of total housing at various dates

	1914	1939	1971	1989
Australia[@]	49	54	69	68
Britain	10	33	52	68
France		46*		53*
Denmark		33[+]	46[+]	58[+]

Notes:
[@] dates 1911, 1933, 1971 and 1981
* dates 1945 and 1991
[+] dates 1950, 1970 and 1991
Sources: Power, A. (1993) *Hovels to High Rise*, London: Routledge; for Australia, Williams, P. (1984) 'The politics of property: home ownership in Australia', in Halligan, J. and Paris, C. (eds.) *Australian Urban Politics: Critical Perspectives*, Melbourne: Longman Cheshire.

requires an investigation into developments in capital markets well beyond the scope of this book. One of the particular thrusts of Ball, Harloe and Martens' book is to stress that it is necessary to go beyond the direct interventions of governments to explain developments in housing systems. Nevertheless government support for, including subsidy of, those earlier 'specialised circuits' has been important in their development and subsequently in making finance for owner-occupied housing now an interesting business proposition for other financial institutions. The discussion will now examine these in detail.

Tax relief for house buyers

Perhaps the most widespread mode of support for house purchase has been tax relief for house buyers. It is important to recognise that this is a form of subsidy. If people can secure tax relief in respect of the payment of interest on loans, that relief reduces the actual amount being paid below the prevailing market rate. Such a form of relief has been a salient feature of policy in Britain (particularly since a change in the system of taxation of property in 1963), the United States, Denmark and the Netherlands (this is obviously not an exhaustive list). In some countries (for example, the United States) there is tax relief on a variety of forms of borrowing. Where, on the other hand, it is largely confined for private individuals to house purchase loans it is susceptible, on the other, to what has been called 'leakage' to other purposes (Lansley, 1979, pp. 106–70), as lenders use the benefits bestowed by these *de facto* cheap loans to subsidise other activities. Sometimes this may be explicit where new mortgages are deliberately sought to finance some other expenditure. Often, however, it is implicit, inasmuch as borrowers benefit from the way housing credit reduces pressures upon their resources.

Such is the importance of mortgages that it must be recognised that a high proportion of all the owner-occupied houses are, in effect, not yet paid for. In Australia, a country which has had a very high level of owner-occupation for a long while, about half of all owner-occupiers are 'purchasers' as opposed to outright 'owners' (Jones, 1990). In Britain where the growth of owner-occupiers has been more recent 'purchasers' account for a higher proportion of owner-occupiers.

Production subsidies for houses for sale

In various countries governments have subsidised the production of houses for sale in much the same way as they have subsidised the production of rented social housing (for example, in France, see Ambler, 1991; and in the Netherlands, see Ball *et al.*, 1988). Similarly in West Germany subsidy of production was a popular approach for a while. Eventually a major corruption scandal regarding a leading producer, Neue Heimat, contributed to discrediting it (see Power, 1993, ch. 12).

The 'social' benefits of production subsidies are principally achieved through controls over the types of house that are subsidised. This is a fairly indiscriminate form of subsidy. A desire to assist the building industry because of a need to speed up the rebuilding of towns after the Second World War or because building is a key source of employment has influenced the readiness of governments to adopt this form of help. In these circumstances the 'leaking' of benefits from consumers to producers is particularly likely. As with rented housing the use of indiscriminate production subsidies was largely discontinued in the last quarter of the twentieth century.

An alternative approach, again found in the Netherlands (Emms, 1990), involves reduced rate loans to low-income buyers for a specific period of time. An alternative used in France involves relief from property tax for a period (Ambler, 1991, p. 195). Ball, Harloe and Martens point out that the direct subsidy of house buyers has been widespread in the United States (1988, pp. 96–7). In the United Kingdom the indiscriminate mortgage interest subsidy has come under attack from the 'left' because of its regressive nature and from the 'right' because of its relatively untargeted form of assistance with housing costs.

Mention has already been made about the way concerns about stimulating the building industry have influenced production subsidies. A full account of the ways in which owner-occupation is *de facto* subsidised would have to take into account issues like government influences upon the supply of land for building, issues about land taxation, concerns about the legal cost of house transactions and laws relating to inheritance. The discussion could get into deep water about the circumstances under which government interventions in these areas provide subsidies and those in which they in fact impose costs upon owner-occupiers.

In general, however, what is clear about the growth in the importance of owner-occupation in many industrialised societies is that governments have widely regarded this as a desirable phenomenon and have sought to encourage it. What follows from the comments on social stratification which have already been made in this chapter is that such encouragement reinforces social divisions in housing. In Britain, for example, only 11 per cent of owners and managers and 13 per cent of professionals are renting their houses, the rest are owner-occupiers. By contrast 54 per cent of unskilled workers and 46 per cent of semi-skilled workers are tenants (HMSO, 1994, table 8.24, p. 117).

Various attempts have been made to examine the benefits different groups secure from housing subsidies. The more indiscriminate forms of production and mortgage-related subsidies for owner-occupiers tend to be relatively regressive in effect, particularly when they increase with the size of the house or the size of the mortgage. The actual benefits of interest rate subsidies (including tax relief) tend to vary with those rates, and grew large during the era in which monetary policy pushed interest rates up. There will be no attempt to provide examples here as they tend to be country and time specific. However, there is little doubt that a combination of relatively relaxed approaches to the subsidy of owner-occupiers and the careful targeting of support for social housing, as particularly manifest in Britain since 1979 (see Malpass, 1990; Hills, 1988), has had regressive effects.

Housing and families

Household formation

So far the discussion has looked at housing consumption with little regard to anything other than the socio-economic status of the consumer, but it is family units (including one-person families) who are the consumers. The close equation between housing and family units is most evident in censuses which, in most western countries, equate families and the occupiers of a common housing unit as a 'household'. This entails difficulties when efforts are made to assess the extent of unmet housing needs, since within households there may be hidden or suppressed separate households who have not formed a separate unit because accommodation is unavailable or they lack the resources to acquire it.

The fact that this is more than an issue of how households are counted becomes evident if it is considered that household compositions regularly change – individuals reach adulthood and move away from the family of origin, marriages break down and death alters the framework of a family unit. There are cultural assumptions about the desirability of a newly married couple establishing a separate household or, more controversially, about the extent to which it is reasonable for young unmarried people to live away from the parental homes. The issues about appropriate care for the old or disabled, discussed in Chapter 6, are influenced by views about the desirability of separate living arrangements. The actions of others – relevant kin, employers, friends and, of course, governments – influence how these mutations occur.

A general feature of the evolution of family life in most industrialised countries has been a tendency for the population to be distributed amongst an increasing number of households. Young people have been leaving the parental home earlier, marriages have been breaking down more frequently and complex multi-generational households have been becoming rarer. Changing work opportunities requiring geographical mobility influence these trends. These developments interact with housing policies in complex ways. They increase the demand for housing even in the absence of population growth. The logical consequent response tends to take the form of the provision of relatively small units. Yet any shift towards smaller units may itself exacerbate the trend to which it is a response by reducing the availability of accommodation for larger households.

Governments frame policies based upon their views on some of these questions. They may regard some aspects of separate household formation as entirely acceptable and to be encouraged by policies. In most European societies, for example, while kin are often expected to play a role in community care, the notion that efforts should be made (through phenomena like sheltered housing) to sustain elderly people in their own homes is generally accepted.

By contrast policies are much less evident to assist young single people to form separate households from their parents. In Britain, for example, social assistance policies make separate household formation by childless people under the age of 25 difficult. The single homeless also get little help from housing authorities. Alternatively, Britain differs from many of its European neighbours in that it still has (albeit weakening) grant policies towards the support of university students which facilitate residence away from the parental home.

The growth in single-parent households, which is principally a consequence of marriage and relationship breakdown but may arise out of deliberate choice, raises particularly important policy issues. These are likely to be matters of concern to the providers of social housing, since most single-parent households are female headed and many of these families face severe income deficiency problems. Inadequate responses by housing authorities arise:

1. Because authorities lack the resources to respond satisfactorily.
2. Because the difficulties faced by this group of families are not properly recognised.
3. Because some authorities believe that a sympathetic response to this group is undesirable because it will encourage the phenomenon to which it is a response.

This last point of view is a variant on the stance taken by ideologues like Murray (1990) who see single parenthood as a symptom of moral decay encouraged by public policies designed to support single mothers. There is a related position which may be taken with regard to the provision of accommodation which may be in some sense or other a 'refuge' from a violent spouse.

This section has put a complex variety of points together. The essential argument is that housing policies are also to some degree family policies, at least as far as those who lack the resources to deal with their needs through the market are concerned. The demands upon the publicly supported housing sector are influenced by changes in family life; public authorities may also influence or attempt to influence family arrangements.

Inheritance

Finally, a rather different family issue more pertinent to the owner-occupied sector. One of the arguments against subsidy for owner-occupation which has not been mentioned before is that in the long run buyers acquire an asset. Yet, the defenders of subsidies argue that individuals can rarely realise those assets; they continue to require to be housed until the end of their life. However, this means that their heir or heirs realise the asset. This may be channelled into help with their housing problems, but in practice this succession rarely occurs at a time when the next generation are just setting up home, given the longevity of most elderly people. Quite a lot of the property that passes to future generations is of comparatively little value, because it is old or because it is in the wrong place. British studies have suggested that there is not yet a great deal of wealth passing on in this way, and that it will take a long while for the British growth in owner-occupation to have a big impact upon inheritance (there has been an extensive British debate on this theme, with Saunders, 1990, stressing the importance of this issue but with Forrest *et al.*, 1990 and Hamnett, 1991, indicating that the data suggest the more cautious conclusion summarised above).

Where this issue does come to a head is in situations in which elderly people who may be described as income poor but asset rich (because of their houses), and require substantial public expenditure upon their care. This has led to some policy developments designed either to force their potential heirs to contribute to the cost of their care or to force the old people to sell or remortgage their houses. This theme was mentioned in Chapter 6.

Conclusions

The main thrust of this chapter has been to suggest that housing arises as a social policy issue in a wide variety of ways. It is a common error to see only social housing as social policy. It is important to recognise how the initial response to perceived housing problems in many societies was to try to regulate the private rented sector, but that governments supplemented that (partly because of the difficulties about such market interventions) by trying to influence the provision of housing more directly. This latter response did not only involve subsidies for the most disadvantaged in the housing market. Public policies, though they have purported to have a 'social housing' concern, have involved a variety of interventions in the owner-occupied sector, some of which have spread benefits relatively far up the socio-economic 'ladder'.

At the same time housing policy interventions have reflected divisions in society. Far from correcting social inequalities in some societies social housing policies have concentrated disadvantaged people in poorly designed, ill-sited and stigmatised estates and have in fact reinforced them.

In the same way housing policies need to be seen as broadly responding to rather than creating changes in family life, but in doing so they have also contributed to trying to influence the changes taking place not so much by assisting family change (as suggested by Murray, 1990), but by creating severe hardships for those whose behaviour – a young person who wants to leave home or a woman trying to escape an unhappy marriage – deviates from norms embodied in policy. Inasmuch as there has been a housing response to these issues it has exacerbated the social divisions in the sector by allocating the least desired units to these most disadvantaged people.

Guide to further reading

Ball, Harloe and Martens's *Housing and Social Change in Europe and the USA* (1988) is a lively analytical comparative book on housing policy. Harloe has also produced a comparative study of rented housing, *Private Rented Housing in the United States and Europe* (1985). Apart from the Ball, Harloe and Martens book there has been little comparative analysis of owner-occupation.

A start on the comparative analysis of direct benefit support for tenants is found in Kemp's article 'Income-related Assistance with Housing Costs' (1990), while European comparative material is set out in Emms's *Social Housing: A European Dilemma* (1990) and Power's *Hovels to High Rise* (1993).

CHAPTER EIGHT

Employment policy

Introduction

In the discussions of income maintenance, health, social care and housing policy the focus has been upon benefits and care which are very often provided directly or indirectly, or subsidised by the state. In this chapter the focus is rather different since work is generally seen as something provided within a market context. Even if the provider of work is the state, there is normally a market-type transaction involved in which the state is a 'buyer' of labour. The focus for a discussion of employment policy as 'social' policy is thus upon 'interference' with the normal working of the labour market. Such interference does not necessarily only come from the state. Families and communities may seek to influence the way the employment market works – trying to force employers to favour particular applicants for work or to influence the terms of a labour market contract. The considerations which dictate such interventions will be very like those which influence the state: dissatisfactions with the outcomes of market processes. Much political activity around issues about employment can indeed be seen as efforts to persuade the state to take on formally regulatory tasks where societal pressures – collective actions to influence labour contracts – are ineffective.

A difficulty about identifying employment policy as 'social' policy is that market interventions are not only adopted for welfare ends. States interfere with employment markets to try to increase their effectiveness in waging war – with conscription replacing market methods of securing a labour force and the terms of the work relationship then imposed upon those conscripted. They also interfere in labour markets in the cause of the enhancement of economic efficiency, when their concerns are not so much the welfare consequences of the way markets are working as their outcomes for the economy as a whole. With this kind of intervention there may be considerable difficulties in separating economic and welfare objectives. Unemployment, low pay, poor working conditions, discrimination in the labour market (phenomena to be discussed in more detail in this chapter) may be seen as both 'problems' to be attacked for welfare reasons but also as 'inefficiencies' in the labour market. In other words, when these phenomena are examined from a societal point of view, they are likely to be seen both in terms of their welfare impact upon individuals and as failures to use economic resources in as efficient a manner as possible. Alternatively there may be a conflict between social concerns and labour market efficiency concerns.

These last issues take the discussion close to fundamental ideological disputes about markets. Some of the discussions in earlier chapters have considered propositions about 'market failure' as justifications for state interventions. In the field of employment policy the focus upon the labour market takes the discussion right into the centre of disputes about the desirability of market methods of regulating social life. Welfare concerns figure substantially in those disputes, but they do not stand alone. Views on this subject may be seen as organised around two 'poles' – one involving a pure market perspective which sees interference with the labour market as likely to lead to such inefficiencies that diswelfare (as a whole) is the result and the other involving a pure 'socialist' perspective which sees the market as something to be swept away in the name of both efficiency and welfare. Between these 'pure' polar positions, there is a spread of views. There can be said to be a general tendency for those whose views are close to the market perspective to be least concerned about the individual diswelfares consequent upon market processes and those who are close to the 'socialist' perspective to be most concerned about them. Thus, in the 'middle' of this spectrum of views there will be many who wish to delineate a range of justifications for interference with markets on welfare grounds. However, as suggested above, the fact that interference with markets may be justified in terms other than welfare ones complicates these arguments. Karl Marx had much to say about the exploitation of the proletariat and the process of 'immiserisation' under capitalism, but his thesis was ultimately not merely that capitalism was unjust but that it would collapse or be overthrown because of its own contradictions or inefficiencies.

Hence, this chapter has to look at specific welfare-oriented interventions in the labour market within this bigger debate. It will therefore need to focus upon these specific issues while recognising their place in a wider debate about capitalism. In doing this it also needs to recognise that 'pure' models of capitalism and socialism are constructs used within ideological disputes and are of little use to describe the actual labour markets of individual societies. That point will be readily accepted as far as the socialist model is concerned in this era after the collapse of the Soviet bloc, but it equally needs to be recognised that the pure capitalist form is an abstraction. Capitalist societies evolved out of earlier modes of economic organisation in which labour markets were regularly the subject of social interventions, often supported by the state. While the 'high noon' of classical economic theory in Britain or the United States in the nineteenth century was a period in which efforts were made to sweep away all forms of interference with the working of markets, these efforts never achieved all they wanted. Outside those two countries the evolution of the capitalist economy was often a much more clearly state-managed process, with labour market regulation as a continuing process (see Hobsbawm, 1994, for an analysis of twentieth-century history in the terms outlined above).

While it is helpful to analyse the social aspects of employment policy in relation to such phenomena as the recognition of unemployment as a specific problem for capitalist economies, the identification of the weakness of the labour side of the employment contract and the developing concern about discrimination in the labour market, it must be recognised that the evolution of the real world has not involved simply a shift from unregulated to regulated labour markets.

In this chapter the social aspects of employment policy will be examined in terms of forms of intervention. These are defined as the following:

1. Influencing the supply of labour.
2. Influencing the demand for labour.
3. Action against unemployment involving a complex interaction between influencing both supply and demand (and therefore given detailed separate attention).
4. Influencing choice by employers.
5. Imposing conditions on labour market contracts.

In looking at these issues it will be recognised that the state will not necessarily be merely a direct regulator of the labour market. The state has other roles which also have an impact. The state is itself a labour market actor as an employer. What work it supplies and the terms under which it supplies it have an impact upon the labour market as a whole. Similarly the state subsidises private market activities – the provision of houses, hospitals, schools, armaments – and in this way has a variety of indirect effects upon employment. As a provider of social benefits – particularly cash benefits – the state may affect labour market participation by employees. These considerations will be brought into the discussion where appropriate.

Influencing the supply of labour

Much state intervention to influence the supply of labour can be seen as designed to have an impact upon labour as an economic commodity, not as social welfare policy. Yet it has strong connections with social security. In Chapter 2 it was shown that the earliest public relief policies saw the support of those without work as a local responsibility. The itinerant poor could be driven back to their original communities. Hence, once towns began to grow and industrial activities developed unevenly across a nation (near to supplies of raw materials, ports, capital cities, etc.), an approach to relief which tended to inhibit labour mobility could be seen as undesirable on economic grounds. The state had to take steps to universalise relief, ensuring that it was available in new communities and perhaps indemnifying those communities for costs that they might find difficult to meet during periods of recession (de Swaan, 1988).

Once, however, labour mobility became seen as a matter for state concern more positive ways of influencing the supply of labour, other than just removing barriers to mobility, got on the political agenda. Hence states began to contribute to the spread of information on work opportunities through labour exchange systems (developed in a number of European countries around the end of the nineteenth century).

Simply facilitating the exchange of information – linking supply and demand – may be extended into policies designed to assist movement of labour through subsidies to help to cover costs of residential relocation. This has been a feature of active labour market policy in a number of countries: for example, Swedish measures to assist people to move from their northern counties (Mukherjee, 1972).

Mobility may be between countries as well as within countries. Nation states may actively assist people to migrate in search of work. In the 1940s and 1950s, for example, Australia subsidised immigrants from Europe. Nation states are likely to be ambivalent about this phenomenon. Movement *out* is indicative of a national failure to meet the needs and aspirations of its citizens. As Lee had sadly said of Ireland:

> *... this was a society that devoted much of its energy to skilfully socialising the emigrants into mute resignation to their fate .... Parents ... were essentially collaborators in the socio-economic system that decreed mass emigration and natural population decline as prerequisites for the comfort of the survivors. (1989, p. 644)*

Movement *in* is likely to be regarded with suspicion by the indigenous population, particularly when it involves an influx which is seen as ethnically different. The 'guest worker' contributing to the economy but likely to go home if unable to work is the ideal for a state which does not want to face up to the social implications of labour mobility (the nation state equivalent of the itinerant worker forced back to the parish in earlier times – Castles and Kosack, 1973; Husbands, 1988).

Overall, then, much state activity to influence labour supply in these general terms may be seen as economic rather than social policy, but it is economic policy with considerable social implications. These may be taken into account by the state. Measures to stimulate the movement may be accompanied by the subsidisation of that movement and perhaps by a recognition of other needs of workers and their families who move in this way. Immigration and internal migration both have implications for housing policy and for the provision of education, health care and social care in the areas to which people move. Entitlements to social benefits, including income maintenance, need to be portable, which they normally are for internal migrants in the modern state. In the case of movements between countries this portability is less likely, and access to other services may also be restricted by citizenship, length of residence or contribution rules (discussed further in Chapter 11). Here is a key way in which the development of common supra-national labour market areas (like the European Union) has implications for the harmonisation of social policies (see Watson in Gold, 1993).

Attention to the special needs of immigrants within social policy may be rendered all the more important by the presence of special cultural and linguistic needs on the part of workers or their families. Furthermore, even without formally state-sanctioned limitations on access to services, discriminatory behaviour by those who are the 'gatekeepers' for services may exacerbate the problems encountered by migrants.

The fact that nationalistic and racist attitudes may engender policies which limit the free flow of labour means that states may act to limit labour supply as well as to stimulate it. Some of the earliest social policy interventions by states did this by preventing the access of women and children to the labour market (see further discussion below). Another way in which states influence the supply of labour is through policies which supply replacement incomes to those who are not in the labour force. This issue was examined in Chapter 4.

There are differences between societies, or within societies over time, in the extent to which policies are actively used to either encourage or discourage labour supply. As far as the elderly are concerned there has been a shift in recent years from policies which encourage older people to remain in the labour force to ones which aim to discourage them. At a time of job shortage there may be a demand to 'make room for the young' (see Kohli *et al.*, 1991, p. 11). Nevertheless there are calls to reverse this policy (see OECD, 1994c) on the ground that the size of the 'dependent population' is rising relative to the working population. This view seems to confuse questions about the cost of support for those out of the labour force with questions about the availability of jobs. Removing or reducing state benefits to some of these individuals may reduce costs for the state or for private retirement schemes, but it can have little impact upon the availability of work (see further discussion in Chapter 12).

It might more generally be argued that 'voluntary' unemployment could be encouraged when jobs are short. In practice there is a universal concern that benefits for the able-bodied unemployed should not reduce labour market participation. The arguments about the impact of support for this group upon the supply of labour will be discussed later.

Measures to keep children out of the labour force were accompanied by the development of state support for education. While the main issues about education are to be discussed in Chapter 9, some points must be made here about the impact of education on labour supply. So far the whole discussion of labour supply has treated labour as homogeneous, but in fact workers enter the labour force with varying attributes. While these partly depend upon innate abilities, they also depend upon previous experience, education and training. Hence education influences the characteristics of the supply of labour.

In examining issues about education and training it is pertinent to refer back to the discussion in Chapter 2 on economic 'externalities'. In a free market for labour any efforts made by an employer to enhance the skills of his or her own labour force may create a situation in which competitors may secure a benefit which someone else has paid for. The early capitalist employer who sought to teach young workers to read, write and calculate enhanced the 'quality' of the supply of labour but then faced a problem about preventing rivals 'poaching' workers. The socialisation of these costs by the development of state education offered a solution to this problem.

The problem is, however, an endemic one since it extends beyond basic education to anything which may be done to enhance the skills of a labour force. In the modern situation in which many jobs demand high skills and many of those skills are best developed in the work situation employers continue to encounter the 'poaching' phenomenon. The problem is exacerbated by the fact that the poached employee takes both acquired skills and perhaps job-specific information.

There are therefore a range of issues about the respective roles of state and employers in regard to training. Efforts may be made to ensure that as much training as possible is 'socialised' within publicly funded training institutions, or training may be regarded as a shared responsibility with the state intervening to try to ensure that those employers who do train are subsidised and those who do not are taxed. Another partial solution to the problem is to prevent the mobility of the trained through contracts which prevent job change for a period of time. This last solution, however, runs right against efforts to make the labour market one in which both parties can freely buy and sell.

Just as the issue of labour mobility in general has international ramifications in the modern world, so does the issue of the mobility of skilled labour. Nations may be seen as the 'poachers' of labour. There are special problems here where very high skills are involved for which training is particularly expensive. A salient example of this within social policy concerns the medical profession. There are flows of doctors from countries where their incomes are low to ones where they are high. If the former have borne the costs of their training the cost implications may be considerable.

More generally, just as it was indicated above that the development of supra-national labour markets raises issues about the portability of social benefit rights so too do issues arise about the development of common approaches to training (see Rainbird in Gold, 1993). It may be objected that these issues about the economic consequences of enhancement of the skills of the labour force have little to do with social policy, but the skill training is a benefit to the individual likely to enhance his or her income, job security and job satisfaction. Training and education policies which distribute these benefits differentially have substantial social welfare implications. Education and training are widely seen as solutions to problems of social disadvantage in societies. Within the European Union training is seen as very central to European Community social policy, and the European Social Fund is very largely a mechanism to subsidise training for disadvantaged people (see Gold, 1993). The issues about training as a policy response to unemployment will be discussed further below.

Influencing the demand for labour

The issues about state influence upon the demand for labour could take the discussion even further into the realms of economic policy. Yet again it is important not to disregard the important social effects of such activities or to ignore some inevitable interactions between economic and social policy. This issue particularly comes up in debates about appropriate responses to problems of unemployment. That will be given attention in the next section. This section will establish some of the parameters for that discussion.

The initial discussion about labour supply considered influences upon the free movement of labour. But geographical imbalances between the location of work and the location of potential workers can be solved another way, by movement of the work. The location of some work is determined by natural phenomena – for example, you can only mine coal where there are coal seams! In many other cases, however, immovable natural phenomena (where raw material comes from, where ports can be located, etc.) are only a few amongst the many considerations to be taken into account in the choice of location of an enterprise. In some cases these phenomena are of little or no importance. Very often these considerations are dwarfed by another constraint upon movement, that a large fixed investment has already been made at a specific place. In all the situations in which work location is not absolutely determined the issues for an entrepreneur about coping with a shortage of labour might be expected to be determined by an economic calculation about the respective costs of moving the enterprise or financing the movement of labour. Need this concern the state?

There are a variety of justifications which can be advanced for state involvement in influencing workplace location. The nation state may want to try to gain an advantage over other nation states where entrepreneurs could equally locate. Similar considerations may influence the behaviour of local governments within states. There may be state security implications with regard to different locations. National economic interest may be deemed to override the interests of specific entrepreneurs. The state may feel it is necessary to intervene when entrepreneurs fail to perceive long-run as opposed to short-run considerations because of sunk costs or limited information.

State interventions with regard to the location of enterprises may also be justified on social grounds. Movement of labour may be deemed to impose unreasonable costs upon those forced to leave homes, families and communities. The change to the social characteristics of an area consequent upon labour migration – leaving collective institutions under-used, leaving behind an ageing population, and so on – may be deemed to be too devastating to countenance. Where countries have ethnic, linguistic or religious minorities concentrated in particular areas movements of workers may be deemed to be likely to have undesired consequences. Political calculations may be relevant here: migration affects the electoral bases of party support. All of these issues assume heightened significance when there is a shortage of work in the society as a whole.

Hence states adopt policies to influence the location of work for a variety of reasons. The policies may include both regulation and public expenditure. The former involve planning measures to determine locations which can or cannot be used. The latter involve subsidies to encourage movement or to make particular locations attractive for new plants.

So far the discussion of states as influences on the demand for labour has been limited to a model of the economy which assumes that there is a limited amount of work available and that this work is provided by the private sector, but the state is also a provider of work itself, a subsidiser of privately provided work, and a purchaser of goods and services from the private sector. All three of these give the state opportunities to influence the location of work, taking into account the social and political considerations outlined above.

Furthermore, in the modern world states also attempt to manage the economy as a whole and thus may be able to influence the total volume of work available as well as its location. In the former Soviet bloc states, and to some extent still in China, the role of the state has been to try to treat the desired volume of work to be provided as the starting-point for economic planning as opposed to an indefinite resultant of market activity. In the capitalist world Keynesian economic theory (Keynes, 1936) seemed to offer a similar prospect. That prospect seems now to have been damaged by the increased globalisation of economic activity, which takes the determination of much economic policy out of the hands of the individual nation state, and by difficulties in manipulating aggregate employment levels without causing inflation. There is a view, which this author shares, which suggests that there is much that can still be done to influence aggregate employment through creative use of the public sector, but that obviously has tax implications for the private sector which many consider to have a strongly limiting effect (OECD, 1994b). This leads to the more detailed discussion of unemployment and the social policy issues about its alleviation or prevention.

Unemployment and social policy

The 'discovery' of unemployment

Unemployment is a consequence of an imbalance between the supply of labour and the demand for labour. For that reason it requires separate consideration following the general discussion of policy influences upon supply and demand. Remedies for unemployment involve suggestions of ways to influence both the supply of workers and the availability of work. Furthermore, for some economic analysts the very issue of unemployment is seen as a consequence of unwarranted state intervention in the labour market.

In Chapter 2 there was some discussion of the way in which, during the nineteenth century, relief policies began to accept that able-bodied adults (particularly males) without work might be regarded as in need of consistent help as opposed to simple control measures designed to coerce them back into the labour force as quickly as possible. This change of attitude was partly a product of fear of this group of people – as potential rioters, vandals and criminals – but partly an acknowledgement that the labour market did not necessarily balance supply and demand easily and quickly, as suggested in the simpler formulations of classical economic theory.

Historians' discussions of unemployment in the United Kingdom, the first of the highly industrialised societies, have suggested that it was roughly in the 1880s (when incidentally the word 'unemployment' was first included in the Oxford English Dictionary) that attention began to be applied to the possibility that the relationship between the supply of labour and the demand for labour might merit attention in policy discussions (see Harris, 1972; Burnett, 1994, ch. 5). This recognition coincided with the identification of the problem of the 'trade cycle', the shift over time between periods in which the demand for labour and for commodities was going up rapidly and pushing up prices and periods when it was relatively slack, with resultant under-use of labour.

The discussion of unemployment which emerged from this recognition involved a range of perspectives (see notably a relatively sophisticated treatment of this by Beveridge (1909) early in the twentieth century). At one extreme were views that it was very much a consequence of temporary labour market adjustment difficulties. At the other extreme it was seen as evidence of deep flaws in justifications of capitalism, which glorified the 'hidden hand of the market' (see Showler in Showler and Sinfield, 1981, for a good discussion of the alternative views and the way the debate developed). That range of perspectives is still evident in debates about unemployment today with corresponding implications for the way the related policy issues are identified. It is appropriate to look at the spectrum of perspectives in a little more detail, and at the policy prescriptions associated with them.

The most widely accepted modification of the perspective on the labour market offered by early classical economic theory involves accepting that there is 'frictional unemployment'. Neither buyers nor sellers of labour have complete information, there are delays as each side learns and adjusts its behaviour. Employers have to find out where there are workers and workers where there are jobs. Each may also have to learn to adjust the 'price' (wage) at which they make their bargain, by reference to what is going on elsewhere in the labour market. The most basic 'policy' associated with this theory involves intervention to speed up the learning process – the establishment of 'labour exchanges' at which the two sides of the labour contract can pool information – employers registering information about jobs and workers registering their availability. Sometimes one or the other of the parties themselves establishes this simple 'market' device. It is also the case that private agencies may meet this need, charging fees to either or both 'sides', but there are collective action barriers to the funding of such agencies (see discussion on p. 31) in that it may not be worth while for any single or small group of people to make the initial investment in an exchange or to sustain its running costs, hence local and national governments have often taken on the responsibility.

The problem of frictional unemployment is complicated by geography. Job opportunities may be declining in one area but increasing in another (this issue has already been discussed above). Systems to facilitate information exchange may be sufficient to deal with this problem, but it may be seen as necessary to attempt to facilitate the movement of either workers or work. In the past the social and economic structures were such that much of the necessary movement was slight and within the boundaries of nation states. Now the adjustment problems may be global. It is to be questioned whether, as the scale of these so-called frictional problems has widened, it remains appropriate for economic analysis to deal with them as if they are simply information and time-related problems. This is particularly the case when the boundaries of nation states (with all their influences not only on population movements but also on forms of economic organisation) get in the way of adjustments. It is little consolation to the victims of regional or national decline to be told that their problems merely arise from friction in the behaviour of labour markets. They are likely to look to corrective actions which either involve radical state interventions along the lines discussed above or extended income maintenance policies.

The Keynesian perspective

More radical perspectives in economic theory move away from widening the usage of the term 'friction'. They suggest that economies may be working in ways which simply do not create enough jobs. Within orthodox economics the main version of this thesis is associated with the work of John Maynard Keynes (1936). His thesis rests principally upon the weaknesses in the micro-economic theory of labour market adjustment which arise because of the fact that a series of rational behavioural responses by individuals produce collective effects which deepen the problems to which people are trying to adjust. Hence, an entrepreneur adapts to deterioration in the market (which may be induced initially by a variety of phenomena including bad harvests and wars) by cutting back and becoming more reluctant to take risks. That adaptation, however, simply exacerbates the problem for others. It reduces the work available and the money circulating in the economy. In doing so it makes similar adjustments with similar effects necessary for others. A vicious circle ensues. Hence the trade cycle, discovered in the nineteenth century, involved a set of socially reinforcing activities by individuals which deepened tendencies to economic decline. Eventually individuals realise they have over-reacted and a recovery will begin. There are corresponding alternative effects as conditions get better, creating a tendency to excessive optimism, leading to inflation and ultimately to a crisis. The next downward movement may then not need any external phenomena to trigger it, it will simply be the ultimate reaction to an excessive upswing.

The processes above are made more complex by the existence of financial markets, where speculative behaviour amplifies the processes described. Since such markets have grown massively since Keynes's time this is an aspect of his work which is being emphasised in contemporary reassertions of the Keynesian position:

> *. . . Keynes was the father of the argument that the financial markets are inveterately short-term; that their preference for liquidity oppresses the real economy. His famous dictum that 'when the capital development of a country becomes a by-product of the activities of a casino, the job is likely to be ill-done' captures the essence of his position . . .. It is one of the most devastating critiques of the stock market as a means of channelling resources into investment ever written. (Hutton, 1995, pp. 243–4)*

Keynes's view was that governments could act against these market phenomena. They could invest, in a sense speculating against a declining market. Correspondingly they could take money out of the system in a boom. In this discussion the concern is, however, with the policies recommended to deal with a depression. While they may be seen as quintessentially economic policies their social effects are of fundamental importance. The Keynesian strategy to deal with a depression involves efforts to generate employment. Indeed, for technical reasons to do with differences in the propensity to save or spend in different sectors of society, Keynes saw the direct creation of work as a particularly appropriate measure.

Another significant feature of Keynes's perspective is that while it involves a view that markets will not easily adjust naturally, it is expected that they will eventually. Their adjustment can be nudged along by government 'management of the economy'. By contrast therefore with economic perspectives deriving from socialist thinkers, and particularly from the work of Karl Marx, Keynes's view was that capitalism can be a viable system to generate economic well-being for all, if it is wisely managed by governments.

It is important to interpose at this stage that the Keynesian view about the role governments can play in the management of the economy has been interpreted in alternative ways. Weir (in Weir *et al.*, 1988, p. 171) contrasts the 'social Keynesianism' suggested by the account offered above with '"commercial Keynesianism" – tax cuts aimed at stimulating the economy with a minimum of government direction'. The latter approach, Weir suggests, has always been dominant in the United States.

The socialist perspective

Nineteenth- and early twentieth-century socialists saw the trade cycle as evidence of the fundamental instability of capitalism and argued that its damaging swings would simply increase to crisis proportions (in addition to the work of Marx the contribution of Hobson, 1896, is important). The fact that governments have been partly able to bring these under control have contributed to undermining the socialist predictions (though the main problem for socialist thought has not been this but rather the difficulties that have been encountered by socialist methods of management of the economy and state – a topic beyond the scope of this discussion).

Other aspects of the socialist critique of capitalism still, however, deserving of attention are the following:

1. Suggestions that there is little justification for the assumption that 'in the long run' the supply of labour and demand for labour can balance naturally in a market system.
2. Arguments that in order to work efficiently the capitalist labour market needs a 'reserve army of labour' operating at the margins of the system, available for work at low wages when needed but easily discarded.

Both of these propositions have implications for social policy in a capitalist economic system. The first suggests that casualties of the system will be endemic. The second indicates that capitalism is likely to need policies which hold that reserve army in a state in which it is fit for work and unlikely to place conditions on its availability – in other words a benefit system which is adequate for the survival of the reserve army but not generous enough to make offers of work seem unattractive when they come along.

The causes of unemployment in the modern world

It has been shown, then, that the spectrum of views about unemployment range from those which see it as merely a consequence of 'friction' in the working of the labour market, through views which see macro-economic management as crucial if unemployment is to be avoided, to a perspective which sees unemployment as an endemic feature of capitalism. To explore these views further in relation to an era in which unemployment has become very widespread and the comfortable middle-ground position offered by Keynesianism has become seen as problematical, it is necessary to look at the following:

1. The implications of the heterogeneity of the labour force.
2. The arguments about technological unemployment.
3. The issues about the 'price' of labour.

All of these, furthermore, need considering in the context of the increasing 'globalisation' of the economy, which makes it difficult for national policies to address economic problems without reference to what is going on in the rest of the world.

A potential workforce is a diverse collection of people, with varied innate abilities and acquired skills. The jobs available to them are also diverse, particularly in an advanced industrial economy. These considerations greatly enhance the difficulties of matching supply and demand. Labour market friction theory has been prepared to try to come to terms with this, yet it typically addresses 'mismatch' as a labour supply problem. Two important social policy implications follow from that approach. Where the issue is one of a lack of people with relevant skills, training programmes are likely to be recommended. Where the issue is one of redundant skills which workers are reluctant to abandon or wage demands based upon those skills, any benefit support system is likely to be expected to apply pressures for change.

A more sophisticated approach to labour market complexity has recognised that it tends to generate a stratified system in which it is more appropriate to speak of a number of separate labour markets rather than a single one. The kinds of bargain reached between workers and employers in these different markets are likely to be radically different. Pools of available workers are likely to be regarded as finite. Employers may prefer to poach from rivals rather than look outside a conventionally defined pool. This stratified view of the labour market will be reinforced by social status, and by racial and gender divisions in society. Various analysts have written of 'dual' or more complicatedly 'segmented' labour markets (Doeringer and Piore, 1971; Gordon, 1972; Aglietta, 1987). Policy responses, including other social policies, are likely to reflect and reinforce these divisions (this is discussed further in Chapter 11). The relationship between the factors which push up wage costs and the factors which cause unemployment was assumed by Keynesian theory to render it impossible for rising unemployment and rising inflation to occur together (stagflation). Modern analyses have sought to come to terms with the breakdown of that assumed relationship. One suggested explanation for that can be found in labour market segmentation. It is suggested that legal and trade-union enforced mechanisms protect those in jobs from the economic pressures experienced in the depressed labour market for those in weaker 'market situations'. The former continue to pressure for wage rises unaffected by the overall weakness of the labour market (see Jackman in McLaughlin, 1992; Ormerod in Michie and Grieve Smith, 1994).

The wider issue of 'technological unemployment' involves the suggestion that what the modern world is facing is not simply a set of issues about skill mismatch but the wholesale disappearance of employment opportunities. This is particularly linked with the decline of manufacturing employment in contexts in which productivity per worker is growing dramatically in some sectors. While the usage of the term 'unemployment' in English was identified earlier as not much more than a hundred years old, angry movements protesting that machinery was replacing people in employment can be found much earlier. In agriculture the introduction of the wheat-threshing machine provoked riots in Britain at the very beginning of the nineteenth century and a little later protests about the displacement of hand-loom weavers by machines played a significant role in early working-class radicalism (Burnett, 1994).

The displacement of the hand-loom weavers has been much analysed by historians anxious to use it in support of modern arguments about the strengths and weaknesses of capitalism (see Burnett, 1994, ch. 2, for an account of this debate). But it may be doubted as to whether lessons for the modern world can be learnt from this painstaking examination of historical evidence. Contemporary technological change is taking place in a much more globalised economic system in which the advanced economies face considerable difficulties either in developing adjustments in their business systems which will effectively compete with newly emergent economies or in establishing new consumer needs in the 'first' world which can be met by vast new labour-intensive investments. The weaknesses of the global economic system relate more to difficulties in overcoming distributional problems than to difficulties in solving production ones. The relatively productive prosperous economies are left with a range of difficulties in providing work for all, requiring social policy responses *either* in the form of deliberately government-created work *or* subsidised work *or* social benefits.

The previous paragraph, however, sets out one view (which the author finds plausible), but there are others. The most salient alternative is one which attributes the problem of unemployment in the advanced 'western' economies to the high price of labour, and goes on to lay much of the responsibility for this upon social policies (broadly defined) and social benefit systems in particular (see OECD, 1994b, for a 'moderate' version of this thesis). The broad point has already been mentioned – the existence of a variety of measures such as laws which protect workers' jobs and laws which strengthen trade unions' capacities to protect jobs and wages. The more specific point concerns the levels of benefits available to those out of work. This means in particular benefits for the unemployed, but as was demonstrated in Chapter 4 other benefits – for the elderly, the sick and parents – may also have labour market effects.

Income maintenance measures for unemployed people may, by virtue of the levels at which they are pitched, exercise an effect upon the labour market by establishing a minimum, below which individuals will simply refuse to accept work. Typically, benefit systems for unemployed people are accompanied by rules which enable the authorities to cut or totally eliminate support for those who leave jobs, refuse work or do not try to seek employment. There is, however, a moral problem, and perhaps a political problem, if these sanctions are applied when the jobs available are remunerated at levels which bring individual or household incomes below state-prescribed minimum benefit levels. If these levels have been proclaimed to be based upon any notion of minimum human needs, there will be an obvious inconsistency.

One way round this problem is for the state to provide benefits for people to supplement the remuneration from very low-waged work. Yet this involves, for the hard-nosed defender of 'laissez-faire' in the labour market, just as much a state distortion of the economy as any other benefit or subsidy. For the more pragmatic members of this school of thought this combination of economic and social policy is perhaps legitimate, but it has been shown in Chapter 4 that this sort of intervention faces problems such as the 'poverty trap'.

There are two further points to be made about the general stance of those who blame contemporary unemployment upon 'generous' benefit systems. The first point is a theoretical one. The notion that the price of labour can be reduced to a level at which the market will clear seems to be based upon the nonsensical view that there is no practical lower limit for wages – even if the worker starves. Nineteenth-century 'classical economists' put that theory to the test in the Irish famine with appalling consequences (see Woodham Smith, 1962). Adjusting the benefit system to ensure, moreover, that the starving will stagger to work conflicts, as suggested above, with the need for a reserve army of labour fit to work.

The other point has also already been made that matching supply and demand implies overcoming massive skill imbalance or geographical imbalance problems (including supra-national ones) which presuppose substantial expenditures by some agency. In this sense protecting the income of a middle-aged redundant skilled manual worker in a declining region may seem a relatively cheap alternative. Certainly it is an alternative that will have no significant adverse effect upon the working of the labour market.

If the redundant industrial workers of Europe, like many of their nineteenth-century compatriots driven off the land, were prepared to make the colossal sacrifice of sailing to the labour-hungry markets of today (in the 'little tigers' of East Asia, for example), they would not receive even the chilly welcome offered by the America of old. Indeed the limited migration in the Pacific – from mainland China and from the Philippines, for example – is kept under close state surveillance, and much of it is illegal and highly risky.

This section has indicated the range of alternative explanations of contemporary high unemployment in many advanced economies, and the kinds of policies used or proposed to try to deal with the issue. Since countries differ in their unemployment rates comparisons between them are used in the arguments about appropriate policies. It is necessary therefore to look at some of the evidence on unemployment rates. But any presentation of data on unemployment needs to be preceded by a discussion of some of the difficulties about the data sources. These difficulties derive from the problem that unemployment itself is not as simple a phenomenon as it appears to be. 'Facts' about the incidence of unemployment are nearly as fiercely politically contested as the explanations for those facts.

Issues about unemployment statistics

The decisions people make about whether actively to seek work are going to depend upon how they obtain resources to maintain themselves and upon the other activities available to them. For example, on reaching a state's compulsory school-leaving age a young person may be able to get further education and may be able to persuade his or her parents to support this venture. At the other extreme he or she may want to, and need to, seek work as soon as possible. There are other options – private income or a parent's support may make possible a round-the-world trip or participation in other leisure activities before seeking work. A similar set of options may be open to someone towards the end of their life, to choose when to leave the labour market and to live on resources accumulated during the working life.

The state may have a role to play in some of these decisions about whether to work or not. Furthermore the state's role may be as a provider of incomes under various justifications. Reference has already been made to the discussion in Chapter 4 about the way in which the borderline between benefit recipience because of unemployment and that because of retirement, sickness or family commitments may be hard to determine, and may be determined as much by administrative rules relating to benefit entitlement as by whether or not work is really wanted.

Hence, there is a need for a way of defining unemployment which distinguishes between worklessness because work cannot be found and formal worklessness by choice. At the same time it is not satisfactory to fall back upon the classification of people in terms of the administrative categories associated with the available state support systems.

Data on unemployment may be derived from answers to survey questions about aspirations. The figures derived from this source may be highly dependent on the questions asked. For example, alternative ways of surveying this issue may range from simple enquiries about whether people would like to obtain paid work, through questions like 'Are you actively seeking work?', to interrogations which try to establish whether positive job search behaviour is occurring. Ironically, results are going to depend upon opportunities as well as aspirations. Surveys at times of acute job shortage are likely to underestimate ideal aspirations.

Alternatively data may be derived from official administrative records, based upon numbers registering with employment offices or claiming benefits. Findings based upon these sources will be highly sensitive to administrative rules, which encourage or discourage formal registration. Obviously, for example, a register based upon claims for benefits will exclude those – who by virtue of dependency rules, age or means tests – are not entitled to them. At the same time they may include people who need to register to get benefits but who have no wish to obtain work.

Another problem about data on unemployment is that they will be collected and published by those who wish to make political points. In fact much of the collecting of data is done by governments who, while they may profess to desire to measure unemployment accurately for the purposes of economic planning, are likely to have an interest in being able to show that they are doing well in dealing with a problem on which they experience strong criticism.

Overall, there is a problem about the extent to which people's perceptions of the evidence on unemployment are influenced by their views about how the phenomenon is caused. Those on the 'right' who emphasise the ways in which the effective workings of markets are inhibited are likely to deduct from their figures the people whom they deem to be not making 'real' efforts to find work – there are some of these, but to what extent should counting them extend to all people unwilling to go anywhere and do anything at any price. The 'right' has also made some attempts to estimate the size of a naturally difficult-to-count group, people who say they are unemployed when they are not in order to cheat the benefit system (attempts to estimate these from aggregate data get into some heroic guesses – see Hakim in McLaughlin, 1992, for a discussion of this topic).

Those who take a diametrically opposed view to that of the 'right' may suggest that the real unemployment figures should contain: pensioners who would really still like to be at work, disabled people who could work in sheltered conditions, parents who would seek work if they could solve their child-care problems cheaply, and so on. In societies where there have been traditionally severe barriers to female labour market participation and those barriers are gradually and rather reluctantly being brought down, there is an obvious difficulty about the definition of the size of female unemployment. A related measurement problem here concerns the extent to which part-time workers (another largely female group) who would ideally like more work should be included in a count of the unemployed.

Finally, it is worth commenting on the relationship between this measurement problem and the classical economic assumptions about the ultimate feasibility of matching supply and demand. The size of the potential workforce is itself influenced by the demand for labour. It is not a relatively fixed commodity like land, or one the availability of which rises or falls relatively predictably over time like some natural resources. While demography plays a part in determining the size of the labour force, actual labour market participation may shift in quite a volatile way over a short period of time in response to changing demand. This theme will be picked up again in a rather different way in Chapter 12.

Differences between nations in the incidence of unemployment and attempts to draw policy lessons from those differences

The preceding section has provided a substantial 'health warning' about comparative unemployment statistics. Their compilers, organisations like the OECD, try to ensure that common assumptions are applied, but there are still problems. The statistics are most useful if looked at essentially in fairly gross comparative terms – if the rate in country x is twice that in country y there are clearly some rather different things going on even if the accuracy of specific figures cannot be trusted in either. Inevitably in practice a great deal of attention focuses upon the outliers in a world table, rather than on comparisons between countries close together in the distribution. In this context changes over time are also significant if countries' own rates change dramatically in a period of time (as has certainly been the case in much of

Table 8.1 Comparative unemployment rates (percentages)

Country	1962	1972	1982	1992
Austria	1.5	1.0	3.1	3.5
Australia	2.8	2.6	7.1	10.7
Canada	5.4	6.2	10.9	11.2
Denmark	2.1	1.6	9.8	11.3
France	1.4	2.8	8.1	10.2
Japan	1.3	1.4	2.4	2.2
Netherlands	0.8	2.9	11.4	6.7
Norway	2.1	1.7	2.6	5.9
Sweden	1.1	2.2	2.6	4.8
Switzerland	0.2	0.0	1.2	9.0
UK	2.9	4.2	11.3	10.0
USA	5.3	5.5	9.5	7.3

Source: OECD *Economic Outlook*, quoted in Layard, R., Nickell, S. and Jackman, R. (1994) *The Unemployment Crisis*, Oxford: Oxford University Press; reproduced by permission of the OECD.

Europe in the recent past) (see European Commission, 1994, ch. 1, for a discussion of some of the problems of comparison).

Table 8.1 sets out data on a cross-section of OECD member countries. The selection of these has been influenced by a wish to illustrate some differences that have been the subject of debate. The discussion that follows will deal with aspects of that debate, particularly its concern with the impact of policy upon unemployment. Figures are set out for four dates at ten-year intervals. There are great fluctuations between ten-year points, but in order to avoid an overwhelming number of dates this limited selection has been used. In fact the dates chosen standardise for the effects of temporary fluctuations rather well because none of them were particularly high points in the international trade cycle.

Discussions about policies to combat unemployment tend to be polarised in terms of political ideology. The position of the 'right', as has already been seen, suggests that the problem of unemployment is best contained by a minimum of interference with markets and by severely restricted benefits for the unemployed. The directly contrasting position, the 'left', requires governments to be active in influencing the labour markets, to be major actors in the economy themselves and to be generous providers of benefits.

In this debate a contrast is sometimes drawn between the liberated 'free market' economy and the highly regulated 'corporatist' economy. In these terms, the countries in the above list can perhaps be divided into: Japan, Switzerland and the United States in the first camp, with the United Kingdom joining them after 1979; Sweden, Norway with perhaps Austria, Denmark,

France and the Netherlands in the second. Note that this is a dual variant of the Esping-Andersen three-type social policy model discussed in Chapter 3. Australia and Canada are seen as difficult cases to 'fit' in either approach to modelling.

Using this contrast, which perspective 'wins' the argument? Probably the answer is neither. In the first group Japan shines through as a success (though at the time of writing even that country seems to be running into difficulties) and the United States seems to have avoided the worst of the impact of world economic problems since the end of the 1970s. Something is now, however, going very wrong in Switzerland, and there are grounds for arguing from these data that joining the 'hard-liners' has done the United Kingdom nothing but harm. In the second group Sweden and Norway stand out as relatively good performers throughout the period, though in both cases the relative rises to 1992 have been very high. Austria, often a special case for social policy analysts – as a corporatist rather than socialist system (Mishra, 1984) – also has a good record. The European Economic Community (EEC) countries in this group – Denmark, France and the Netherlands – had poor records by both of the later dates (incidentally one EEC country that normally appears in discussions like this has been left out, that is Germany where unification makes for comparison difficulties).

The difficulty with this sort of analysis is that special considerations need to be introduced in order to take it any further. Therborn carried out a comparative study on this theme in 1986 in which he concluded that any explanation of *Why Some Peoples are More Unemployed than Others* (the title of his book) had to look at the policy record. The fact that Japan and Switzerland (at the time of his study) were found along with the Scandinavian countries and Austria amongst the high performers could, he argued, be put down to peculiar interventionist policies of their own. In the Swiss case that intervention involved policies to move the 'reserve army' in and out of the country as 'guest workers' (this has probably now become more difficult to achieve, see Castles and Miller, 1993, p. 69). The argument with regard to Japan is more complex, but involves saying more or less that, despite being a comparative low welfare policy country, Japan is more corporatist, more ready to engineer employment than it appears. With regard to the high welfare policy countries which have been nevertheless poor performers with regard to unemployment – notably France and the Netherlands – Therborn's conclusions are complex, but again involve arguing that there has been a lack of a consistent policy approach.

A more recent comparative analysis by three economists (Layard *et al.*, 1994) combines political and economic explanation, and in doing so finds some grounds for concern about the impact of income maintenance benefits. They draw a contrast between the poor recent record of the EEC countries and the relative success in the former European Free Trade Area countries (ironically most of them are joining the European Union at the time of writing) and Japan. They argue on the basis of their econometric analysis:

> *This appears to be due to differences in social institutions, with the latter countries having highly corporatist wage-setting arrangements and/or shorter entitlements to benefits (combined in Sweden with major training and employment programmes for the unemployed). These arrangements both inhibited unemployment's original rise and ensured that unemployment did not persist. (Layard,* et al., *1994, p. 8)*

In Table 8.1 there are three other countries about which little has been said. In the case of the United States what has been significant is that while unemployment was relatively high there in 1962 and 1972, and indeed earlier, that country did not experience the subsequent big rise experienced in the EEC. Layard, Nickell and Jackman (1994) suggest that the limited duration of income maintenance benefits helped to prevent a sustained rise, but they also note that the greater self-sufficiency of that economy may be relevant. Such a view seems to be supported by the evidence of the way Canada went from bad to worse in a period in which she agonised about her relationship to the powerful American economy. Finally, Australia is an example of a country with strong unions, limited welfare systems and little political intervention in the labour market which slipped badly in the 'employment league' over this period. However, perhaps the central Australian problem involves adaptation to the changing economic structure of the Pacific: this has become a source of a challenge there and even more so in New Zealand, a country where a most dramatic rise in worklessness has occurred.

It is appropriate to consider further the two contrasting strategies for coping with unemployment. The data have suggested the comparison is difficult and that broader economic trends – affecting the EEC, the European Free Trade Association (EFTA), the Americas and Australasia rather differently – need to be taken into account. But the two strategies may also be seen as competing fashions – one championed by Sweden under social-democratic rule, the other championed by the United States. Weaker versions of the two approaches figure in some of the arguments Britain has been having with the rest of the European Union. In economic terms this has been seen as a contrast between two alternative strategies to cope with competition in the modern world. One involves lowering labour costs by attacking not only wage levels but also conditions of work and the security of workers. Implicit in this, at least in the British case, is the encouragement of temporary and part-time work together with small (often one person) businesses taking contracts from larger enterprises at terms employees would never tolerate. The alternative is the development of a highly trained and motivated labour force which, in return for high rewards, good conditions and job security, will play a role in pushing forward technological change. Hence:

> *The dispute between the British government and the other European Community governments over the Social Chapter can clearly be interpreted in these terms, with those supporting the Social Chapter seeking to pursue the high-wage/high productivity route. (Sawyer in Michie and Grieve Smith, 1994, p. 181)*

Perhaps, however, it is not so much a matter of choice between two routes as the development of a dual structure (see p. 187 above) in which the participation of some is encouraged through training and good working conditions while the 'reserve army of labour' is disciplined with little job security and poor benefits.

This return to the dual or segmented labour market theme is a reminder that to compare countries simply in terms of unemployment rates may offer a misleading impression of labour market policy. Much the same point was made in Chapter 5 about health indices. An apparently satisfactory national unemployment rate may conceal the fact that the experience of worklessness is very concentrated upon a limited group (Sinfield, 1981). British data show that there is a relatively small segment of the population with experience of unemployment, but within that segment long-term and frequent unemployment is very likely. Minority racial group membership, low skill, inferior education and residence in a deprived region are all strongly correlated with experience of unemployment (Pissarides and Wadsworth in McLaughlin, 1992).

Another feature of a segmented labour market in which income maintenance benefits are not easily accessed by disadvantaged groups is that formal data on worklessness can be relatively hidden (see Metcalf in McLaughlin, 1992). That is the potential flaw in Layard *et al.*'s assumption, quoted above, that restricted benefit durations limit unemployment. Formal data sets tend to underestimate levels of unemployment amongst women who are often discouraged from active efforts to seek work and who tend to have difficulty in claiming benefits for themselves.

It may be argued that social policy should have a role in alleviating inegalitarian consequences even if it can do nothing about the incidence of unemployment as a whole. This is an argument both for generous income maintenance benefits for the workless, particularly the long-term unemployed, and for a concentration of the efforts of training schemes upon that group. To some extent the targeting of schemes like the European Social Fund does aim to achieve the latter. The problem is that the orthodox economic perspective sees national efficiency as best advanced by limiting benefits to the 'reserve army' and targeting training upon those most likely to be effective labour market participants.

The economic efficiency approach to unemployment always sees it as a problem to be weighed in the balance against another problem, inflation, in a post-Keynesian trade-off (but see Ormerod, 1994, for a critique of economic thinking on this association). It is inclined to be more concerned about the under-use of resources than about the social waste of unemployment, and even the under-use of resources may be seen as advantageous inasmuch as the workless constitute a 'reserve army' waiting on the side, making a contribution to the disciplining of those in work. Hence, social policies for the unemployed are principally concerned to deal with supply of labour rather than demand for labour issues, and even radicals easily fall into the economistic view that a good supply (a well-trained potential labour force) will create its own demand.

Influencing choices by employers

The discussion has moved from that of policy influences upon labour supply and labour demand to a general discussion of unemployment. But there are two other ways in which public policies may influence the labour market – by influencing who employers choose for work and by influencing the terms of the labour contract.

Influencing choices by employers may consist of preventing the employment of particular people. Alternatively it may involve preventing discrimination and trying to ensure the employment of particular groups. In historical order state interventions to prevent certain choices by employers came first. Many of the laws seeking to do this have subsequently been abandoned. As noted on p. 178, in various countries laws were passed limiting the employment of women and children. Employment of the latter is still strongly regulated while laws preventing female employment are now widely regarded as unjustifiably discriminatory. There are disputes about the origins of laws of this kind: were they humanitarian interventions to prevent exploitation of the weak and vulnerable, or were they designed to protect the work opportunities of adult male workers? (Walby, 1986).

Even more contentious state interventions to prevent some individuals getting employment were laws such as the 'apartheid' laws in South Africa or the laws restricting the activities of Jews in Nazi Germany. Would it be stretching the term 'social policy' too far to consider these here? These laws were intentionally premised upon 'social goals', albeit ones most of us regard as obnoxious. By contrast an important area of state intervention into the field of employment which can readily be described as social policy involves legislation to try to outlaw discrimination by employers. Such legislation while having social effects does not fall outside liberal free market ideas. On the contrary, assuming most discrimination violates economic rationality, this kind of state intervention may be welcomed by market liberals inasmuch as it involves forcing employers to choose the best qualified regardless of race, sex, age or disability.

More controversial is legislation which requires some form of positive discrimination. It is important not to automatically characterise this as legislation which forces employers to disregard the best qualified. This may be the case, but very often it can be shown that apparently race-blind, gender-blind, etc., procedures have implicit biases which do not simply favour the 'best' applicant. Earlier discrimination by others – schools, for example – may have 'loaded the dice' in favour of white males. It also needs to be borne in mind that most selection processes are qualitative and unscientific, and that selecting the alleged 'best' may not be very crucial when most applicants could do the job.

Nevertheless, positive discrimination, involving an expectation of quotas of recruits from designated groups, rarely gets official government support. It has been seen as not merely compensating for hidden biases, but also as forcing the choice of less adequate applicants in the interests of counteracting past biases against their race or gender (Edwards, 1987).

One special case of positive discrimination which has received some government support concerns disabled people. British legislation in 1944 imposed a requirement upon firms to aim to achieve a specific proportion of disabled people in their workforce. If below quota they were expected to give priority to disabled persons (Showler, 1976). In practice this legislation was easy to evade and weakly enforced. With the re-emergence of high unemployment and a government disinclined to give social goals any priority in employment policy this legislation has become more or less a dead letter.

Imposing conditions on labour market contracts

The last form of state intervention to be considered is an aspect of social policy brought into prominence in Europe by the European Union. This concerns the imposition by the state of rules relating to contracts of employment. In the European Union context older traditions of state paternalism and modern efforts by unions to secure standards for work contracts have received support from a recognition that if labour costs vary significantly between countries because of different employment standards then the countries with lower standards will secure competitive advantages. There is also a concern that if labour mobility is to be encouraged workers will want to take work-related rights with them as they move.

This perspective is opposed by an alternative view upheld by free market liberals that contracts of work should be freely negotiated by employer and employee. To some extent this view has also been upheld by trade unions representing groups of skilled workers who have been able to drive their own bargains with employers. A difference of view on this subject has been part of the conflict between Britain and the rest of the European Union, mentioned earlier in this chapter.

The items which come under this heading are many. They range from comparatively uncontroversial rules about health and safety, through rules about hours and holidays, guarantees of maternity and sick leave, rules about participation rights and union membership; to rules which affect pay rates themselves. While these have been given particular attention within a contemporary European debate they are important features of employment legislation in many countries, including some of the East Asian countries like Japan and Taiwan which are regarded in the West as free market economies.

In the context of the high unemployment rates discussed above, rules relating to the terms under which part-time or temporary work contracts are given may be important aspects of social policy. There are substantial differences in the extent to which these forms of work are available in different countries, having an important impact upon the terms available to women in the labour market.

Finally, perhaps the most important intervention in this category is legislation to try to impose minimum wages. This issue was first raised in the discussion of models of social welfare in Chapter 3, where it was suggested that a minimum wage might offer a firm foundation for an egalitarian social welfare system, even for one with limited rights to income maintenance benefits. The presence of a minimum wage can set a satisfactory floor level for income maintenance policies and avoid some of the problems of comparisons between incomes in and out of work.

It is important, however, to recognise the difficulties with policies designed to guarantee minimum wages, and to acknowledge that there is a lack of comparative studies which explain what effect minimum wage policies really have (see a review of this issue in Commission on Social Justice, 1994). A statutory minimum wage may be set so low that it has only a symbolic effect upon real reward patterns. It may operate merely to set a low baseline from which all wage negotiators start, and its up-rating may have a predictable inflationary effect. Alternatively, it may be widely ignored in actual pay contracts.

From the economistic, free labour market perspective minimum wage legislation may reduce the amount of work available for all. It will certainly affect international competitiveness. Perhaps in this case the choice is between the segmented labour market, with the disadvantaged segments in the labour force securing remuneration below the sort of levels a minimum wage would guarantee, or a less segmented system with a minimum wage but higher levels of unemployment. Certainly, it has to be acknowledged that the ideal of a satisfactory minimum wage is easier to sustain in a fully employed society. Whether or not these two aspirations are conflicting takes the discussion back to the argument between the two models of the labour market – the competitive free market versus the 'social market'. The concluding section of this chapter summarises that argument.

Conclusions

Adam Smith the 'founding father' of classical economics was quite clear that the market systems operate within a social and cultural climate which both underpin them and give moral support to them. That is particularly the case with labour markets:

> *. . . the labour market cannot be visualised as a market like any other . . .. Human beings are not tradeable commodities. As . . . Robert Solow argues, the theoretical categories that might be applied to analysing trade in chocolate bars, fish or computers cannot be extended to labour because we have to confront the issues of fairness, morale and human motivation that permeate human action. Orthodox classical theory completely misinterprets these forces, instead imposing a simple economism that can only explain part of the story. (Hutton, 1995, pp. 99–100)*

Accordingly labour market intervention of some kind is ubiquitous. The idea that there is, in particular places, or has been, at particular times, a pure labour market unaffected by social or political considerations is a myth perpetrated by simplistic economic theory. Even punitive measures against the unemployed and against labour organisations were state labour market measures of a kind.

Hence, contemporary debate about the way the *nation state* should 'manage' the labour market can increasingly be identified as involving two distinctive positions, as follows:

1. The advocates of a 'free economy and a strong state' (Gamble, 1994) who see a need for an authoritarian state to attack trade unions and social policies which raise the price of labour to ensure that the nation competes effectively in world markets.
2. The exponents of a view that the best way to enhance national efficiency is for the state to play a positive role in stimulating high-technology investment and that this involves investment in labour too, in both education and training measures; generally this perspective regards welfare concerns as appropriate, seeing high quality in the labour force as more important than low costs.

The emphasis upon these as remedies advocated for 'nation states' was deliberate. Both may be seen as strategies which take solving national problems in a global context as involving a search for competitive advantage. The first suggests that the industrialised nations can best compete with the developing ones by being more like them. The second suggests that it is possible for some nations to maintain technological advantages over others.

In the management of their economies governments are using both strategies in different combinations. In doing so they may be enhancing divisions in the labour force. Severely marginalised 'reserve armies of labour' are growing, with people forced to compete for scarce, insecure poverty-level jobs. The American record in keeping unemployment down needs to be judged in terms of the extraordinarily low wages paid to many in that society – 'nearly one job in every five in the US does not carry sufficient income to raise a family of four' (Hutton, 1995, p. 19, quoting Robert Reich, the US Labor Secretary). Here is a 'third world' economy within a 'first world' country.

At the same time the high-technology response to problems of competition involves a heavy emphasis upon flexibility and insecurity in the labour force. Endless popular accounts of how we should all adapt to the future suggest that we must be prepared to retrain or change jobs several times in a lifetime. High rewards are increasingly linked to short-term contracts, productivity-related bonus payments, and so on. It is far from evident that increasingly technological employment can generate these benefits for whole populations.

If either development is seen out of a national context in a world economy there must be questions to be asked about their sustainability. The model, on the one hand, which stresses wage level competition offers no way forward for the economies where low wages are endemic. If, on the other hand, governments in these economies can follow the East Asian path of growth they must intensify competition for those who have already chosen the high-technology alternative. Economics, the 'dismal science', seems either way to present a model of remorseless competition.

Yet, an optimistic view of world economic development stresses that we are collectively getting more prosperous. If the 'luddites', who opposed technological change in the early years of the industrial revolution because it was destroying jobs, had had their way we would all remain very poor. The challenge for the modern world is to find ways which *either* distribute jobs *or* redistribute the benefits from production in ways which enable all to share continuing global growth. That is a social policy task.

Guide to further reading

The OECD Jobs Study (1994b) and Layard, Nickell and Jackman's *The Unemployment Crisis* (1994) sets out what is broadly the conventional wisdom on this policy area. Some of the essays in Michie and Grieve Smith's edited collection *Unemployment in Europe* (1994) offer challenges to this. A stimulating, but unfortunately now rather dated comparative discussion of government responses to unemployment is to be found in Therborn's *Why Some Peoples are More Unemployed than Others* (1986).

The importance of policies dealing with employment and the labour market within the European Union is inevitably stimulating a variety of comparative work. The Commission's own *Employment in Europe* (1994) is an important source of data and analysis. Gold's *The Social Dimension* (1993) is a good factual source on European policies while Simpson and Walker's *Europe: For Richer or Poorer?* (1993) and Coenen and Leisink's *Work and Citizenship in the New Europe* (1994) are two edited collections which contain some thought-provoking essays.

The globalisation theme, relevant to this chapter and to Chapter 12, is readably and challengingly explored in Lipietz's *Towards a New Economic Order* (1992) and Reich's *The Work of Nations* (1991).

CHAPTER NINE

Education policy

Introduction

While there is a great deal of formal and institutionalised activity in the field of education, it is also the case that in many respects individuals educate themselves. There are parallels here with health. It is not unknown for children to teach themselves to read. Once they have that capacity many children secure a great deal of knowledge for themselves. Before the coming of universal formal education in many societies many people were self-educated, and colloquially people still refer to the knowledge and wisdom acquired through participation in everyday life. Later in the education process some people undertake higher education part-time and with a minimum of formal help, and some students perform adequately on full-time courses with little attendance at lectures and seminars. Finally, the highest level of formal education, studying for a PhD, is widely acknowledged as a lonely process in many subjects, where self-motivation is vital and contact with others often minimal.

While in all these cases the role of the formal education system may be low this does not mean that other people are irrelevant. To emphasise the 'self' in the acquisition of education is not necessarily to characterise children as 'noble savages' able to develop skills and knowledge without the support of others. Whether education is acquired within or outside formal institutions the success of individuals is likely to depend a great deal upon the support of families and friends. With such support a great deal can be achieved with a minimum of formal provision, as in earlier times when education was simply a family matter. Without the support of family and friends formal inputs may be of little use. When, later in this chapter, some of the issues about differential educational achievement are explored it will be found that alongside the issues about differences in access to 'inputs' there are also many issues about the implications of family, and social, support and encouragement.

These issues about support are also relevant to issues about the role of the market in relation to education. Clearly education is something which may be purchased, and the discussion below will look at some issues about the place of privately purchased education systems in societies. However, it is important to recognise that there are a range of ways in which publicly provided education systems are supported by private expenditures. The costs of education extend beyond the costs of the provision of teachers and buildings to, for example, books, writing materials and technology (computers, laboratory equipment, etc.). There are many situations in which all or part of these costs are met by parents or students. Some of the more impoverished education systems depend heavily on these additional private inputs, but even in the best-funded systems there is scope for private expenditures by individuals to enhance the resources available to them. This kind of private supplementation of a public system depends heavily on the commitments of individuals and families and accordingly influences educational inequalities.

The cost issues may extend further. There may be costs of travel to schools and colleges. There may be maintenance costs – for food and accommodation – which are additional to the living costs to be met by families, once pupils are there. Finally there are what are called 'opportunity costs', participation in education may be at the expense of other activities. Those other activities may include work, so families have to forgo the earnings of children and young people to enable them to secure education. Thus, while public education systems are very important in industrialised and urbanised societies, there will be many ways in which their use both requires the support of families and imposes costs upon them.

The point above about 'opportunity costs' also draws attention to the fact that the motivation of individuals and families in respect of education may be influenced by the extent to which it facilitates entry into an occupation. Looking at the same issue from the point of view of an economic enterprise it may want to recruit educated employees. As was seen in the discussion of training in Chapter 8 enterprises may train, and by the same token educate (no attempt will be made to draw a distinction between the two here), but they are likely to prefer to be able to recruit people who cost little to train for their specific needs.

What other social institutions play a role in education outside the family and state? Families may band together to meet educational needs collectively. However, there is no need to pause here on this comparatively rare phenomenon. In practice most formal education was developed by others before communities had the resources to contemplate it. The issues about community participation come in therefore as issues about local control of institutions which are provided by others.

A particularly salient institution in the development of education in many societies has been organised religion. Religious bodies have an interest in education as a means to inculcate a set of beliefs. The importance of this depends upon the complexity of the corpus of religious knowledge. It also depends upon the extent to which it is regarded as necessary for the laity to understand the more complex aspects of the religion. In this respect a religion which expects the laity to participate and to share in religious practice, as opposed to one which merely requires them to accept the leadership of a priestly elite, is likely to have a strong interest in education. Some accounts of the origins of education systems in western societies have therefore drawn attention to forms of protestantism which have rejected episcopal leadership and expect the laity to understand the bible. Such a perspective requires bible study and therefore the ability to read, and the capacity to participate in discussions about the interpretation of the scriptures. A feature of the evolution of protestantism after the Reformation was the translation of the bible into vernacular languages from Latin (Green, 1990, ch. 2).

However, it was not only protestantism which took an interest in the development of religion in Christian societies. Once religious factions were in competition for the adherence of the laity the inculcation of belief systems became an issue for all the protagonists. This generalisation seems applicable to Christendom after the Reformation. It may also be an issue today where there are opposing proselytising religions – particularly on the boundaries between the Judaeo-Christian world and the Moslem one.

Here, then, organised religion has been, at least as far as Christendom is concerned, a rival to the state for control over education systems, but in practice the development of nation states in Europe and the conflicts over religion went hand in hand as part of the same story. The identification with, or protection of, particular religious beliefs played a key part in state formation. Later attempts to separate religious controversy from nationalism (in divided states like the Netherlands or in new states created from a mixed body of immigrants as in the United States) made it important for states to try to reach arrangements about the provision of education which prevented religion being a divisive force. Direct state provision of education, with religious teaching banned or carefully controlled, or the disbursement of subsidies to religious bodies in ways designed to accommodate different interests, emerged as alternative ways to deal with this issue (Holmes, 1985).

This introductory section has deliberately avoided the issues about the state as provider of education. The state's role in all industrialised societies is great. This section has endeavoured to indicate the variety of ways in which the family, the market and the 'community' are also involved, but in a variety of complex interactions with the state. The next section looks at this issue the other way round.

Table 9.1 Percentages of education expenditure coming from public sources

Australia	93
Canada	92
Denmark	99
Finland	91
France	84
Germany (West)	96
Greece	92
Ireland	93
Japan	77
Netherlands	95
Norway	98
Switzerland	98
USA	74

Source: OECD (1990) *Education in OECD Countries 1987–88*, Paris: OECD, p. 115; reproduced by permission of the OECD.

Why is the state so dominant in education?

Before exploring the reasons for the dominance of the state in education it is appropriate to set out the evidence on which such a statement is based. Table 9.1 compares public and private expenditure on education for some of the nations on which the OECD have published data (note: various countries are omitted, including two whose policies have been given much attention in this book – the United Kingdom and Sweden – because the OECD report no data on private expenditure in those countries). The point about state dominance is made using expenditure data not provision data – as in other areas of policy, there are significant publicly funded private providers.

In explaining the dominance of public provision, subsidy and control in education, some of the themes explored in Chapter 2 will be re-examined where they have a particular importance or peculiar characteristics in the field of education. Two separate, and sometimes conflicting, themes dominate explanations of the emergence of public educational provisions – one of these concerns will be called 'citizenship' while the other concerns economic interests. These will be examined separately and then brought together (this discussion draws partly upon the work of Archer, 1979, and Green, 1990).

It has already been established that individuals have an interest in securing education. It gives them access to a range of ideas, symbols, beliefs, etc., which may be loosely described as 'culture'. It therefore opens up possibilities of religious and political participation. In this sense education may be seen as being transformed over the ages from a preserve of an elite – kings, nobles and priests – to something more widely shared. Opening the system up in this way was amongst the demands of democratising movements. To what extent did democratisation bring demands for mass education and to what extent did demands for democracy follow upon the expansion of education? The answer is that there was a complex interaction between the two.

It is, however, possible to identify reasons why elites and states promoted education before democratisation. The special interest of religion has already been identified. Furthermore, where a state's claim to rule over a territory was based upon the assertion that there was a single religious community, it was in the state's interest to promote that religion and ensure its dominance. But the establishment of nation states depended on other aspects of culture as well as religion. Language in particular was also important. Also important were things like the acceptance of a common currency, common ways of measuring and common conventional and legal practices to deal with matters of dispute. Education could play an important part in achieving a measure of unity, particularly if it began to impose a common language. Remember that even the main languages of Europe had various forms and that also many smaller languages which survive in various weakened forms today – Welsh, Catalan, Occitan – were once the sole means of communication in their heartlands. Green's (1990) exploration of the role of education in state formation looks at these issues, particularly in relation to Germany in the eighteenth and nineteenth centuries. In some studies of the role of education in colonial societies, and other countries where there is external domination, it has been suggested that education may play a key role in 'cultural domination' (Welch, 1993).

Green's analysis goes on to show how, as the activities of states increased in complexity, so their educational needs increased. The development of an army, a civil service and a legal system had to move outward from dependence upon a narrow educated elite to draw in a wider range of citizens. Moreover even the education of an elite is something that states find it risky or inefficient to leave entirely in private hands. It can in those circumstances be a subversive force, or at least address itself very much to the needs of the elite rather than the state. There have been variations between societies in the extent to which these have been synonymous, depending upon national homogeneity – a bigger problem for Prussia than for England (see Green, 1990). The tendency was inevitability for states to want to control elite education. Then as has been suggested with regard to health policy, aspirations to control tend to draw states into subsidy or direct provision.

The evolution of educational forms, under the dominance of elites, meant that in many respects what was regarded as important – after the basics – was often the subjects that had been studied before the state took an interest.

These derived from the concerns of religious elites, supplemented and sometimes challenged – in the European case – by the classical studies which had had such a liberating impact on the culture of European elites during the Renaissance. This had an interesting impact upon the use of educational qualifications for selection for key roles in society and the public service, which is still a source of controversy. The issue is encapsulated in a comment made in 1833 by Macaulay, a key figure in the development of the British civil service:

> *Whether the English system of education be good or bad is not now the question. Perhaps I may think that too much time is given to the ancient languages and to the abstract sciences. But what then? Whatever be the languages – whatever be the sciences, which it is, in any age or country the fashion to teach, those who become the greatest proficients in those languages and those sciences will generally be the flower of the youth – the most astute – the most industrious – the most ambitious of honourable distinctions. (Hansard, 1833)*

Most defenders of traditional education use a more simplistic argument than Macaulay's: that, despite the fact that much of their content is irrelevant to the tasks subsequently to be performed, their subjects train minds. Macaulay's interesting perspective, on the other hand, is open to alternative interpretations. One is that the education system performs a selection process – sorting out the 'flower of the youth' from others. A sorting process of this kind may have some general benefit. However, it is important to bear in mind that this sorting process may be made more necessary by the shortage of elite positions than by a shortage of people able to assume those positions (this is the 'positional competition' brilliantly analysed by Hirsh, 1976). Another possibility, certainly seen by its critics as a characteristic of British elite education, is that the 'flower of the youth' are in fact pre-selected by their upper-class origins. They then receive a private elite education designed to confirm their status and set them apart from the common herd. Their real advantage lies in their origins not in the fact that they have mastered a classical language.

The discussion of the reasons states may have for involving themselves in education because of concerns about 'citizenship' has been widened by this examination of the education of elites. There are very different concerns embedded in narrow arguments that people should be educated to read and write a common language, and to participate in basic political and legal institutions, than those which relate to the education, socialisation and selection of governing elites. However, the two are connected by democratisation. One key demand of democratic and radical movements has been for state interventions to open up elite education – to ensure that the 'flower of the youth' are drawn from all social groups. Another has been that the education of citizens should be a common process, in which elite and mass share, as far as possible, common educational experiences. That perspective is expressed most effectively in the writings of John Dewey, who was an influential figure in educational thinking in the United States. Dewey argued:

> *The intermingling in the school of youth of different races, different religions and unlike customs creates for all a new and broader environment. Common subject matter accustoms all to a unity of outlook upon a broader horizon than is visible to the members of any group while it is isolated. . . . A society which is mobile . . . must see to it that its members are educated to personal initiative and adaptability. (Dewey, 1966, p. 2)*

This view of education for social mobility in an open and democratic society will be explored further later.

The issue of competition for scarce opportunities touches on the second theme of this section, the 'economic' arguments for education and their influence upon the state. It is not a passion for democratic participation which motivates most pressure for more state support of education – it is a recognition that education provides a 'meal ticket'. This point is deliberately put colloquially. This is because there is a major fallacy that education provides economically *necessary* qualifications. This may be the case. However, the demands of employers for specific or general qualifications and their selection of employees on the basis of educational qualifications should not be regarded as sufficient evidence in itself that the educational efforts that produced those qualifications are essential to the needs of the economy. The key point is that educational achievement, whether intrinsically necessary or not, is often important for individuals in competition for economically advantageous positions in industrial society. This competition is what generates intense concern about education in democratic political systems, stimulating demands for state provisions and expenditure and fuelling the pressure for equality of opportunity in education.

The discussion in the last section, and the consideration of issues about 'externalities' in Chapters 2 and 8, explored the employers' perspective – seeing the state as socialising costs that would otherwise fall on entrepreneurs. This will not be explored further here. It does need saying, however, that employers' interest in education links with the citizenship and culture issues outlined above inasmuch as economic activity requires the use of shared linguistic and mathematical skills and the capacity to participate in a common economic community. The latter, on the one hand, now implies something much broader than the nation state – witness, for example, some employers' interests in foreign language training. On the other hand it implies an approach to education which is much more pragmatic than the concerns about the sharing of a complex common culture embodied in traditional approaches to elite education. It may also embody views about topics the education system *should not* cover, those encouraging and enhancing aspirations about citizenship rights. Some analyses of educational policy have stressed the strongly 'capitalist' determined model of education, deriving from that perspective. It is argued that employers do not want education to create participating citizens along the lines embodied in Dewey's educational philosophy. They want a disciplined and conformist labour force, cheerfully accepting the inequalities of rewards and power implicit in the labour market contract. Radical analyses show how the demands of capitalism have created a narrow model for state education:

> *The educational system serves . . . to reproduce economic inequality and to distort personal development. . . . It is precisely because of its role as producer of an alienated and stratified labor force that the education system has developed its repressive and unequal structure. In the history of U.S. education, it is the integrative function which has dominated the purpose of schooling, to the detriment of the other liberal objectives. (Bowles and Gintis, 1976, p. 48)*
> *(See also, for extensions of this analysis to other countries, Willis, 1977, and Sharp, 1986.)*

Marxist theory about the need for the state to socialise some of the costs of capital is amplified in various ways with the notion that the state has economic needs of its own. In the field of education this has taken its strongest form in emphases upon the need for substantial educational investments in developing societies. There is a substantial body of comparative work which has sought to explore the relationship between education and economic growth, stimulated by the concerns of bodies like the United Nations Educational, Scientific, and Cultural Organization (Unesco) and the World Bank about the impact of assistance with the development of public education programmes (see Kogan, 1979; Hurst, 1981). This emphasis in aid programmes seems to be very influenced by an American belief in the importance of education opportunity in generating an open and efficient capitalist society.

In developed societies the equivalent to the development concern involves a preoccupation with competition with other nations, and a fear that a nation may lose its competitive edge. Weaknesses in the education system are then seen as not producing enough engineers or not doing enough to encourage scientific innovation or undermining the entrepreneurial spirit. In the 'cold war' years American educational investment was stimulated by fears that, at the time the Russians launched the 'sputnik', the Communists were advancing faster technologically (Holmes, 1985, p. 109). British concerns about competition from Germany and Japan, or general European fears about economic growth in East Asia have similarly been channelled into enquiries about the defects of educational systems (for an example of one of many discussions along these lines see Commission for Social Justice, 1994, chs 2 and 4).

A theoretical perspective which has contributed to and channelled some of these debates is 'human capital theory' (Blaug, 1970). This focuses directly upon the economic value of education, and can be conceptualised in both individual and collective terms. The individual version sees education as making a distinct contribution to the earning power of a person. This is fairly uncontroversial in itself; the problems lie in its application to societies. As suggested above, the reasons why individuals may enhance their earning power through education are multiple, and may owe as much to social conventions about selection as to real increases in their value to society. Herein lies one problem about human capital theory: the real effects of investing in people (that is allegedly enhancing human capital) may be illusory when viewed from a society-wide perspective, however much social processes make it beneficial to the individuals concerned.

A feminist critique of this theory argues that human capital theory's preoccupation is solely with the needs of the formal economy and not with the worth of such investments to society in a wider sense (Matthews, 1984). Conceivably human capital theorists would argue that this is merely a methodological objection to be overcome once ways are developed to measure outputs in the household. A rejoinder to that is that societies develop as a result of education in ways which are in no way reflected in production, however measured. This highlights a concern about the narrow materialism of human capital theory.

This critique offers a philosophical objection to 'human capital theory' in suggesting that sociological and economic processes are being confused in the shift from the individual level to the societal level. Research evidence supports this critique. The mechanisms by which investment in education is transferred through into economic growth are complex and indirect. Many other factors come into play. Effects which may be detectable are likely to be very specific – concerning educational inputs which are probably better conceived as training (enhancing specific job-related skills), and results which are industry or even enterprise specific. The arguments about undervaluing technology, original scientific research or the entrepreneurial spirit involve complex connections, in which many other social factors may be relevant (Hüfner, Meyer and Naumann in Dierkes *et al.*, 1987).

The importance of human capital theory for a discussion of education policy, like many popular social theories, lies not so much in its accuracy as in the influence it has on policy and practice. An Australian discussion captures this very well:

> *The problem is that politically the perception may be that there is simply no other game in town. Mr John Dawkins, Federal Minister for Education . . . commented that the renewed interest in human capital theory was due to the*

> *'heightened recognition of the limits of* macroeconomic *policies to deal with the economic problems' and hence the greater attention being given again to* microeconomic *theories. . . . Within this perspective education and training are seen as microeconomic tools for governments to refine. It is essential to understand that the education debate in Australia is overwhelmingly dominated by this perspective. (Lingard* et al., *1993, p. 39)*

Significantly Dawkins' speech was made at an OECD conference. Like the World Bank in developing countries the OECD plays a role in disseminating the use of this narrow perspective in developed societies. The observations here on the Australian debate could be replicated in other countries. Human capital theory offers a widely accepted argument for public educational investment; discussion later in this chapter will return to the implications of this for the substance of education policy.

How does the state involve itself in the education system?

Chapter 5 identified a number of roles the state may play in relation to health care. Education policy may be presented in the same way. The roles set out in Chapter 5 were the following:

- Regulator.
- Funder/purchaser.
- Provider/planner.

In the case of education it has already been shown that the private sector is comparatively small in most countries. It is also the case that the simplest model of health provision, where the state is both funder and provider, is the commonest one in education provision. It is, however, complicated by administrative decentralisation, inasmuch as the provider is a public education institution (school or college) and its relationship to the state may be mediated through other institutions, in particular local government. As in the case of health, federal systems complicate the role of the state (it can perhaps be said that there are two 'states' involved in these cases).

This discussion will be divided into three sections. First, a fairly brief section on the issue of regulation of the private sector, then a discussion of administrative divisions within the public sector and finally a section on issues about public partnerships with private or voluntary sectors.

Regulation of the private sector

The rationale for state concern about the private sector in education tends to be, as with some regulatory concerns in social care, one which derives from the fact that children are minors. In such circumstances the state may deem it appropriate that it should not leave decisions about education solely to parents, notwithstanding their capacity to make private purchases. In many cases this concern follows logically from legislation which determined that education up to a certain age should be compulsory. Once the state had determined that it should try to reach certain standards in the provision of education it logically had to concern itself with the standards offered outside its remit.

The issues about the regulation of private education may not only concern the core educational product, but they may also extend to standards of accommodation, issues of child health and welfare, and matters of discipline. States take it upon themselves to ensure that private schools are not operated in conditions like those described in Dickens's nineteenth-century novel *Nicholas Nickleby*. Supervision of schools is likely to be achieved by some sort of licensing system, backed up by inspection, to ensure standards are maintained.

These concerns do not necessarily extend to further education, though in relation to this sector issues about trading standards may arise outside the remit of the education system (about the business methods of these bodies, which may exploit vulnerable students anxious for qualifications – students from abroad, etc.).

Administrative divisions within the public sector

In federal systems the provision of school systems, and sometimes higher education systems (for example in Switzerland), is the responsibility of the lower tier. Yet many states have seen federal governments seeking justification for intervention in the lower tier in many areas of social policy, notwithstanding apparent constitutional prohibitions. In the United States federal interventions have been justified in terms of two provisions within the constitution. The interventions that have received the most international attention have been those based upon equal rights clauses in the constitution, which were used to justify federal moves against segregated education in the South (Crain, 1968). These may be seen as regulatory interventions. More important for the day-to-day business of education has been the clause in the constitution which gives Congress the power to 'provide for the common defense and general welfare of the United States ' (Article 1, Section 8). Under this clause the federal government provides cash to support educational activities within the states. The Morrill Act of 1862 provided for grants to higher education. In 1958 the concerns related to the 'sputnik' launch (see p. 209) produced the National Defense and Education Act under which grants are made to support some aspects of secondary education.

In Australia education is similarly a function not identified as a federal one in the constitution, and therefore reserved to the states. But in that country's constitution the federal government can make grants to the states on 'such terms and conditions as' the federal parliament deems fit. This has led to a situation in which about 11 per cent of funding for government schools, and nearly all funding for universities, comes from the federal government.

Once there is a situation in which a federal government is pouring substantial funds into an activity at the state level it has a lever which it can use to influence the form that activity takes. While, in federal systems, the 'lower tier states' continue to have a considerable degree of latitude over detailed organisation arrangements and over the curriculum, there is likely to be intervention on issues about which the federal government feels strongly. This is likely to include a variety of concerns about educational performance and about educational equality. The power in relation to the latter is likely to be reinforced, as in the American case since the 1950s, where the federal government has seen itself as the defender of the 'equal rights' clauses in the constitution. Similarly the Australian federal interventions have been influenced by equity considerations.

Outside federal systems responsibility for schools (but generally not for higher education) is very often delegated to local government. In the relationship between central and local government, as in federal systems, a great deal of central power will stem from funding arrangements. Local government systems often involve local taxation, but this does not raise enough money for its educational costs to be carried entirely in this way.

However, it is inappropriate in the case of central–local relations in respect of education to look to explain central control entirely by reference to funding arrangements. Education legislation in non-federal states (and in the lower-tier units in federal ones) is characteristically heavily prescriptive on matters of school systems, the arrangements for the employment of teachers, curricula and assessments systems. There are likely to be inspection systems to reinforce these concerns.

In various societies some part of the education system is directly administered by central government. This is particularly true of higher education systems. In the French case this extends to higher-level secondary schools, via a decentralised administrative system. In the French case moreover the extent of commune control over the other schools is comparatively slight (Holmes, 1985).

Clearly there is a sense in which, in all systems, the educational institutions themselves represent another administrative tier. The very nature of a school is such that a great deal of crucial day-to-day decision-making will be carried out at that level, and will exert a strong influence on its educational outputs. Variations in educational performance which are neither determined by the system as a whole nor attributable to the social characteristics of the pupils have been the subject of study in various countries, in a search to identify and explain 'the school effect' (Creemers and Scheerens, 1989; Reynolds and Cuttance, 1992). In various countries the need for decentralised management of schools has led to administrative arrangements designed to give schools or groups of schools a measure of autonomy, perhaps accompanied by democratic or quasi-democratic arrangements for parent or community representation separate from other aspects of local government.

At the advanced end of the educational system institutions tend to be larger and tasks more complex. There is a paradox here that, while the importance of these institutions tends to influence the desire for central or federal governments to exercise direct control, complexity and the higher status of staff also contribute to more autonomous management arrangements. These arrangements are influenced by the following two related phenomena:

1. Universities can draw upon a set of collegial norms established back in medieval times when they were accountable if at all to church rather than to state.
2. There is a philosophical position rooted in the liberal challenge to totalitarianism that those engaged in teaching and research should enjoy some freedom in the choice of what they say and do.

The paradox referred to above produces a tension, heightened by the fact that these institutions are believed to be in a crucial position in relation to training for elites and state investment in 'human capital' (see pp. 205–9 above). They may also be a source of challenges to the *status quo* (see Halsey, 1995, for a discussion of some of these issues, with particular reference to Britain).

A not dissimilar conflict applies to some of the issues about local management systems for schools. In the recent history of the British school system there have been a set of changes in which the government has adopted measures involving more central control while proclaiming the desirability of increased community control (Glennerster *et al.*, 1991). The peculiarity of this can largely be explained by government hostility to local government as a key actor in education decision-making (perhaps largely attributable to party ideology differences between the government and the controlling parties in many local governments). The deal offered to schools is self-management with direct central government funding. The deal offered to parents is opportunities to participate more in the local management of schools. Rather more important for most people are provisions expected to facilitate parental choice of schools (as far as competition for scarce places allows) to replace bureaucratic allocation procedures. Consumerism linked with school autonomy are expected to make a quasi-market system work in education, but very much in the context of central supervision in an era where central government is being more directive on curriculum matters than ever before (see Bondi, 1991, for a UK/US comparison which highlights the impact of differences in central control upon responses to contemporary pressures for educational reform).

Public partnerships with private and voluntary sectors

The British example set out in the previous paragraph is often seen as part of the 'new right' assault on traditional approaches to the provision of public services, which is shifting British state systems towards market systems. The limited competition between schools produces, as suggested above, a 'quasi-market' system, but the schools remain fully publicly funded in respect of their mainstream tasks (there is scope for a large digression here about ways in which schools have to compensate for under-funding by private fund-raising). The 'new right' have argued for a more distinctive shift towards privatisation by way of the provision of education vouchers (Maynard, 1975; Coons and Sugarman, 1978). These would enable parents to buy a basic education package at any school of their choice – publicly or privately owned – making up extra costs, likely at most of the better examples of the latter (called in Britain, for quaint historical reasons, 'public schools'). It may be debated whether such a measure would increase parental choice or merely offer a public subsidy to those currently choosing the private system. It could, in the long run, bring more private providers into the system (but note what was said on p. 107 with regard to hospitals about the high risks likely to deter such investments).

There have been voucher experiments in the United States (see Raywid, 1985), but so far no national attempts to establish such systems. Education involves public-private partnerships in many ways in various countries, including Britain. 'Private', however, rarely means 'profit-making' in this context, but rather under the control of a voluntary body. The main source of this 'private sector' has been the aspirations of religious groups many of whom were, as noted above (pp. 203–4), pioneers of education. Such schools are widespread in the Netherlands and France. In Britain the terms under which religious groups run schools involve such a strong measure of state management that they are scarcely thought of as 'private' at all. The following comment on France, where about 16 per cent of pupils are in private schools mainly of this kind, indicates a similar strong control system:

> *Since 1959 those private schools accepting state financial aid had to employ qualified teachers. Contracts were introduced whereby private schools accepting state assistance would adhere to state programmes and timetables according to the judgement of academié inspectors. (Holmes, 1985, p. 71)*

As suggested above, private institutions of a more diverse kind, including profit-making ones, are more evident in the further and higher education sectors. These sectors may accept state funds in various forms, and may thus experience pressures additional to any purely regulatory ones.

The characteristics of education systems

Discussion about administrative arrangements for education has focused solely upon control issues, but there are a series of important policy issues in education which deal with rather different structural considerations: these include when education starts and finishes (and what the related limits are for compulsory education), how education systems are divided along age lines and, often closely related to that last point, the ways in which education systems offer forms of specialisation or stratify by ability as well as age. These are the concerns of this section.

Divisions by age

An OECD compendium of statistics is an excellent source on many of the above issues (OECD, 1990). Table 9.2 reproduces part of a table on compulsory education from that volume. A number of countries – Austria, Belgium, Germany and Spain – require one or two years of part-time education after the compulsory leaving age. The variations in the starting and finishing ages, and in the length of compulsory education, need to be contextualised by looking at numbers in full-time education at points before and after the common leaving dates. While a number of countries have high rates of participation in pre-primary education by the 3–5 age group, with France as the extreme case with 100 per cent, the late starter nations are not exceptionally notable for this (apart from Sweden with a 95 per cent participation rate).

Table 9.3 looks at the other end of the education process, setting out percentages still in full-time education at the age of 17. In this table the leaving ages from table 9.2 have been left in for comparison. There seems to be a tendency for lower voluntary participation to be correlated with lower compulsory participation. Exceptions are Japan, with a high participation rate despite its comparatively early leaving age, and the United Kingdom, which has a heavy drop-out rate despite having a leaving age of 16. It is unfortunate that the available data on this topic are rather old, there has been a considerable increase in the numbers staying on in education in many countries since then (a consequence both of efforts to do more for those with limited educational attainments and of the poor job prospects for this group).

Comparative discussions of organisational divisions within education systems tend to describe systems in terms of three levels: one (from starting

Table 9.2 Age limits and duration of compulsory full-time education in various countries, 1988

	Age limit Min.	Max.	Duration
Australia	6	15	9
Austria	6	15	9
Belgium	6	16	10
Canada	6/7	15/16	9
Denmark	6/7	16/17	9
Finland	7	17	10
France	6	16	10
Germany	6	16	10
Greece	5.5	14.5	9
Ireland	6	15	9
Italy	6	14	8
Japan	6	15	9
Netherlands	5	16	11
New Zealand	6	15	9
Norway	7	16	9
Portugal	6	14	8
Spain	6	14	8
Sweden	7	16	9
Switzerland*	6/7	15/16	8/9
United Kingdom	5	16	11
USA	6	17	11

Note: *varies according to canton.
Source: OECD (1990) *Education in OECD Countries 1987–88*, Paris: OECD, p. 120; reproduced by permission of the OECD.

age until 11), two (from 11 to 19, a stage generally experienced in schools) and three (from 19 onwards, a stage generally undertaken in universities or vocational education colleges). More subtle sub-divisions are possible – many systems separate level two into groups above and below 15 (broadly junior and senior high schools in the United States) and discussions of post-19 education may distinguish divisions related to types of course rather than ages (courses below undergraduate level, at undergraduate level and at post-graduate level).

It is possible to map different systems according to these concepts. The OECD statistics collection is followed by an elaborate series of charts (OECD, 1990). It is not very useful to follow this subject through in detail here. However, some interesting observations can be made about the structuring of the later stages in relation to specialisation within schools and colleges.

Table 9.3 Percentages in full-time education at 17 related to termination ages for compulsory education in various countries, 1986

	Minimum leaving age limit	Per cent of 17-year-olds still in education in 1986
Australia	15	50
Belgium	16	86
Canada	15/16	79
Denmark	16/17	75
Finland	17	91
France	16	80
Germany	16	100
Greece	14.5	55
Ireland	15	41
Italy	14	46
Japan	15	91
Netherlands	16	87
New Zealand	15	54
Norway	16	76
Spain	14	53
Sweden	16	86
Switzerland	15/16	83
United Kingdom	16	49
USA	17	89

Note: in Germany there is compulsory part-time education at this age.
Source: OECD, *Education in OECD Countries 1987–88*, Paris: OECD, pp. 73 and 120; reproduced by permission of the OECD.

Divisions by specialisation or ability

An important division in education policy concerns the extent to which attempts are made to give children a common schooling regardless of ability or performance. Generally countries adopt unitary (comprehensive) systems for children up to the age of 11, unless exceptional handicaps require special attention. In some societies even at this early stage performance differences affect progress between grades in some societies (Switzerland, France, Japan) – children do not automatically move up with their age group.

After the age of 11 systems move at various speeds towards some degree of educational segregation. The rationale for this is seen to be different educational needs based upon future occupational expectations. The main differences concern the extent to which this segregation occurs in different schools and the level at which it begins to occur. The United Kingdom has largely abandoned, between the 1940s and the 1990s, a system in which decisions were made at the age of 11 to sort children by means of tests into two, sometimes three, very different types of schools – grammar schools for those likely to go into higher education or non-manual work and secondary modern schools for the rest. This has been replaced, by incremental changes (depending upon local authority decisions), by a system in which nearly all areas provide comprehensive schools at least up to the compulsory school-leaving age. Yet these schools are still internally stratified, assessments of performance influence the curriculum offered and attendance beyond the compulsory leaving age is largely confined to those with aspirations to qualify for higher education.

Countries which have ascribed to a comprehensive model rather more enthusiastically – getting it established earlier and making more efforts to eliminate divisions within schools – have included the United States, Australia and Sweden. By contrast countries like France, Germany, Japan and Switzerland have paid more attention to earlier evolution towards division of children into schools with markedly different curricula – traditional academic, technological and practical. In these systems the crucial divide comes around the age of 15 or 16.

Comparisons are made difficult by the 'within school' divisions already referred to. They are also complicated by variations in the school-leaving age and by the extent to which children are encouraged to continue in education regardless of performance. Chisholm (in Bailey, 1992) suggests education systems can be analysed in terms of the relationship between selection and participation. In this respect a comparison may be made between Denmark, Germany and the UK. Denmark has a late selection system accompanied by high rates of educational participation. While the German system selects relatively early, becoming clearly a divided one during the middle teenage years, great efforts are made to ensure that all get an education package of some kind – shifting from full- to part-time in some cases – until the age of 17 or 18 (see also Clasen and Freeman, 1994, ch. 6). It can be described as an 'early selection/high participation' system. In the UK, by contrast, early exit from education has been a characteristic of underachievers. While the development of comprehensive education has contributed to moving it in the direction of late selection this has not produced a consequence for participation comparable to that of Denmark.

Higher and further education systems are divided everywhere. Sometimes divisions are identifiable from distinctions made between universities and other institutions. In other systems – the UK and Australia, for example – many institutions have been recently promoted to 'university status'. Opportunities to work for degrees, in institutions which may be described generically as universities, are competed for with varying intensity. Some university systems are clearly stratified – in Japan, the United States and the UK (plus France where the highest-prestige institutions are the *grandes ecoles* not universities). It is interesting to note that while in the United States private institutions occupy the 'top' ranks in this 'hierarchy', in Japan and Taiwan private institutions have developed to respond to a demand for higher education from those unable to win places in the 'elite' state institutions. In some other countries universities serve a broad population (defined as much by the location of their homes as by school performance differences) – Sweden and Germany, for example. Everywhere it is hard to get places on courses that lead to highly valued occupations, particularly when the education is costly (medicine, for example). For many other subjects a distinction may be made between countries where entry is fairly easy but then failure rates within the courses are high (the United States, Italy), and those where entry is more difficult but few then drop out (the UK, Japan).

Expenditure on education

Table 9.4 provides information to enable some comparisons to be made between countries in respect of expenditure on public education. The first column contains data on education expenditure as a percentage of GDP. The second column is designed to give some idea of the priority given to education as opposed to other public expenditure, setting out education expenditure as a percentage of all expenditure. The figures on expenditure as a percentage of GDP suggest a pattern remarkably similar to that for other social policy expenditure. Those on education as a percentage of public expenditure suggest that there is a group of nations whose attention to education expenditure stands out a little in relation to other items – Switzerland, Canada and to some extent the United States. The OECD suggests that 'those countries which devote the highest proportion of their public expenditure to education are the ones where such expenditure is lowest in relation to GDP' (OECD, 1990, p. 56). Is there some suggestion here that the differences between countries in the importance they ascribe to education are rather less great than their differences in commitments to public expenditure in general? Such a view is supported by the very long history of public education in many countries.

The OECD survey from which these data are taken endeavours to examine trends in education expenditure. It suggests a general downward trend in education expenditure as a percentage of public expenditure. This is attributed by the OECD to the fall in the proportion of school age children. Expenditures standardised for pupil numbers do not show the same fall, except in relation to further and higher education. Here, then, costs have been reduced by lowering standards – making this kind of education more of a 'mass participation' phenomenon. It is interesting to relate this development to Le Grand's evidence on the significance of expenditure on higher education as a social policy bias towards the middle classes (Le Grand, 1982).

Table 9.4 Comparative data on educational expenditure for 1987

	Public education expenditure	
	As % of GDP	As % of all public expenditure
Australia	5.3	13.6
Austria	5.9	11.2
Belgium	5.1	9.8
Canada	6.5	15.6
Denmark	7.5	13.2
Finland	5.3	13.7
France	5.6	10.9
Germany (West)	4.2	9.4
Greece	2.7	10.6
Ireland	5.8	9.7
Italy	5.0	9.7
Japan	5.0	12.8
Netherlands	7.0	12.1
New Zealand	5.4	n.a.
Norway	6.8	14.0
Portugal	4.3	12.2
Sweden	7.2	12.2
Switzerland	5.0	14.5
United Kingdom	5.0	11.5
USA	4.8	12.9

Source: OECD (1990) *Education in OECD Countries 1987–88*, Paris: OECD, pp. 115 and 116; reproduced by permission of the OECD.

It contradicts Goodin and Le Grand's (1987) argument about the capacity of that group to protect the services in which they have the greatest interest (see Chapter 11 for further discussion).

Education outputs

As with health policy, comparative data on inputs into the education system provide little basis for arguments about the quality of systems. They may, also, reflect variation between nations in efficiency or in salary levels and other costs. What is needed are output data. But it is not easy to compare crude data on this either – variations in numbers in the system cannot be meaningfully compared except outside the compulsory school years, and even then the crucial questions will not be about numbers participating but about the benefits they are acquiring from participation. This last point is made more relevant by current fears that further and higher education may be regarded politically as a convenient 'parking place' for young people when insufficient new job opportunities are arising.

Nevertheless scholars have endeavoured to develop standardised ways of measuring educational performance, which can facilitate comparisons between countries or over time. The International Association for the Evaluation of Educational Attainment has assembled a range of comparative test material. Heidenheimer, Heclo and Adams report, for example, a study of maths which appeared in 1987:

> *Compared to the previous tests, the United States had not increased the proportion of the age group taking advanced high school math* [sic], *whereas Japan had. Nevertheless, Japanese got much higher grades on all sections of the math exam . . . French students also outscored American students. (Heidenheimer* et al., *1990, p. 39)*

They went on to report that these findings attracted presidential attention in the United States, but were related in complex ways to the way education is organised. Data of this kind attract a kind of 'Olympic Games' approach to national comparisons; there are difficult questions to be answered about how differences may be explained, and about the extent to which they reflect national differences in school effectiveness (see Husen, 1987).

As suggested in Chapter 5, it is important to distinguish output data and outcome data. Ultimately it is the latter which really matters – improved 'end states' for the individuals concerned. Yet in the case of education not only, as in health, will factors unrelated to education affect educational outcome (as suggested at some length in the introductory section), but it must also be recognised that inasmuch as education facilitates sorting for desired occupations (see p. 207) an actual outcome for an individual may be simply an indicator that it has performed this function.

Educational inequality

Comparative studies in education, like comparative studies in health, may mask substantial inequalities within countries. Moreover, inasmuch as these studies are working towards being able to make a practical contribution to concerns about levels of performance in individual countries one consideration, alongside the perhaps dominant 'human capital' enhancement one, is the extent to which education makes a contribution to either the diminution of social inequalities or at least to ensuring that inequalities are not needlessly inherited. In this context the issue about whether it is education or some other social factors which determines outcome is obviously important. The idea that education primarily facilitates sorting for desired occupations may be put in a positive light if the objective is to ensure that this sorting is not carried out in other less egalitarian ways (Evetts, 1973). In other words an important objective for education systems may be to ensure that 'output' is not merely determined by social 'input'.

There are several competing models against which an education system's performance on this issue may be evaluated as follows:

1. The ideal may be that education should not sort individuals for different occupational opportunities at all. It should take all children, whatever their backgrounds, into common schools and give them skills and an introduction to appropriate cultures (this is put vaguely, for reasons which will be made more apparent below). In this sense education would be a process of socialisation for citizenship in an egalitarian society. This is an educational ideal, nowhere translated into practical policies. It does serve as a 'lodestar' for many educationalists, has influenced some educational developments and may be put into practice in some parts of the curriculum (those least likely to be regarded as providing job credentials).
2. An alternative egalitarian ideal is to see education as contributing to equality of opportunity in a society, and particularly as ensuring that its outcomes (which ideally lead on to job opportunities) are not determined by criteria other than innate ability. There are difficulties in determining what that last expression really means (there has been an extensive nature/nurture debate about the determination of performance in education and even about the determination of results in tests which psychologists have claimed to be 'pure' ways of measuring intelligence – see Taylor, 1980; Henry *et al.*, 1988, pp. 190–204). Nevertheless a great deal of attention has been given to efforts to arrive at educational systems which do not discriminate in terms of race, gender and social class. These issues have been very important in American debates about education, with equality of opportunity playing an important role in American democratic ideology (see Bowles and Gintis, 1976, ch. 1, for a discussion of the way this has been seen as fundamental to the American dream – 'education as the new frontier').
3. The third alternative involves the rejection of the other two. It has two alternative but closely related forms. One of these is embodied in the preoccupation with the economic function of education. It suggests that the concern about inequality gets in the way of education doing an efficient job in equipping people for the labour market. The object should be to ensure that the system is efficient for each stratum in society, educating them (or perhaps training is the better word here) to become effective employees. This approach particularly involves an attack on the purer model of equality ((1) above). It is often combined with a cautious version of (2) inasmuch as it is recognised that it is economically inefficient to fail to advance people with talent because of their social

origins. The other form of this perspective is rather more content to see education as socialising individuals for their largely predetermined stations in life. This perspective picks up on the issue of education for citizenship, seeing dangers in letting education raise unrealisable expectations. In the modern world this view is rarely openly advanced, however, radical critiques of education systems suggest that this is how they often operate in practice (Bowles and Gintis, 1976).

The debate set out here is further analysed in Bowles and Gintis, 1976; Finch, 1984 and Burgess, 1986 (particularly ch. 2).

As suggested above the key issues in relation to these perspectives concern the role education plays in relation to social stratification. Issues about social stratification and social policy are explored further in Chapter 11. Here some of the key issues about education will be outlined. The salient dimensions in relation to stratification are class, ethnic origin and gender – often operating in combination with each other. The various ways in which stratification issues arise in education are analysed separately below.

Overt discrimination

Schools may openly reject certain kinds of people. Schools which require parents to pay fees explicitly discriminate in favour of the better off. In this sense the presence of a strong private sector in education will stratify a society's education system as a whole. Rich people are able to frustrate egalitarian aspirations in a society by opting out of the public system if they feel it is undermining the initial advantages possessed by their children.

Single-sex educational institutions obviously discriminate against the excluded sex. Notwithstanding the other arguments for or against the segregation of the sexes in education, any system practising sex segregation needs to be scrutinised carefully to see whether or not there is parity in the facilities offered.

Overt racial discrimination in the initial allocation of educational facilities has become generally taboo in the societies discussed in this book. That is not to say there is not implicit discrimination – arising either directly, by way of class or gender discrimination, or because of inequalities between facilities in different geographical areas. The existence of religious divisions in education may also facilitate forms of 'ethnic' discrimination.

Other forms of de facto *discrimination*

Where selection processes occur in education there are obviously various opportunities for discrimination – ranging from deliberate overt discrimination through the application of criteria which have a discriminatory effect (here the class/gender/race/religion interactions may be significant), to unwitting discrimination which emerges out of unquestioned patterns of behaviour and practices. A central issue here is the extent to which teachers' behaviour is influenced by assumptions – that girls find science difficult, that people of African origin are good at sport or music (and by implication not much else), and so on. A fundamental underlying issue for all forms of stratification is the extent to which expected future outcomes determine current behaviour by teachers. This sort of self-fulfilling prophecy takes the form: there is not much point in troubling with children of this kind, they never do well. Research evidence suggests that unwitting forms of discrimination occur widely, with teachers making less effort with some kinds of children (Deem, 1978; Delamont, 1980; Kelly, 1981).

Educational effects which arise out of cultural biases in the system

This issue is difficult as education is an activity which by definition involves using cultural forms and socialising children into a culture. A fundamental issue, for example, concerns the main language used for instruction. Every child educated in a language other than that used at home encounters some educational disadvantage. That is a factual statement not a judgement – the issue of judgement concerns whether the system should prepare that child for effective participation in another language community or alternatively offer an education in his or her original language which will carry with it disadvantages in competition in the society outside. There are hybrid options – including acceptance of bilingualism so that everyone is educated in more than one language. Readers will, it is hoped, realise that this is a simplified statement and there are many possibilities. (Note, for example, the author's daughter works in a London borough where school children have over 100 different original languages!)

The comments here on language apply also to other aspects of culture – any teaching of literature, history, social sciences, etc., draws upon a limited range of culturally determined sources. An extreme position here is obviously to require education to draw principally upon sources from a single culture (the requirements for history and literature teaching in the British 'national curriculum' have been criticised in these terms; Flude and Hammer, 1990). There are particularly discriminatory dangers when aspects of the inculcation of a culture involve the glorification of the past activities of the 'dominant' culture – victories in wars, the securing of an empire, the establishment of a 'settlement', etc. These 'dangers' may have effects way beyond the teaching of these things in themselves, in contributing to the alienation of some children from the system as a whole.

An extreme reaction against this problem of cultural bias is to try to exclude much of a nation's history and all past literature which embody prejudiced views about particular groups. A less dramatic alternative is to try to balance teaching – dealing with various people's histories and literatures, exploring critiques of hitherto accepted work. The balance is difficult to achieve, not only because of the complexity of the social divisions which may occur, but also because the inculcation of a culture is also the inculcation of values (Welch, 1993). Notwithstanding the fact that this may involve, along the lines already discussed in relation to the work of Bowles and Gintis (1976), socialisation for a subordinate social status, it has to be recognised that such social mobility as does occur requires some assimilation of the dominant culture. There is also a series of complicated points, which philosophers have sought to disentangle and which cannot be explored here, about the extent to which any system however liberal should propagate its own value system and limit its tolerance of alternatives. These have been brought to a head, for example, in relation to conflicts between the Judaeo-Christian tradition and Islam.

This discussion of culture would not be complete without a brief reference to the notion of the 'hidden curriculum'. In various ways the Marxist (Bowles and Gintis, 1976), feminist (see Dale and Foster, 1986, ch. 4) and anti-colonialist (Freire, 1974) critiques of education all draw attention to the many obscure and subtle ways in which schools inculcate values: in the way classes are organised, in the options which are offered (or not offered – cookery instead of science for girls, etc.), in the uses made of ceremonies and ranking systems in everyday school life, in assumptions about the desirability of competitive sport or conformity in dress, and so on). The hidden curriculum socialises but it also discriminates.

The impact of disadvantages pupils bring from outside the education system itself

Perhaps the most difficult issue of all concerning the contribution of education to social equality is the problem, already alluded to, of the relationship between 'inputs' and 'outputs'. The results of the education process, contrary to the aspiration that education should offer a route to social mobility, indicate that social background is a fundamental determinant of educational success (Coleman *et al.*, 1966; Jencks *et al.*, 1972). One response to this has been to argue that these differences are explained by differences in innate ability (Jensen, 1975). Reference was made above to the debate about intelligence. Whatever the balance between 'nature' and 'nurture' in the determination of performance there is no doubt that there is a great deal of underachievement in education which cannot be explained away by the genetic hypotheses.

The policy issue is then: to what extent can, and should, an education system actively seek to compensate for the disadvantages children bring to the education system by virtue of their parents' poverty, poor education, language background, etc. (Rutter and Madge, 1977)? This word 'input' used in the paragraph above masks the fact that this is about continuing disadvantages; children go back every night to their poor home, their household without books, their language of origin, and so on.

There is more to it than this even, since these background disadvantages are reinforced by other factors. Children's friends are likely to share their disadvantaging characteristics and others whom they encounter will reinforce negative images. Schools with egalitarian aspirations operate in a culture which is likely to attack what they are trying to do and to denigrate those they are trying to help.

The only answer to these multiple problems other than despair is to try to compensate for these disadvantages. Additional resources may be made available to schools which are trying to encounter disadvantages like those outlined here. There have been various efforts made – the Disadvantaged Schools Programme in Australia, Headstart in the United States, Education Priority Areas in Britain. They are rarely sufficient to compensate even in terms of an addition to the formal resources to counteract the lack of private resources on which a school is able to draw. They have also come under heavy attack from the 'human capital' school of thought – as offering poor returns on educational investment by comparison with concentrating resources on educational 'high-flyers'.

The widespread evidence of school rejection by disadvantaged children (absenteeism, vandalism, classroom disruption) does not help in this argument. As job prospects have worsened for this group so the temptation to see disadvantaged schools as temporary custodians of a group who are going to make little contribution to society has been encouraged (Willis, 1977). The ideas about competition in education systems, forcing schools to concentrate upon securing examination results which will attract parents who are ambitious for their children, have further undermined efforts to support the education of the group discussed here.

Efforts to study educational inequality comparatively

The one issue which can be explored comparatively concerns the difference between the genders in the use of and success in the education system. A useful yardstick here is offered by female participation in the higher education system. The evidence set out in table 9.5 shows a trend towards higher female participation and equality in some countries. It needs interpreting with caution, however, because some systems are highly stratified or have become more highly stratified as they have expanded. In other words females are still excluded in various ways from some of the more

Table 9.5 Percentage of female undergraduates were in 1975 and 1986

	1975	1986
Australia	n.a.	45*
Canada	46	54
Denmark	38	44
France	46	54
Germany (West)	34	38
Italy	39	47
Japan	23	25
Netherlands	25	38
New Zealand	41	51
Norway	34	51
Sweden	n.a.	46
Switzerland	n.a.	36*
United Kingdom	n.a.	45
USA	46	51

Note: * = data for 1984.
Source: OECD (1990) *Education in OECD Countries 1987–88*, Paris: OECD, p. 76; reproduced by permission of the OECD.

advantaged sectors (for example, high-status universities in Japan, the *grandes ecoles* in France).

Conclusions

This concluding discussion summarises the issues, with particular reference to the politics of education policy. As is the case with health policy there are a range of ongoing issues about control over the system. In many ways that struggle can be characterised as one between the two perspectives which have been highlighted in this chapter: a concern about the contribution education can make to increasing equality (generally expressed in terms of the weaker of the two variants outlined on p. 223), and a concern about the contribution of education to the economy (set out above as the human capital perspective). This is recognisably a 'left' versus 'right' issue in political ideology terms. It is also an issue on which much of the strongest support for the egalitarian ideal has come from inside education. It is similar to the debate about the control over health policy inasmuch as there is a concern to control the professionals, but unlike it because of the absence of a significant anti-professional attack from the 'left'. Unease about professional domination merely weakens the resistance to the attack from the 'right'.

Education policy is a curious and difficult phenomenon to analyse because there is very broad support for it in general terms – as suggested nationalist, economic and democratic arguments all come together on this – but considerable controversy about its content. The very fact that, as suggested in the introduction, getting an education involves a combination of institutional, individual and family inputs, means that everyone is to some extent an 'expert' on the subject. The professional expertise of teachers is very much more readily exposed to challenge by the public than is the expertise of doctors.

The debate concerning the content of education is also very confused by the 'credentialism' which this chapter has emphasised. Actual educational needs are masked by the uses made of evidence on educational achievement in the job selection process. Here, the whole picture is influenced by the characteristics of elite education. Many today share Macaulay's cynicism (p. 207) about this. This puts educationalists, particularly those of an egalitarian disposition, in a considerable difficulty. Elite education embodies fundamental cultural values – about those parts of historical, literary, philosophical, etc., heritages which should be passed down from generation to generation. Herein lies the justifications for education *for its own sake* – not for economic growth or social peace or individual advancement. A utilitarianism perspective may involve rejection of this whole educational model – elites and mass should all share an education oriented towards the needs of the economy. What occurs, however, in practice (specially in the nations that are particularly concerned about their cultural heritages – France and Britain, for example, as opposed to the United States and Australia – though the contrast should not be overdrawn) is that the utilitarian model tends to dominate in 'mass' education while the cultural heritage model survives in elite education. It is the latter, however, which may be crucial for elite job opportunities, hence democratic demands for it to be open to all.

The suggestion is then that this tension lies at the heart of contemporary educational controversy. Public expenditure crises together with rising economic difficulties and attendant unemployment lead many to cry for education expenditure – meaning expenditure on the education of the masses – to be concentrated on subjects of clear economic relevance. The exponents of this position are by no means limited to the ranks of the 'new right'. Indeed there is even a conflict within this group between those of the 'social capital' school of thought and those who are worried about the breakdown of 'traditional values'. The latter may be attributable to a decline of 'traditional' education concerned with the transmission of cultural values – particularly religious ones.

Those on the other side of the political spectrum have a related problem. Egalitarianism in education has often involved a hostility to traditional education because it transmits a conservative set of cultural values. In that sense there can be some identification with the quest for greater relevance in education. The problem is then how to draw a distinction between the narrowly economic concept of relevance and the wider ideal that egalitarians have in mind (see Ball, 1990, ch. 1, for a good discussion of this issue). They are apt to be ground between the social capital school and the traditionalists. Their adherence to the 'comprehensive' ideal of a shared education for democracy is under an assault from those seeking to strengthen the old divided agenda, which separates the issues about a relevant 'mass' education and a traditional elite one. In a situation in which education offers very little to a wide band of people with poor and deteriorating job prospects, it is hard to fight against this divided agenda.

In writing these conclusions the author may have been influenced by British developments. The British system has always been dominated by an elite model deriving from the so-called public schools and the ancient universities. Upward mobility in British society has involved a chase after this ideal through state educational institutions prepared to subscribe to the same model (see a variety of powerful discussions of this, for example, Hoggart, 1957; Jackson and Marsden, 1962). Yet, as already suggested, the French and German systems have many similar characteristics. The way in which the issues manifest themselves must depend upon culture, and particularly upon the underlying strengths of egalitarian ideals in various cultures. The Scandinavian, American and Australian systems may have gone further to eliminate the elite/mass distinction in education, but in their cases it is replaced by the conflict between the utilitarian model and the demand for a mass 'liberal' education (Lingard *et al.*, 1993). In this context the latter is a difficult position to advance in the face of demands for public expenditure cuts and interpretations of rising unemployment which blame the education system for the alleged deficiencies in the 'supply' of labour.

Guide to further reading

Issues about the comparative history of education are well covered in Green's *Education and State Formation* (1990). While concerns from Australia and New Zealand dominate in the edited collection by Lingard and his colleagues *Schooling Reform in Hard Times* (1993), some important contemporary issues are addressed there. Two country-specific books must be mentioned because they are important for the analysis of education policy. One that has already been very influential is Bowles and Gintis's *Schooling in Capitalist*

America (1976). The other is Ball's book on recent events in Britain *Politics and Policy Making in Education* (1990).

The OECD's *Education in OECD Counties 1987–88: A Compendium of Statistical Information* (1990) is an invaluable source of data. Since education data date rather fast, readers should look out for other publications on education from the OECD.

CHAPTER TEN

Environmental policy

Introduction

This chapter deals with an area of public policy which is characterised by measures to curb the behaviour of individuals and organisations in order to improve the quality of life for societies or groups within societies. This distinguishes it from other concerns in the book where the attention has been upon measures designed to provide more specific benefits or services, and the regulation of others has not been particularly salient. The discussion of environmental policy is rarely included in accounts of social policy, yet it undoubtedly has an important impact upon human welfare.

In the view of the author it is particularly appropriate to discuss environmental policy alongside policies designed to provide health services, enhance incomes, influence employment prospects, and so on, because of its important contribution to health and the quality of life, because of its interaction with employment and housing policies, and because of the role it plays in redistributing the costs of economic activity in a variety of senses. It is not an exaggeration to say that some of the more specific kinds of social welfare policy which are trying to compensate people who are the casualties of modern societies may be seen to be beside the point in an unsafe environment. In these circumstances they will be merely offering 'sticking plasters' to deal with injuries which need not have occurred. In particular effective national *health* services need to take on board environmental influences on health (amongst other social and economic causes of ill-health) if they are to be something more than merely national *illness* services.

Identification of the issues

A modern concern?

In the third edition of their book on comparative public policy Heidenheimer, Heclo and Adams start their discussion of environmental policy by saying

'Of all the concerns of governments that we analyze in this book, environmental pollution is the most recent' (1990, p. 308). While they are right to identify the aspiration to develop comprehensive measures to deal with pollution as a very recent development, it is important to recognise that under certain circumstances some aspects of public environmental control, with pollution not necessarily as its primary focus, have been on the policy agenda in some nations for a long while. Ancient concerns about the control of rivers have been seen as sufficiently important in earlier societies to be recognised as playing a key role in the development of nation states. Wittfogel, in particular, saw the roots of ancient bureaucratic empires to lie in the aspiration to control flooding and the distribution of water in China, the Middle East and India (Wittfogel, 1957). More recently collective action to control water played a key role in the development of the Dutch Republic (Schama, 1987). Moving more specifically to the issue of pollution – risks to workers within factories began to be given attention in nineteenth-century legislation. Furthermore in the nineteenth century there were also efforts to curb certain kinds of readily identified sources of pollution, albeit in a way which involved only measures against exceptional nuisances (note the reference to early British public health legislation on p. 155; German pollution control is similarly seen to have its origins in a Prussian 'general trade regulation act' in 1845 – Weidner, 1986).

What is characteristic of modern environmental policy is a recognition that pollution problems are endemic, a consequence of the many activities which create and sustain the levels of material prosperity in advanced industrial societies. They need to be seen in the context of population growth, and the resultant pressure upon space and resources. They also need to be seen in relation to very high and complex levels of consumption. This is well summed up in a comment by the OECD on the economically advanced countries which that organisation represents:

> *The population of OECD countries . . . has become richer and older . . .. Consumption patterns have become increasingly dependent on packaged goods, durable goods and the automobile; consequently, they have generated more waste and pollution and generally consumed more natural resources, such as oil, water and wood. Time-use patterns have been marked by a rapid increase in leisure and tourism activities; this has been partly beneficial for the environment, by stimulating improved protection of the natural environment . . . but it has also generated increased pressures . . .. (OECD, 1991, p. 294)*

There is a sense in which contemporary environmental consciousness can be attributed to a 'post-materialist' view that now people have to find ways of curbing the side-effects of the activities from which they have benefited.

In some respects environmental policy may be regarded, particularly by those nations still struggling to raise material standards, as a luxury only available to those with high standards of living. If, further, the efforts of environmental policy are seen as directed towards the preservation of rare animals or plants or to the maintenance of an 'unspoilt' natural environment this will particularly heighten this 'north'–'south' contrast (using those compass point expressions as shorthand for these global conflicts of interest between developed and less developed nations). In the same way, where the problem is seen to be population growth it will be pointed out by the nations of the 'south' that the amount of pollution generated per person is very much higher in the rich than in the poor countries. These are bases for understandable hostility to some of the efforts to curb pollution in still industrialising countries which come from nations whose earlier activities raised global levels of pollution to high levels.

Production, consumption and pollution

This conflict also highlights the point that, while much of the attack upon environmental pollution involves a search for ways to eliminate pollutants that are produced or to clean up after polluting activities, there is an alternative which is simpler – in the scientific if not the political sense. This is to alter the way in which production or consumption occurs. Production techniques may be adopted that are slower and more extravagant in their use of human resources, but produce fewer waste products (in particular waste products from energy use). Consumption patterns may involve simpler products, less well-packaged products, slower methods of travel, and so on. There may even be a need to question whether certain forms of consumption are really necessary. These are considerations which enter into efforts to define 'sustainable growth'. More radically they lead to the questioning of 'productivist' ideologies which refuse to look beyond the narrow confines of conventional 'economic rationality' (Lipietz, 1992). Significantly there are some connections here with the concerns of Chapter 8 – developing production processes which produce less pollution may also increase the numbers of jobs (so may greater efforts to clean up after pollution).

Another influence upon the increased interest in environmental policies arises precisely from an awareness that it cannot be a private matter – for nations any more than for individuals. The global economic interactions which sustain the prosperity of many nations, together with the tourism referred to in the quotation from OECD above, contribute to the recognition that pollution is an international issue. Ecological disasters with transnational implications – like the nuclear power station explosion at Chernobyl in 1986 – reinforce this awareness.

The public, and often global, significance of many environmental policy issues makes them rather different from most of the issues discussed in the rest of this book. Yet, to look at these issues helps to highlight a weakness in the way other social policy issues are often discussed. Issues about income maintenance or health or education or job provision are too often seen as private ones when in fact there are wider issues about the public benefits and the public resource exchanges associated with them. Examining the communal, national and global concerns which are unavoidable in relation to environmental policy may help to open up the debate about social policy.

Science and the development of the environmental agenda

Environmental policy development owes a great deal to scientific advances which have enabled people to perceive more clearly the damage that is being caused and to understand how it is caused. This has also, through the contribution it makes to the understanding of long-range and long-term effects, assisted the process by which pollution has been put on the global political agenda (see Kormondy, 1989 and Brenton, 1994, for a discussion of the increasing international activity, largely starting from the Unesco conference on the biosphere of 1968 and the United Nations Stockholm Conference of 1972, and carried forward by the Rio conference of 1992).

Heidenheimer, Heclo and Adams' view of the recent development of environmental policy is given powerful support by an examination of the amount of legislative activity by nations since the late 1960s. Figure 10.1 which was taken from Weale's book on this topic (1992, pp. 12–13) brings this out very clearly.

The view that environmental policy is a post-materialist political concern (McCormick, 1989; Kitschelt, 1989) also diverts attention from the fact that the impact of environmental pollution – despite the fact that it is often indiscriminate in its spread – is experienced unequally within industrial societies. Concentrations of pollutants are, in general, likely to be higher close to their sources – factories, power plants, vehicles, etc. Those with higher levels of income and wealth are more likely to be able to make choices about where they live, taking pollution sources into account. Where this is not possible higher incomes offer, to a degree, scope for individualistic solutions to pollution problems – controlling the atmosphere and noise levels within houses and cars, and purchasing food and drink which is less likely to have been contaminated. Indeed, one of the more interesting manifestations of this is the widespread purchase of bottled water in societies where tap water is much cheaper and not necessarily less pure.

The impact of differences in exposure to environmental hazards upon inequalities in health is a topic which is only just beginning to be studied

Measures	Canada	France	Germany	Netherlands	Sweden	United Kingdom
Organisational:						
Expert council	Canadian Environment Advisory Council, 1972	High Committee for the Environment, 1970	Council of Environmental Experts, 1972	Temporary Council on Air Pollution Control, 1970	Environmental Advisory Committee, 1968	Royal Commission on Environmental Pollution, 1969
Ministry/agency	Department of the Environment, 1970	Ministry for the Protection of Nature and the Environment, 1971	Interior Ministry acquires responsibility for environmental issues, 1969 Federal Environment Office (research), 1974 Federal Ministry of the Environment, 1986	Ministry of Public Health and Environmental Protection, 1971	National Environmental Protection Board, 1969 Franchise Board for Environmental Protection, 1969	Department of the Environment, 1970
Policy developments						
Air	Clean Air Act, 1971	Air Pollution Law, 1961 Decree on Air Pollution, 1974	Federal Immission Control Act, 1974	Air Pollution Act, 1970	Environmental Protection Act, 1969	Health and Safety Act, 1974
Surface waters	Canada Water Act, 1970 Canada Shipping Act, 1970 Fisheries Act, 1970 Northern Inland Water Act, 1970	Water Law, 1964	Federal Water Resources Act, 1957 Federal Water Law, 1976 Effluent Charge Law, 1976	Surface Water Pollution Act, 1969	Environmental Protection Act, 1969	Rivers Act, 1951 Control of Pollution Act, 1974
Chemicals/toxics	Environmental Containments Act, 1975	Law on Chemical Substances, 1977	Chemicals Law, 1980	Chemical Wastes Act, 1976	Act on Chemical Products, 1986	Deposit of Poisonous Wastes Act, 1972 Control of Pollution Act, 1974
EIA	Environmental Assessment and Review Process, 1973	Requirement for Environmental Impact Assessment, 1976	Requirement for Environmental Impact Assessments, 1975	General Administrative Order, 1987	Proposals in 1990/91	Only under EC Directive, 1985
Integrated pollution control	Environment Protection Act		None	General Environmental Provisions Act, 1979	Environmental Protection Act, 1990	Environmental Protection Act, 1990

Figure 10.1 Developments of pollution control policy during the 1960s and 1970s

in any depth (Phillimore, 1993). Such studies often have to relate evidence on environmental hazards in particular districts to other factors in particular kinds of work. In doing so they have also to deal with the fact that for many people there is an invidious choice between exposure to environmental and work-based hazards on the one hand and unemployment or poorly paid work on the other. This is an echo at the more individual level of the issues about comparisons between nations referred to above.

This brings the discussion back to the role of expertise in the identification of environmental problems. In this book the issues about income maintenance, service provision and employment have been seen to have been put on the political agenda through the development of democratic political participation. The role of self-interest in politics has been apparent in these cases. In relation to pollution it is not so evident. In some cases, indeed, democratic political participation has been seen to work against effective pollution control where actions against environmental hazards are seen as direct threats to jobs (Crenson, 1971; Blowers, 1984). In these cases it is not merely that there is the sort of insidious trade-off problem identified above, but it is also the case that the trade-off is often perceived to be between a direct material threat and an uncertain health hazard.

There are several factors which make the latter hard to perceive. Some pollution problems are readily apparent to everyone – they can be smelt, seen, heard or even felt. However, many pollution phenomena, including the most dangerous, are not open to straightforward sensory perception. This is the case with nuclear radiation hazards. It is also the case with many chemicals suspended in water or air, in particular metals like lead and asbestos. In these cases measurements are needed to inform people that a pollution hazard is present. Methods may not be available to do this. Where they are they often use scientific techniques not easily carried out by citizens as a matter of course. Moreover, even when such measurements are carried out the evidence from them may not be made available to the public. The emitters are likely to want to conceal that evidence, and officials and governments may collude with this concealment.

Once measurements are taken there may still be issues about the risks related to any particular form of pollution. Chemical suspensions in air and water are ever present, dangers exist when they are excessively concentrated, but what is an excessive concentration – how much over how long a period? The poisoning processes which occur from pollution are not generally dramatic, they occur over a long time span. The evidence that poisoning is occurring is accumulated gradually, and in some circumstances the resultant diseases are argued to have other causes. In the case of nuclear radiation, for example, there has been a long-standing controversy about whether a slightly raised incidence of comparatively rare diseases in particular places or amongst particular workforces are attributable to radiation exposure

(Barker and Peters, 1993). The difficult policy issue that this raises concerns the extent to which a 'precautionary' approach is justified that curbs pollution just in case of long-run or later-to-be-detected dangers (*ibid.*).

Here again the contributions of experts to the policy debate are rather crucial, in this case to the determination of the level of risk. It may also be noted that the defenders of secrecy on some of these issues rest their case upon the very complex relationships between emission levels and their consequences – they protest that they do not want to raise unnecessary concerns.

Expertise is not only involved in identifying the presence of pollutants and in determining their effects, it is also involved in tracing pathways, interactions and long-term effects. Two good examples of this, contributing to the evolution of the environmental policy agenda, concern acid-rain and the ozone layer. In the case of acid-rain meteorological observations were necessary to identify the relationship between emissions from combustion processes and the subsequent precipitation of chemicals in rain at places separated often by considerable geographical distances. The relationship between British emissions on the one hand and tree loss and lake acidification in Scandinavia on the other, for example, had to be carefully established. Scientific complexity and national self-interest combined to make the debate about acid-rain a difficult and long, drawn-out affair (Wetstone and Rosencranz, 1983). The issues about the impact of emissions on the ozone layer are even more complex, here the potential problems are global and the adverse effects will take a long while to manifest themselves. There is still a great deal of controversy regarding these issues.

Another important issue about interaction, illustrated by the acid-rain issue, concerns the relationships between the different strategies for disposing of pollutants. There are choices about whether to disperse pollutants to the air, into water (rivers or the sea), or to bury them in the ground. Yet chemicals in the air get carried into lakes and rivers, chemicals in rivers get deposited on the land, and chemicals from land-fill sites leach out into water courses. Dispersal into air, water or land which, in the past, has been seen to be unproblematical because of the capacity of these media to absorb (and ultimately dilute) pollutants becomes less and less satisfactory over time. Now, not only is it recognised that many rivers are carrying more pollutants than they can absorb, but worries are also emerging about strategies which involve disposing of pollutants into the sea. Some seas in particular are vulnerable as 'sinks' where matter dispersed into them and into their feeder rivers are becoming concentrated (the Mediterranean and the Baltic, for example, see Kinnersley, 1994).

These interaction effects make the determination of environmental policies difficult. First, because they make it necessary for policy strategies to be holistic – concerns about reducing air pollution, keeping rivers clear or controlling land-fill activities need to be integrated, despite the fact that very different agencies, interest groups and kinds of expertise are likely to be involved. Second, because it is difficult to put effective geographical boundaries around policies and regulatory agencies. Pollutants travel from one administrative area to another, in many cases they travel from one nation state to another. Seas like the Mediterranean obviously have many nation states around them. Air basins are even more complex, and an issue like ozone-layer depletion is a worldwide one. It is also, as a third point in this list, appropriate to remind readers of the general point made earlier that the simplest way of all to reduce pollution is to curb the activity which causes it – to cut motor vehicle emissions by making them travel more slowly, to cut fuel consumption for heating by insulating buildings better, and so on.

This discussion makes clear that pollution control policy involves some very complex collective action problems (Weale, 1992). The next section will explore some of the particular issues about collective action, which make environmental control policy very clearly a *public policy* issue yet at the same time one where conventional political processes often function very ineffectively.

Environmental control as a collective action problem

Throughout much of this book social policy issues and problems have been portrayed as phenomena which may be regarded as both matters for attention by individuals (functioning as market actors), by families and by communities as well as concerns of the state. It has been recognised that much controversy about social policy involves arguments between those who see it as a central concern for the state and those who consider that the state should play a much more minimal 'night-watchman' role. By contrast environmental policy is increasingly recognised as a fundamental feature of the 'night-watchman' role.

Some observations have been made about what individuals with resources may do to reduce the impact of pollution upon themselves. It has also been suggested, however, that such strategies may be limited and may fall foul of unexpected effects. Individuals can buy bottled water, but they may find it more difficult to get access to an unpolluted lake or beach (note the interesting OECD discussion of the implications of tourism, 1991, pp. 242–9).

Hence part of the case for seeing environmental control as a collective action problem lies in the difficulty individuals have in adopting strategies which protect themselves satisfactorily. Perhaps what helps to put environmental policy on the modern political agenda is the increased difficulty elites have in escaping from pollution. The nineteenth-century owner of 'dark satanic mills' polluting the environments in which his employees lived could escape to a country mansion in unspoilt countryside. That is more difficult today.

'Externalities'

An even more important reason why environmental policy is seen as a collective concern may lie in the fact that the pursuit of economic self-interest generates pollution but rarely generates motives to do anything about it. The concept of 'externalities' was explored briefly in Chapter 2 and pollution was quoted as a very clear example. Production processes generate unwanted by-products. If those by-products can be pumped out into rivers and seas, blown into the air or (perhaps less commonly) dumped on wasteland, they will be disposed of at minimal cost to the enterprise. The owners of the enterprise may suffer no ill-effects from these actions. Or if they do worsen the quality of their own environments, the effects of their own actions upon themselves may be marginal and shared with the rest of the 'community' they have polluted. The word 'community' is put in inverted commas here; it has been used loosely and could refer to a very large group indeed.

The externality problem needs to be analysed first in terms of the example of a single polluter, and then by recognising that this polluter may be one amongst many. The actions of a single polluter may be curbed by neighbours, who are bearing the costs of the action. Economic theory about the extent to which this is possible concerns the extent to which there are identifiable exchange relationships. These may be wider business relationships, selling goods to each other, or the exchanges may concern the externalities themselves. Neighbours may restrain noise because they recognise they 'take in' each other's externalities. The problem is that these exchanges are rarely balanced. Consider for example two enterprises on the banks of a non-tidal river: emissions to the river from the upstream enterprise will affect the environment of the other, but the reverse will not apply.

Relationships between neighbours are not necessarily governed solely by exchange considerations – friendships, community spirit and wider ethical considerations may also inhibit behaviour which damages others. But this is the beginning of the identification that there is a collective action issue here, where wider considerations about our common lives influence behaviour. This becomes, once more complex institutions arise, a justification for state action to restrain behaviour which has adverse effects upon a wider community.

Here again, the discussion needs to be linked to the issues that have already been discussed concerning the particular 'natural history' of pollution. The ethical issue of 'Who is my neighbour?' is very complex when externalities from a productive enterprise affect people far away or people not yet born. While there can be an appeal to general ethical principles it can hardly be expected that a simple 'community consciousness' leading to voluntary action to limit an externality will be sufficient to cope with the problem.

Now add to the analysis the fact that it is rare that the problems of externalities come singly (see Le Grand and Robinson, 1984, ch. 5, for a good examination of the complex economics involved). Imagine again the issue of a single enterprise pouring waste products into a river. In many cases, so long as the size of that enterprise is limited, if the river has no other polluters along its banks it may well be able to absorb those products – diluting them and transforming them into less harmful forms with no danger to the wildlife of the river or to anyone seeking to take water from the river. This is a nice idyllic picture, corresponding quite closely to past reality in many societies. Modern reality is very different. There will be many potential polluters along the banks of this hypothetical river (and before readers start to think that the author only sees industry as a polluter it should be said that human and animal wastes, agricultural chemicals and pesticides are likely to be amongst the sources of damage to the river quality).

'The tragedy of the commons'

All waste products have to go somewhere, hence the real world political problem posed by the example explored in the last paragraph is not about how to stop emissions, it is about how to control them in such a way that the river quality is maintained to an acceptable standard and the people who wish to discard by-products into the river feel that they have been fairly treated relative to others. What there is here is the kind of collective action problem which has been described as 'the tragedy of the commons' (Hardin, 1968). Where there is common land on which peasants are entitled to graze livestock, if there is no regulation of numbers each individual will see it as not in their interest to restrict use. They will reason that a few more animals will not make any difference. Yet when all behave in this way the consequence is the destruction of the common pasture. All suffer in the long run.

In this case there is likely to be some recognition of what is going on and some sort of community spirit. Hardin's thesis need not necessarily lead to pessimistic conclusions about the scope for collective action (Ostrom, 1990). The commoners will probably band together to make some rules about the numbers of stock each may put on the common (near where the author lives there is a common that has been regulated in precisely this way for many years).

The issues concerning pollution are similar to this, but have already been shown to be much more complex. Accordingly there is a powerful case for states to engage in action to regulate. But as has already been said, pollution may cross national boundaries – long rivers and semi-enclosed seas, in particular, already pose critical problems – hence collaboration between states is often needed too (see Bennett, 1992, chs 3 and 4, for some good case study examples).

While this chapter has been entitled 'environmental policy' the discussion in this section has focused upon issues about the control of pollution. This is a fundamentally important environmental policy issue, but it is not the only issue. To explore this point further it is worth looking again at the hypothetical river. There are more reasons why the river should not be treated as everyone's drain than simply that it is not very pleasant for those living by it or using it for transport. The river is likely to be a source of water. Severely polluted water can be reprocessed to be used for drinking and washing, but at a substantial cost. In many countries river water is used for irrigation; where large amounts are extracted in this way it has consequences for flow elsewhere. People may wish to swim in the river and engage in other aquatic recreations. Fish are a source of food, and fishing is a popular recreation. The maintenance of a river containing plants and fish contributes to it as an amenity, pleasant to sit and walk beside. An environmental policy for that river involves taking all these things into account, recognising that the multiple uses of the river and the problems which arise if those uses are not held in some sort of balance with each other. Techniques have been developed to try to assist with issues of this kind (notably 'environmental impact assessment', see Carter, 1977).

In other words environmental policy is not merely about minimising the worst consequences of pollution, it is also about maintaining naturally shared amenities (the common parts of societies) in conditions in which conflicting interests in using them are held in some sort of balance. This poses particularly severe problems in circumstances in which, like the common grazing land, legitimate and generally careful use by many people brings unintended consequences in its wake. For example, popular beauty spots suffer from problems of erosion from over-use or the wild creatures whom people want to see are scared and perhaps deterred from breeding by an excess of visitors to their habitat.

Policy options and instruments

The main approaches

The last section has established the way in which environmental issues come to be on the public policy agenda; this one will explore the devices governments use to deal with them. The most straightforward of the policy options involves direct state action to deal with the problem or to clear up afterwards. In the case of solid and liquid waste disposal there may be government waste disposal services. These may be simply funded out of local or national taxation, like services to remove materials from homes and

Table 10.1 Types of regulatory power

Powers relating to	General planning powers	Specific powers
Start-up	1	2
Change of activities	3	4
Continuous surveillance	5	6

business premises. There may be charges if they have to deal with large or exceptional loads. In the case of liquid waste the common device in urban societies is simply a drainage system. Again arrangements have to be made to deal with the exceptional. There will be problems for sewage treatment and disposal systems if there are enterprises putting exceptional pressure upon the system or if the material being discharged is toxic and requires special treatment procedures. Government may regulate such discharges and impose charges. Some of the special issues concerning permit and charging systems will be explored further below. Solid and liquid waste disposal responsibilities may be sub-contracted from government organisations to private firms.

In the light of the comparative newness of many pollution control policies, societies with extensive industrial legacies have problems from the past to clear up. Abandoned factories and mines, lagoons and solid waste dumps from earlier times impose a variety of costly problems upon governments, which cannot easily be recharged to anyone else.

Much environmental legislation gives central or local government regulatory powers. Two key distinctions concern the extent to which the powers are comprehensive ones determining the permissibility of the activity as a whole or specific ones relating to explicit activities (particularly emissions), and the extent to which powers relate solely to the start of an activity or impose continuous surveillance. These distinctions are illustrated in Table 10.1.

General planning powers

Many countries have developed comprehensive forms of planning legislation (alternative 1 in Table 10.1) which enable authorities to determine whether activities can be established in specific places. This sort of legislation is likely to give powers to consider any new activity in the context of the activities already going on in that area. This may operate in two rather contrasting ways.

There may be attempts to determine zones for industrial, agricultural and residential uses. A new venture may have to establish that it is compatible with the activities already being carried out in the area and will not damage those or the general amenities of the area. Alternatively there may be planning restrictions that are imposed because of existing levels of activity in the area, a new venture may be deemed to overload the area in terms of pollution emissions, traffic use, etc. (Wood, 1989).

Specific planning powers

An alternative or supplementary regulatory approach may require enterprises to secure permits to carry out specific activities (alternative 2 in Table 10.1). This approach is widely used with static emission sources and readily identifiable discharges (see various examples from the United States, Britain and Germany in Downing and Hanf, 1983). These may be specifically concerned with what is allowed to go up chimneys or be discharged into a water course. New ventures may have to go through a double process of securing both general planning permission and specific permits for such activities. Where different regulatory agencies are involved there may be confusion and inconsistencies.

Regulations relating to changing activities

Alternatives 3 and 4 in Table 10.1 are supplementary to 1 and 2. There is a distinction to be made between regulatory systems which operate only to determine the initial siting of an activity and those which require reapplications whenever new developments occur or new activities are contemplated. One of the difficulties in environmental policy is that systems have moved over time from very rudimentary controls to more continuous regulation. Once activities have been established under simple legislation it may be difficult to control future developments.

Continuous surveillance

Alternatives 5 and 6 in Table 10.1 take the notions embedded in 3 and 4 much further in requiring that enterprises accept as a condition of initial permission to operate some expectation of continued surveillance over their activities. This approach places the regulatory authority in a much stronger position to exercise control. It may also allow the possibility of enforcing the improvement of standards of pollution control as new techniques become available. A device used here may be the renewable permit – the enterprise is allowed to operate under a set of conditions which are reviewed from time to time.

Most complex regulatory systems today involve continuous surveillance. The laws relating to them impose punishments for breaches of the terms of permits. There are various options: fines, closure of the operation, the imprisonment of the violating owner or staff. The difficulty the enforcement agencies face is that the more draconian options have consequences for other than the offenders. Employment may be affected if the punishments stop activities, either directly or indirectly by imposing prohibitive costs upon them. The elimination of an important economic activity may have ramifications well beyond those directly affected. In the last analysis there may be issues about the viability of whole communities (see Crenson, 1971) or even nations. It may be noted here that this point may contradict an earlier remark that environmentalism may be a positive influence on employment levels. This reaffirms the importance of collective action, often beyond the limits of the nation state, to ensure that 'dirty' production processes do not offer specific enterprises competitive advantages over others.

A consequence of enforcement difficulties is that regulatory systems tend to involve the use of 'carrots' as well as 'sticks'. Where there are violations of pollution control regulations, officials may be expected to offer advice; they may also be able to use public funds to support plant modifications which will bring the operation into conformity with the requirements of the law.

Comparing control systems

The next section will consider some of the issues about differences between environmental control systems. While the ideas discussed have derived largely from comparative studies, the efforts of those studies to distinguish between national approaches to environmental control, in ways which might enable good and bad approaches to be distinguished, have been largely unsuccessful. The OECD have published data on national expenditures on this policy area. Apart from showing that expenditures are generally low, they do not readily facilitate even limited comparisons in the way that the figures on health, education and income maintenance have done. The problems about making comparisons arise in part from the impact of the size of the problem of pollution (in this respect it is not surprising to find relative unpolluted countries like Sweden and Norway, amongst the lower spenders). There is also a problem that it is not self-evident that the most expensive regulatory systems will be the most efficient. The OECD attempt to identify private as well as public control and abatement expenditure; it is hard to be convinced about the reliability of the former. Despite these sceptical comments the OECD data are set out in table 10.2.

Table 10.2 Pollution abatement and control expenditure as a percentage of GDP, mid 1980s

	Public	Private	Total
Canada	0.89	0.36	1.25
USA	0.60	0.86	1.47
Japan	1.17	0.08	1.25
France	0.56	0.33	0.89
Germany (West)	0.78	0.74	1.52
Netherlands	0.95	0.30	1.26
Norway	0.54	0.27	0.82
Sweden	0.66	0.27	0.93
UK	0.62	0.62	1.25

Source: OECD (1991) *The State of the Environment*, Paris: OECD, p. 255; reproduced by permission of the OECD.

The implementation of pollution control policy

There are significant differences between nations in the formal mechanisms used to implement pollution control policy. Knoepfel and his colleagues generalise as follows:

> *The approach of the United States relies on coercion, while the United Kingdom, Japan and France prefer persuasion techniques. Polluters in the United States are treated as foes to be fought in the courts; in Britain, Japan and France polluters are considered friends who must be convinced and sometimes assisted. (Knoepfel* et al. *in Dierkes* et al., *1987, p. 174)*

Later in the same article reference is made to 'legalist traditions of administrative behaviour in Italy, Spain and West Germany' (*ibid.*, p. 175). Yet the article as a whole suggests that the comparisons between countries relate very much to 'policy style' (Richardson, 1982) rather than output. Outcomes are to a greater extent determined by the power of the interests involved. It is then perhaps the case that the defeat of the regulators in court battles or deliberate decisions not to use the more draconian powers (perhaps as a result of earlier defeats) produces, in the countries with the apparently more formal systems, similar outcomes to the permissive implementation systems in other countries (see Kelman, 1981; Vogel in Dierkes *et al.*, 1987; note also a forthcoming volume edited by Hanf and Jensen).

These considerations have led to particular interest in the regulatory policy systems which involve bargaining and discretion rather than bringing formal and direct law enforcement into play. Regulation of complex economic activities, in respect of their waste products, is a difficult matter. To determine the extent to which waste can be minimised, the ways in which it may be made safe and the best techniques to deal with it require considerable expertise. It is difficult to formulate a series of laws which can be applied fairly across a wide range of enterprises, using different processes and with different capacities to adapt to use the most up-to-date technologies. Rules which some companies can comply with easily may drive others out of business. Clearly regulation requires some effort to achieve a trade-off between the minimisation of pollution and the achievement of efficient and cheap production. In some cases this can be a 'positive sum' game – less polluting processes are more efficient or waste products can be put to further productive uses. The latter is, for example, the ideal in much agricultural activity, when animal waste can be used as fertiliser. However, where it is rather more of a 'zero sum' game difficult judgements have to be made between alternative evils.

What all this implies is that it may be regarded as appropriate to regard regulatory activity as one which works not with absolute rules but with principles about the best practice established by expert officials and operationalised using discretionary powers (see Hill in Downing and Hanf, 1983; and Ham and Hill, 1993, ch. 9, for a wider discussion of the issues about discretion in administration). What this often involves, given that officials need to work very closely with the objects of their regulatory activities, is a process of bargaining between regulator and regulatee (Peacock, 1984; Hawkins, 1984). Such bargaining will deal not merely with costs and consequences, but will also be likely to take into account past behaviour (Has the compliance record of the regulatee been satisfactory?) and the likely impact of any outcome on the behaviour of others. Hanf has described this process as one of 'co-production' in which the determinants of regulatory behaviour need to be seen as 'embedded in the social worlds within and outside the regulatory agency' (Hanf in Hill, 1993b, p. 109; Hanf in Moran and Prosser, 1994).

The disadvantage of this phenomenon is that it makes much regulation a private activity, not open to scrutiny by politicians and the public. However, as suggested earlier, inasmuch as the detection of pollution and the interpretation of its effects requires expertise this is partly inevitable.

Nevertheless it has led to controversy about the extent to which regulation can be effective if carried out in this way. It has been alleged that regulators working in circumstances like this are subject to 'capture' by the industries they are regulating – they are often former employees of that industry, they have to work closely with those they regulate, and they are likely to form a view of what control is feasible largely determined by those whose activities they are required to curb. The regulatory agencies dispute this interpretation of their activities, stressing that their close understanding of the processes they are regulating make it difficult for the regulatees to deceive them or to hide undesirable practices. They stress that an informed regulator can educate and encourage better practices, helping an enterprise to achieve better pollution control more effectively that way than through formal sanctions (see Frankel, 1974; Ashby and Anderson, 1981, for alternative views on this issue in relation to the control of air pollution in Britain – the organisational arrangements have since changed, but the issues about process remain relevant). The success of this approach may also depend upon the extent to which there is consensus about the desirability of the policy goals. It may be that in the Scandinavian context where 'framework laws' are typically used to this end with officials and regulatees willing to fill in the details this may be the case, while elsewhere little may be achieved (see case studies in Hanf and Jensen, forthcoming, contrasting Sweden and Italy but also noting slow progress in restraining pollution from Danish agriculture).

In the interpretation of this argument the examination of the role played by sanctions may be important. Court cases where polluters are prosecuted for the violation of agreements help to establish the parameters of a control system, indicating what is clearly unacceptable and warning possible future violators. It is evidence to the public that the regulatory system does have some 'teeth'.

Finally, institutional complexity may further complicate enforcement processes in these circumstances – arising both from divisions of powers between 'levels' of government (central – regional – local) and between different central departments with competing interests (environmental policy ministries versus industry or agriculture ministries). (These themes are also well explored in Hanf and Jensen's forthcoming edited collection.)

Differences between national regulatory systems assume a particular importance where some nations suspect that others are not doing all they might to reduce a problem which is a shared concern. As already observed, pollution is increasingly recognised as a supra-national problem. In a river flowing across a border, a sea which is a 'sink' for several nations or an air flow system which transports pollutants far and wide, some sort of common approach is necessary. Where efforts have been made to set up supra-national government systems to deal with common trading areas, as in the European Union, it may be possible to legislate to try to achieve a control system shared by several countries. Without this, agreements are required to adopt related approaches, particularly agreements concerning the amounts of emissions allowed from each country – as with the transmission of sulphur dioxide in the wind or emissions into an international river or sea. Pollution control has become an important topic for international diplomacy.

The European Commission endeavour to use 'directives' to achieve common policy responses. These have been evident in relation to environmental problems. Directives have to be implemented through absorption into the legal and administrative systems of each member country. The Commission may take action against ineffective implementation of its directives.

Such action is likely, where there is a lack of satisfactory data, to be concerned as much with form as substance (see Haigh, 1989).

The discussion has implied that an ideal regulatory system is one where there are clear publicly available rules – setting out best practices, activities which will be unacceptable, limits which must not be exceeded and targets for good practice – enforced by officials with sufficient discretion to be able to take into account particular difficulties, disregard isolated accidents and take a view about what is acceptable practice over a sustained period. One difficulty concerning pollution control is that emissions will fluctuate, being affected by variations in economic activity and changes in weather (particularly in agriculture) as well as by variations in the care with which enterprises operate. Monitoring systems have to be set up, therefore, which enable a long view to be taken of emissions. It is not satisfactory either to have a system where behaviour is exemplary only when inspection is known to be in progress or to have one where isolated accidents lead to draconian penalties. That is a point that could be applied to many inspection systems and regulatory activities; it is particularly important in relation to pollution control since its ultimate object is the achievement of as satisfactory an environment as possible, not the absolute prevention of pollution.

Inasmuch as pollution control requires flexible approaches, with enforcement responsibilities delegated to officials with discretionary powers there is an obvious danger that state responses will be 'symbolic' (Edelman, 1971). Governments will want to be seen to be concerned, but they may be unwilling to grasp the political, economic and administrative difficulties entailed in being effective. The impact of emergent 'green' parties in various countries has led to responses by the older parties, which may be abandoned when the threat to parliamentary majorities from these new minorities subside (see Hanf and Jensen, forthcoming). In the longer run governments may fail to put the necessary resources and formal support systems in place in order to facilitate effective implementation (see Ham and Hill, 1993, chs 6 and 9, for a further discussion of this aspect of 'implementation deficit').

Monitoring, specific emissions and the general environment

As monitoring methods have become more sophisticated and it has become more clearly recognised that the movement of air and water is complex, pollution control objectives have come to be increasingly specified in terms of target levels for areas of water (rivers, etc.) or air. In the case of rivers this can be specified in terms of qualities necessary to sustain wildlife. In the case of air the setting of ideal parameters is a little more complex, but as it is known that the incidence of certain diseases (asthma, for example) is affected by air quality it is possible to set goals for a city or region. Where one of the problems to be addressed is associated with the flow of air (as in the case of the acid-rain problem), the technical problems are more difficult, but it is still possible to specify emission limits for a whole area (by contrast with simply doing it for specific emitters). This approach helps so long as adjustments can be made for flows, to deal with the problems raised above in regard to comparisons between the effectiveness of different national systems. European Commission policies and international agreements may be able to establish targets for air or water quality by specific dates (see, for example, the reference to air pollution targets in OECD, 1991, p. 48), with corresponding arrangements for a common monitoring system.

The development of this approach implies that there can be 'trade offs' – if emission levels from individual sources fluctuate wildly peak outputs from one source may not matter if the general level remains low, or more critically some continuously high emissions may be tolerated when they can be offset against others which are less hard to control. The difficulty about framing regulatory practices in these circumstances is that those who are regulated will need to be satisfied that they are being fairly treated. Farmers who take great care to limit slurry discharges to a river will not be very happy if a neighbour's continual carelessness is tolerated simply because the river quality remains high. One approach used in some places (for example in relation to some aspects of air pollution control in the United States) involves tradeable permits. Permits allow a certain amount of emission. The total number of permits issued is set at a low enough level to achieve a general air quality objective. Those enterprises able to keep their own emissions below their permit level are then able to sell their unrequired excess to others.

Economic approaches to environmental regulation

Earlier in this discussion it was pointed out that often those producing solid and liquid waste are required to pay for its disposal, with either a charge for its removal or a charge for permission to discharge it somewhere (into a river, etc.). Theoretically the same principle could be applied to discharges into the air (though here satisfactory monitoring is likely to be a problem). The idea of charges or taxes for emissions has been picked up by economists and related to the problem of 'externalities'. It is argued that:

> *. . . the price of a good or service should fully reflect its cost of production and the cost of resources used, including environmental resources. Use of air, water or land for the emission, discharge or storage of wastes is as much a use of resources as other 'conventional' factors of production . . . it is the free use of such resources which is the prime cause of environmental degradation. (OECD, 1991, p. 258)*

This has led to the formulation of the 'polluters pay principle' which suggests that devices are needed to make 'polluters "internalise" the costs of use or degradation of environmental resources' (*ibid.*). Obviously charges for emissions do this in some way, so in a sense do fines for transgressions. The idea that there may be explicit charges related to amounts of permitted emissions takes this further. To this is added the idea that such permits might be tradeable (see the reference to this above, p. 250).

The polluters pay principle is a device offered by economists in an age of disillusion with direct administrative regulation. It derives from an exercise of economic theorising involving the notion that a simple cost device can be put in the place of all the human complexities of regulatory policy. It seems to offer an approach which will obviate all the difficulties discussed above about bargaining, co-production and regulatory capture (Pearce, 1993).

The polluter pays principle has been widely endorsed 'as a principle' (see discussion in Weale, 1992, ch. 6) and is influencing governments inasmuch as it disposes them to strengthen existing charging systems. It is found most clearly in policies which tax energy sources. However, there are several problems about extending this alternative to offer a comprehensive approach to pollution control. One is that such a cost may not be an incentive to stop polluting, particularly when it can be passed on to consumers in situations of monopoly and oligopoly. Another is that while other costs are, in general terms, imposed by market forces the imposition of a pollution tax needs to be determined by government. There is no easy methodology for determining such a tax, and in any case politicians are unlikely to be prepared to treat it as simply a technical issue. In other words the creation of a workable structure of taxes to enforce the polluter pays principle on a large scale would be likely to be just as difficult as current regulatory methods, and just as likely to need regular revision (thereby imposing what economists describe as 'transaction costs' – see Williamson, 1975, 1985 – though, in theory, these can be passed on to the polluters too).

Where, as in relation to international pollution control issues, case-monitoring issues are complex, and it is generally appropriate for these to deal in aggregate data and not concern themselves with individual emissions, the underlying theory embodied in the polluter pays principle may merit attention. In relations between nations it offers an approach to the concern that countries should not derive trading advantages from allowing cheap and dirty productive processes to operate. Countries may be set targets requiring control responses which therefore impose general costs upon their economies.

Conclusions

The daunting problem about pollution is that the world is now facing large issues about the spread of pollution and its long-term effects. Single dirty rivers or a limited range of dirty factory emissions blowing across a frontier are comparatively easy issues to address. Issues like the widespread degradation of seas and the evolution of long-term climatic change as a result of the long-term collective impact of emissions, most of which will not have been regarded as harmful in themselves, raise much more fundamental problems. The economic analyses of the issues about externalities and the 'tragedy of the commons' suggest pessimistic conclusions about the prospects of coming to grips with these issues (see Weale, 1992, for a good, and comparatively optimistic, analysis of this). The models of political and economic behaviour which suggest that short-term self-interest is the dominant driving force in policy change have been invoked in various places in this book as offering plausible explanations of the evolution of social policy. If they are right they offer little comfort as the world confronts its environmental problems. Ironically, other models – which either emphasise the impact of elites and altruism or which see social policy progress as stimulated by broad humanistic ideological movements – suggest ways in which such universalistic problems may be addressed. There is an increasing volume of writing which stresses how important it is for the world to come to grips with these issues. They offer an important argument to counter those analyses of the 'crisis' of the welfare state which see governments as impotent in the face of global economic forces. They see opposition to simplistic 'productivist' ideologies as vital for our survival (see, for example, Lipietz, 1992, and the discussion of 'greenism' in George and Wilding, 1994). This theme will be discussed again at the end of Chapter 12.

It is, however, not entirely appropriate to conclude this chapter with an emphasis on the large, long-run and difficult agenda, since environmental policy is *both* about the big issues of global risk *and* about a whole range of quite specific and localised issues which can be easily addressed. These issues are important for social welfare and interact in significant ways with more individualised health, housing and income maintenance issues. As stressed early in the chapter, while pollution affects everyone its impact is generally heaviest upon those who are disadvantaged in other respects. Moreover, that point may even be made with regard to the global issues – if global warming results in a rise in sea levels the Dutch will probably invest massively to protect themselves, but many people in Bangladesh will probably drown.

Guide to further reading

When the author was wondering how to approach the chapter on environment policy Weale's *The New Politics of Pollution* (1992) was published, offering a lively analysis of the issues. Bennett's *Dilemmas: Coping with Environmental Problems* (1992) provides some very nicely presented case studies which illustrate the complexity of this area. Markham's *A Brief History of Pollution* (1994) is a good introduction to the issues, while Kinnersley's *Coming Clean* (1994) explores the issues about water pollution.

More specific comparative work, as opposed to general introductions which rightly stress that pollution is an essentially international or global issue, is harder to find. Downing and Hanf's *International Comparisons in Implementing Pollution Laws* (1983) contains some useful material but is rather dated. Hanf and Jensen have edited a new collection of essays; their publication is likely in 1996 or 1997.

PART III

Social policy, society and the state

CHAPTER ELEVEN

Who gets what: social divisions of welfare

Introduction

Earlier in this book it has been suggested that social policies have a variable impact and that there are divisions within systems which affect who gets what. Social policies occur in societies which are divided or stratified in various respects. Salient divisions occur in relation to socio-economic status or class, gender and ethnicity. Social policies are bound to be affected by these divisions and perhaps influence them. Much of the rhetoric of social policy suggests that it ought to have an impact upon those divisions, contributing to the advancement of equality (see Le Grand, 1982, ch. 1). The 'welfare state' has been portrayed in these terms both by its defenders and by its critics. Yet, as Bagguley has suggested (in Burrows and Loader, 1994, p. 78), the expression 'welfare state' is particularly used by those who are 'conceptual prisoners' of the dream that state social policies could change society. A more modest aspiration for social policy is that it may play a role in alleviating or mitigating the worst effects of capitalism. But there are alternative possibilities. One is that far from reducing divisions in society social polices reinforce or increase them. Furthermore, social policy may itself be a creative influence upon stratification – producing divisions of its own. Another view is that social policies have no significant effect upon divisions, they merely reflect them.

It is important to examine social policy in these terms, to consider the ways in which its operation interacts with and has an impact upon social structures. To do this it is necessary to explore some of the basic elements in social structures and then to look at the extent to which social policies can be seen to be divided along similar lines. That can then lead on to consideration of some of the more dynamic aspects of the relationship between social policy and society.

The approach to comparative analysis adopted by Esping-Andersen and by Korpi and Palme, which was discussed in Chapter 2, is rooted in the notion that some social policy systems may reflect and contribute to social solidarity. The concept of 'decommodification' is used by Esping-Andersen to suggest that some policy systems achieve a universalism, which treats all sections of society alike. The decommodified systems of Scandinavia are contrasted with corporatist and liberal systems which more clearly reflect labour market divisions and market ideologies. Yet these are attempts to classify national systems as a whole; the inclusiveness of the Scandinavian systems is seen relative to other systems. This does not preclude the continuation of some divisions in those systems. Decommodification is a relative concept. Furthermore, as a number of critics have pointed out (Ginsburg, 1992; Williams in Burrows and Loader, 1994), issues about women and ethnic minorities are given little attention in this analysis.

This discussion will emphasise divisions within systems, eventually coming back to address comparative questions about the extent to which some systems are more divided, or divided in different ways to others. It will be carried out primarily in terms of the three key elements in social stratification: class, gender and ethnicity (though other elements in stratification will be discussed briefly after that). There will be separate sections dealing with class, gender and ethnicity, in which it will be necessary to explore briefly the meanings of these three concepts before examining their manifestation in social policy. This will be done in a sketchy, and therefore sometimes inevitably tendentious way. This is a book about social policy and not about social stratification; it cannot, therefore, explore all the complex issues involved in the analysis of the latter (for a good guide to this literature, see Crompton, 1993). At the same time, as suggested above, it cannot ignore stratification. For analytical purposes it is necessary to deal with each aspect of stratification separately. The order in which they are considered should not be taken to indicate a view of their relative importance. Feminists, for example, have justifiably criticised the primacy given to class analysis, ignoring other sources of inequality or assuming they can be read off from class. The analysis here may be open to the same criticism. Yet the way in which much argument about stratification has been shaped around class analysis, particularly Marxist class analysis, and responses to that, makes it appropriate to look at that first. The aim is to reach an integrated position in the end.

Social class and social policy

Concepts and theory

Social class concepts are used in a variety of ways both in everyday discourse and in sociological analysis. It is easy to arrive at a situation in which people are talking past each other because of their different usages. In the context of this book it is necessary to examine some basic sociology in order to establish the parameters of the discussion to follow. In doing so elements from an elaborate debate about social class will be set out as succinctly as possible.

Perhaps the most common popular usage of class sees it in subjective terms, with cultural overtones about who people identify with, feel comfortable with and are able to talk to (sometimes quite literally in the last case – given differences in language usage). This approach ignores the income, occupation and power differences in society which these subjective and cultural phenomena reflect and often reinforce. It makes the achievement of a classless society a matter of breaking down these cultural barriers, a comfortable 'egalitarian' objective for those who do not want to sacrifice more material privileges.

There is an alternative approach to defining class in subjective terms which offers a direct challenge to it. The most strident formulation of this occurs in Marxist theory – defining class in terms of the relationship to the means of production. If stripped of its tendency to work with a simple class division into ownership and non-ownership, its link with a prediction of increased polarisation and its association with a direct attack on capitalism, this approach has the following merits:

1. That it focuses upon the very concrete and evident differences between people in terms of income, wealth and power.
2. That it recognises that these differences are relational (if a cake is divided unequally some have less *because* others have more).

These basic points need to be confronted *before* going on to any arguments about justifications. People may want to argue that differential participation in the creation of the cake justifies unequal shares; the point here is merely to establish that measurable differences, with consequences for other activities, arise out of the sharing process and that that process involves a relationship.

Most modern usages of class in these terms have moved a long way from Marx's capitalist/proletariat distinction. They owe a great deal to the German sociologist Max Weber and to more recent developments of his work (see Dahrendorf, 1959; Bendix and Lipset, 1967; Giddens, 1973). The characteristics of these usages are as follows. It is recognised that labour market relationships are important but cannot be simply dichotomised into ones involving either buyers or sellers of labour. Most labour market participants are sellers of labour but selling involves different levels of skill in varied situations. At the most advantaged end are, for example: people with skills that are much in demand, people who have secured managerial roles within capitalist enterprises, professionals who have secured state monopolies and bureaucrats who acquire rights to their jobs so strong that they may almost be regarded as property. At the disadvantaged end are the traditional proletariat who have nothing to sell but their labour power, who (in the event of competition for work) may be further divided amongst themselves in terms of differences of age, health and experience (gender and race considerations will be brought into the analysis later). Between these two extremes are various gradations of 'market situation', dependent upon education and skill but also upon the success of groups in securing legal statuses and/or trade union protection for themselves.

In trying to throw the wide range of considerations into the analysis, factors which facilitate entry to advantaged positions and factors which protect individuals once into those positions have been mixed together. A further feature of a class structure is that individuals endeavour not merely to protect themselves but to pass advantages on to others, notably to their children. In capitalist societies differential advantage in the labour market leads to differential rewards. Then the main way advantages are passed to the next generation is through the effective use of those monetary rewards within the family. The comparative openness of the labour market in many industrial societies, inasmuch as posts are not inherited or passed on through patronage but are the subject of competition, makes family economic advantage only one of the factors which influence the life chances of children. In other words the class structure is an open one in which family members may rise and fall between generations. This fact, when also associated with a lack of cultural divisions between the classes, is also referred to by those who argue that their societies are classless. Against this, social mobility studies indicate that a parent's position in the class structure is still a very strong predictor of his or her children's likely future position (Goldthorpe, 1980). However, it is important not to confuse very real divisions at any one point in time with the possibilities of change over time and between generations in a context of a changing society.

The relatively abstract theory set out above is translated into operationalised social class concepts. A limited number of socio-economic groups are identified. These are classified by occupations but with the recognition that a 'high' position in that classification normally implies a high income and vice versa (taking a long view not a short one – regard may need to be had to stability and the opportunities to increase income over time without an occupational change). Non-manual and professional jobs tend to dominate the top end of any such classification, while manual ones (particularly low-skilled ones) dominate the bottom end. In the middle the manual/non-manual distinction, once comparatively clear in such systems, is today very blurred. There are some groups who are hard to classify. The self-employed – Marx's bourgeoisie – range from very minor business people with poverty-level incomes to major magnates. There are obvious problems about classifying someone without a labour market attachment (the discussion will return to this issue with regard to women). Past employment or the nature of the employment sought by those out of work may be an unsatisfactory basis for classification.

Earlier socio-economic 'class' indices have been used in the examination of the performance of social policy systems – notably in relation to health and education, where there are distinct links between final outcomes (likelihood of survival of birth, likelihood of success in the education system, etc.) and socio-economic status. There will be various explanations for these differences and they cannot, without consideration of other factors, be used to *judge* the outputs of social policy systems. Social policies – particularly income maintenance, employment and education policies – may have an important part to play in relation to the dynamics of a class structure.

'Social divisions of welfare'

It has been suggested that there are 'social divisions' in social welfare systems which reflect, and may reinforce, social divisions in society. Seminal essays on this theme, by Titmuss (1958) and by Sinfield (1978), drew attention to the way both tax reliefs and untaxed fringe benefits may convey privileges to some, largely better off, workers so that their incomes in adversity (particularly when they are sick or retired) are state subsidised in ways not available to other, largely worse off, workers. These two forms of welfare, subsidised by the state but often not identified in the 'welfare package', are described as 'fiscal' and 'occupational' welfare.

A related vein of British work has shown that better-off families may secure considerably more state-subsidised services than worse-off families (Le Grand, 1982; Townsend, 1979, but note qualifications to this conclusion offered in Hills, 1993). Two crucial ingredients in these British findings are that the better off are likely to make much more use of the most expensive elements in the education system (particularly higher education) and that they are likely to make more effective demands upon a state health care system. However, the thrust of this work is a little different to that in Titmuss's and Sinfield's essays. It points to under-use by poorer people of universally available services as opposed to subsidies for private privileges. These are rather different issues, calling for very different remedies by those who are unhappy with the inequalities demonstrated.

Nevertheless, it is worth considering to what extent the implications of both approaches to differential experience of social policy can be generalised to model the association between class inequalities *before* and those *after* social policy inputs. This relationship could be traced in simple terms of a comparison between the welfare expectations of two broad 'classes' distinguished by work, an upper non-manual class and a lower manual one. That sort of approach was dominant in discussions of a topic like this around the time Titmuss wrote his essay on the 'social divisions of welfare' in 1958. It is not so applicable today largely because of the increasing merging in the middle already referred to. It is perhaps more appropriate now to work with a three-'class' model which recognises the following:

1. That the market situations and tax situations of the very well off have improved in various societies (notably the United States and Britain) (George and Howards, 1991).
2. That policy developments in favour of the traditional working class have, wherever employment can be maintained, contributed to a merging of that group and the lower earners amongst non-manual workers.
3. That falling opportunities for unskilled manual work and the related high unemployment have separated this group off from the rest of the old working class.

One way of dealing with the last of these three developments has been to characterise the resultant lowest group as an 'under-class' (Myrdal, 1962; Wilson, 1981, 1987; Dahrendorf, 1985; Field, 1989). This usage, however, has been linked with arguments about the behavioural characteristics of the disadvantaged, emphasising not social but psychological processes (Murray, 1984, 1990). Mann condemns the attempt to identify the economic and social forces that create this division as 'sloppy' sociology (Mann, 1994, p. 94) which encourages a popular media usage which, in treating the underprivileged as in this sense 'outside' of society, blames the victims and derives harsh policy prescriptions from its focus on behaviour. Rank offers powerful evidence in support of Mann's view from his study of 'welfare' recipients in the United States. He shows them to share the dominant values (even to the extent of stigmatising their fellow benefit recipients!) (Rank, 1994). The under-class concept implies, at best, the absence of a relationship to other classes; at worst, a deliberate opting out of society. In the latter sense it is used with stigmatising intent. It is therefore not used here.

Moore similarly argues that the pejorative connotations of the term 'under-class' create problems for a realistic analysis of the issues. He directs attention to the extent to which the situation of this group might be analysed in terms of the concept of 'citizenship', where the absence of work opportunities leads to exclusion from full social participation (Moore in Coenen and Leisink, 1993). Other contributors to the same symposium take a similar line, arguing that Marshall's analysis of citizenship (Marshall, 1963) saw social rights as supplementing civil and political rights and partly counterbalancing the disadvantages bestowed by the class system. The problem in regard to this is the extent to which those social rights depend in practice upon labour market participation (Coenen and Leisink, 1993, particularly ch. 1). Here then is a key issue for the analysis of social policy.

A social divisions model

A connection between the divisions in society and the 'social divisions of welfare' may be made by tracing the nature of the latter. In the discussion below three 'groups' will be identified in terms of their likely experience of social policy. The expression 'groups' rather than classes is used in order to try to avoid confusion with the sociological analysis of class. The groups identified will be called simply (1), (2) and (3). There are strong connections between these groups and 'class' stratification, but the purpose of the exercise is to identify how social policy works. Where it seems likely that this is a reflection of the more general stratification system that will be identified, the usage of the concept of 'group' is designed to try to avoid eliding policy effects and wider social factors. The initial treatment will leave the issues relating to gender to be followed up in the next section. Furthermore no attempt will be made to suggest the influence ethnicity will have upon who gets into which group, as this too is to come later.

Before beginning this analysis there is a need to interpose one qualification. One of the difficulties about the analysis of stratification concerns the relationship between a description of a situation at a specific point in time, which tends to be static, and the fact that the object is to explain an essentially dynamic aspect of social life. This is evidently a problem if, as will be the case below, labour market attachment is seen as of central importance. The third of the groups discussed below is defined largely in terms of failure to secure an adequate labour market attachment. How then can those at the beginning of an actual (or potential) working life be described? An important modern phenomenon is temporary difficulties in securing work followed by market entry for most young people. It may, on the one hand, make comparatively little sense to describe those in this situation, who by virtue of family and educational advantages, are likely to be only temporarily workless as members of a disadvantaged and vulnerable group. On the other hand, some of them will fail to benefit from their initial advantages. There is a need to recognise their hopefully temporary dependency, seeing their situation as dependent on the capacity of their family of origin to offer support while they are in this situation. It is in this context that the difficulties the children of those without effective labour market attachments also face in securing this 'benefit' assume particular policy significance.

Employed people in 'group' (1) will be unlikely to experience breaks in their working lives before retirement. If they are temporarily sick their employers will make up their pay. They may thus be practically unaware of entitlements to insurance benefits when sick or unemployed. Once retired, private pension schemes are likely to determine their income; they will probably have state insurance pensions too but in many societies these will be dwarfed by private scheme entitlements. This will apply as much to state employees as to private ones. These are forms of 'occupational welfare' often subsidised by tax relief (fiscal welfare). If they live in a society with a good state health system they will make use of it, but they will readily turn to private schemes if it lets them down. They may use the state education system for their children (there are some very interesting differences between societies in the extent to which the well off use the state system), though if they do they will be very fussy about school standards and may make efforts to ensure access to the 'best' schools in the public system. Their children's educational achievement will in any case be heavily influenced by additional inputs from home. Employers and systems of tax relief may subsidise private health or education expenses. They are very unlikely to occupy subsidised rented housing; in many societies they are likely to be owner-occupiers and may perhaps benefit from tax subsidies to that sector. They will choose to live, as far as practicable, in areas where pollution levels are low. Yet they will be, as high-level consumers and high energy users (bear in mind above all travel), high producers of pollution. Public employment services will be irrelevant to them. Social services will largely be inaccessible to them because of means tests.

'Group' (2) will be the main beneficiaries of the mainstream welfare systems. Insurance benefit systems will be important in reducing the impact of temporary absences from work and in providing support in retirement (there are here some important differences in the extent to which different countries have ensured that public schemes provide high levels of income replacement). Tax- or insurance-funded health schemes will be very important in preventing severe difficulties in the event of serious illness. Children will be sent to the nearest available state schools. This will only be regarded as a problem if there are many poorer (or ethnically different) people in the catchment area. Housing choices may minimise this 'problem'. Depending on the country they will either be the owner-occupiers of modest, mainly modern, houses or the tenants of the better-quality property available from a social landlord. In either event they will have been likely to have taken some care to avoid stigmatised areas. The kind of work they do may expose them to pollution sources. A need to be near work may, furthermore, make pollution difficult to avoid. These are important factors in putting pollution issues on the modern political agenda. Public employment services may be used, particularly early in the career in countries where labour market training has been given attention. This group will also be low users of social care services.

'Group' (3) can now largely be defined by contrast with group (2). Low wages and low levels of job security will tend to undermine social insurance entitlements; means tests will very often determine their incomes. Indeed the 'poverty trap' (see p. 85) will make it difficult to move away from a state-determined minimal level in many societies. Housing will be likely to be poorer-quality social housing (with initial desperate need and then limited income minimising choice), though they may be in very poor-quality old private rented or owner-occupied housing. School and health care choices will be minimal, and they will not be particularly effective at making demands upon professional staff. They will be likely to live and work in a poor environment, exposed to risks from pollution. The employment service will be an important, but also a very controlling element in their lives ('workfare' – see Jacobs, in Coenen and Leisink, 1993). They are likely to be able to get access to social care services, but this may bring social controls with it too.

The situations of those in group (3) feature as a key ingredient in the debate about the 'under-class' (see p. 262). The pattern of disadvantage to which that label has been applied is much more salient in high unemployment and low wage economies, particularly where certain areas of the manual labour market have collapsed and opportunities have been low for a long while. A similar point may be made by means of historical comparisons (Mann, 1992). It follows from what is being said here about the way social policies work – how limited labour market participation undermines insurance rights, how low income limits housing choices and how this implies limited location choices and thus limited choices about other services – that the downward spiral involved reinforces the problems encountered.

Using the model comparatively

The three-group model outlined here is an attempt to generalise across industrial societies. A few comments within the analysis acknowledged variations between countries. In devising the model the author was inevitably influenced by his own country, Britain, where the advance of the 'welfare state' accompanied and contributed to the erosion of the old non-manual/manual divide; this movement towards classlessness was then undermined by two things. One of these was the massive advance of unemployment and economic insecurity. Over a fifth of the British are living at or below the minimum income level determined by the scales for means-tested benefits (Child Poverty Action Group, 1993). The other was the widening of the income gap through increased rewards and reduced taxation at the top of the income distribution during the 1980s (Commission on Social Justice, 1994). This was accompanied by deterioration of the more universal public services – health and education – increasing the incentives for group (1) to use private services.

The availability of secure employment is particularly important for the prevention of the growth of a large group (3). Many European countries, other than Britain, have comparatively small numbers in this group because of a combination of minimum wages laws, measures to combat part-time and insecure employment, and policies to try to avoid concentrating the burden of unemployment. In the United States, on the other hand, the phenomenon of the 'dual labour market', with a significant group of very poorly paid and insecure work, has been recognised for a long while (Wachtel, 1972; Rank, 1994).

The model seeks to explicate the relationship between economic arrangements and social policies. Social policies, as suggested at the beginning of this chapter, may reinforce or counteract stratification. The notion of 'solidarity' in income maintenance schemes is important. A great deal turns upon how social insurance has developed.

Alongside any analysis of the 'dual labour market' in the United States, for example, there needs to be some consideration of the dual character of social policy. Weir, Orloff and Scokpol argue:

> *The critical feature of New Deal social policy that would continue to shape public intervention for the next half century was the bifurcation of policy into two tiers: a top tier of increasingly generous, politically legitimated social insurance programs and a bottom layer of politically vulnerable programs aimed at the poor. Once established, this pattern of policy channelled the development of federal government capacities along particular lines and affected possibilities for alliances of social interests. (1988, p. 287)*

In other countries great efforts were made to make social insurance a scheme for all, with pension arrangements sufficiently good to ensure participation at the top end of the income distribution, and the 'insurance' element muted to prevent people with weak labour market attachments from falling out of the scheme. In such circumstances it plays an integrating role, minimising social divisions. This is the case in Norway and Sweden. Yet, as suggested in Chapter 3, it is difficult to separate the success of these countries' programmes to keep people in the labour market from their inclusive approach to income maintenance – the two policies reinforce each other (Furniss and Tilton, 1979).

The other important role social policies play in reducing the divisions outlined above is in the provision of services which are regarded as universal across the groups. This applies to education and health in a number of countries. It could apply to housing – socialist aspirations pointed in this direction, but the importance of market processes in this field eroded their effect. Nevertheless there are differences between those countries where social housing is widely accepted (Germany and Denmark, for example), and those where it is regarded as very much 'welfare housing' for the poor (United States, Britain since 1980). It has been argued that social care is perhaps the most clearly socially divided of all the services (largely because of the rejection of universalism in the field of pre-school care). Again the Scandinavian countries are a slight exception to this.

'Universalism'

Before concluding this part of the discussion, it is worth while to dwell a little on the principle of universalism in social policy. In this context it involves the provision of a single, relatively uniform service for all citizens regardless of income or class.

Can universalism in social policy play a role in countering divisive features within a social structure? There is confusion in some discussions of this issue between the case for universalism within a service, on the grounds that this is desirable in itself, and the case for universalism because it advances equality in society (Le Grand, 1982). The fundamental problem, as Le Grand's analysis shows, is that, in an unequal society, people 'bring' their inequalities into a universalistic welfare system. People with higher incomes, higher-status jobs and better education can more easily take time off to visit the doctor, relate to the doctor more comfortably, know the right questions to ask and how to argue for what they want. The range of ways in which such people can assist their children to take the best advantage of state education are even more evident. In any case, as far as 'final outcome' is concerned health status or educational achievement is a resultant of a combination of use of the services and the presence or absence of other social and economic advantages *(ibid.)*.

The issues about universalism in income maintenance are more complex, since benefit systems explicitly redistribute. The alternative relationships between what is paid in and what is paid out were explored in Chapter 4. Simple egalitarianism would demand unequal contributions and equal benefits. The problem with this, as universalist advocates like Titmuss recognised (1968), is that it generates a situation in which the better off have very strong incentives to try to avoid participating or to add private systems which enhance their prospects of avoiding a severe fall in income in old age. A compromise position then involves recognising the need to modify an absolute redistributive approach by one which accepts that higher contributors will be able to take more out, in the interests of universal participation (see also Korpi and Palme, 1994).

In the circumstances set out in the last two paragraphs the arguments for universalism within social policies are as follows. First, there are ways in which good services for the poor may contribute to social mobility. These are explicit in education, inasmuch as a state education system can make a contribution to social mobility. Somewhat similar, if weaker, arguments apply to the health advances to be achieved as a result of a good health care system. Of course, it may conversely be argued that a system that concentrated subsidy on schools and health services for the poor would do this better – this leads on to the second argument.

Second, it is suggested that a fragmented system – in which different schools, different health services or separate pension schemes are provided for different socio-economic groups – involves a very explicit state endorsement of inequalities in society. Conversely, a universal system enhances this cohesion and solidarity, a point Titmus made poignantly when he was dying of cancer – referring to his participation in an out-patients clinic where the only discrimination involved treating patients in the time order of their arrival (1974).

Third, such clear acknowledgement of inequalities can itself contribute to widening them. The second-class service will tend to be inferior, operating close to a minimal level of acceptability and attracting relatively poor staff. A related point is that the strong demands of better-off people for quality services – expressed both through direct demands upon service providers and through the political system – will contribute to rising standards for all (see Goodin and Le Grand, 1987).

Finally, as far as health services and income maintenance are concerned (and this could apply to social care services), there are arguments for universality which have nothing to do with social divisions *per se*. There is a case for public intervention to ensure that exceptional problems do not disadvantage people relative to their socio-economic equivalents. A universally available health service ensures that the rich as well as the poor do not experience devastating health bills. In these circumstances the poor get treatment they might otherwise have to reject and the rich avoid a sharp reduction in their income and wealth. In this respect social policy may prevent downward mobility even if it cannot assist upward mobility. There are also issues about children as a concern of the whole society, and thus appropriate charges on the state and not just on their parents (see Pedersen, 1993, for an account of arguments on this in Britain and France).

Gender, social stratification and social policy

The previous section began by tracing the roots of the approach to the definition of social class which links it to 'market situation'. The whole section deliberately, and rather artificially at times, avoided bringing in other factors which contribute to social stratification. It did not deal with gender and only introduced the family inasmuch as social structure is reproduced in the next generation.

The classic sociological literature on social stratification was almost silent on the issue of gender until challenged by the feminist movement in the 1970s. There were a few exceptions to this, notably Marx's colleague Engels, but they tended to be ignored. The definition of class in terms of market position was occasionally challenged with the question: How do you define the class position of women if they are not labour market participants? The stock answer was 'in terms of the class position of their husbands or fathers' (Goldthorpe, 1983; see Crompton, 1993, for a critique).

The feminist challenge was obviously directed at the assumptions about the dependent and subordinate position of women embodied in that approach, but the approach was also bad sociology. It led to confusion over the interpretation of the situation of women who were labour market participants and to a lack of attention to the social stratification issues concerning women who lost this implied male 'protection'. Furthermore it led to the disregard of issues about the way resources may be shared within the family.

Variants of feminist theory

The feminist challenge to the invisibility of women in social stra[illegible] theory took various forms. The three main forms are often labell[illegible] feminism', 'socialist feminism' and 'radical feminism' (see Dale [illegible], 1986 or Williams, 1989, for a discussion of them and their ap[illegible] to social policy). It is perhaps unfortunate that these ideas are [illegible] in ideological language – and seen to be in some senses in oppo[illegible]ach other – as each has something important to say about the way [illegible]hips between genders occur in society.

Liberal feminism concentrates upon the barriers to equal competition between men and women in society (discussions of feminism seem reluctant to pin this label on contemporary theorists, as most have moved beyond it; however, it is the perspective which has made most inroads into conventional, male dominated, policy debates – see Dale and Foster, 1986, pp. 49–51). It offers a critique of many forms of discrimination – in the workplace, in education, and so on. It seems to suggest that the key issue is the removal of the barriers to equal labour market participation. Then women will assume places of *their own* in a gender-blind stratification system. This approach gives some attention to female labour market disadvantages consequent upon roles as mothers and as carers for other relatives, but sees the solution to these problems as lying in laws which take these things into account (in relation to job security, promotion and pension rights), together with improved provisions for child care.

Socialist feminism (Hartmann, 1979; Barrett, 1980; Eisenstein, 1984) builds upon this analysis to see the difficulties women face in achieving equal labour market participation in a context of unequal and exploitative relationships. Women's disadvantages in getting less from the education system, in getting less support in advancement into the world of work, and in needing to withdraw from labour market participation at times to assume nurturing and caring roles are seen as creating divisions in the labour force. They enable women to be relegated to the lower strata in a dual labour market to be treated as part of the reserve army of labour. The remedies which stem from this perspective are very like those which stem from the liberal feminist critique, with, however, the additional emphasis that the whole structure of exploitation needs attention if fundamental progress is to be made.

Neither the liberal nor the socialist perspective entirely opens up the issues about the role of the family. They both stress the need for egalitarian relationships within the family. If women are to be full labour market participants their partners need to make adjustments, and ageing parents cannot make assumptions about female availability to undertake caring tasks. It is, however, the radical feminists who have concentrated attention upon the nature of male power – exercised *both* inside and outside the family (Millet, 1970; Brownmiller, 1975; Delphy, 1984). They have pointed out that there is another 'market' relationship, implicit if not explicit, within the family in which such resources, care and protection women obtain are 'bought' through the performance of sexual, caring and household duties. This is, at heart, a forced exchange – secured through a combination of direct power and indirect cultural dominance. This perspective, naturally, emphasises a concern about male violence in relation to this. It sees a male-dominated society and state as condoning the use of physical force in family relationships.

The radical feminist perspective sometimes involves the rejection of the family as an institution. Concern here is with its contribution to sociological analysis. As such it suggests a need to 'open up' the family to examine the reality of the power and exchange relations occurring within it. Romantic love (a male cultural subterfuge?) encourages us to see the exchanges within the family as voluntary, private and rooted in shared commitments. Yet the difficulties about these assumptions are very clearly exposed when marriages and other 'romantic' partnerships collapse, or when force is used within them.

The implications of gender for the social divisions model

This discussion of the way issues about gender divisions in societies have been put on the modern sociological, and philosophical, agenda suggests a range of important considerations for social policy. This discussion will try to fit the gender issues into the three-group model discussed in the last section. The issue concerning looking inside the family assumes particular importance in relation to the advantages possessed by group (1), when those for women are derived from a 'dependent' position in relation to a male. It is clearly possible that when the distribution of resources within the family is unpacked, women may be found not only to be in a vulnerable position but actually deprived of opportunities to benefit from the privileges and wealth of the family unit (Pahl in Walker and Parker, 1988).

This is not only an issue about resources. There are issues about power within the family and about occupational and other choices to be taken also into account. The allegedly 'privileged' position of women defined by dependency into group (1) may be founded upon acceptance of a 'private' caring role. There is an important feminist agenda here about the need to make caring tasks 'public', recognising them as contributions to society not merely as private acts.

Parents are less likely to buy expensive education for their daughters than for their sons. Within that education teachers are likely to make unjustifiable assumptions about the differences between the sexes in abilities and in capacity for some kinds of future employment (Spender and Sarah, 1980; Kelly, 1981). The key professions providing the services purchased by group (1) are male dominated and male practitioners may make sexist assumptions about the experiences and needs of women (for example, in health care – see Roberts, 1981; Stacey, 1988).

Clearly widowhood and divorce are particularly likely to expose weaknesses in a model of private provision which is very linked to employment in a male-dominated labour market. Widowhood, and particularly divorce, are likely to terminate access to private pensions, employer help with health and education expenses, and so on, if these are benefits derived from husbands' employment. Such events are likely to 'relegate' women from group (1) to group (2). They do not have a corresponding impact upon males.

Women can access some of the benefits described above through their own employment. However, many of the most advantaged occupations are ones which women have found it difficult to enter. Moreover, even when they do secure such employment their chances of reaping full benefit from that fact may be affected by the absence of satisfactory provisions to cope with absences on account of parenthood (see Bryson, 1992, ch. 8).

Many of the things that have been said about women in group (1) also apply to group (2). Here the heavy dependence upon the mainstream state services – education, health and income maintenance – makes for particular problems if male dominance is embedded within them. If unequal treatment of women is to be avoided great attention needs to be paid to unrecognised assumptions. It is worthy of note that, for example, disquiet has arisen over the apparently egalitarian development of co-education, on the grounds that the needs of boys may dominate the agenda (a particularly difficult problem if the boys make greater demands because they are less mature and more disruptive). A 'gender-blind' approach is also questionable when female needs are distinctly different from male needs, as in some areas of health care (by definition in obstetrics and gynaecology but also in some other specialisms). These issues in health and education raise questions about the extent to which equal opportunities in access to employment is a sufficient advance towards equality between the genders in these fields. There is a case for positive discrimination to ensure, for example: the availability of female medical practitioners and female teachers at the male-dominated advanced end of the education system.

In income maintenance the issues are rather different for group (2). The key issue (discussed in Chapter 4) is the link made between labour market participation and social insurance. A pattern of female labour market participation which is less complete than the norm for adequate insurance protection means that women will be disadvantaged when sick, unemployed or retired. The problems here are a combination of an unavoidable fact of nature, that women bear children, and a variety of social assumptions (which the women involved may choose to accept) concerning women's roles in relation to the care of those children. To these may be added social assumptions about other caring roles. All of these things are then compounded by male expectations, as both husbands and employers, about who should make the adjustments to work patterns when caring tasks arise. It is possible, as was shown, to devise income maintenance systems which give due weight to the implications of these reasons for withdrawal from the labour force; this is an important feature of the evolution of some social insurance systems away from rigid insurance assumptions (Sainsbury, 1993).

In addition to these issues concerning care there are likely to be assumptions about which gender has priority in situations of job scarcity or in relation to new job opportunities – assumptions which even the weakest versions of the belief in gender equality will want to challenge, but which are very deeply embedded in many societies.

In Chapter 4 it was pointed out that many of the early social insurance systems, designed in a more patriarchal age and one in which female labour market participation was much lower, dealt with the issues discussed above by regarding married women as the dependants of their husbands. There should not be a need to spell out the objection to this at this stage in the argument. However, as a system of social protection which linked female fortunes to those of male breadwinners, this approach did have the merit of protecting the widows of men in group (2) so that loss of the breadwinner through death had no more serious economic consequences than that likely to occur if he became unemployed. Indeed, if the man were mean about handing over money his death might be less financially damaging for the woman than his unemployment!

These relatively cheerful assumptions about 'dependency' under social insurance only applied to widowhood. Moreover, even in the case of widowhood, the relative longevity of working-class women relative to men, once the dangers of childbirth were past, was likely to result in exceptionally long periods of benefit dependency for women (Groves in Lewis, 1983; see also her contribution in Glendinning and Millar, 1992). More seriously insurance provision for widows in these traditional schemes did not extend to separated and divorced women or to women whose dependent status was in a partnership rather than a formal marriage.

The consequence of relationship breakdown, other than through death of a husband, is likely to be for female non-labour market participants a relegation into group (3) with income dependent upon means tests and a variety of other service choices severely curtailed (in the way set out in the description of that group) (Glendinning and Millar, 1992). Furthermore even when such women are labour market participants they will often be – given the family and employment assumptions outlined above – in casual, part-time, temporary and/or low-paid employment. In which case the termination of a relationship will have much the same consequences as if they had no work at all.

In many modern societies where women are likely to be labour market participants they are expected to be insurance contributors in their own right. However, this can lead to anomalies if the older provisions for women as dependants remain. There will tend to be a problem of double counting, where married women secure pensions in their own right but in the process lose the benefits that would have been provided by their husband's contributions (as in Britain and the United States).

This discussion of women in terms of the three-group model has concentrated on female disadvantages in situations in which their male partners or 'equivalents' would be likely to be in groups (1) and (2). The discussion has demonstrated the wide range of situations in which the combination of disadvantages and discrimination in the labour market and the weaknesses of social protection schemes will tend to mean that many women who are 'unprotected' financially by relationships with men, or particularly who lose that protection, are likely to be in group (3).

Women and care

Before moving on from this consideration of women's experience of social policy a little more needs to be said about the issue of women as carers. The key points have already been mentioned. Not only are there likely to be assumptions within societies and within families that women should assume caring roles with regard to children, but there will also often be assumptions about similar responsibilities towards adults with disabilities and health problems. This has been described as 'compulsory altruism' (Land and Rose, 1985) – an expectation that unpaid caring for elderly parents (in particular), but also for other relatives, will be undertaken by females without financial rewards and perhaps at the cost of abandoning opportunities to participate in the paid labour force (see also Finch and Groves, 1983). Inasmuch as governments regard community care as family care and, thus, reducing demands upon public funds, this means female care. The availability of female relatives may be used as a specific criterion for the denial of social care services.

Similar assumptions may extend to self-care. It has been shown (Arber and

Ginn, 1991) that elderly men coping on their own despite disabilities and health problems are more likely to secure statutory care services than elderly women, who are assumed to be better able to care for themselves.

Somewhat similar assumptions may be applied in relation to voluntary caring activities and even to state provision of care – that such tasks may be expected to be performed by women for little or no reward. In the case of paid work these assumptions about female altruism may reinforce labour market disadvantages (see Evers *et al.*, 1994). It has been pointed out that much of the growth in female labour market participation has occurred in 'welfare state employment' – caring roles which have 'gone public' (Hernes, 1987). While this is a welcome development it carries with it the problem that these tasks may be regarded, because they have come out of the family, as lower status, deserving of lower rewards and dispensable when there is a lack of public resources.

Equal opportunities?

'Universalism' was earlier evaluated as a response within social policy regarded as mitigating divisions. What is the similar remedy as far as the inequalities between the genders are concerned? The obvious answer is 'equal opportunities policy'. The discussion of liberal feminism partly examined this. What the other forms of feminism indicate is that equal opportunities policy on its own does not tackle the structured forms of inequality associated both with the treatment of women as a key element in the 'reserve army of labour' (socialist feminism) and male power exercised both in society and within the family (radical feminism). Simply requiring policies to be operated in ways which maximise female participation in economic institutions and minimise dependency assumptions (in income maintenance, for example) may disadvantage rather than advantage women if all many can achieve are inferior and poorly paid work roles from which they return in the evening to partners who expect disproportionate contributions to domestic and caring tasks.

Race, ethnicity and social policy

Any discussion of racial or ethnic divisions in society starts with a definitional problem stemming from the fact that those divisions are socially and culturally determined. They may be linked with physical differences, but those differences are often exaggerated, difficult to detect at the margin and have none of the connections to abilities and attributes which earlier biological theories of racial differences suggested. Furthermore divisions within societies may be discovered for which there are no biological cues at all but where patterns of discrimination have been developed and social barriers to contact have been set up of a similar kind to those found in other societies where divisions are based on physical racial characteristics. Examples are societies where language or religion is the key criterion used by individuals to act in a discriminatory way. In many divided societies these criteria are linked to doctrines of nationalism rather than racism.

This diversity of phenomena makes it difficult to develop a satisfactory terminology. To speak of race relations runs the risk of appearing to subscribe to the theories which have been used to justify racism. It is not very appropriate terminology for many national, religious or linguistic divisions. Some writers cope with this difficulty by using 'race' in inverted commas (see, for example, Williams, 1989, p. ix). Others have turned to the concept of 'ethnicity' (Glazer and Moynihan, 1975); this will be used as a shorthand term for this group of social divisions.

The diversity and complexity of ethnic divisions

The expression 'ethnic divisions' and therefore the discussion in this section covers a wide range of divisions in societies including the following:

1. Divisions whose origins lie deep in the processes by which nation states were formed – as in the case of Belgium, Northern Ireland and the Balkans.
2. Patterns of domination which arose from the conquest of territories – as with the indigenous minorities in Australia, New Zealand, the United States and Canada, and the majority black population of South Africa.
3. Patterns deriving from the importation of people to perform menial tasks in societies – slavery and the introduction of indentured workers.
4. Situations arising from movements of people in search of work – ranging from the massive migrations into the United States, through the movements of people from colonies and former colonies to Europe, to much more local movements of workers (for example, between the countries of Europe, some of which may be regarded as temporary – itself a source of problems for those treated as 'guest workers' regardless of their needs or aspirations).
5. Migrations of refugees.

That list covers divisions in societies which have been linked with the formation of modern nation states – 'the extension of state power over ever-larger areas, and the incorporation of hitherto distinct ethnic groups' (Castles and Miller, 1993, p. 37) – and others which have arisen from the involuntary and voluntary movement of peoples. The latter phenomena are of fundamental importance in recent times, yet the earlier state developments 'help to determine the conditions for the implantation of new immigrant groups' (*ibid.*).

Related to the different ways in which ethnic divisions arise but also to other aspects of the cultural and ideological milieu in which they occurred are differences in the intensity of conflict and discrimination. At one extreme are patterns of blatant and outright discrimination, sometimes – as in the past in South Africa and the southern states of the United States – linked with segregation and the enforcement of a separate legal status. At the other are distinctions and divisions of a much more subtle kind. Moreover, any divisive system, particularly a powerful one like the institutions of slavery or apartheid, leaves a legacy of divisions which are very hard to eradicate. The beneficiaries of such divisions, however much they ascribe to egalitarian principles, will not readily relinquish those benefits. The victims of the divisions continue to suffer and to pass on to future generations disadvantages stemming from the weak position from which they started.

There are strong links between ethnic divisions and class divisions in many societies (a source of political and theoretical argument about how these respective phenomena should be interpreted). For Marxist theory, ethnicity inasmuch as it is acknowledged, is a phenomenon which divides the proletariat, weakening its capacity to struggle against the bourgeoisie. That perspective begs the 'chicken and egg' question: Which came first, the economic divisions or the social divisions? There are very good reasons, given the comparatively recent emergence of capitalist economic institutions and the ways in which their emergence occurred in a period of intense nationalist activity for regarding ethnic divisions as often prior to, or at least linked with, economic divisions. Patterns of colonial domination and slavery involved economic exploitation, but they were not necessarily a product of the struggle between the classes in the Marxist sense (for a discussion of sociological approaches to this aspect of stratification, see Rex, 1986).

What is important for contemporary analysis are the ways in which ethnic and economic divisions interact, and often reinforce each other. If one can imagine a society which suddenly became 'race-blind' it would still have within its social stratification reflections of earlier patterns of racial discrimination because of the extent to which earlier racism had disadvantaged its victims. Since the reality is only at best a slow evolution towards that liberal ideal, the ethnic and socio-economic divisions are mixed together in a complex way.

One way of representing this mix in order to analyse differences involves seeing a country's socio-economic structure as a triangle with a flattened top (or a volcano with its top blown off). Then there will be various ways in which ethnic divisions will be manifest in that structure. Figures 11.1 and 11.2 offer two logical possibilities for a society with just two ethnic groups.

Figure 11.1 represents a society with a rigid ethnic division – a system in which one group is absolutely dominant, allows no one in the subordinate

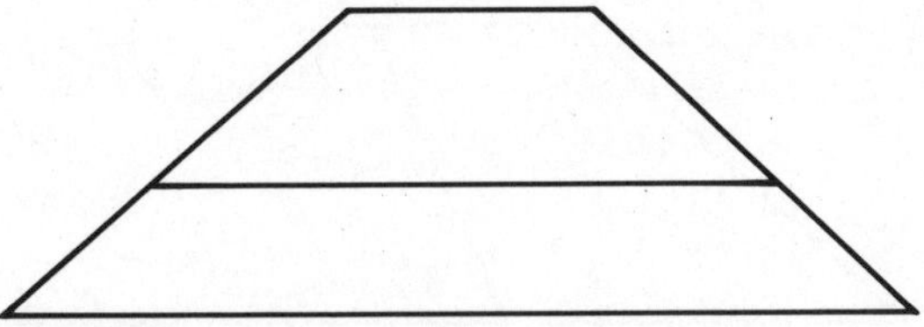

Figure 11.1 Models of ethnic divisions 1

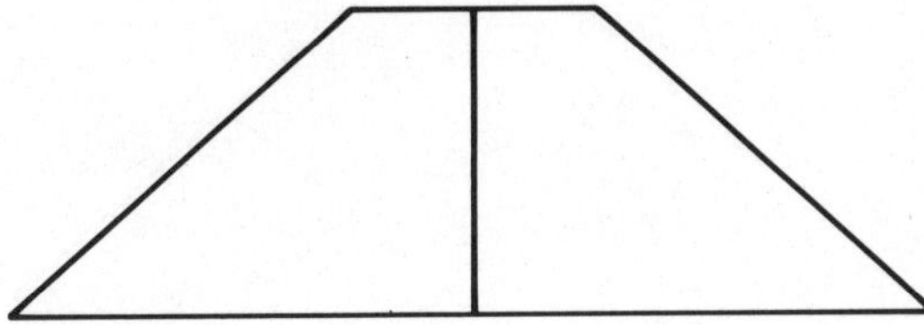

Figure 11.2 Models of ethnic divisions 2

group to rise beyond a certain level and correspondingly prevents its own members from falling. This was more or less the situation in the American deep south after the formal ending of slavery was followed by efforts to maintain the status quo as far as possible. Blacks were kept down to their 'station', poor whites were rare.

Figure 11.2 represents a society with separate institutions for the two groups, with positions of power, wealth and influence available to each group in a context of very separate social relations. This is more a pluralist ideal than a reality for two reasons. First, where – as is likely to be the case – it is also accompanied by geographical separation it is likely to produce a breaking down into separate nations (as in Cyprus). Second, where such high levels of mutual tolerance occur the cultural separation is likely to be gradually eroded so that it no longer makes sense to see the country as 'ethnically' divided (as in the case of the evolution of the phenomenon of 'pillarisation' in the Netherlands emergent out of religious differences in that country – Lijphart, 1975).

Figures 11.3 and 11.4 offer some alternative models, corresponding rather more closely to the way the relationships between class and ethnicity are likely to manifest themselves. Figure 11.3 provides a simplistic model of a society where there is still a strong correlation between ethnic status and socio-economic status. The subordinate group is over-represented at the bottom of the 'triangle' and under-represented at the top. The variant in figure 11.4 shows a situation in which elite positions remain unoccupied by the subordinate group.

Many real societies are divided in ways resembling figures 11.3 and 11.4.

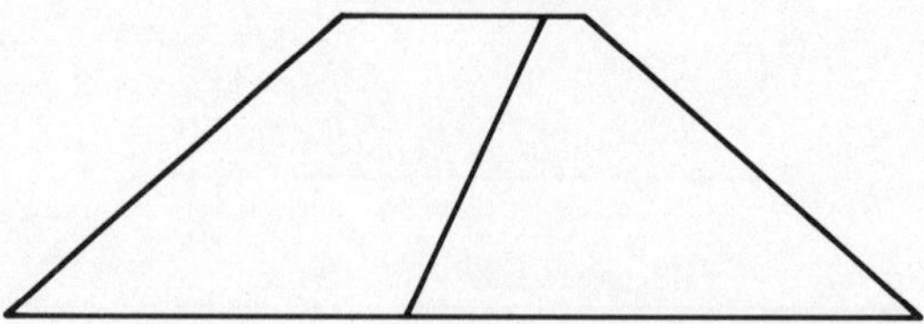

Figure 11.3 Models of ethnic divisions 3

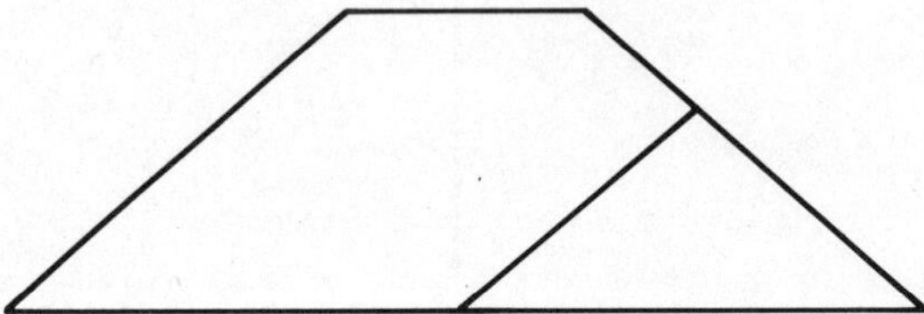

Figure 11.4 Models of ethnic divisions 4

In practice other things need to be taken into account. There are often more than two ethnic groups. There will often be people who are products of sexual relationships between the groups. In either of these cases there may then be a structure in which a number of strata can be identified. Complicating the diagrams above might involve trying to draw parallel diagonals on them. In fact simple graphical representation is likely to be difficult; the lines will be irregular and blurred.

This discussion has not involved the mention of numbers. In the discussion of ethnic relations the expression 'minority groups' has sometimes been used. Yet the issues about numbers and about under-representation should not be confused, some oppressed ethnic groups are majorities.

Another complication, briefly mentioned in relation to figure 11.2, concerned the spatial distribution of groups within a society. It is important to bear in mind that economic inequalities may also be spread spatially. These correspondences are very central to debates about nationalism. In relation to public policy there will be relevant issues about partial self-determination within a nation state to reflect such divisions (but it may then reinforce them – see the later discussion).

Citizenship

In examining the implications of ethnic divisions for social policy it is useful to return to the concept of citizenship (see p. 262). This might have been explored further in the section on gender. The feminist struggle involves a quest for full and equal citizenship for women – through political enfranchisement, the elimination of laws giving men command over the persons and property of wives and daughters, and the provisions of legal guarantees of equal access to employment and social benefits.

In relation to ethnic groups issues of the denial of citizenship in the formal sense are very salient. Systems of institutionalised and legalised discrimination deny full citizenship. It is important to recognise that this aspect of citizenship will involve political rights (the right to vote, etc.), civil rights (absence of formal discrimination) and social rights (rights to social benefits).

The denial of these rights, and particularly social rights, does not merely occur in societies with substantial formal systems of official discrimination. In many societies the rights of minorities are undermined by measures controlling immigration and denying full citizenship to new entrants from other countries (Layton-Henry, 1992). They may also be affected, more subtly, where social policies prioritise some cultural patterns relative to others or fail to recognise the salience of some cultural characteristics and culturally determined needs (perhaps either deliberately, or not).

These forms of discrimination contribute to the creation of situations in which denials of full citizenship tend to reinforce economic – particularly job market – disadvantages. There are further specific ways in which migrants are pushed into exceptionally exploited positions. One of these is where entry is allowed only to perform some particularly menial and ill-rewarded task. The recruitment of domestic workers in many societies falls into this category – linking gender roles and ethnic disadvantages in a particularly exploitative way (see Ungerson in Evers, 1994, ch. 3). An even more disturbing situation arises with illegal migrants, vulnerable to exploitation and blackmail from those who purport to help them.

The advanced industrial countries which are the focus of attention in this book have nearly all encountered substantial amounts of recent immigration (the main exceptions are the Scandinavian countries and Japan). This is likely to have been related to labour shortages and to a search for new work opportunities by people from less prosperous economies. It, however, has also been affected by previous imperial connections – the extent to which countries like Britain and France spread their culture within their colonies and created an image of a 'mother country' to which people from those colonies could turn for work or education (ironically called, in the title of one book on British race relations, *The Empire Strikes Back* – Centre for Contemporary Cultural Studies, 1982).

The issue about citizenship which connects social policy with social stratification concerns the social rights which immigrant workers are given. The concept of the 'guest worker' (particularly evident in Germany and Switzerland) is of an immigrant who comes to the country simply to work. That worker's long-run security may be regarded as no concern of the 'host' country, it may well be happy for the worker to pay taxes and social security contributions but not to make demands upon the benefit and care systems which those pay for. The worker's family obligations – to provide for and educate children, to support other adults, and so on – may likewise be regarded as of no concern of the 'host', who may indeed sometimes make it difficult for him or her to bring 'dependants' with them (Castles and Kosack, 1973; Castles, 1984; Castles and Miller, 1993).

This is an extreme form of the denial of social citizenship. Others may be a little less malign. Immigration to work may lead to the granting of rights after a period of stay in the country. The countries which boasted of their paternalistic stance towards their colonies were perhaps more readily shamed into enabling immigrants to become full citizens. The treatment of refugees, unable to look back to their place of origin, also demands – if human rights pledges are to be honoured – progression towards citizenship in the new country (Joly and Cohen, 1990).

As far as social rights are concerned it is important to bear in mind the variety of ways in which equality may be denied in practice. The following are some examples:

1. If income maintenance benefits depend upon past contributions most newcomers to a country may be disadvantaged by late entrance.
2. The late entrance problem may also undermine opportunities to get access to other benefits where waiting times are used to regulate access to resources – for example, with social housing
3. If a society contains both people from a specific ethnic group who are formally supposed to have full citizenship rights and others who do not officials may discriminate against and stigmatise the first group whenever they may be confused with the second (there is a special issue here about purges against illegal immigrants which are likely to catch legitimate ones in the 'course nets' used to deal with the problem).
4. The state may nevertheless be suspicious of claimed dependencies, particularly when they rest upon cultural patterns strange to the dominant society (hence efforts to get wives, children and other dependent relatives into the country may be difficult, and obligations to send money back to them may be disregarded by income maintenance systems) (Gordon and Newnham, 1985; Gordon, 1986; Castles and Miller, 1993, pp. 208–12).

Ethnicity and culture

The last point in that list leads on to a larger issue about ethnic minorities and social policy. This concerns the way in which cultural differences are dealt with in the delivery of services – health, social care and education. There is an often proffered 'liberal' solution to this, which is flawed (even in its own terms). This is the view that such services should be ethnicity 'blind' – people regardless of race, creed or language are to be treated like everyone else. That, it is argued, is what an equal rights policy requires. There are a number of problems about this.

First, it is a line of argument offered to resist scrutiny by officials who are actually discriminating. One cannot be confident about an egalitarian policy without the collecting of evidence to ensure that it is in operation (Henderson and Karn, 1987).

Second, to operate without regard to people's actual needs and preferences may be discriminatory. Supplying houses or income maintenance benefits which do not enable people to meet their actual social obligations may severely disadvantage them. Supplying services which violate deeply held beliefs and feelings – disregard of religious practices and holidays, medical services that have no regard to family cultural practices, education that imposes instruction in an alien religion – may alienate and lead to under-use of badly needed services.

Third, induction into full citizenship requires acceptance that the history, the traditions, the culture and the language of the individual have a value along with that of the dominant society. To do anything less is to send the message that many of the things that create the individual's own sense of identity are not important – an implicit way of making him or her feel a second-class citizen (Stone, 1981).

The last of these considerations has important but difficult implications for education. It is arguable that the child of an immigrant has the best prospects in the new society if he or she concentrates upon imbibing the new culture, and of course language. But the price to pay for doing this is alienation from family and other roots. If that painful process is undergone (as various poignant autobiographical accounts testify), there is no guarantee that the dominant society will accept the individual as fully assimilated (particularly if he or she has a different skin colour). In the face of discrimination a person may cope better with a pride in their 'roots' than if they have undergone a process which has systematically undermined that.

In this sense it is important to recognise the dynamic nature of culture. Individuals are not choosing between a culture from which they come and one which offers assimilation. Both are changing:

> *The dynamic nature of culture lies in its capacity to link a group's history and traditions with the actual situation in the migratory process. Migrant or minority cultures are constantly recreated on the basis of the needs and experiences of the group and its interaction with the actual social environment. (Castles and Miller, 1993, pp. 33–4)*

There is a difficult line to be drawn, in any effort to accommodate the conflicting demands of the new culture and the old one, between the one extreme outlined above and the other extreme of providing a separate socialisation process for a separate people. That will be one which will reinforce separation and pass on disadvantages. People will then tend to remain separate whether they like it or not.

This is an issue about which there are strong feelings. There is a view taken by radical elements within some discriminated against groups that the prospects for the liberal model are so poor that separate institutions are preferable. Castles and Miller argue that culture is increasingly becoming politicised – exclusionary practices are based upon culture rather than overt arguments about racial superiority while 'the politics of minority resistance crystallise more and more around cultural symbols' (*ibid.*, p. 35).

Language differences pose particular problems inasmuch as failure to gain proficiency in a dominant language often leads to severe economic disadvantages. Bilingualism offers a solution though dominant groups are rarely as ready to learn the less important language as subordinate groups are to learn theirs (a point that should not be lost on all those who, like the writer of this book, have the special advantage of having one of the world's dominant languages as their native tongue).

There are also some very difficult issues where cultural differences involve beliefs and practices about which there are deeply held values on either side. A central example here is family practices, involving appropriate relationships and behaviour between men, women and children.

The implications of ethnicity for the social divisions model

The threads of this discussion of ethnicity can now be pulled together, relating it to the three-group model used in earlier sections. Figures 11.1 to 11.4 suggest that any class analysis of society may need to take into account barriers to the upward mobility of ethnic groups. The discussion has indicated that those barriers may take a variety of forms – from explicit arrangements to deny full citizenship through to more subtle phenomena which perhaps reflect the impact of past institutions. These are going to have an impact upon the representation of disadvantaged ethnic groups within the three groups in a variety of ways. But then, what role do social policies play? There are two key points to make.

First, earlier discussions have seen the distinction between the first two groups to be that those in 'group' (1) tend to be the main users of private systems (pensions, schools and health care systems, in particular), while those in 'group' (2) are the mainstream users of and beneficiaries from state services. Ironically, if there are tendencies for the needs of an ethnic minority to be disregarded within the state system then those relatively successful in economic terms may be more likely to use private systems than their counterparts in the majority group. Private schools set up to meet cultural and linguistic needs and health services which have regard to minority beliefs and practices may have a particular appeal to this group.

Second, for many of the less successful within an ethnic minority there may be particularly strong forces which tend to ensure that they are found within 'group' (3) rather than 'group' (2). Reference has already been made to insurance rules which may disadvantage migrant workers and people who arrive in a new society in the middle of their working life. Forms of discrimination will limit people to less well-paid and less secure work; this will be reflected in disproportionate representation amongst the unemployed. Residential segregation may be the result of explicit discrimination or produced by a combination of low 'market power', and the selection of areas where there is security and the availability of appropriate institutions (places of worship, voluntary organisations, etc.). It may then have an impact upon choices of houses, schools and health services.

Theories about the 'under-class' (Murray, 1984), or an earlier variation on this same theme – propositions about the 'culture of poverty' (Lewis, 1968), are expressed in terms which involve implicit allusions to ethnic minorities. Behaviour which is a response to, and even perhaps a way of coping with, disadvantage, when manifested by a minority ethnic group, is regarded as a natural characteristic of that group. The response becomes treated as the cause of the behaviour. In societies where explicit racism is taboo, at least in intellectual or journalistic analyses of social problems, talk about the 'under-class' or the 'problems of the inner cities', and so on, may be a covert kind of racist rhetoric (see Moore's analysis of this in Coenen and Leisink, 1994). This may then encourage variations in official responses, based upon whether or not 'deviants' belong to minority ethnic groups.

Alternatively, positive discrimination in social policy may involve an attempt to add to efforts to avoid simple discrimination a recognition that the impact of earlier discrimination will have imposed economic and cultural disadvantages upon a minority group. Positive discrimination may involve quotas to bring the representation of certain groups within an occupation or educational institution up to their proportion in the population. Such actions thus involve discrimination against better-qualified members of the defined majority group or groups. Fierce philosophical arguments have raged about the justifiability of this approach (Edwards, 1987). It is comparatively rarely practised; a belief that is widespread features in the fantasies of racist rhetoric in societies where cautious efforts are being made to outlaw simple discrimination.

This section has endeavoured to generalise about ethnic stratification across modern industrial societies. In doing so it has inevitably mixed together a variety of phenomena (which may or may not arise in combination): divisions arising in the context of migration and the according of limited 'guest worker' status, longer-standing divisions in a society, racial divisions (in which physical differences facilitate discrimination), language differences and religious differences. These variations influence the social divisions in societies and the ways in which social policies respond to them or reflect them.

It is useful to return to the concept of 'citizenship' – asking to what extent particular situations involve one of the following:

1. The total denial of formal citizenship rights ('apartheid' or the 'guest worker' phenomenon).
2. A variety of limitations upon full participation because of the impact of length of residence (as in social insurance) or culture (as in education) upon full participation.
3. Discrimination which is officially taboo but widely practised (inside public services as well as in the private sector).
4. Disadvantage which is a difficult-to-eradicate legacy of earlier denials of full citizenship.

It is important not to be fooled by official statements which suggest that only the last applies, and the way institutions work in practice must be examined closely. In doing so bear in mind that social policy – as the analysis in Chapter 2 indicated – is used to control and to channel as well as to respond to emergent divisions in society.

Other social divisions

The three forms of social stratification discussed above – class, gender and ethnicity – are by far the most important. They do not, however, exhaust the possibilities. This section will look briefly at two more forms which are important for social policy. These are disability and age. Their particular importance lies in the fact that social policies are often responses to these two issues, yet they may contribute to their roles as sources of social divisions.

The basic issue about disability as a basis for social division was well expressed by the title of a long-running British radio programme about the subject. It was called 'Does he take sugar?' The issue is that disabled people are treated as 'dependants', to be looked after but not able to participate in their own right as full citizens. In this sense their own difficulties in participating in society – in getting work, in travelling, and so on – are compounded by policies which make them the recipients of compassion rather than treat them as people with rights. This is a general problem for disabled people as a whole, but it is particularly evident if they have disabilities which render their participation in society difficult. In this sense physical mobility barriers to participation are more easily overcome than blindness or deafness, and the implications of these disabilities are more easily handled by others than intellectual disabilities, which impede learning and communication.

People with disabilities provide a challenge to modes of service and benefit delivery. Chapter 6 raised one of the key issues about this – that state-provided services or benefits for carers treat disabled people as dependants whereas benefits which enable the disadvantaged to buy care acknowledge their rights as decision-makers for themselves. There are related issues about the scope for choices in health care and education. In respect of the last-named policy area there are also issues to be addressed about the extent to which any extra help can be a part of a 'normal' service, not something provided away from other children in special institutions.

There are also important issues about the provisions of employment opportunities for disabled people. There are a variety of responses possible to employment difficulties. In choosing between them it is necessary to distinguish between the fact that, in some circumstances, disabled people may be less efficient employees from the fact that employers may discriminate against them without that 'economic' justification. If, as a matter of course, employment is subsidised the latter problem may not be properly addressed. On the contrary, employers may be only too eager to gain a premium for taking on some workers, stigmatising people well able to participate in the labour force. Similar problems may occur with regard to quotas which compel the employment of some disabled people. The hard fact is that a competitive labour market in a less than fully employed society is one in which disabled people find it difficult to participate – the steering of them towards 'sheltered' work, labelling them as different, may be difficult to avoid.

There are similar issues about age divisions in society. Immaturity in childhood and frailty in old age make individuals dependent. A variety of regulations, services and benefits offer protection, but to what extent do these lead to the treatment of people, at either end of life, as unjustifiably unable to participate? There is a general issue here concerning the extent to which either the young or the old are consulted about the services offered to them. As far as the old are concerned this may explicitly conflict with the fact that they have, formally speaking, full citizenship status as voters.

There is also a particular problem about labour market participation. This too applies at both ends of the life cycle, though at the young end it is linked with expectations about participation in education. At the other end of life, retirement may be forced upon people with no alternative but impoverished dependent status. While this may be a labour market response, like that applying to the disabled in which the allegedly least productive amongst employees are rejected, it may also be a stereotyped response to the reaching of a specific age. In this sense the development of a crucial support policy for elderly people, pensions, has also contributed to the creation of a comparatively arbitrary end point to labour market participation. Again, much depends upon labour demand (see further discussion in Chapter 12).

Any more detailed analysis, however, is bound to take the discussion back to the other aspects of inequality. Thus, for example, the extent to which premature retirement is an undesired and problematic state is likely to be affected by economic opportunities earlier in life, and thus by class, gender and ethnicity.

Geographical aspects of social divisions

The possibility that the distribution of two or more ethnic groups across the territory occupied by a nation state will be uneven has already been discussed. The same point applies, generally rather less strongly, to the other aspects of social stratification. Class divisions will be influenced by the geographical distribution of economic opportunities. Countries are likely to have prosperous regions (in which higher socio-economic groups are over-represented), and deprived and perhaps declining regions (in which lower socio-economic groups are over-represented. These differences may have demographic correlates – the young moving in search of work and the old staying behind. There may also be regions particularly favoured by the old, specially those of the old prosperous enough to make choices, on – for example – climatic grounds (Florida, for example). Demographic imbalances may also produce gender imbalances: the consequences of women outliving their male partners (with consequent implications for overall inequalities), for example.

The implications of these geographical phenomena for social policy are that they raise concerns about 'territorial justice'. Effective responses to inequalities may require the biasing of policies in favour of specific geographical areas. Equal spread of resources for health care or education may need to take into account both 'need' and 'demand' as well as the simple distribution of population. Where services are funded from local tax bases it may be the case that deprived areas have high needs but low incomes. Redistributive policies at national levels, or even exceptionally at supra-national levels (as with the regional and social policies of the European Commission), may be developed to have regard to these disjunctions.

There may arise in these circumstances a tension between territorial justice and local self-determination. This will be a particularly important issue where there are ethnic differences between regions. To secure high levels of participation and services which are responsive to local needs and culture, a high level of local control is required. Yet the elimination of territorial imbalances may require resources to be poured into the area from a central source. Resource transfers tend to bring with them controls over local decision-making.

The final point to make here is that the units developed to effect between-region adjustments and responses may be inadequate. Any specific geographical area is likely to contain a mix of people, including a mix of the deprived and the privileged. The larger the unit, the less clearly will the deprived segments within it be identified. Hence, specific interventions justified in terms of the concentration of a needy group in an area may fail to reach their target, solely benefiting the already advantaged. Evidence of such phenomena needs to be fed back to examination of the choice of 'instruments' – in this sense specific benefits for individuals or households reach their ultimate 'targets' better than general injections of cash into a local service or general efforts to increase levels of employment (see Higgins *et al.*, 1983, for a discussion of these issues).

Conclusions

This chapter has related general issues about social stratification to specific issues about social policy. Using a three-group model influenced by social policy divisions, it has shown how policies partly mitigate divisions in society but may also reinforce them. It is suggested that the crucial issues here concern the nature of what has been called 'group' (2). The main beneficiaries of direct public social policy provisions are seen as being men in this group. Their security is maintained so long as their attachment to the labour market is maintained. Women join this group if they can become secure labour market participants. Otherwise they are 'dependants' of men in this group. The importance of caring tasks in social policy has peculiarly ambiguous implications for women in this group. Women have alternative statuses as the main providers of care either inside or outside the formal labour market; these statuses may be advantaged if they involve secure and adequately remunerated jobs inside it. They will, however, be disadvantaged if they are outside it.

Bryson, who has separate chapters in her book on 'men's' and 'women's' welfare states, brings out the issues well in her concluding sections to each chapter:

> *Men's welfare state still largely pivots on the role of the breadwinner . . .. Occupation remains the crucial basis for the distribution of all three forms of welfare – social, occupational and fiscal . . . major welfare gains have come through the actions of male-dominated trade unions . . .. (1992, p. 188)*

> *Women's welfare state in the past consisted largely of social welfare, which could be claimed via dependence on a husband or as a widow or a parent. Gradually . . . women have been drawn more into the labour force. With these changes . . . come opportunities to partake of occupational and fiscal welfare. However, because women have largely been absorbed into the secondary labour markets, their access to the benefits of employment are restricted. (*ibid, *p. 223)*

Ethnic 'minority' groups likewise have difficulty in joining the protected club because of citizenship rules, disadvantages due to late participation in social protection schemes, discrimination and inherited socio-economic disadvantages. Not surprisingly, those who combine both of the disadvantages mentioned above – ethnic minority women – are particularly likely to be outside this social protection system (Williams, 1989).

While the key dynamic involves the relationship between the mainstream social policy protection accorded to 'group' (2) and the disadvantaged 'group' (3), the role of 'group' (1) in this dynamic should not be forgotten. Those who make the rules for the social protection system are likely to be in this group. The more they perceive the comparatively universal benefits provided for 'group' (2) – social insurance and state-provided or -supported health care and education systems – as extravagant and in need of better targeting, the more they accelerate the processes under which economically weaker individuals drop into 'group' (3). Devices that impose means tests or relegate various kinds of help to the needy and diminish incentives to participate in insurance schemes tend to sort the occupants of 'group' (2) into those who can make the strenuous efforts necessary to join the privately protected in 'group' (1) and those who drop down into 'group' (3).

The propensity to adopt policies which have the effect described in the last paragraph depends upon the extent to which the elites themselves, and those most likely to offer them crucial electoral support, benefit from state services. As already noted a general benefit that flows from a universal health care, education or pension system is likely to have effective political support.

Social stratification systems are dynamic. This analysis has been rather different to those characteristic of the 1960s, which stress the non-manual–manual divide in many industrial societies, because it is believed that this is less important than the growing rift between the secure and the insecure in the labour market. Social policy can play a role in relation to such a dynamic. Robust inclusive protection schemes mitigate the factors which lead to the growth of 'group' (3). Conversely, it has been suggested that an outright attack on universalist social policies will polarise a social structure much more profoundly. Disregard of gender and ethnic inequalities in social policy reinforces polarisation along these dimensions, with evident political consequences if ethnic divisions are enhanced.

In this respect, contrasts can be drawn between states. It was acknowledged above that the three- 'group' model was influenced by the British experience. The author has used it earlier for the analysis of income maintenance developments in that country (Hill, 1990), where a combination of high unemployment and attacks on the Beveridge model of social insurance has eroded the salience of 'group' (2). By contrast, the importance of solidaristic social policies in Scandinavia is seen as concentrating a high proportion of the population in 'group' (2) (that is the implication of Korpi and Palme's, 1994, analysis). Solidarity extends to women inasmuch as they are able to be labour market participants. Integrative responses have been adopted towards minorities, but ethnic homogeneity in those countries has meant that this aspect of stratification is comparatively unproblematical. Here, perhaps, a positive policy towards refugees is increasingly coming under strain. The United States is a society in which race and gender are particularly significant with regard to the gulf between the advantages of 'group' (2) and the disadvantages of (3) (Weir *et al.*, 1988, part III). The same may be said about Germany, with respect to ethnic divisions (see Ginsburg, 1992, for a similar series of contrasts).

The Netherlands and Australia, which have been identified before as rather difficult to classify (see chapter 3), have made more efforts than others to deal with ethnic divisions, but both have been seen as having very male-dominated social policy provisions. The argument here tends to answer the questions posed at the beginning of this chapter on the impact of social policy in a fairly negative way. The influence of social policy is secondary to the influence of market forces and discriminatory practices, and its character is largely determined by these. Undoubtedly political activists have sometimes turned to social policy in the hope that it can do more than that. Income maintenance policies have been seen as instruments for the pursuit of a much more equal distribution of ultimate incomes. Education policies have been seen as contributing to equality through social mobility and/or the sharing of a common culture. Housing policies have been seen as having the capacity to create heterogeneous communities. Universal health and social care have been seen as eliminating fundamental life chance inequalities and reminding us of our common humanity. The analysis in the earlier policy-specific chapters has indicated how limited the achievements of these egalitarian aspirations have been.

The next chapter will analyse more fully aspects of the retreat from that dream. However, it is useful to recognise a fundamental problem for that dream contained in the way social policy has been constructed in capitalist societies. It has been seen as essentially residual to economic policies, at best as some combination of a system to deal with those social issues where market forces do not work very well (in health care and education, for example) and a system to deal with the casualties of the market economy.

In this respect it is useful to highlight the three policy areas discussed rather little in this chapter: housing, employment and pollution control. Housing has been seen mainly as a market good; focus on policy has been upon helping the housing market to work and providing limited help to those unable to participate in the market. Employment policy has similarly focused upon casualties – those without work, concentrating upon helping them get into the labour market. It has been very influenced by changes in overall labour market conditions and has been inhibited in many societies by a political reluctance to make full employment a higher priority than other economic goals. Pollution control has experienced similar limitations. It has been seen in terms of serious 'externalities' which are susceptible of attention without imposing exceptional costs upon enterprise. More widely, the achievement of high levels of consumption and the maintenance of those levels (with their consequent benefits for employment) have been seen as of higher priority than curbing the growth of environmental problems.

In all three of these cases social policy goals have been seen as subordinate to economic goals. It has not been seen as possible – as it has in many societies in the special cases of health care and education policy – to envisage a framework for policy which is more or less independent of market considerations. The next chapter will analyse how even that has now come under challenge.

Guide to further reading

Lois Bryson's *Welfare and the State* (1992) has as its central concern the issues discussed in this chapter. It has been an important influence on my work.

The classic essays on social divisions in welfare are Titmuss's 'Social Divisions of Welfare' in his *Essays on the Welfare State* (1958) and Sinfield's 'Analysis in the social division of welfare' (1978).

Moore's discussion of citizenship in Coenen and Leisink (eds.) *Work and Citizenship in the New Europe* is an important modern contribution on that subject, whilst Mann deals effectively with the 'under-class' argument in his 'Watching the defectives: observers of the underclass in the USA, Britain and America' (1994) and in his book *The Making of an English 'Underclass'* (1992).

The issues about women and welfare are central to Bryson's book. The collection edited by Sainsbury, cited as further reading for Chapter 3, *Gendering Welfare States* (1994) is also important. Other key essays on this topic include Land and Rose's 'Compulsory Altruism for some or an altruistic society for all' (1985) and Sainsbury's 'Dual welfare and sex segregation of access to social benefits: income maintenance policies in the UK, the US, the Netherlands and Sweden' (1993).

The citizenship literature examines some of the issues about ethnic divisions in social policy. Another useful perspective on this is offered by the work of Stephen Castles and his collaborators (Castles and Kosack's *Immigrant Workers and Class Structure in Western Europe* (1973), Castles's *Here for Good: Western Europe's New Ethnic Minorities* (1984) and Castles and Miller's *The Age of Migration* (1993)). Issues about ethnicity obviously emerge in much American literature on social policy, the book by Weir, Orloff and Skocpol (see recommended reading for Chapter 2) picks up the key themes well. On the issues about ethnicity and social policy which arise where indigenous people have experienced a European invasion see Patterson in Yelaja (ed.) *Canadian Social Policy* (1987) and Keen in Najman and Western (eds.) *A Sociology of Australian Society* (1993).

CHAPTER TWELVE

Whither social policy

Introduction

This final chapter will explore issues about the future for social policy. A book of this kind written in the 1960s would have been likely to have observed some challenges to the idea that advanced industrial societies could be welfare states and some questioning of what that would really mean, but few suggestions that any of the pioneer nations would turn their backs upon the policy developments of which they were generally proud. It would probably have concentrated upon weaknesses in the various policy systems and looked at the feasibility of improvements. It might have concluded that welfare state growth would continue to depend upon increments of economic growth that could be applied to social policy advancement.

In the 1970s the challenges to social policy intensified. The sharp oil price rise was unsettling to many economies. It came at a time when deflationary monetarist policies were beginning to become the conventional economic wisdom. These identified public expenditure control and public borrowing control as key 'cures' to economic problems. For countries like the United Kingdom, Australia and New Zealand where balance-of-payments problems loomed large as part of the crisis the international economic 'doctors' were quick to prescribe public expenditure cuts. While the long period of Conservative rule in the 1980s and 1990s led many in the United Kingdom to be inclined to attribute public expenditure restraint to the 'new right' government of Margaret Thatcher, it was a Labour government which initiated the cut-back process. Callaghan, the Labour Prime Minister, responded to demands for cuts as a condition for the receipt of an International Monetary Fund loan and lectured his party conference in 1976 that a government could no longer spend its way out of a recession. Then, in 1979, Margaret Thatcher was able to exploit electorally a populist mood of suspicion about social expenditure, linked to the appeal of promised tax cuts (see Kavanagh, 1990). It was in the late 1970s and early 1980s that a series of academic analyses were published which suggested that 'the welfare state' might be in crisis

(Rose and Peters, 1978; OECD, 1981; Berthoud, 1985). Yet, the manifestations of that 'crisis' varied from country to country; outside the United Kingdom, Australia and New Zealand developments occurred more slowly and in some countries there was little attempt to attack social policy expenditure (particularly Scandinavia; for a comparative analysis carried out in the early 1980s, see Mishra, 1984).

Writing in the 1990s it has to be observed that the challenge to social policy has remained strong, though not perhaps as strong as some of the more extreme of the 'new right' ideologues have suggested (see Glennerster and Midgley, 1991, for an assessment). What is significant is that while for a time in the 1980s it might have been suggested that variations in the political responses to the challenge to social policy might exacerbate the divisions between the welfare leaders and the welfare laggards (see Chapter 3), now the worldwide picture looks more uniform. The militant governments of the 'right', in Reagan's America and Thatcher's United Kingdom, did not turn back the clock as much as their rhetoric suggested they would. On the other hand the Scandinavian model has begun to be questioned by governments in those northern countries. The swing to the 'right' in Sweden has been of particular importance (Marklund, 1992). It has also been significant that some pro-welfare state governments in countries facing particularly worrying long-run economic prospects – like Labour governments in New Zealand and Australia – have initiated curbs on welfare state expenditure (Taylor, 1990; Cass and Freeland in Hills *et al.*, 1994). In other words, debates about social policy cut-backs, or at least restraint upon the growth of social policy, have become fairly universal.

In this chapter these debates will be examined. The starting-point will be the more extreme forms of these debates expressed in theories which postulate that there is a 'welfare state crisis'. It is not helpful to use the word 'crisis' casually to describe any kind of economic, ideological or political challenge. Much of the crisis rhetoric is excessive. To talk of a 'crisis' implies a fundamental and irresistible sequence of events, leading to radical change. The crisis theory is useful in drawing attention to some of the tensions between social and economic policy, but does not lead us to a particularly useful discussion about what is actually happening.

Moving on from crisis theory the chapter will look at the forces which are pushing social expenditure upwards. While it will be argued that those who want to talk of crisis exaggerate the impact of these phenomena, it will be accepted that they provide a serious political challenge. This challenge may apply not merely to how countries organise their welfare states but also to how they run their economies. A section will explore the particular importance for social policy of changes to economies which seem to be affecting the labour market.

This discussion will lead on to an examination of the political response to the social expenditure trends. It will look at the form the response takes

– bringing the discussion back to the analysis of the respective roles of market, family, community and state. It will suggest that there has been a shift, even amongst welfare state supporters, from a commitment to the advancement of statism to a 'mixed economy of welfare'.

Crisis theory

As previously suggested, it is confusing if the word 'crisis' is used loosely to describe simply some intensification of the political dilemmas about priorities for social policy. It is more appropriate to reserve that concept for a combination of events which are likely to produce a radical transformation of social institutions. The concept of crisis in this sense appears in Marxist theory. This postulates the evolution of capitalist institutions to a point at which the polarisation of society is so absolute and the conflict between the classes so intense that revolution will occur.

The Marxist version of crisis theory

Marxist analyses of the development of the welfare state have seen it as playing a role in postponing the arrival of the crisis within capitalism (see Chapter 2), but then facing tensions which undermine its ameliorative effect (O'Connor, 1973; Gough, 1979; Offe, 1984). These writers argue that, over time, the price to be paid for the achievement of social and industrial peace through social policy expenditure tends to rise. This follows logically from their argument that such measures postpone rather than abolish the realisation of the capitalist crisis (see also Wolfe, 1977). In particular the role of social policy in 'legitimising' an unequal and exploitative society – dealing with the casualties of market processes and offering social benefits to buy off proletariat discontent – becomes increasingly expensive. Here then, it is suggested, is a force which drives welfare expenditure ever upwards. This imposes costs upon production which will undermine competitive efficiency and will tend to be resisted by the bourgeoisie. A conflict arises, these theorists argue, that cannot be resolved through normal political processes in a capitalist society. If political decisions are made to cut costs they intensify discontent, yet if cuts are not made increasing public sector costs undermine enterprise.

The Marxist way forward is the elimination of capitalism. Since no society is, at present, adopting that way out, this version of crisis theory seems rather unconvincing. In its defence it may be argued that there may be other phenomena which represent responses to the crisis on both sides. On the proletariat side discontent with the hardship generated by the evolution of capitalism may not be channelled effectively into political and/or revolutionary responses but may take the form of withdrawal from social participation, with personal attempts at accumulation and the expression of frustration being manifested in crime. Marx himself identified in nineteenth-century Europe a submerged disadvantaged group below the vanguard of the politically active proletariat, the lumpenproletariat who could not be counted on as a reliable political force. This is, perhaps, the 'under-class' in some modern analyses of social stratification (as discussed in the last chapter). On the bourgeoisie side the response may be not the extension of social policies but a resort to more direct forms of social control through policing and a search for ways to protect property more effectively (Hall *et al.*, 1979; Hall and Jacques, 1985).

The new right version of crisis theory

There is an equivalent to the Marxist theory of crisis to be found in theories particularly linked with the opposite side of the political spectrum. The 'economic theory of democracy' has suggested that politics involves an auction in which party competition to win elections drives up social expenditure, particularly when the costs can be hidden, delayed or spread (see Tullock, 1976; Brittan, 1977). The rising expectations of citizens fuel these political demands, and so long as politicians respond to them this has a feedback effect to produce more demands.

Echoing the work of neo-Marxist theorists like O'Connor, 'new right' theorists argue that welfare expenditure is unproductive, it is dependent upon the productive part of the economy. The imposition of increasing welfare costs is seen as threatening economic efficiency and competitiveness within economies. It is suggested that social policy places demands upon state investment which tend to crowd out investment in productive enterprise (Bacon and Eltis, 1976). There is also concern about the levels of taxation required to support social policies. These are seen as damaging the productive sector, deterring entrepreneurial risk taking and reducing work efforts (Joseph and Sumption, 1979).

While the Marxist theory postulates the development of a conflict which cannot be resolved without radical, perhaps revolutionary change, new right theory argues that there is a way forward. This requires political elites to resist the demands upon them. This involves a conflict between the needs of capitalism and the demands of democracy (see Brittan, 1977). Some writers have suggested, moreover, that limitations upon the taxing or spending powers of governments should be enshrined in constitutions (Buchanan and Wagner, 1977). Alternatively, it may be argued that elites have a duty to educate electorates to accept the damage that unreasonable demands for expenditure will do to the economy.

Whether this new right theory should be called 'crisis theory' in the terms laid down at the beginning of this section is debatable. Unlike Marxist theory it specifies a non-revolutionary way forward. Some exponents of this view have, however, sought to specify levels of public expenditure which they identify as a crisis point, where economic disaster will follow if nothing is done. There are nevertheless grounds for doubt as to whether identifying such points is feasible. These doubts rest principally upon ambiguities embedded in the data upon which such judgements are based.

New right crisis theories either focus upon the relationship between productive and unproductive activities or upon the relationship between private and public sectors (with these two often treated as synonymous, despite the fact that the latter may be a source of production and the former includes private services of all kinds). A particularly popular version of this argument looks at public expenditure as a proportion of the gross domestic product (GDP) in a society, suggesting that there is some threshold at which the former is dangerously high (see Heald, 1983, for a critical discussion of this).

Evaluating the evidence for a crisis

There are various problems about these judgements. There are difficulties in measuring GDP accurately and in defining some activities as productive and others as unproductive. Why should the manufacturing of drugs and medical equipment be defined as productive while the tax-provided resources consumed during their use by state health services are deemed to be unproductive? There is much productive activity with consequences positively damaging to societies – for example, weapons, tobacco, addictive drugs, pornographic videos, etc. It seems odd to have a theory which sees these as 'good' for society and publicly provided caring services as bad! The classification of private services sold to fellow nationals as contributing to GDP but public tax-supported services as drains upon it has some validity if your concern is levels of taxation but little if you are dealing with allegations about a lack of national productivity.

On the public expenditure side a number of writers have pointed to a confusion in the arguments between public sector consumption and the organisation by the public sector of transfer payments. It is argued that the provision of income maintenance benefits and other kinds of cash subsidy involve merely the state shifting money from one group of citizens (tax payers) to another (Heald, 1983; Hill and Bramley, 1986). These are massive elements in welfare state expenditure and are particularly prominent in the growth of public expenditure. If they are deducted from the proportion of GDP 'consumed' the result is figures which are much less alarming, in either absolute or growth terms. That seems an important qualification, but is it sufficient? Is not a state-funded service, in which taxes are used to pay salaries to provide free or subsidised education or health care not also, in the same sense, 'merely' a transfer activity? Services are bought by the state on people's behalf using the money they have provided, effecting in the process some redistributive effects.

The overall point is that some comparatively arbitrary definitions are used to arrive at figures that have been treated with great reverence in the debate about the 'burden' of social policy. It is important, however, not to take the scepticism expressed in the last two paragraphs too far. The theories that are particularly suspect are those which rest upon concerns about productivity and investment. The suggestions above do not provide a basis for refuting concerns about effects of public expenditure upon competitiveness between countries or about the impact of the 'burden' of taxation upon individuals.

The first of these issues is particularly important: to refute concerns about levels of social expenditure expressed in these terms there is a need to explore issues about competitiveness between countries. A simple but merely suggestive rather than explanatory approach to this question is offered by scrutinising the data about differences in expenditure between countries. Inasmuch as the high welfare spenders are not the least competitive internationally and the low spenders the most competitive there are grounds for rejecting simplistic arguments about this subject (see Hill and Bramley, 1985, ch. 6; Pfaller *et al.*, 1991). Included in this are many other variables, but it must not be forgotten that social policy makes a contribution to national efficiency.

The issue about the burden of taxation for individuals is rather different. It has a superficial plausibility. People do not want to see all their efforts to produce income for themselves undermined by state appropriation. Yet people also recognise that some of that appropriation is directly or indirectly for their benefit. In some areas, most obviously in relation to health care and pension expenditure, there is a very simple trade-off–high taxation for these implies a low need for private expenditure on them, and vice versa.

What is difficult to answer is the question: At what level does that appropriation operate as a disincentive to effort? Considerable efforts by economists to answer that question have yielded inconclusive results (Brown, 1983; Kay and King, 1983). Obviously these efforts focus upon 'marginal effects' – top rates of taxation which deter extra working-hours or efforts. In this context it is important to bear in mind the 'poverty trap' discussed in Chapter 4 which showed that some of the most punitive 'real' taxation effects apply to low-income people trying to emerge from dependence upon means tests, rather than to high-income entrepreneurs.

The main idea of the argument set out thus far is to suggest that the crisis theories advanced, including the Marxist one, tend to be rather deterministic in nature. There are grounds for distrusting these kinds of theories and for denying that social policy expenditure is, or has recently been, the direct source of a crisis for the economies of the advanced industrial nations. That is not, however, to argue that there are no crises with other causes, or that social policy expenditure has not been seen as an element, perhaps even a crucial element, in the emergence of those crises. In this sense it may matter little whether or not the above theories are right; what is significant is that people, or more specifically political elites, believe them to be right.

Politicians and administrators have, in most of the countries discussed in this book, believed that they faced crises which had been affected by high levels of public expenditure or public expenditure growth. While in some societies – the United States and Britain, in particular – high defence expenditure could be identified as an element in this, but what was evident overall was the high and growing levels of social policy expenditure. The sense of crisis was amplified by the media – who trade in fashions and scares. Thus it has been conveyed to the public, creating support for measures of the kind demanded by the new right.

The discussion will return to some of the issues in regard to what is happening to many industrial economies later, but first it is important to look more carefully at what is happening to social policy expenditure and why.

The growth of social policy expenditure

Until the twentieth century levels of public expenditure were low in all nations. The state paid for a minimum of activities, principally concerned with defence and the maintenance of internal order. Taxation was low, principally a combination of indirect taxes and direct imposts on the relatively small number of prosperous people. Local schemes of poor relief were generally funded by local charges upon property. In wartime expenditure temporarily escalated. Governments tried to cope with this as far as possible by borrowing, getting in the process into a range of problems of indebtedness that forced them to resort to taxation (sometimes with revolutionary consequences).

The emergence of publicly funded social policy changed all that. It led to a steady growth of public expenditure, punctuated by dramatic bursts associated with wars and leaving behind a population more accustomed to taxation. Gradually the direct tax net extended downwards to take in ever greater proportions of the working population. The long-run consequences have been stated in Chapter 3 with public expenditure today a substantial proportion of the gross domestic product and social policy expenditure accounting for around two thirds of that.

Table 12.1 charts the growth of public expenditure as a percentage of GDP in various countries between 1960 and 1974 – the point at which most countries began to regard this growth as a problem, while table 12.2 examines

Table 12.1 Public expenditure trends in various countries, 1960–74 (total government outlay as a percentage of GDP)

	1960	1968	1974
Austria	35.7	40.6	41.9
Denmark	24.8	36.3	45.9
France	34.6	40.3	39.3
Germany	32.4	39.1	44.6
Netherlands	33.7	43.9	47.9
Sweden	31.0	42.8	48.1
United Kingdom	32.2	39.3	44.8
United States	27.0	30.7	32.2

Source: OECD (1992b) *Historical Statistics 1960–1990*, Paris: OECD, p. 68; reproduced by permission of the OECD.

Table 12.2 Public expenditure trends in various countries, 1977–92

	1977	1982	1987	1992
Austria	46.1	50.1	51.9	50.2
Denmark	48.9	61.2	57.3	59.5
France	43.6	50.3	50.9	52.0
Germany	47.6	49.0	46.7	49.4
Netherlands	51.1	58.7	58.9	54.7
Sweden	57.0	64.8	57.8	67.3
United Kingdom	41.6	44.5	40.7	44.1
United States	31.2	33.9	33.4	35.4

Source: OECD (1993) *Economic Reports*, Paris: OECD; reproduced by permission of the OECD.

public expenditure trends between the mid-1970s and the early 1990s. The latter shows that the dramatic growth pattern indicated in table 12.1 ended in this period, suggesting both that the growth of expenditure was not as irresistible as some versions of crisis theory suggested. On the other hand the new right can claim little success (for example, in the United States or the United Kingdom) in turning back the clock (see, for example, the evaluation of Margaret Thatcher's efforts in the United Kingdom in Hills, 1990). These are only curbs in expenditure as a percentage of GDP; they are not in absolute terms. An examination of the factors affecting social policy growth, other than deliberate additions to policy provisions, offers evidence

Table 12.3 Numbers (millions) under 14 and over 65 in various countries

Country	1950	1980	2010 est.	2040 est.
Australia	2.8	5.1	6.6	9.5
France	14.3	19.5	19.5	22.8
Japan	33.9	38.2	47.6	48.0
Netherlands	3.7	4.8	4.8	5.7
Sweden	2.4	3.0	2.8	3.2
United Kingdom	16.7	20.2	19.9	21.1
United States	53.4	77.0	89.73	119.6

Source: OECD (1988) *Ageing Populations*, Paris: OECD, table a.1; reproduced by permission of the OECD.

on why growth is difficult to control but also casts doubt on the more extreme scenarios about a remorseless advance of social dependency.

Factors affecting social policy expenditure growth

Increases in the size of the 'dependent' population

It is possible to identify two segments of the population at either end of the age spectrum who may be defined as particularly likely to be dependent upon social policy: those under working age (in somewhat greater need of health services and personal social services very early in life and the main recipients of education expenditure) and those over working age (recipients of pensions and, with advancing age, increasing users of the health service and personal social services).

The 'dependent' population defined in this way is seen as a 'problem' for many societies. A characteristic of advanced industrial nations is that they have low birth rates but substantial numbers of people perhaps born in an era of much higher birth rates, who are now living many more years. Hence, the 'dependent' population is growing. The issue is encapsulated statistically in terms of proportions of people either below the age of labour market participation or over the age of retirement. Table 12.3 reproduces data from a cross-section of countries, showing this 'dependent' population (people under the age of 15 or over the age of 65) in 1950 and 1980, and then including projections which have been made suggesting what the numbers will be in 2010 and 2040. The projection to 2010 will be reasonably accurate, most of the people involved have already been born, and death and birth rates

Table 12.4 'Dependent' numbers as percentages of total population

Country	1950	1980	2010 est.	2040 est.
Australia	35	34	33	39
France	34	36	34	40
Japan	41	33	37	42
Netherlands	37	34	32	41
Sweden	34	36	34	40
United Kingdom	33	36	35	38
United States	35	34	32	38

Source: OECD (1988) *Ageing Populations,* Paris: OECD, table a.2; reproduced by permission of the OECD.

are unlikely to change markedly. The estimates for 2040, which show further increases in the dependent population, will be much less reliable since birth rates may change significantly over a much longer period.

These data suggest that pressure on social expenditure increased markedly in the period 1950 to 1980 and will continue to do so in some of the countries shown. There are some interesting contrasts, however. Australia, the United States and (particularly) Japan have much more of this 'demographic pressure' ahead; the European countries by contrast have gone through much of the 'worst' of the initial growth but have another growth spurt ahead. If there were a birth rate increase that would affect the 2040 estimate, but unless that occurs soon it could well merely exacerbate the size of the 'dependent' population.

There are, however, some important alternative ways of looking at data of this kind. First, while increasing numbers of dependants increase costs for nations as a whole, economically this may be more easy to bear in a context in which the prime age adult group is increasing at the same time. Hence, table 12.4 expresses the figures set out in table 12.3 as percentages of the total population in each country at each point in time.

Looking at the figures in this way the position in the European countries, other than the Netherlands, is shown to have involved a rise in the dependent proportion which is now being followed by a slight fall before a further rise. In the United States and Australia there is a slight fall across the first three points in time and then a predicted rise, while the data for Japan shows a U-shaped pattern of a fall followed by a rise. What is significant in the case of Japan is a shift from a very high child population at the first date through to a very high elderly population at the later dates.

However, the rise of the alleged problem of 'dependency' is regarded as particularly attributable to the rise in the number of the elderly against a background of a comparatively constant or falling child population. Table

Table 12.5 Numbers (millions) over 65 in various countries

Country	1950	1980	2010 est.	2040 est.
Australia	0.7	1.4	2.6	4.9
France	4.8	7.5	9.4	12.7
Japan	4.4	10.7	24.0	27.2
Netherlands	0.8	1.6	2.3	3.4
Sweden	0.7	1.4	1.4	1.8
United Kingdom	5.4	8.3	8.4	11.8
United States	12.4	25.7	35.8	61.3

Source: OECD (1988) *Ageing Populations*, Paris: OECD, table a.1; reproduced by permission of the OECD.

Table 12.6 Elderly as percentages of the 'dependent' population

Country	1950	1980	2010 est.	2040 est.
Australia	23	28	38	52
France	33	39	48	56
Japan	13	28	50	50
Netherlands	21	34	48	60
Sweden	30	45	51	56
United Kingdom	32	41	42	56
United States	23	33	40	51

Source: OECD (1988) *Ageing Populations*, Paris: OECD, table a.1; reproduced by permission of the OECD.

12.5 therefore shows numbers of elderly people in the populations of the sample countries and table 12.6 shows the elderly in each country as a proportion of the 'dependent' group.

The first of this pair of tables (table 12.5) shows that the rise in the absolute numbers of the elderly is a universal phenomenon for this sample of countries; the difference between the European countries and the rest is that it is more significant in the early period in Europe but then flattening off. The last table brings out the importance of ageing for this 'dependency' issue most clearly. The change going on in Japan is particularly dramatic. An unexpected rise in birth rates in the years ahead could change that picture, but as pointed out above it would, initially, have the effect of temporarily increasing the 'dependency' ratio.

Table 12.7 Per capita social expenditure by age group: Netherlands, 1981 (in guilders)

Policy area	0–19	20–44	45–64	65–79	80+
Social security	1,700	2,190	5,910	12,020	13,350
Education	3,930	560			
Health care	790	640	1,060	2,710	7,020
Social services	110	50	130	930	5,010
Total	6,530	3,440	7,100	15,660	25,380

Source: Netherlands Social and Cultural Planning Office quoted in OECD (1988) *Ageing Populations*, Paris: OECD, p. 34; reproduced by permisssion of the OECD.

There is another reason for concentrating upon the issue of ageing when looking at dependency ratios. The evidence suggests that the burden elderly people impose upon social spending is very much higher than that imposed by the young. The OECD (1988, p. 34) suggests that while this varies from country to country the average ratio of national expenditure on elderly people was some 2.7 times that on children.

That same report included an interesting table from the Netherlands showing amounts of various elements in public social expenditure for the different age groups (see table 12.7). It brings out clearly the issues about the cost of an an elderly population in a nation providing a high level of social welfare services (see also the Australian data on health expenditure in Chapter 5).

Table 12.7 also highlights another issue, the particularly high cost of the 'old elderly'. In the United Kingdom, which has been seen to be one of the earliest countries to experience the impact of ageing, people over the age of 80 more than tripled in number and increased from 1 per cent of the population in 1951 to 3 per cent in 1981 (Central Statistical Office, 1992, p. 27). The OECD report (1988) emphasised that growth in the very old as a proportion of the elderly population is a particular feature of the age structures of those countries which aged in the 1950 to 1980 period. In these countries the very old will increase rapidly as a proportion within their relatively stable elderly populations in the period up to the year 2010. Thereafter the proportion will fall, assuming medical developments do not significantly increase life expectation, simply because the young elderly numbers will start to increase again as the post-Second World War 'baby boom' generation passes the age of 65.

As far as health care is concerned the more medicine can do to prolong life the more it has to cope with high demands on its services in that extra period it has added to people's lives. Perhaps one of the most difficult things for politicians to come to terms with is the inevitable rise in costs associated with an ageing population. Efforts to increase efficiency and lower costs in the face of this pressure can achieve little except by explicitly damaging the service available. One particular contradiction here is that while politicians will be reluctant to see the elderly as an undeserving group they are nevertheless likely to be an economically inactive group, contributing little to the growth of tax revenues. Similar considerations apply to pension schemes. The very poor pension provisions of past state schemes have led to concerns about the poverty of the elderly and to pressure for pension improvements. Many improvements are coming gradually in these ageing societies, as 'pay-as-you-go' contributory schemes reach maturity. These rising costs prompt a search for alternatives which impose lower burdens on public expenditure. This cannot readily be achieved without repudiating long-run pension promises.

Inasmuch as politicians worry about burdens ahead (the post-2010 retirees), it is still possible to do something – three interrelated options are a shift to the 'funding' of pensions, privatisation and a change in the retirement age. Several difficulties have to be tackled. First, since current public pensions are generally provided on a 'pay-as-you-go' basis, with current payments funded from current contributions, a change will in effect make the current paying generation pay twice – once for current pensioners and then additionally into a fund for themselves. Second, as pointed out in Chapter 4, privatising of pensions may remove the burden on the public purse, but it does not remove the burden on the productive generation. Third, as far as the retirement age is concerned what really matters as far as 'dependency' is concerned is when people cease to work. In many European countries at the time of writing the *de facto* average retirement age is coming down as the unavailability of work for all forces many to leave the labour force early.

The whole discussion about dependency has been conducted in terms of a rigid distinction between, on the one hand, children and elderly people defined by a fixed age, and on the other, the age groups in between. While it will be true that some demands upon social policy are best defined in aggregate in these terms (this is generally true of health costs), others depend upon the availability of choices – to retire and take up a pension, to go on working, to come out of or go into education, and so on.

More importantly much of the discussion is cast in terms of a 'burden' upon a working population falling within fixed age points. In practice labour market participation both within the 'prime age' and within the elderly population may vary considerably. This point will be illustrated with reference to the workforce of England and Wales at four census dates: in 1931, 1951, 1971 and 1991 (HMSO, various dates). Unemployment was high at the first and last of those census dates but was relatively low at the two dates in between. Yet the size of the workforce rose steadily between 1931 and 1991 and as a proportion of the population it was higher in 1991 (47 per cent) than on any of the previous census dates.

Furthermore when comparing 1971 and 1991, if the unemployed are added to the figure for the labour force the upward trend in the numbers and the proportion of the population who want to work is even more striking. A crude 'economically active'/'economically inactive' distinction as used in the census report shows a shift from a ratio of 47 : 53 in 1971 to 52 : 48 in 1991. The position is complicated by the numbers working part-time, which have increased substantially, but the essential point here is about numbers wanting to be economically active in some way. The most important conclusion to draw from this is that despite the growth of the elderly population across this period, as shown in the earlier tables, the proportion of the population participating in the labour force has increased.

The crucial influence on this was the increase in female labour market participation. Similar trends may be traced in other societies. In this context it is interesting to note differences between relatively similar societies. Economic activity rates of women in the countries of the European Union have been rising steadily. Yet they still differ, for women aged 25 to 49, between a high of nearly 90 per cent in Denmark and a low of 50 per cent in Ireland. In the Netherlands it is around 60 per cent.

Given better opportunities for work the labour market participation rate could be even higher. In England and Wales high unemployment had, by 1991, produced various forms of withdrawal from labour market participation. The 1971 census return identified about 450 thousand people as 'permanently sick'. The figure for the 1991 census was about a million and a half!

The *de facto* average retirement age has been falling. In the full-employment era in England and Wales many individuals worked beyond the official retirement age. As job opportunities have declined so has this phenomenon. The number of men still in employment after the age of 65 was 596,000 in 1951 and 467,000 in 1971. By 1991 it had dropped to 247,000.

At the same time increasing numbers, particularly of men, have left the labour force before retirement age. In 1971 the number of males in England and Wales below the age of 65 who described themselves as 'retired' was 132,000. In 1991 it was 370,000. A 1993 European Commission report showed, for example, in Germany and the Netherlands a 'noticeable decline in the activity rate (of men) to well below 20% even before the statutory pension age is reached' (Commission of the European Communities, 1993c, p. 27). This pattern was evident in a less dramatic form in the other member states (see Kohli *et al.*, 1991). Some countries actually adjusted formal pension ages downwards to accommodate this trend. Thus, the OECD shows falls in the 'average retirement age in public old-age schemes' for males in various countries, as set out in table 12.8.

Table 12.8 Average retirement age in public old-age schemes for males

	1970	1990
Austria	64.2	62.0
Canada	66.7	63.3
Germany*	65.2	62.7
France⁺	64.0	62.0
United States	66.8	63.7

Notes: *manual workers
⁺men and women

Source: OECD (1994c) *New Orientations for Social Policy*, Paris: OECD, table 7, p. 90; reproduced by permission of the OECD.

One response to this last trend has been to advocate efforts being made to deter early retirement (see, for example, OECD, 1994c). This begs the questions as to whether this is a genuine choice or a response to the unavailability of work for all (see also Quinn and Berurkhauser in Martin and Preston, 1994, for a similar analysis in respect of the situation in the United States). Clearly the most expensive cases of early retirement – where people are bought out of the labour force with generous (often private) pension packages are likely to involve willing acceptance, yet even these (if viewed in aggregate terms) release jobs for other people.

This discussion has suggested that 'dependency' might be defined in terms of absence of employment rather than in terms of age. Doing so, and at the same time noting the data about rising unemployment rates and increasing withdrawal from the labour market, suggests that worries about the future might be appropriately focused upon difficulties economies have in supplying employment for all who want it. Such a conclusion needs analysing with care in terms of the different experiences of men and women, the nature of the employment on offer and the extent to which social policy has seen employment as a key ingredient in the 'contract' between the individual and the state. These issues will be further explored later in the chapter, after other factors which are affecting social policy growth have been analysed.

Growth in the costs of providing services

A rather different theme in the debate about social policy expenditure concerns the extent to which unit costs of providing services tend to rise, so that the welfare state costs more even without meeting any additional needs (for analyses of this issue in relation to Britain see Hills, 1993). Some of these cost increases come about as a result of advances in technology. This is particularly evident in the area of health care. The expression 'advances in technology' is used loosely to include the development of new drug therapies as well as new operations and new devices to assist with diagnoses. The impact of these developments on health care costs is complex. New technology, while more expensive, may also be designed to produce savings: for example, simplifying operations so that hospital stays can be shortened. Difficulties may arise in these circumstances from organisational, staffing and plant (building) rigidities which make such savings hard to realise in practice.

The equivalent in education will be demands for the use of new technology such as computers. In some of these cases the developments may again be said to improve the service, but unless they yield economies of scale (on which more will be said below), they will not enable any more people to receive the service.

Costs are also pushed up by changes to the prices charged by those who supply the medicines and the technology. If the price for any standard item used by the service increases at a rate faster than inflation then, relatively speaking, costs will rise by comparison with other costs as a whole. Health services, particularly state health services, are – as large monopoly or oligopoly buyers – able to drive hard bargains with their suppliers. However, the 'battalions' may be at least as big, or bigger, on the other side. The drug companies, for example, are largely very powerful multi-nationals able to argue that they need high returns to pay their high research and development costs (the development of new drugs to reach safe standards takes many years). In an article published in 1991 Manga and Weller reported that drug costs in Ontario had risen on average '21.3 per cent per annum for the past decade' (in Altenstetter and Haywood, 1991, p. 218).

There are other critical 'suppliers' of services eager to get the best possible deal on 'prices'. These are particularly the staff, whose 'prices' are wages, salaries and fees. Before rushing into any judgements about whether 'unreasonable' or 'monopolistic' demands come from this source it is necessary to look at a problem about returns to services, particularly public services. If a nation enjoys a particular annual growth, accompanied by a specific inflation rate, workers will, in general, be looking for rises in their incomes which will give them a share in the growth and compensate them for inflation. If they work for a manufacturing enterprise that growth may be identifiable as a growth in the profitability of the firm; there should then be little difficulty in making a case for a rise along these lines. What if, however, the activity involves selling a personal service to other citizens (including doing this indirectly by selling to the state) in circumstances in which the only possibility of achieving growth depends upon working harder or more effectively? That is the situation of many social welfare service workers. It is quite likely that they will expect those bargaining on their behalf for a wage increase to argue both that they are working as hard as they can and that they deserve a share in the growth of the nation as well as compensation for inflation. If negotiators succeed with this argument service costs will go up (see Heald, 1983, for a good discussion of this issue). Governments faced with this source of cost pressure may try to resist giving more than compensation for inflation (indeed they may even go further as curbing public sector costs has been seen as one weapon to use against inflation). If they choose this method they will reduce the rewards of these public service workers relative to others. This may not matter to employers if there is an ample supply of such workers. Suppose, however, they are in competition with other employers for a scarce supply of workers, and other employers are more easily able to raise wages. Then they are in a difficult position.

In the special case of high-prestige professional workers like doctors the situation may be even more complicated. This group have secured a position in many societies where they can control their supply. They will compare their rewards with other high income groups, some of whom will (for economic or political reasons) be able to secure large increases. Exceptionally they may even be able to move out into those other occupations. They will often be able to win popular support for their claims. If they threaten to withdraw their service, even partially, this will cause alarm. Finally they may have alternative ways of earning within their profession. This will apply particularly to doctors in dispute with a public authority if there are opportunities to practise privately. It is also important to bear in mind that the market for professionals, and particularly for doctors, is international.

Governments may tackle this particular cost control problem another way by seeking an efficiency gain in return for a pay rise. The problem with this approach is that governments have an easy way to try to do this, which may be absolutely meaningless in practice. They can say, and indeed often do say, that pay increases for a service must be funded out of an existing budget 'by efficiency savings'. In the example above about new technology it may be possible to increase the efficiency of its use – extending the hours or increasing 'public throughput'. In the case of personal services efficiency savings are likely to involve a change in the ratio of staff to users (doctors to patients, teachers to pupils) which is likely to diminish the quality of the service.

These issues about pay for service workers have a particular significance for the costs of the service as a whole wherever staff costs form a high proportion of total costs, as they do in health services, education and social care. They do make a contribution to the rise of social expenditure. They are, as has been suggested, fought quite hard by governments and are an important influence on the quest for alternative ways of organising and delivering services.

These quests are also influenced by a rather more sinister interpretation of the phenomena discussed here. Perhaps because he is himself a public service worker the author has tended to stress the inevitability of cost increases and the difficulties of securing efficiency gains. There is an alternative view, which deserves some attention, which stresses the implications of the relative monopoly positions in which some of these service workers operate.

The 'economic theory of democracy' (see p. 23) expounds a view that political competition tends to push up public expenditure, as politicians 'bribe' the electorate to win power. A companion theory to that suggests that they are supported in these efforts by bureaucratic service providers – the doctors, the teachers, the care workers and all the ancillary and managerial staff linked with them – who stand to gain from this growth. They are able to do this because public bureaucracies tend to be monopoly providers of goods and services. Economic theory on monopoly stresses the absence of constraints upon costs when these can be passed on to consumers. It suggests that in the absence of market limitations a monopolist will tend to over-supply commodities. It is argued by this school of 'public choice' theorists that it is these phenomena which will apply in the public sector (Buchanan and Tullock, 1962; Tullock, 1967; Niskanen, 1971).

This may have an impact both upon the capacity of these public service workers to push up their own rewards and upon their ability to enlarge their services. Demand for services is very often in the control of those who supply services, they are their own 'gatekeepers' (Foster, 1983). Public choice theorists would suggest that there will be a kind of conspiracy between those who demand and those who supply services which will push up public expenditure.

There are a variety of different arguments against this perspective. The 'conspiracy' described above may be regarded as a benign one, in which professional ambition leads to public needs being put on the agenda (see the discussion in Chapters 2 and 5).

Unconstrained monopolists in public services may advance goals which would be disregarded in a situation of competition. Dunleavy has suggested that in such situations bureaucracies may internalise costs in ways which advance the general good (Dunleavy, 1985, 1986, 1991). Examples of this include such things as exemplary employment practices and equal opportunities policies. In general public and political accountability may be enhanced better with a single responsive organisation than with competition between separate services.

This argument leads on to the more general point that, in making choices between explicit monopoly provision and market provision, inefficiencies in the former need to be traded off against control problems with the latter. This may come to a clear case in favour of the former when in practice market constraints are ineffectual.

The issues about a powerful profession like medicine are interesting here. One view is that a combination of a profession with strong control over its members and over entry to its ranks and a single provider organisation exacerbates the dangers to the public (Friedson, 1970). An alternative view is that the power of the profession is best constrained by a monopoly buyer, the state.

The exposition of public choice theory has led to a diligent search for ways to avoid situations in which 'perverse incentives' may be built into the day-to-day work of public organisations. Enthoven's examination of the British National Health Service in these terms is interesting, particularly inasmuch as it is inspired by a series of related control problems in the private system in the United States (Enthoven, 1985). The development of control devices to deal with these phenomena has been previously discussed, particularly in Chapter 5.

It is quite difficult, in practice, to separate the analysis of those need factors which drive up the demand for services and these supply factors which also affect growth (see Hills, 1990, for a thorough exploration of these two in the British case). The issue of 'dependency' analysed in the previous section is made all the more difficult by the increased cost of that dependency analysed in this. The discussion needs therefore to return to the wider economic and political aspects of this.

The impact of the rising cost of welfare in the context of the changing economy

There are good grounds for suggesting that the 'problem' of rising dependency has been exaggerated and equally that the rise of costs of provision can be contained. In this sense the author agrees with Hills (1993) that anxieties about the burden of welfare have been exaggerated, particularly in societies relatively far down the welfare spending 'league' (see table 3.1) like the United Kingdom, Australia and the United States. However, it is important to bear in mind that these rising costs are occurring against a background of an increasingly globalised economy, a changing economic relationship between nations and changing labour markets. This is not an economics textbook, so the implications of these first two developments, which are very complex, will be alluded to fairly briefly. The third, on the other hand, is very important for social policy (as earlier discussions on the family and economy, policy responses to unemployment and the dependence of income maintenance systems on work participation have indicated).

It is naive not to recognise that when economists and politicians argue that economies cannot cope with social policy expenditure increases they are working with a model of the world economic system, rightly or wrongly, in which the prices of commodities are increasingly set globally and in which the high-cost economies have increasing difficulties in competing with low-cost ones. Those comparisons rest not only upon differences in labour costs but also on differences in taxation levels, in fact these phenomena are linked. Paying for social policy improvements further raises taxation. There are ways to try to deal with these issues. Globalisation of costs, to eliminate the competitive advantages enjoyed by low-cost systems, is one such approach. This is seen in the area of pollution control where the externalities imposed on all lead the more advanced economies to try to curb some of the practices of the cheaper ones. Ideally rising standards throughout the world will eliminate some of the contrasts between low-wage and high-wage economies, but it would be rash to expect these developments to be cost free for those nations that have benefited from exploitation of the low-cost economies. Insulation of the rich economies from competition from the poor ones is seen as an increasingly difficult practice to sustain. As suggested at the end of Chapter 8 scenarios advanced by economists eager to protect welfare in the advanced economies often seem to rest upon a faith in the maintenance of a global division of labour in which those economies concentrate upon high-technology activities with high rates of return to input of labour (see the contributions by Sawyer and by Glyn and Rowthorn in Michie and Grieve Smith, 1994). That solution, however, seems to have implications for levels of employment; this will be further discussed.

Many industrialised countries have moved through an era in which a steadily higher proportion of the population was drawn into the labour market, into a period, since 1975, where unemployment and evidence of withdrawal from the labour market suggest that work cannot now be provided for all who want it. Another feature of that evolution involved a marked shift in the pattern of employment from industry to services (see table 12.9).

Table 12.9 Shares of employment in industry, agriculture and services in various European Union countries

	Agriculture	Industry	Services
Belgium	2.7	30.5	66.8
Denmark	5.7	27.6	66.7
Germany	3.5	40.1	56.4
France	6.0	30.0	63.9
United Kingdom	2.4	34.6	63.0

Source: Commission of the European Communities (1993a) *Employment in Europe*, Brussels: Commission of European Communities, pp. 51–2.

Another feature of the evolution of employment in many countries has been a consistent rise in female labour market participation. In these circumstances the subsequent down-turn in employment has been particularly marked for males rather than females. However, one reason for this is the extent to which the female participation is in part-time work. In Britain 60 per cent of women in employment are in part-time work. The figures are similar for the Netherlands (where women form a relatively low proportion of the workforce) and Denmark (where they are a high proportion). About a third of employed women in Germany and a quarter in France are in part-time work (Commission of the European Communities, 1993, ch. 6). There is, however, more to it than this; there are good reasons for suggesting it is not only its part-time nature that characterises this female labour market participation – it is also relatively less well paid and less secure. In other words, a scrutiny of trends in the European labour market suggests that the economy is adapting to its economic difficulties by reducing the deal offered to workers, in the process replacing a predominantly male labour force expecting (at least since 1945) secure relatively well-paid employment (much of it in manufacturing) with a much more casualised labour force, in which women are a key element. These trends are particularly strong in Britain.

The British adaptation to the changing world economy has some characteristics which are its own. Britain has the disadvantage of being the oldest of the industrial economies and it may have adapted particularly badly to the changing situation (this is an area of much controversy, beyond the scope of this book). However, its experience is not radically different from that of some other economies (particularly those just across the North Sea from it). The trend towards casualisation may have been peculiar to the British economy (together perhaps with the American, in which there have long been many areas where unions have been weak) – an issue explored in Chapter 8. However, it has been shown that Britain is by no means the only economy worried by high unemployment.

Conclusions: scenarios for the way forward

It seems to be the case that all the developed economies face a similar need to cope with a lowered (and still falling?) capacity to generate employment. Their responses may then consist of one of the following scenarios (or some combination of them):

1. Sustaining employment for lower returns (lower wages, less security, fewer fringe benefits, shorter hours).
2. Intervening to attempt to generate high technology-/high knowledge-based employment.
3. Requiring higher levels of dependency upon the family.

4. Requiring higher levels of dependency upon the state.
5. Expecting the state to play an even bigger role in the generation of employment.

The first two of these may be broadly characterised as 'economic policy' responses. They were discussed extensively in Chapter 8, and at its conclusion it was suggested that 'social policy' responses might be needed too. The characteristics and implications for social policy of each of these responses are as follows.

The economic or 'productivist' scenarios

Response 1 has already been presented as the typical British one, at least between 1979 and the time of writing (1995). A number of commentators have shown that it has many inegalitarian features embedded in it (Simpson and Walker, 1993; Commission on Social Justice, 1994). As suggested in Chapters 8 and 11 it has actually involved 'segmentation', with a strong contrast between those who survive in 'good' work situations and those who have to put up with bad ones. This division is, moreover, in many respects a gender one. For men it is to some extent the case that those who cannot get secure work get no work. Difficulties in providing for families on some of the poor wages on offer contribute to this. Comparatively few unemployed men are supported by employed wives in Britain. This is to a substantial extent a function of low returns available in the jobs available to women. It is also affected by the rules relating to the benefit system (the family means test and the assumption of female 'dependency'). Ironically both no-earner households and two-earners households are growing as a proportion of households in modern Britain (see Hills, 1993, p. 26).

Response 1 together with the segmentation that accompanies it has already been shown to be a factor in the changing social divisions of welfare (see Chapter 11). It is, in the British case, contributing to the collapse of the employment-related social insurance approach to income maintenance. The thrust of the discussions of the future of income maintenance tends to be upon a search for further ways of subsidising low wages through means tests and of making it easier for female single parents to combine work and care despite low wages (OECD, 1994b; Commission on Social Justice, 1994).

Response 2 adopts a less pessimistic view of the capacity of the population to rise to the challenge of changing technologies. It was portrayed in Chapter 8 as the response to the 'luddites' throughout the ages – human societies can develop through the harnessing of technology to raise collective standards of living. However, in Chapter 8 a note of doubt about this optimistic scenario was introduced: Can it bring opportunities for all, both within nation states and in the world as a whole?

Privatised solutions: the family in a key role

Response 3 gives the problem back to the family, which it sees as the 'forum' for redistribution of the products of the economy. Such are the aspirations of women in the industrial societies and such is the lip-service paid to equal opportunities that it is not openly on the official agenda, but to what extent is it what is actually happening in societies where relatively low levels of female labour market participation are combined with strong attempts to reinforce traditional family values (Ireland, Italy) or where social benefit systems are linked to employment (Netherlands) (see Sainsbury, 1994)?

The dominant perspective at the time of writing is one which involves one or the other of the two 'economic policy' scenarios together with an increased role for family and community, with the state in a more 'residual' role than was the case. Politicians in democratic societies want to be seen to be still advancing the welfare of their societies. For the 'new right' that particular objective has been seen to be achievable by restoring the competitiveness of the economy – 'a rising tide raises all the boats' they argue. Yet, as they have come to recognise that this goal is not so easily attainable, pragmatic politicians have sought other ways to enhance welfare without raising public expenditure. Ideas about 'privatisation', quasi-market systems to make public services more efficient and the 'mixed economy of welfare' have come to be emphasised. These seem to offer new approaches to welfare goals and at the same time advance 'capitalist' interests and values.

The mixed economy of welfare as a way forward?

The idea of the mixed economy of welfare was introduced in the very first chapter of this book. It was a theme picked up in various ways throughout the book. The author has been concerned to emphasise that social policy always involves a mixture of state responses with market, community and family care, and provision systems. In this sense the renewed emphasis in the rhetoric of social policy is only an attempt to strengthen or renew the non-state elements in welfare provision. However, it has been given a number of features which though mentioned earlier – particularly in the chapters on health and social care – need highlighting here. These are the following:

1. Devices to ensure that individuals and family undertake more of the costs of social welfare systems.
2. Devices to get individuals to invest towards the future costs of welfare (in this sense a revival of insurance with a shift towards private rather than 'social' insurance inasmuch as the latter is merely taxation by another name).

3. Devices to increase the roles of family members and community volunteers in caring tasks.
4. Methods to enable private organisations to play a bigger part as the providers of care.
5. Quasi-market systems, performance-related pay and incentive systems designed to make public providers behave more like private providers.

(For a more extensive discussion of the connection between these ideas and 'new right' ideology see Mishra, 1990; Glennerster and Midgely, 1991 and Taylor, 1990.)

The first three of these approaches are directly designed to shift the costs of social policy away from the state. It is important to remember that they do not shift the real costs away from society inasmuch as they enable support systems to be provided more efficiently. The last two are seen as ways to increase efficiency. The extent to which they do so depends substantially upon the extent to which market systems are cheaper than non-market systems (see Self, 1993). As suggested in Chapter 2, this is influenced by the extent to which real competition is more efficient and can be achieved.

The globalisation of policy thinking is such that these ideas for curbing the costs of social policy travel rapidly around the world. They are seen as effective responses to the rising costs of social policy. There are grounds for scepticism about what they can achieve; these have been voiced at various places in this book. Many have not yet been adequately tested, indeed many are hard to test.

An alternative perspective: the state in a key role enhancing social solidarity

The two scenarios labelled 4 and 5 above can be taken together as both give key roles to the state. These are the responses to the issues about welfare which have been to a large extent adopted by the Scandinavian countries, involving both efforts to maintain full-employment and 'solidaristic' benefit policies (described by Esping-Andersen and discussed in Chapters 3 and 11).

An emphasis upon the provision of full employment fits better with value systems which demand that people should work in order to be supported. Yet societies accept a variety of legitimate 'dependency' situations – particularly on the part of the young and the old. Falling work opportunities following upon (and to some extent accompanying) rising levels of female labour market participation mean that egalitarianism in respect of relations between the genders requires the state to accept either the service provision or the income transfer implications (or probably both).

This scenario has come under fierce attack from a group extending far beyond the original ranks of the 'new right'. The fall of confidence in the state's capacity to provide for full employment – particularly through the use of high taxes to guarantee high levels of labour intensive public services (as at the time of writing in Sweden, see Marklund, 1992) – seems to be leading to a retreat from adequate systems of income maintenance support for those out of work. Lipietz has suggested that the welfare state is a 'very specific form of solidarity' between those in work and those out of work which can only survive if the latter group is not too large relative to the former (Lipietz, 1992, p. 92).

The OECD has warned Sweden, obviously encouraged by that country's government, that it cannot sustain its social policies (OECD, 1994a, see quote on p. 52). The OECD's own *Jobs Study* accepts that any job creation is likely to be in the service sector, but goes on to say that these must 'be generated by the private sector, because in nearly all countries budget deficits and resistance to tax increases rule out significant expansion of the public sector' (1994b, p. 33). Politicians of the 'left', eager to get into power (in Britain or Germany) or remain in power (in Australia), have sought to convince electors that they will not increase taxes (at the time of writing a new coalition has formed in the Netherlands with odd 'bedfellows', with a prime minister on the 'left' supported by parties on the 'right', pledged to bring public expenditure under control).

It is this reaction to the expenditure implications of this scenario which contributes to a widespread sense that there is a 'crisis' for the welfare state ideal. Various analyses of contemporary society by political scientists or political economists have written of the demise of the 'Keynesian welfare state' (Burrows and Loader, 1994; Pierson, 1991). This involves the abandonment of the belief held by political elites that public expenditure could play an active role in advancing employment opportunities and social policy goals at the same time.

It must be acknowledged that the 'globalist' critique which can be applied to the 'economic policy' solutions (see above and Chapter 8) also applies to these two 'statist' social policy solutions. The challenge to those who still believe in them is then how to extend them:

> *Solidarity and local initiative can develop only by extending their horizon to the whole world. . . . Without . . . supra-regional levels to establish ground rules, there is a great danger that regions will find themselves in 'free competition' with each other to the disadvantage of the worse-off. There can be no local solidarity without national and international solidarity. (Lipietz, 1992, p. 110)*

It is, however, the wider impact of globalisation – the globalisation of the economy and the recognition of the universality of social hazards – that is crucial in widening the social policy agenda. A central issue here is the extent to which orthodox, and generally dominant, economic thinking sees solutions to world problems in terms of a need for growth (OECD, 1994b), yet it is dangerous to pursue that growth without attention to both distributional and environmental consequences.

Within our own societies we may participate in debates about policy delivery and the organisation of social policy. Yet if these are not located in an awareness of wider global forces they will be exercises in 'rearranging the deckchairs on the Titanic'. Equally they will come to grief if they are located in the simple economistic belief that rising national prosperity will readily benefit all. We live in a world in which the collapse of the Soviet empire, with conclusive evidence for those not already convinced that it was corrupt and inefficient, has discredited social planning. Yet, there is still abundant evidence that it is equally dangerous to fail to plan and to leave all to market forces.

Eric Hobsbaum in his formidable survey of world history between 1914 and 1991 argues that a feature of post-Second World War developed market economies, by comparison with pre-War ones, was 'that the mass market had been stabilised by the shift of labour to tertiary occupations, which had, in general much stabler employment, and by the vast growth in transfer incomes . . .' (Hobsbaum, 1994, p. 572). *Both* of these developments were central to the growth of the 'welfare state'. Later therefore he looks forward in the following way:

> *Suppose – the scenario is not utterly fantastic – present trends continued, and led to economies in which one quarter of the population worked gainfully, and three quarters did not, but after twenty years the economy produced a national income per capita twice as large as before. Who, except public authority, would and could ensure a minimum of income and welfare for all?* (ibid., *p. 577)*

Earlier, Hobsbawm had acknowledged that the main threats to a scenario like that are the pollution such a rise in productivity would cause and the difficulties in achieving a globally even spread in the growth. But surely the alternative scenarios suggested by these reservations would also call on 'public authority' to deal with the regulatory and redistributional problems associated with them. Without such interventions they suggest very gloomy scenarios indeed, as threatening to the welfare of the rich as to that of the poor.

Final conclusions

In the first three chapters of this book the many factors which led to the growth of state social policy, as an accompaniment to economic, urban and political development, were explored. Many of these factors are still relevant.

Turning back the clock on social policy development is difficult, certainly the statistics quoted earlier suggest that the rate of growth of social policy expenditure has merely been curbed. It has been shown (Taylor-Gooby, 1985, 1991) that people are broadly in favour of the main forms of public social policy expenditure. Now, in the view of this author, people need to come to terms with the fact that state social policy – broadly defined – offers in many cases the best way of socialising costs that will otherwise fall heavily, unpredictably and inequitably on individuals and families. The social divisions analysed in Chapter 11 are likely to be enhanced. The economic orthodoxy which terrifies politicians of the 'left' from championing public expenditure growth with its inevitable tax implications needs to be challenged. So too does the narrow nationalism within which so many responses to these issues are framed. These challenges are vital to the cause of the advancing of a caring, responsible and safe world.

Guide to further reading

Mishra's work on comparative social policy is always stimulating. His books *The Welfare State in Crisis* (1984) and *The Welfare State in Capitalist Society* (1990), both deal with issues about the future of welfare. Hills has provided *The Future of Welfare: A Guide to the Debate* (1993); his data are specifically for a British audience but his approach to setting out the issues clearly could well be emulated elsewhere.

This book's dependence on OECD as a source of data will be evident. Publications by the OECD which are particularly useful for an overview on the ways social policy is developing are *New Orientations for Social Policy* (1994c) and *Ageing Populations* (1988).

Recommendations relating to the globalisation theme have been set out at the end of Chapter 8. As the author was completing this volume a book on the problems British society is facing which made a big impact was Hutton's *The State We're In* (1995). While this is very specific to Britain it has some provocative things to say concerning the implications of contemporary economic developments and the increasing divisions in society. Comparable, but rather more academic, analyses are offered for Australia in Bell and Head (eds.) *State, Economy and Public Policy in Australia* (1994) and for Canada in Abele (ed.) *How Ottawa Spends: The Politics of Competitiveness* (1992).

Bibliography

Abele, F. (ed.) (1992) *How Ottawa Spends: The Politics of Competitiveness 1992–93*, Ottawa: Carleton University Press.

Aglietta, M. (1987) *A Theory of Capitalist Regulation: The US Experience*, London: Verso.

Alford, R. (1972) 'The political economy of health care: dynamics without change', *Politics and Society* (Winter).

Altenstetter, C. and Haywood, S. (eds.) (1991) *Competitive Health Policy and the New Right*, Basingstoke: Macmillan.

Ambler, J. S. (ed.) (1991) *The French Welfare State*, New York: New York University Press.

Arber, S. and Ginn, J. (1991) *Gender and Later Life*, London: Sage.

Archer, M. (1979) *The Social Origins of Educational Systems*, Beverly Hills, CA: Sage.

Ashby, E. and Anderson, M. (1981) *The Politics of Clean Air*, Oxford: Clarendon Press.

Ashford, D. E. (1982) *British Dogmatism and French Pragmatism: Center-Local Relations in the Welfare State*, London: Allen & Unwin.

Ashford, D. E. (1986) *The Emergence of the Welfare States*, Oxford: Blackwell.

Atkinson, A. B. (1993) *Beveridge, the National Minimum, and its Future in a European Context*, Welfare State Programme Discussion Paper 85, London: London School of Economics.

Bacon, R. and Eltis, W. (1976) *Britain's Economic Problem: Too Few Producers*, London: Macmillan.

Bailey, J. (ed.) (1992) *Social Europe*, London: Longmans.

Baldock, J. and Ungerson, C. (1994) 'All our futures: becoming a consumer of care in old age', paper given at the Social Policy Association conference, Liverpool.

Baldwin, P. (1990) *The Politics of Social Solidarity*, Cambridge: Cambridge University Press.

Baldwin, S. and Falkingham, J. (eds.) (1994) *Social Security and Social*

Change, Hemel Hempstead: Harvester Wheatsheaf.

Ball, M., Harloe, M. and Martens, M. (1988) *Housing and Social Change in Europe and the USA*, London: Routledge.

Ball, S. J. (1990) *Politics and Policy Making in Education*, London: Routledge.

Barker, A. and Peters, B. G. (eds.) (1993) *The Politics of Expert Advice*, Edinburgh: Edinburgh University Press.

Barrett, M. (1980) *Women's Oppression Today*, London: Verso.

Becker, G. (1975) *Human Capital*, Chicago: Chicago University Press.

Bell, D. (1978) *The Coming of Post-Industrial Society*, Harmondsworth: Penguin Books.

Bell, S. and Head, B. (eds.) (1994) *State, Economy and Public Policy in Australia*, Melbourne: Oxford University Press.

Bendix, R. and Lipset, S. M. (eds.) (1967) *Class, Status and Power*, 2nd edn, London: Routledge.

Bennett, G. (1992) *Dilemmas: Coping with Environmental Problems*, London: Earthscan.

Berthoud, R. (ed.) (1985) *Challenges to Social Policy*, Aldershot: Gower.

Beveridge, W. (1909) *Unemployment: a Problem of Industry*, London: Longman.

Beveridge, W. (1942) *Social Insurance and Allied Services*, Cmd. 6404, London: HMSO.

Blaug, M. (1970) *The Economics of Education*, Harmondsworth: Penguin Books.

Blowers, A. (1984) *Something in the Air: Corporate Power and the Environment*, London: Harper & Row.

Boddy, M. (1980) *The Building Societies*, London: Macmillan.

Bolderson, H. (1986) 'Comparing Social Policies: Some Problems of Method and the Case of Social Security Benefits in Australia, Britain and the U.S.A.', *Journal of Social Policy*, 17 (3), pp. 267–88.

Bolderson, H. and Mabbett, D. (1991) *Social Policy and Social Security in Australia, Britain and the USA*, Aldershot: Avebury.

Bolderson, H. and Mabbett, D. (1994) 'Deconstructing targeting', paper given at International Social Security Association research meeting, Vienna.

Bondi, L. (1991) 'Choice and diversity in school education: comparing developments in the United Kingdom and the USA', *Comparative Education*, 27 (2), pp. 125–34.

Bowles, S. and Gintis, H. (1976) *Schooling in Capitalist America*, New York: Basic Books.

Bradshaw, J. (1995) 'The levels of social assistance in eighteen countries', *Benefits*, 12, pp. 16–20.

Bradshaw, J., Ditch, J., Holmes, H. and Whiteford, P. (1993) *Support for Children*, Department of Social Security Research Report 21, London: HMSO.

Brenton, T. (1994) *The Greening of Machiavelli*, London: Earthscan.

Briggs, L. (1994) 'Meeting the challenge: Australian labour market trends and the income support system', paper given at International Social Security Association research meeting, Vienna.

Brittan, S. (1977) *The Economic Consequences of Democracy*, London: Temple Smith.

Brown, C. V. (1983) *Taxation and the Incentive to Work*, London: Oxford University Press.

Brownmiller, S. (1975) *Against Our Will: Men, Women and Rape*, New York: Simon & Schuster.

Bryson, L. (1992) *Welfare and the State*, Basingstoke: Macmillan.

Buchanan, J. M. and Tullock, G. (1962) *The Calculus of Consent*, Ann Arbor, MI: University of Michigan Press.

Buchanan, J. M. and Wagner, R. E. (1977) *Democracy in Deficit*, New York: Academic Press.

Burgess, R. G. (1986) *Sociology, Education and Schools*, London: Batsford.

Burnett, J. (1994) *Idle Hands: The Experience of Unemployment 1790–1990*, London: Routledge.

Burrows, R. and Loader, B. (eds.) (1994) *Towards a Post-Fordist Welfare State?*, London: Routledge.

Butrym, Z. T. (1976) *The Nature of Social Work*, London: Macmillan.

Cahill, M. (1994) *The New Social Policy*, Oxford: Blackwell.

Carter, L. W. (1977) *Environmental Impact Assessment*, New York: McGraw-Hill.

Castles, F. (1985) *The Working Class and Welfare*, Sydney: Allen & Unwin.

Castles, F. (ed.) (1989) *The Comparative History of Public Policy*, Cambridge: Polity Press.

Castles, F. and Mitchell, D. (1992) 'Identifying welfare state regimes: the links between politics, instruments and outcomes', *Governance*, 5(1), pp. 1–26.

Castles, S. (1984) *Here for Good: Western Europe's New Ethnic Minorities*, London: Pluto.

Castles, S. and Kosack, G. (1973) *Immigrant Workers and Class Structure in Western Europe*, Oxford: Oxford University Press.

Castles, S. and Miller, M. J. (1993) *The Age of Migration*, Basingstoke: Macmillan.

Centre for Contemporary Cultural Studies (1982) *The Empire Strikes Back*, London: Hutchinson.

Child Poverty Action Group (1993) 'Poverty: the facts', *Poverty*, 84 (supplement).

Clasen, J. and Freeman, R. (eds.) (1994) *Social Policy in Germany*, Hemel Hempstead: Harvester Wheatsheaf.

Cochrane, A. and Clarke, J. (eds.) (1993) *Comparing Welfare States*, London: Sage.

Coenen, H. and Leisink, P. (eds.) (1993) *Work and Citizenship in the New Europe*, Aldershot: Edward Elgar.

Coleman, J. S. *et al.* (1966) *Equality of Educational Opportunity*, Washington, DC: US Government Printing Office.

Collick, M. (1988) 'Social policy: pressures and responses,' in Stockwin, J. A. A. (ed.) *Dynamic and Immobilist Politics in Japan*, Basingstoke: Macmillan.

Commission of the European Communities (1993a) *Employment in Europe*, Brussels: Commission of the European Communities.

Commission of the European Communities (1993b) *European Social Policy: Options for the Union*, Brussels: Commission of the European Communities.

Commission of the European Communities (1993c) *Social Europe*, 1/93, Brussels: Commission of the European Communities.

Commission of the European Communities (1994) *Employment in Europe*, Luxembourg: Commission of the European Communities.

Commission on Social Justice (1994) *Social Justice: Strategies for National Renewal*, London: Vintage.

Coons, J. and Sugarman, S. (1978) *Education by Choice: The Case for Family Control*, Berkeley, CA: University of California Press.

Crain, R. L. (1968) *The Politics of School Desegregation*, Chicago: Aldine.

Creemers, B. and Scheerens, J. (eds.) (1989) 'Developments in school effectiveness research', special issue of *International Journal of Educational Research*, 37, pp. 685–825.

Crenson, M. A. (1971) *The Unpolitics of Air Pollution*, Baltimore: The Johns Hopkins Press.

Crompton, R. (1993) *Class and Stratification*, Cambridge: Polity Press.

Culyer, A. J. (1980) *The Political Economy of Social Policy*, Oxford: Martin Robertson.

Dahrendorf, R. (1959) *Class and Class Conflict in Industrial Society*, London: Routledge.

Dahrendorf, R. (1985) *Law and Order*, London: Stevens.

Dale, J. and Foster, P. (1986) *Feminists and State Welfare*, London: Routledge & Kegan Paul.

Darley, G. (1990) *Octavia Hill*, London: Constable.

Deacon, A. (1976) *In Search of the Scrounger*, London: Bell.

Deber, R. (1993) 'Canadian medicare: can it work in the United States? Will it survive in Canada?', *American Journal of Law and Medicine*, XIX (1 and 2), pp. 75–93.

Deem, R. (1978) *Women and Schooling*, London: Routledge & Kegan Paul.

Delamont, S. (1980) *Sex Roles and the School*, London: Methuen.

Deleek, H., Van Den Bosch, K. and DeLathouver, K. (1992) *Poverty and the*

Adequacy of Social Security in the European Community, Aldershot, Avebury.

Delphy, C. (1984) *Close to Home: A Materalist Analysis of Women's Oppression*, London: Hutchinson.

Department of Social Security (1993) *Households below Average Income 1979–1990/91*, London: HMSO.

Dewey, J. (1976) *Democracy and Education*, New York: The Free Press.

Dierkes, M., Weiler, H. N. and Antal, A. B. (eds.) (1987) *Comparative Policy Research: Learning from Experience*, Aldershot: Gower.

Dixon, J. and Scheurell, P. (eds.) (1989) *Social Welfare in Developed Market Economies*, London: Routledge.

Doeringer, P. and Piore, M. J. (1971) *Internal Labor Markets and Manpower Analysis*, Lexington, MA: D. C. Heath.

Doling, J. and Davies, M. (1984) *The Public Control of Privately Rented Housing*, Aldershot: Gower.

Donnison, J. (1977) *Midwives and Medical Men*, London: Heinemann.

Downing, P. B. and Hanf, K. (eds.) (1983) *International Comparisons in Implementing Pollution Laws*, Boston, MA: Kluwer Nijhoff.

Drover, G. and Kerans, P. (eds.) (1993) *New Approaches to Welfare Theory*, Aldershot: Edward Elgar.

Dunleavy, P. (1985) 'Bureaucrats, budgets and the growth of the state: reconstructing an instrumental model', *British Journal of Political Science*, 15, pp. 299–328.

Dunleavy, P. (1986) 'Explaining the privatization boom: public choice versus radical approaches', *Public Administration*, 64 (1), pp. 13–14.

Dunleavy, P. (1991) *Democracy, Bureaucracy and Public Choice*, Hemel Hempstead: Harvester Wheatsheaf.

Dyson, K. H. F. (1980) *The State Tradition in Western Europe: A Study of an Idea and Institution*, New York: Oxford University Press.

Edelman, M. (1971) *Politics as Symbolic Action*, Chicago: Markham.

Edwards, J. (1987) *Positive Discrimination, Social Justice and Social Policy*, London: Tavistock.

Eisenstein, Z. (1984) *Feminism and Sexual Equality: Crisis in Liberal America*, New York: Monthly Review Press.

Elias, N. (1978) *The History of Manners*, Oxford: Blackwell.

Elias, N. (1982) *Power and Civility*, Oxford: Blackwell.

Emms, P. (1990) *Social Housing, A European Dilemma*, Bristol: School for Advanced Urban Studies.

Enthoven, A. C. (1985) *Reflections on the Management of the NHS*, London: Nuffield Provincial Hospitals Trust.

Esping-Andersen, G. (1990) *Three Worlds of Welfare Capitalism*, Cambridge: Polity Press.

Etzioni, A. (1969) *The Semi Professions and their Organization*, New York: The Free Press.

Evans, P. B., Rueschemeyer, D. and Skocpol, T. (eds.) (1985) *Bringing the State Back In*, Cambridge: Cambridge University Press.

Evers, A., Pijl, M. and Ungerson, C. (1994) *Payments for Care: A Comparative Overview*, Aldershot: Avebury.

Evetts, J. (1973) *The Sociology of Educational Ideas*, London: Routledge & Kegan Paul.

Field, F. (1989) *Losing Out: The Emergence of Britain's Underclass*, Oxford: Blackwell.

Fimister, G. (1986) *Welfare Rights in Social Services*, London: Macmillan.

Finch, J. (1984) *Education and Social Policy*, London: Longman.

Finch, J. and Groves, D. (eds.) (1983) *A Labour of Love: Women, Work and Caring*, London: Routledge.

Flora, P. and Heidenheimer, A. J. (eds.) (1981) *The Development of Welfare States in Europe and America*, New Brunswick, NJ: Transaction Books.

Flude, M. and Hammer, M. (eds.) (1990) *The Education Reform Act 1988*, London: Falmer Press.

Forrest, R. and Murie, A. (1991) *Selling the Welfare State*, London: Routledge.

Forrest, R., Murie, A. and Williams, P. (1990) *Home Ownership*, London: Unwin Hyman.

Foster, P. (1983) *Access to Welfare*, London: Macmillan.

Freire, P. (1974) *Pedagogy of the Oppressed*, Harmondsworth: Penguin Books.

Friedman, M. (1962) *Capitalism and Freedom*, Chicago: University of Chicago Press.

Friedman, M. and Friedman, R. (1981) *Free to Choose*, Harmondsworth: Penguin Books.

Friedson, E. (1970) *Professional Dominance*, New York: Atherton.

Furniss, N. and Tilton, T. (1979) *The Case for the Welfare State*, Bloomington, IN: Indiana University Press.

Gamble, A. (1994) *The Free Economy and the Strong State*, 2nd edn, Basingstoke: Macmillan.

George, V. and Howards, I. (1991) *Poverty Amidst Affluence*, Aldershot: Edward Elgar.

George, V. and Wilding, P. (1994) *Welfare and Ideology*, 2nd edn, Hemel Hempstead: Harvester Wheatsheaf.

Giddens, A. (1973) *The Class Structure of the Advanced Societies*, London: Hutchinson.

Gilbert, B. B. (1966) *The Evolution of National Insurance in Great Britain*, London: Michael Joseph.

Gilbert, B. B. (1970) *British Social Policy 1914–39*, London: Batsford.

Ginsberg, N. (1992) *Divisions of Welfare*, London: Sage.

Glazer, N. and Moynihan, D. P. (eds.) (1975) *Ethnicity*, Cambridge, MA: Harvard University Press.

Glendinning, C. and McLaughlin, E. (1993) *Financial Support for Informal Care*, London: HMSO.

Glendinning, C. and Millar, J. (1992) *Women and Poverty in Britain: The 1990s*, Hemel Hempstead: Harvester Wheatsheaf.

Glennerster, H. (1992) *Paying for Welfare: The 1990s*, Hemel Hempstead: Harvester Wheatsheaf.

Glennerster, H. and Midgley, J. (1991) *The Radical Right and the Welfare State: An International Assessment*, Hemel Hempstead: Harvester Wheatsheaf.

Glennerster, H., Power, A. and Travers, T. (1991) 'A new era for social policy: a new enlightenment or a new leviathan?' *Journal of Social Policy*, 20 (3), pp. 389–414.

Gold, M. (ed.) (1993) *The Social Dimension: Employment Policy in the European Community*, Basingstoke: Macmillan.

Goldstein, H. (1973) *Social Work Practice: A Unitary Approach*, New York: Columbia University Press.

Goldthorpe, J. H. (1980) *Social Mobility and Class Structure in Modern Britain*, Oxford: Clarendon Press.

Goldthorpe, J. H. (1983) 'Women and class analysis: in defence of the conventional view', *Sociology*, 17 (4), pp. 465–88.

Goodin, R. and Le Grand, J. (eds.) (1987) *Not only the Poor: The Middle Classes and the Welfare State*, London: Allen & Unwin.

Gordon, A. (1982) *Economics and Social Policy*, Oxford: Martin Robertson.

Gordon, D. M. (1972) *Theories of Poverty and Unemployment*, Lexington, MA: D. C. Heath.

Gordon, P. (1986) 'Racism and social security', *Critical Social Policy*, 17, pp. 23–40.

Gordon, P. and Newnham, A. (1985) *Passport to Benefits*, London: CPAG.

Gough, I. (1979) *The Political Economy of the Welfare State*, London: Macmillan.

Gould, A. (1988) *Conflict and Control in Welfare Policy: The Swedish Experience*, London: Longman.

Gould, A. (1993) *Capitalist Welfare Systems: A Comparison of Japan, Britain and Sweden*, London: Longman.

Gouldner, A. W. (1971) *The Coming Crisis of Western Sociology*, London: Heinemann.

Grant, C. and Lapsley, H. M. (1993) *The Australian Health Care System*, Kensington: School of Health Services Management, University of New South Wales.

Gray, J. (1992) *The Moral Foundations of Market Institutions*, London: Institute of Economic Affairs.

Green, A. (1990) *Education and State Formation*, Basingstoke: Macmillan.

Griffiths Report (1988) *Community Care: Agenda for Action*, London: HMSO.

Gunningham, N. (1974) *Pollution, Social Interest and the Law*, London: Martin Robertson.

Haigh, N. (1989) *EEC Environmental Policy and Britain*, 2nd edn, Harlow: Longman.

Hall, P. (1957) *The Social Services of Modern England*, 3rd edn, London: Routledge & Kegan Paul.

Hall, P., Land, H., Parker, R. and Webb, A. (1978) *Change, Choice and Conflict in Social Policy*, London: Heinemann.

Hall, S., Critcher, C., Jefferson, T., Clarke, J. and Roberts, B. (1979) *Policing the Crisis*, London: Macmillan.

Hall, S. and Jacques, M. (1985) *The Politics of Thatcherism*, London: Lawrence & Wishart.

Halsey, A. H. (1995) *Decline of Donnish Dominion*, paperback edn, Oxford: Oxford University Press.

Ham, C. (1992) *Health Policy in Britain*, 3rd edn, London: Macmillan.

Ham, C. and Hill, M. (1993) *The Policy Process in the Modern Capitalist State*, Hemel Hempstead: Harvester Wheatsheaf.

Ham, C., Robinson, R. and Benzeval, M. (1990) *Health Check: Health Care Reforms in an International Context*, London: Kings Fund Institute.

Hamnett, C. (1991) 'A nation of inheritors? Housing inheritance, wealth and inequality in Britain', *Journal of Social Policy*, 20(4), pp. 509–36.

Handler, J. (1973) *The Coercive Social Worker*, Chicago: Rand McNally.

Hanf, K. and Jensen, A.-I. (eds.) (forthcoming) *Governance and Environmental Quality in Western Europe*, Hemel Hempstead: Harvester Wheatsheaf.

Hansard (1833) *House of Commons Speech by Macaulay*, Col. 525, London: Hansard.

Hardin, G. (1968) 'The tragedy of the commons', *Science*, 162, pp. 1243–8.

Harloe, M. (1985) *Private Rented Housing in the United States and Europe*, Beckenham: Croom Helm.

Harrington, M. (1985) *The New American Poverty*, Harmondsworth: Penguin Books.

Harris, J. (1972) *Unemployment and Politics*, London: Oxford University Press.

Harris, J. (1977) *William Beveridge: A Biography*, Oxford: Oxford University Press.

Harrison, S. and Pollitt, C. (1994) *Controlling Health Professionals*, Buckingham: Open University Press.

Hartman, C. (1986) 'Housing policies under the Reagan administration', in Bratt, R., Hartman, C. and Meyerson, A. (eds.) *Critical Perspectives on Housing*, Philadelphia, PA: Temple University Press.

Hartmann, H. (1979) 'The unhappy marriage of Marxism and feminism', *Capital and Class*, 8.

Hatland, A. (1984) *The Future of Norwegian Social Insurance*, Oslo: Universitetsforlaget.

Hawkins, K. (1984) *Environment and Enforcement*, Oxford: Clarendon Press.

Hayek, F. A. (1960) *The Constitution of Liberty*, London: Routledge & Kegan Paul.

Heald, D. (1983) *Public Expenditure*, Oxford: Martin Robertson.

Heclo, H. H. (1974) *Modern Social Politics in Britain and Sweden*, New Haven, CT: Yale University Press.

Heidenheimer, A. J., Heclo, H. H. and Adams, C. T. (1990) *Comparative Public Policy*, New York: St. Martin's Press.

Henderson, J. W. and Karn, V. A. (1987) *Race, Class and State Housing*, Aldershot: Gower.

Hennock, E. P. (1987) *British Social Reform and the German Precedent: The Case of Social Insurance 1888–1914*, Oxford: Oxford University Press.

Henry, M. *et al*. (1988) *Understanding Schooling*, London: Routledge.

Hernes, H. (1987) *Welfare State and Women Power*, Oslo: Norwegian University Press.

Higgins, J. (1981) *States of Welfare*, Oxford: Blackwell.

Higgins, J. (1988) *The Business of Medicine: Private Health Care in Britain*, London: Macmillan.

Higgins, J., Deakin, N., Edwards, J., and Wicks, M. (1983) *Government and Urban Poverty*, Oxford: Blackwell.

Hill, M. (1990) *Social Security Policy in Britain*, Cheltenham: Edward Elgar.

Hill, M. (1993a) *Understanding Social Policy*, Oxford: Blackwell.

Hill, M. (ed.) (1993b) *New Agendas in the Study of the Policy Process*, Hemel Hempstead: Harvester Wheatsheaf.

Hill, M. and Bramley, G. (1986) *Analysing Social Policy*, Oxford: Blackwell.

Hillery, G. (1955) 'Definitions of community', *Rural Sociology*, 20.

Hills, J. (1988) *Twenty-First Century Housing Subsidies: Durable Rent-Fixing and Subsidy Arrangements for Social Housing*, Welfare State Programme Discussion Paper 33, London: London School of Economics.

Hills, J. (ed.) (1990) *The State of Welfare*, Oxford: Clarendon Press.

Hills, J. (1993) *The Future of Welfare: A Guide to the Debate*, York: Joseph Rowntree Foundation.

Hills, J., Ditch, J. and Glennerster, H. (eds.) (1994) *Beveridge and Social Security: An International Retrospective*, Oxford: Clarendon Press.

Hirsch, F. (1976) *Social Limits to Growth*, Cambridge, MA: Harvard University Press.

HMSO (various dates) *Census Reports for England and Wales*, 1931, 1951, 1971 and 1991, London: HMSO.

HMSO (1994) *Social Trends 24*, London: HMSO.

Hobsbawm, E. (1994) *Age of Extremes: The Short Twentieth Century 1914–91*, London: Michael Joseph.

Hobson, J. A. (1896) *The Problem of Unemployment*, London: Methuen.

Hoggart, R. (1957) *The Uses of Literacy*, London: Chatto & Windus.

Holmes, B. (ed.) (1985) *Equality and Freedom in Education*, London: Routledge.

Hudson, B. (1994) *Making Sense of Markets in Health and Social Care*, Sunderland: Business Education Publishers.

Hunt, G. (1990) 'Patient choice and the NHS review', *Journal of Social Welfare Law*, 4, pp. 245–55.

Hupe, P. L. (1993a) 'The politics of implementation: individual, organisational and political co-production in social services delivery', in Hill, M. (ed.) *New Agendas in the Study of the Policy Process*, Hemel Hempstead: Harvester Wheatsheaf.

Hupe, P. L. (1993b) 'Beyond pillarization: the (post-) welfare state in the Netherlands', *European Journal of Political Research*, 23, pp. 359–86.

Hurst, P. (1981) 'Education and development in the third world: a critical appraisal of aid policies', *Comparative Education*, 17 (2), pp. 115–255.

Husbands, C. T. (1988) 'The dynamics of racial exclusion and expulsion: racist politics in Western Europe', *European Journal of Political Research*, 16 (6), pp. 701–20.

Husen, T. (1987) 'Policy impact of IEA research', *Comparative Education Review*, pp. 29–46.

Hutton, W. (1995) *The State We're In*, London: Cape.

Hvinden, B. (1994) *Divided Against Itself: A Study of Integration in Welfare Bureaucracy*, Oslo: Universitetsforlaget.

Illich, I. (1977) *Limits to Medicine*, Harmondsworth: Penguin.

Immergut, E. M. (1993) *Health Policy, Interests and Institutions in Western Europe*, Cambridge: Cambridge University Press.

Jackson, B. and Marsden, D. (1962) *Education and the Working Class*, London: Routledge.

Jacob, J. M. (1988) *Doctors and Rules*, London: Routledge.

Jencks, C. *et al.* (1972) *Inequality: A Reassessment of the Effects of Family and Schooling in America*, New York: Basic Books.

Jensen, A. A. (1975) *Educability and Group Differences*, New York: Harper & Row.

John Paul II (1991) *On the Hundredth Anniversary*, Boston, MA: St. Paul Books.

Joly, D. and Cohen, R. (eds.) (1990) *Reluctant Hosts: Europe and its Refugees*, Aldershot: Avebury.

Jones, C. (1985) *Patterns of Social Policy: An Introduction to Comparative Analysis*, London: Tavistock.

Jones, C. (ed.) (1993) *New Perspectives on the Welfare State in Europe*, London: Routledge.

Jones, M. (1972) *Housing and Poverty in Australia*, Melbourne: Melbourne University Press.

Jones, M. A. (1990) *The Australian Welfare State*, 3rd edn, North Sydney: Allen & Unwin.

Jones, K. (1993) *Asylums and After*, London: Athlone Press.

Jordan, B. (1974) *Poor Parents*, London: Routledge & Kegan Paul.

Joseph, K. and Sumption, J. (1979) *Equality*, London: John Murray.

Kamenka, E. (1989) *Bureaucracy*, Oxford: Blackwell.

Kamerman, S. B. (1983) 'The mixed economy of welfare', *Social Work*, 28, pp. 5–11.

Kamerman, S. B. and Kahn, A. J. (1983) *Income Transfers for Families with Children*, Philadelphia, PA: Temple University Press.

Kavanagh, D. (1990) *Thatcherism and British Politics*, second edition, Oxford: Oxford University Press. Kavanagh 1990.

Kay, J. and King, M. A. (1983) *The British Tax System*, London: Oxford University Press.

Kelly, A. (ed.) (1981) *The Missing Half*, Manchester: Manchester University Press.

Kelman, S. (1981) *Regulating America, Regulating Sweden*, Cambridge, MA: MIT Press.

Kemp, P. (1980) 'Income-related assistance with housing costs: a cross- national comparison', *Urban Studies*, 27 (6), pp. 795–808.

Kerr, C., Dunlop, J. T., Harbison, F. H. and Myers, C. A. (1973) *Industrialism and Industrial Man*, Harmondsworth: Penguin Books.

Keynes, J. M. (1936) *The General Theory of Employment Interest and Money*, London: Macmillan.

Kinnersley, D. (1994) *Coming Clean: The Politics of Water and the Environment*, Harmondsworth: Penguin Books.

Kitschelt, H. (1989) 'Explaining contemporary social movements: a comparison of theories', paper given at annual meeting of American Political Science Association, Atlanta, Georgia.

Klein, R. (1989) *The Politics of the NHS*, 2nd edn, London: Longman.

Klein, R. and O'Higgins, M. (eds.) (1985) *The Future of Welfare*, Oxford: Blackwell.

Knapp, M. R. J. (1984) *The Economics of Social Care*, London: Macmillan.

Knapp, M. R. J. (1989) 'Private and voluntary welfare', in McCarthy, M.(ed.) *The New Politics of Welfare*, Macmillan: London.

Kogan, M. (1979) *Education Policies in Perspective*, Paris: OECD.

Kohli, M., Rein, M., Guillemard, A.-M. and Gunsteren, H. (1991) *Time for Retirement: Comparative Studies of Early Exit from the Labour Force*, Cambridge: Cambridge University Press.

Kormondy, E. J. (ed.) (1989) *International Handbook of Pollution Control*, Westport, CN: Greenwood Press.

Korpi, W. and Palme, J. (1994) 'The strategy of equality and the paradox of redistribution', paper given at the Social Policy Association conference, Liverpool.

Kraan, R. J. *et al.* (1991) *Care for the Elderly: Significant Innovations in three European Countries*, Boulder, CO: Westview.

Land, H. and Rose, H. (1985) 'Compulsory altruism for some or an altruistic society for all', in Bean, P., Ferris, J. and Whynes, D. (eds.) *In Defence of Welfare*, London: Tavistock.

Lansley, S. (1979) *Housing and Public Policy*, London: Croom Helm.

Layard, R., Nickell, S. and Jackman, R. (1994) *The Unemployment Crisis*, Oxford: Oxford University Press.

Layton-Henry, Z. (1992) *The Politics of Immigration*, Oxford: Blackwell.

Le Grand, J. (1982) *The Strategy of Equality*, London: Allen & Unwin.

Le Grand, J. (1990) *Quasi-markets and Social Policy*, Bristol: School for Advanced Urban Studies.

Le Grand, J. and Robinson, R. (1984) *The Economics of Social Problems*, 2nd edn, Basingstoke: Macmillan.

Lee, J. J. (1989) *Ireland 1912–85*, Cambridge: Cambridge University Press.

Leon, D. A., Vägerö, D. and Olausson, P. (1992) 'Social class differences in infant mortality in Sweden: a comparison with England and Wales', *British Medical Journal*, 305.

Lewis, J. (ed.) (1983) *Women's Welfare – Women's Rights*, Beckenham: Croom Helm.

Lijphart, A. (1975) *The Politics of Accommodation: Pluralism and Democracy in the Netherlands*, Berkeley, CA: University of California Press.

Lingard, B., Knight, J. and Porter, P. (eds.) (1993) *Schooling Reform in Hard Times*, London: Falmer Press.

Lipietz, A. (1992) *Towards a New Economic Order*, Cambridge: Polity Press.

Lipsky, M. (1980) *Street-Level Bureaucracy*, New York: Russell Sage.

Macintyre, S. (1985) *Winners and Losers*, Sydney: Unwin Hyman.

Macnicol, J. (1980) *The Movement for Family Allowances*, London: Heinemann.

Malpass, P. (1990) *Reshaping Housing Policy*, London: Routledge.

Malpass, P. and Murie, A. (1990) *Housing Policy and Practice*, 3rd edn, Basingstoke: Macmillan.

Mann, K. (1992) *The Making of an English 'Underclass'*, Buckingham: Open University Press.

Mann, K. (1994) 'Watching the defectives: observers of the underclass in the USA, Britain and Australia', *Critical Social Policy*, 41 (2), pp. 79–99.

Markham, A. (1994) *A Brief History of Pollution*, London: Earthscan.

Marklund, S. (1992) 'The decomposition of social policy in Sweden', *Scandinavian Journal of Social Welfare*, 1, pp. 2–11.

Marmor, T. R., Mashaw, J. L. and Harvey, P. L. (1990) *America's Misunderstood Welfare State*, New York: Basic Books.

Marshall, T. H. (1963) 'Citizenship and social class', in *Sociology at the Crossroads*, London: Heinemann.

Martin, L. G. and Preston, S. H. (eds.) (1994) *Demography of Aging*, Washington, DC: National Academy Press.

Maruo, N. (1986) 'The development of the welfare mix in Japan', in Rose, R. and

Shiratori, R. (eds.) *The Welfare State East and West*, New York: Oxford University Press.

Matthews, J. J. (1984) *Good and Mad Women: The Historical Construction of Femininity in Twentieth Century Australia*, Sydney: Allen & Unwin.

Maynard, A. (1975) *Experiment with Choice in Education*, London: Institute of Economic Affairs.

McCarthy, M. (1986) *Campaigning for the Poor*, Beckenham: Croom Helm.

McCarthy, M. (ed.) (1989) *The New Politics of Welfare*, London: Macmillan.

McCormick, J. (1989) *The Global Environmental Movement*, London: Bellhaven Press.

McKeown, T. (1980) *The Role of Medicine*, Blackwell: Oxford.

McLaughlin, E. (ed.) (1992) *Understanding Unemployment*, London: Routledge.

Means, R. and Smith, R. (1994) *Community Care*, Basingstoke: Macmillan.

Michie, J. and Grieve Smith, J. (eds.) (1994) *Unemployment in Europe*, London: Academic Press.

Millet, K. (1970) *Sexual Politics*, New York: Avon Books.

Minford, P. (1984) 'State expenditure: a study in waste', *Economic Affairs* (supplement), 4 (3).

Mishra, R. (1977) *Society and Social Policy*, London: Macmillan.

Mishra, R. (1984) *The Welfare State in Crisis*, Brighton: Wheatsheaf.

Mishra, R. (1990) *The Welfare State in Capitalist Society*, Hemel Hempstead: Harvester Wheatsheaf.

MISSOC (1993) *Social Protection in the Member States of the Community*, Brussels: Commission of the European Communities.

Mitchell, D. (1991) *Income Transfers in Ten Welfare States*, Aldershot: Avebury.

Moran, M. and Prosser, T. (eds.) (1994) *Privatisation and Regulatory Change in Europe*, Buckingham: Open University Press.

Moran, M. and Wood, B. (1993) *State, Regulation and the Medical Profession*, Milton Keynes: Open University Press.

Morris, R. J. (1976) *Cholera 1832: The Social Response to an Epidemic*, London: Croom Helm.

Mukherjee, S. (1972) *Making Labour Markets Work*, London: PEP.

Munday, B. (ed.) (1993) *European Social Services*, Canterbury: University of Kent.

Murray, C. (1984) *Losing Ground*, New York: Basic Books.

Murray, C. (1990) *The Emerging British Underclass*, London: IEA.

Musgrave, R. A. (1959) *The Theory of Public Finance*, New York: McGraw-Hill.

Myrdal, G. (1962) *Challenge to Affluence*, New York: Pantheon.

Najman, J. M. and Western, J. S. (eds.) (1993) *A Sociology of Australian Society*, Basingstoke: Macmillan.

National Housing Strategy (1991) *The Affordability of Australian Housing*,

Canberra: Government Publishing House.

Niskanen, W. A. (1971) *Bureaucracy and Representative Government*, New York: Aldine-Atherton.

Nordlinger, E. A. (1981) *On the Autonomy of the Democratic State*, Cambridge, MA: Harvard University Press.

Nozick, R. (1974) *Anarchy, State and Utopia*, Oxford: Blackwell.

O'Connor, J. (1973) *The Fiscal Crisis of the State*, New York: St Martin's Press.

O'Connor, J. S. (1993) 'Gender, class and citizenship in the comparative analysis of welfare state regimes: theoretical and methodological issues', *British Journal of Sociology*, 44 (3), pp. 501–18.

OECD (1981) *The Welfare State in Crisis*, Paris: OECD.

OECD (1987) *Financing and Delivering Health Care*, Paris: OECD.

OECD (1988) *Ageing Populations*, Paris: OECD.

OECD (1990) *Education in OECD Countries 1987–88: A Compendium of Statistical Information*, Paris: OECD.

OECD (1991) *The State of the Environment*, Paris: OECD.

OECD (1992a) *The Reform of Health Care*, Paris: OECD.

OECD (1992b) *Historical Statistics 1960–1990*, Paris: OECD.

OECD (1993) *Economic Reports*, Paris: OECD.

OECD (1994a) *Economic Surveys 1993–94: Sweden*, Paris: OECD.

OECD (1994b) *The OECD Jobs Study*, Paris: OECD.

OECD (1994c) *New Orientations for Social Policy*, Paris: OECD.

OECD (1994d) *Caring for Frail Elderly People*, Paris: OECD.

Offe, C. (1984) *Contradictions of the Welfare State*, London: Hutchinson.

Orloff, A. S. (1993) 'Gender and the social rights of citizenship: state policies and gender relations in comparative research', *American Sociological Review*, 58 (3), pp. 303–28.

Ormerod, P. (1994) *The Death of Economics*, London: Faber & Faber.

Ostrom, E. (1990) *Governing the Commons*, Cambridge: Cambridge University Press.

Palmer, G. R. and Short, S. D. (1994) *Health Care and Public Policy: An Australian Analysis*, 2nd edn, South Melbourne: Macmillan.

Pampel, F. C. and Williamson, J. B. (1989) *Age, Class, Politics and the Welfare State*, Cambridge: Cambridge University Press.

Park, R., Burgess, E. and MacKenzie, R. (1923) *The City*, Chicago: University of Chicago Press.

Parker, H. (1989) *Instead of the Dole*, London: Routledge.

Parker, H. (1993) 'Citizen's income', in Berghman, J. and Cantillon, B. (eds.) *The European Face of Social Security*, Aldershot: Avebury.

Parry, J. and Bloch, M. (eds.) (1989) *Money and the Morality of Exchange*, Cambridge: Cambridge University Press.

Parry, N. and Parry, J. (1976) *The Rise of the Medical Profession*, London: Croom Helm.

Parsons, T. (1951) *The Social System*, Glencoe, IL: The Free Press.

Pascall, G. (1986) *Social Policy: A Feminist Analysis*, London: Tavistock.

Peacock, A. (ed.) (1984) *The Regulation Game*, Oxford: Blackwell.

Peacock, A. (1991) 'Welfare philosophies and welfare finance', in Wilson, T. and Wilson, D. (eds.) *The State and Social Welfare*, London: Longman.

Pearce, D. (1993) *Economic Values and the Natural World*, London: Earthscan.

Pedersen, S. (1993) *Family, Dependence and the Origins of the Welfare State*, Cambridge: Cambridge University Press.

Pelling, M. (1978) *Cholera, Fever and English Medicine*, Oxford: Oxford University Press.

Pfaller, A., Gough, I. and Therborn, G. (1991) *Can the Welfare State Compete?*, Basingstoke: Macmillan.

Phillimore, P. (1993) 'How do places shape health? Rethinking locality and lifestyle in north-east England', in Platt, S. (eds.) *Locating Health: Sociological and Historical Explanations*, Aldershot: Avebury.

Pierson, C. (1991) *Beyond the Welfare State*, Cambridge: Polity.

Pinker, R. (1979) *The Idea of Welfare*, London: Heinemann.

Piven, F. F. and Cloward, R. A. (1972) *Regulating the Poor*, London: Tavistock.

Piven, F. F. and Cloward, R. A. (1977) *Poor People's Movements: Why they Succeed, How they Fail*, New York: Pantheon.

Plant, R. (1974) *Community and Ideology*, London: Routledge.

Porter, B. (1983) *Britain, Europe and the World*, London: Unwin Hyman.

Power, A. (1993) *Hovels to High Rise*, London: Routledge.

Prosser, T. (1983) *Test Cases for the Poor*, London: Child Poverty Action Group.

Pusey, M. (1991) *Economic Rationalism in Canberra*, Cambridge: Cambridge University Press.

Rainwater, L., Rein, M. and Schwartz, J. (1985) *Income Packaging in the Welfare State*, Oxford: Oxford University Press.

Rank, M. R. (1994) *Living on the Edge: The Realities of Welfare in America*, New York: Columbia University Press.

Raywid, M. A. (1985) 'Family choice arrangements in public schools: a review of the literature', *Review of Educational Research*, 55, pp. 435–67.

Reich, C. (1964) 'The new property', *Yale Law Journal*, 74, pp. 1245–57.

Reich, R. B. (1991) *The Work of Nations*, London: Simon & Schuster.

Reissman, D. A. (1977) *Richard Titmuss: Welfare and Society*, London: Heinemann.

Rex, J. (1986) *Race and Ethnicity*, Milton Keynes: Open University Press.

Rex, J. and Moore, R. (1967) *Race, Community and Conflict*, London: Oxford University Press.

Reynolds, D. and Cuttance, P. (1992) *School Effectiveness: Research, Policy and Practice*, London: Cassell.

Richardson, J. (ed.) (1982) *Policy Styles in Western Europe*, London: Allen & Unwin.

Rimlinger, G. (1971) *Welfare Policy and Industrialization in Europe, America and Russia*, New York: Wiley.

Roberts, D. (1960) *Victorian Origins of the British Welfare State*, New Haven, CT: Yale University Press.

Roberts, H. (ed.) (1981) *Women, Health and Reproduction*, London: Routledge.

Robinson, R. (1979) *Housing Economics and Public Policy*, Basingstoke: Macmillan.

Rose, R. (1984) *Do Parties Make a Difference*, London: Macmillan.

Rose, R. and Peters, G. (1978) *Can Governments go Bankrupt?*, New York: Basic Books.

Rose, R. and Shiratore, R. (1986) *Welfare State East and West*, Oxford: Oxford University Press.

Rowley, C. and Peacock, A. (1975) *Welfare Economics: A Liberal Restatement*, Oxford: Martin Robertson.

Rutter, M. and Madge, N. (1977) *Cycles of Disadvantage*, London: Heinemann.

Ryan, A. (1991) 'Merit goods and benefits in kind: paternalism and liberalism in action', in Wilson, T. and Wilson, D. (eds.) *The State and Social Welfare*, London: Longman.

Sainsbury, D. (1993) 'Dual welfare and sex segregation of access to social benefits: income maintenance policies in the UK, the US, the Netherlands and Sweden', *Journal of Social Policy*, 22(1), pp. 69–98.

Sainsbury, D. (ed.) (1994) *Gendering Welfare States*, London: Sage.

Saltman, R. B. and Otter, C. von (1992) *Planned Markets and Public Competition*, Buckingham: Open University Press.

Sassen, S. (1991) *The Global City*, Princeton, NJ: Princeton, University Press.

Saunders, P. (1990) *A Nation of Home Owners*, London: Unwin Hyman.

Schama, S. (1987) *The Embarrassment of Riches*, London: Collins.

Schieber, G., Poullier, J.-P. and Greenwald, L. (1993) 'Health spending, delivery and outcomes in OECD countries', *Health Affairs*, 12 (2), pp. 120–9.

Schon, D. (1971) *Beyond the Stable State*, London: Maurice Temple Smith.

Segal, L. (ed.) (1983) *What is to be Done About the Family?*, Harmondsworth: Penguin Books.

Segalman, R. (1986) *The Swiss Way of Welfare*, New York: Praeger.

Seldon, A. (1986) *The Riddle of the Voucher*, London: Institute of Economic Affairs.

Self, P. (1993) *Government by the Market?*, Basingstoke: Macmillan.

Semmel, B. (1961) *Imperialism and Social Reform*, London: Oxford University Press.

Sharp, R. (1986) *Capitalist Crisis and Schooling*, Melbourne: Macmillan.

Showler, B. (1976) *The Public Employment Service*, London: Longman.

Showler, B. and Sinfield, A. (eds.) (1981) *The Workless State*, Oxford: Martin Robertson.

Simey, T. and Simey, M. (1960) *Charles Booth: Social Scientist*, London: Oxford University Press.

Simpson, R. and Walker, R. (1993) *Europe: For Richer or Poorer?*, London: CPAG.

Sinfield, A. (1978) 'Analysis in the social division of welfare', *Journal of Social Policy*, 7 (2), pp. 129–56.

Sinfield, A. (1981) *What Unemployment Means*, Oxford: Martin Robertson.

Smeeding, T. M., O'Higgins, M. and Rainwater, L. (1990) *Poverty, Inequality and Income Distribution in Comparative Perspective*, Hemel Hempstead: Harvester Wheatsheaf.

Spender, D. and Sarah, E. (1980) *Learning to Lose: Sexism and Education*, London: The Women's Press.

Stacey, M. (1988) *The Sociology of Health and Healing*, London: Unwin Hyman.

Starr, P. (1982) *The Social Transformation of American Medicine*, New York: Basic Books.

Stoline, A. and Weiner, J. P. (1988) *The New Medical Market Place: A Physician's Guide to the Health Care Revolution*, Baltimore, MD: Johns Hopkins University Press.

Stone, M. (1981) *The Education of the Black Child in Britain*, Glasgow: Fontana.

Sullivan, M. (1994) *Modern Social Policy*, Hemel Hempstead: Harvester Wheatsheaf.

Swaan, A. de (1988) *In Care of the State, Health Care, Education and Welfare in Europe and the USA in the Modern Era*, Cambridge: Polity Press.

Tarn, J. (1973) *Five Per Cent Philanthropy*, Cambridge: Cambridge University Press.

Taylor, F. (1980) *The IQ Game: A Methodological Enquiry into the Heredity–Environment Controversy*, Brighton: Harvester.

Taylor, I. (ed.) (1990) *The Social Effects of Free Market Policies*, Hemel Hempstead: Harvester Wheatsheaf.

Taylor-Gooby, P. (1985) *Public Opinion, Ideology and State Welfare*, London: Routledge.

Taylor-Gooby, P. (1991) 'Attachment to the welfare state', in Jowell, R., Brook, L., Taylor, B. and Prior, G. *British Social Attitudes: 8th Report*, Aldershot: Dartmouth Press.

Therborn, G. (1986) *Why Some Peoples are More Unemployed Than Others*, London: Verso.

Titmuss, R. M. (1958) *Essays on the Welfare State*, London: Allen & Unwin.

Titmuss, R. M. (1962) *Income Distribution and Social Change*, London: Allen & Unwin.

Titmuss, R. M. (1968) *Commitment to Welfare*, London: Allen & Unwin.

Titmuss, R. M. (1973) *The Gift Relationship*, Harmondsworth: Penguin Books.

Titmuss, R. M. (1974) *Social Policy: An Introduction*, London: Allen & Unwin.

Townsend, P. (ed.) (1970) *The Concept of Poverty*, London: Heinemann.

Townsend, P. (1979) *Poverty in the United Kingdom*, Harmondsworth: Penguin Books.

Townsend, P. (1993) *The International Analysis of Poverty*, Hemel Hempstead: Harvester Wheatsheaf.

Towsend, P., Davidson, N. and Whitehead, M. (eds.) (1988) *Inequalities in Health*, Harmondsworth: Penguin Books.

Tullock, G. (1967) *The Politics of Bureaucracy*, New York: Public Affairs Press.

Tullock, G. (1976) *The Vote Motive*, London: Institute of Economic Affairs.

Ungerson, C. (1995) 'Gender, cash and informal care: European perspectives and dilemmas', *Journal of Social Policy*, 24 (1), pp. 31–52.

Veit Wilson, J. (1994) *Dignity not Poverty*, London: Institute for Public Policy Research.

Wachtel, H. (1972) 'Capitalism and poverty in America: paradox or contradiction', *American Economic Review*, 62(2), pp. 187–94.

Waerness, K. (1984) 'Caring as women's work in the welfare state', in Holter, H. (ed.) *Patriarchy in a Welfare Society*, Oslo: Universitetsforlaget.

Walby, S. (1986) *Patriarchy at Work*, Oxford: Blackwell.

Walker, R. and Parker, G. (eds.) (1988) *Money Matters: Income Wealth and Financial Welfare*, London: Sage.

Watson, D. (1980) *Caring for Strangers*, London: Routledge & Kegan Paul.

Weale, A. (1983) *Political Theory and Social Policy*, London: Macmillan.

Weale, A. (1992) *The New Politics of Pollution*, Manchester: Manchester University Press.

Weatherley, R. (1992) *From Entitlement to Contract: Reshaping the Welfare State in Australia*, working paper 7, Administration, Compliance and Governability Program, Canberra: Australian National University.

Weidner, H. (1986) *Air Pollution Strategies and Policies in the F.R. Germany*, Berlin: WZB.

Weindling, P. (1989) *Health, Race and German Politics Between National Unification and Nazism 1870–1945*, Cambridge: Cambridge University Press.

Weir, M., Orloff, S. and Skocpol, T. (eds.) (1988) *The Politics of Social Policy in the United States*, Princeton, NJ: Princeton University Press.

Welch, A. R. (1993) 'Class, culture and the state in comparative education: problems, perspectives and prospects', *Comparative Education*, 29 (1), pp. 7–27.

Wetstone, G. S. and Rosencranz, A. (1983) *Acid Rain in Europe and North America*, Washington, DC: Environment Law Institute.

Whiteside, N. (1988) 'Unemployment and health in historical perspective', *Journal of Social Policy*, 17 (2), pp. 177–94.

Wilding, P. (1982) *Professional Power and Social Welfare*, London: Routledge.

Wilensky, H. L. (1975) *The Welfare State and Equality*, Berkeley, CA: University of California Press.

Williams, F. (1989) *Social Policy: A Critical Introduction*, Cambridge: Polity Press.

Williams, P. (1984) 'The politics of property: home ownership in Australia', in Halligan, J. and Paris, C. (eds.) *Australian Urban Politics: Critical Perspectives*, Melbourne: Longman Cheshire.

Williamson, O. (1975) *Markets and Hierarchies*, New York: The Free Press.

Williamson, O. (1987) *The Economic Institutions of Capitalism*, New York: The Free Press.

Willis, P. (1977) *Learning to Labour*, Westmead: Saxon House.

Wilsford, D. (1991) *Doctors and the State*, Durham, N.C.: Duke University Press.

Wilson, W. J. (1981) 'Race, class and public policy', *American Sociologist* 16 (2), pp. 125–34.

Wilson, W. J. (1987) *The Truly Disadvantaged*, Chicago: University of Chicago Press.

Wistow, G., Knapp, M., Hardy, B. and Allen, C. (1994) *Social Care in a Mixed Economy*, Buckingham: Open University Press.

Wittfogel, K. A. (1957) *Oriental Despotism*, New Haven, CT: Yale University Press.

Wolfe, A. (1977) *The Limits of Legitimacy*, New York: The Free Press.

Wood, C. (1989) *Planning Pollution Prevention*, Oxford: Heinemann Neunes.

Woodham Smith, C. (1962) *The Great Hunger: Ireland 1845–1849*, London: Hamish Hamilton.

Woodroffe, K. (1962) *From Charity to Social Work in England and the United States*, London: Routledge.

World Health Organisation (1992) *World Health Statistics Annual*, Geneva: World Health Organisation.

Yelaja, S. A. (ed.) (1987) *Canadian Social Policy*, 2nd edn, Waterloo, Ontario: Wilfred Laurier University Press.

Index